Sons
of Adam,
Daughters
of Eve

Books by Ishbel Ross

SONS OF ADAM, DAUGHTERS OF EVE

TASTE IN AMERICA

CHARMERS AND CRANKS
Twelve Famous American Women Who Defied the Conventions

AN AMERICAN FAMILY
The Tafts 1678–1964

CRUSADES AND CRINOLINES

GRACE COOLIDGE AND HER ERA

SILHOUETTE IN DIAMONDS
The Life of Mrs. Potter Palmer

THE GENERAL'S WIFE
The Life of Mrs. Ulysses S. Grant

FIRST LADY OF THE SOUTH
The Life of Mrs. Jefferson Davis

ANGEL OF THE BATTLEFIELD
The Life of Clara Barton

REBEL ROSE
Life of Rose O'Neal Greenhow, Confederate Spy

PROUD KATE
Portrait of an Ambitious Woman, Kate Chase

JOURNEY INTO LIGHT

CHILD OF DESTINY
The Life Story of the First Woman Doctor

ISLE OF ESCAPE

FIFTY YEARS A WOMAN

LADIES OF THE PRESS

HIGHLAND TWILIGHT

MARRIAGE IN GOTHAM

PROMENADE DECK

Sons
of Adam,
Daughters
of Eve

 Ishbel Ross

Harper & Row, Publishers
New York, Evanston,
and London

FIRST EDITION

LIBRARY OF CONGRESS CATALOG CARD NUMBER: 67-13691

Contents

1. Abigail's Bid for Independence   1
2. The Early Pacemakers   21
3. A New Era Begins   53
4. Power in the White House   81
5. Troublemakers and Pioneers   107
6. Beauties, Sirens and Spies   136
7. A Cause Takes Root   155
8. The Hard Road   175
9. The Feminine Establishment   189
10. Charm School   225
11. View from the Summit   242
12. The Vote That Counts   263
13. The Tree of Knowledge   276

Notes   299
Bibliography   313
Index   329

✖ Illustrations

The following are grouped in a separate section after page 150.

Martha Washington
Mrs. John Adams
Dolley Madison
Mrs. John Tyler
Mrs. James Monroe
Mrs. Ulysses S. Grant
Mary Todd Lincoln
Mrs. Grover Cleveland
Mrs. Theodore Roosevelt
Mrs. Woodrow Wilson and President Wilson with King Albert and Queen Elizabeth of Belgium
Mrs. William Howard Taft
Mrs. Franklin D. Roosevelt in the White House in 1940
Mrs. John F. Kennedy with André Malraux, French Minister of Culture, and Mme. Malraux in the National Gallery of Art in 1962
Mrs. Lyndon B. Johnson and Mary Lasker
Margaret Fuller
Kate Field
Mercy Otis Warren
Mrs. Jefferson Davis
Jessie Benton Frémont
Kate Chase Sprague
Monument in the Capitol to Elizabeth Cady Stanton, Susan B.

Anthony, and Lucretia Mott

The women of Cheyenne, Wyoming, casting ballots in 1869

Victoria Woodhull asserting her right to vote

Alice Paul, founder of the National Woman's Party

Lucy Stone

Jane Addams

Carrie Chapman Catt

Virginia C. Gildersleeve and Millicent C. McIntosh

Margaret Sanger before a Senate judiciary subcommittee in 1932

Frances Perkins

Oveta Culp Hobby

Senator Margaret Chase Smith

Alice Roosevelt Longworth

Clare Boothe Luce

Marietta Tree

Mrs. J. Borden Harriman receiving a citation of merit from President
    Kennedy in 1963

Anna M. Rosenberg being sworn in as Assistant Secretary of Defense;
    with George C. Marshall, Robert A. Lovett, and Felix Larkin

Dorothy Schiff

Katharine Graham with British Ambassador David Ormsby Gore
    and his wife, and Harold Wilson

Constance Baker Motley with President Johnson

Frances P. Bolton

Sons
of Adam,
Daughters
of Eve

Abigail's Bid for Independence

ஃ Women have been playing the game of politics since the days of Aspasia and Cleopatra, fresh and ambitious though their goals may seem in the twentieth century. Four centuries before the birth of Christ, Aspasia, as beautiful as she was brainy, was influencing Pericles in his exposition of politics and was composing some of the speeches on which his fame eventually rested. "I wish some of our great men had such wives," John Adams wrote of Aspasia, evidently unaware that he had a pristine example under his own roof, and that together they would go down in history as the founders of one of the nation's most notable dynasties.

Thus, early in its history, America had more than a suggestion of feminine influence in the President's House, but it was so skillfully applied that historians have tended to downgrade Abigail's political importance and play up her instinctive skill as the accomplished wife of an austere and forceful man. None of the emancipated women of today, endowed with the power to vote, to hold public office and even to run for the Presidency, could match the influence exercised by Abigail in state affairs, as well as in the home. As the wife of one President and the mother of another, she had a share in the counsels of the young republic. One political observer said that she should have been the Administratrix of the newborn nation.

It had been John Adams' good luck to choose such a wife, but she was not alone in her milieu. Eighteenth-century women in America, as in Britain and France, repeatedly showed power and influence, wit and stamina, affecting the careers and counsels of their husbands. The spirit that pervaded their parlors and salons, and their strength when faced with the emergencies and needs of a new civilization, made them potent on the political as well as the social scene. Great moments evoke great responses, and the women of the Revolutionary era had the stamina and intelligence to meet the crisis with style and endurance.

Their warriors came and went during the months of war, in the constantly shifting pattern of attack and defense. Often close to the battle scene, women learned to dissemble, to cajole the enemy in order to outwit him, to stay his progress when they could, or sometimes to flee as he advanced. Functioning as individuals, and sometimes in groups, they used their inherent instincts to match the sweep of creative effort going on around them. Backing up their men, they were committed to the struggle that affected the future of their sons as well as their husbands. Their strength and fortitude during this period far transcended their normal round of feminine duties.

Abigail's own influence, like that of most clever women, was infused by indirection into the family pattern. She would have shrunk from a public display of power, yet she figured uniquely in the history of woman's independence. It was all done in an unconscious and instinctive way. Without any desire for the limelight, keeping the signs of her influence invisible, she has left a clear picture of her own place in the sun through her sustained and brilliant correspondence with her husband—the only President's wife to have left so substantial and intimate a record of her husband's life. John Adams recognized its value and urged Abigail to save all their letters. She, on the other hand, wished to have hers destroyed. She did not recognize her own political significance as she played the wifely role to the hilt—with love, understanding and ingenuity.

But the aura of power created at the seat of government by Abigail was vitiated to some extent by the long succession of withdrawn and invalid wives in the White House. Although none had to cope with anything as fundamental as the first three pacemakers—Martha Washington, Abigail Adams and Dolley Madison—a few were openly powerful and unabashedly ambitious. Some practiced nepotism. Two or three bedeviled their husbands. Here and there dazzlers emerged, like Mrs. Madison, Mrs. John Tyler and Mrs. John F. Kennedy. These three, along with Mrs. Grover Cleveland and Mrs. Calvin Coolidge, were perhaps the most obvious charmers in White House history. The majority have been graceful hostesses and unostentatious women who have made little impression on the public.

Although there are few recorded instances of Presidents' wives inspiring important political action except by indirection, there are countless examples of the ways in which they have helped their husbands along the road to the Presidency. Down the years they have shared with Presidents' mothers the shaping of the course. Who would dare to appraise their bedroom and parlor influence, shadowy though some of them seem as makers of presidential history? The extent of their direct political power may be open to debate, but it was discernible in the early days of the Republic, and Arthur Schlesinger, Jr., has pointed out that the wives of the Revolution reigned if they did not rule.

The influence of First Ladies in general may be traced quite clearly in the life stories of Abigail Adams, Dolley Madison, Julia Tyler, Mary Lincoln, Julia Dent Grant, Lucy Webb Hayes, Edith Carow Roosevelt, Helen Herron Taft, Edith Bolling Galt Wilson, Florence Harding, Eleanor Roosevelt, Jacqueline Kennedy and Claudia Alta Taylor (Lady Bird) Johnson.

Julia Tyler was frankly a hedonist, who lit her own candle and employed the first press agent at the White House. Mary Lincoln, craving power for both "Mr. Lincoln" and herself, defeated her own ambitions with her psychopathic moods and rages. Theodore Roosevelt's swift climb to fame was slowed at times by his wife Edith's concern for the education of their children. At significant moments she kept him from impetuous action. Mrs. Taft's resistance to her husband's longing for a seat on the Supreme Court was based on her desire to give their children all the scholarly benefits instinctively sought by the Tafts. Mrs. Woodrow Wilson, who ran a regency from the White House, filled this role because of her husband's illness. She was not essentially grasping for power, but she used it freely when it was hers to command. During her short stay in the White House Mrs. Harding was perceptibly power-hungry, although her husband had no desire for his high office, and was maneuvered into it.

Mrs. Eleanor Roosevelt, in her own right as well as in the political aid she gave her husband, was the most influential of all Presidents' wives. But among those who have invested the role with glamour, Mrs. Kennedy stands alone, not only for her beauty and style but because of the extraordinary circumstances of her husband's death and the unforgettable impression she made on the public in the days that followed. She has been without peer in piquing national and international interest—the only White House occupant to touch the same nerve as Alice Roosevelt Longworth, a President's daughter and headline favorite of the early twentieth century, still exercising her advisory powers in Washington in her eighties.

Although few First Ladies have been impressive in their own right, at least four—Abigail Adams, Dolley Madison, Julia Grant and Grace Coolidge—leavened the taciturnity and aloof manner of their husbands. They also figured among those who have most visibly brought womanly comfort and serenity into the Executive Mansion. Others with these special qualities have been Mrs. Rutherford B. Hayes, Mrs. Grover Cleveland, Mrs. Benjamin Harrison, Mrs. Theodore Roosevelt, Mrs. Herbert Hoover, Mrs. Dwight D. Eisenhower and Mrs. Harry Truman, as quietly persuasive and as little known to the public as Mrs. Harding was shrill and demanding.

One of the most influential of Presidents' wives never lived in the White House, but her shadow stretched across it as long as Andrew Jackson was in office. Bitter and vengeful because of the scandalous talk that had driven his beloved Rachel to her grave, he broke up his Cabinet over Peggy Eaton, whose reputation made her a social outcast in official circles. In earlier days personal animosities came to the surface, and the prejudices of Presidents' wives influenced their husbands in astonishing ways. Mrs. James Polk could not endure Martin Van Buren. Mrs. Lincoln loathed General Grant, Salmon

Portland Chase and Chase's daughter Kate. Mrs. Grant disliked General George B. McClellan. Mrs. Taft was the unseen but potent foe of Theodore Roosevelt long before the open split occurred between her husband and Teddy. Mrs. Wilson despised Colonel E. M. House, and in each instance the viewpoint of these women left scars on the historical scene.

From time to time Presidents have had to bend and sway to the pace set by their families, to their own personal misfortunes, to illness and economic stress, or to death and scandal. The administrations of Franklin Pierce and William McKinley were seriously affected by the invalidism of their wives. Zachary Taylor's wife, Margaret, did not wish her husband to be President, and she kept out of sight, allowing rumors to spread that she sulked in a back room and smoked a corncob pipe. Mrs. Coolidge was stunned when her husband inherited the Presidency, but she fulfilled her mission with worldly ease. Mrs. Grant, in her own intuitive way, was among the most powerful of all wives, for her faith in Ulysses in the days of his misfortunes as well as his triumphs helped him immeasurably throughout his checkered career.

Another winner in the feminine sweepstakes was Mrs. Rutherford Hayes (Lemonade Lucy), who suited her age and generation. She pleased members of her own sex and had considerable influence, political as well as social. Her calm good looks and simple attire matched her puritanical instincts. She was a temperance zealot and upheld the conventional standards for home and family—the image that has always been most approved around the White House. Until recent years the goal has been one of feminine detachment, lest any sensibilities be jarred by the suggestion of petticoat influence at the heart of government.

Even Eleanor Roosevelt clung to this pretension. But since her time it has been increasingly difficult for Presidents' wives to let their days flow by with an innocuous round of teas, functions and openings. Something more is demanded of them now. They must show an interest in the issues and problems of the day, in the arts, in history, in world politics (although the less they say about it the better), in humanitarian causes, in housing and minority groups. Detachment and absorption in their own families to the exclusion of larger interests no longer find favor with a young, restless and questing generation. When Eleanor Roosevelt came to grips with the social problems of the day, a new era was born—in active achievement, in documented effort, in the widespread publicity that reached fantastic proportions in the administrations of President Kennedy and President Johnson.

Everyone knows today what the President's wife is doing, and often what she is thinking. She is in the forefront of her husband's administration. The aura of invalidism and retiring ways that blanketed the White House during much of the nineteenth century has died in the fierce glare of today's exposure to the public. The First Lady must be ready to jump into action on many fronts and to represent her husband with a pertinent speech. Moreover, she is expected to spark off movements of her own, like Mrs. Kennedy's promotion of the arts and restoration of the White House, and Mrs. Johnson's beautification plans for the United States.

The spread of style, fashion and sophistication in government circles has radically changed what is expected of a President's wife. Increasingly the wives of presidential candidates loom up as national assets not to be overlooked. If they are photogenic, eloquent and smartly dressed, so much the better. Today they are allowed to be brainy and witty, too. But in the early days their outward image was not a problem, and Martha Washington, Abigail Adams and Dolley Madison, the first women to figure in American history as potent influences in the national counsels, underplayed their hands. They always took care to emphasize their feminine qualities and to absolve themselves of political interference. Yet Martha shared the rigors of the battlefield and the winter at Valley Forge as gracefully as she did the pomp of the presidential days. Dolley enlarged the social horizons and strengthened the man of intellect and reserve she had married. Abigail's judgment and intellectual force came to the surface repeatedly, even while she practiced all the feminine arts and graces, and wherever she chanced to be—running the family farm at Quincy or observing the elaborate protocol of the French and British courts. Her great-grandson, Henry Adams, wrote of Abigail, "None of the female descendants of Abigail Adams can ever be nearly so familiar as her letters have made her; and all this is pure loss to history, for the American woman of the nineteenth century was much better company than the American man."

No two women could have been more unlike than Martha Washington and Abigail Adams. One reflected the luxury and opulence of the South; the other the austerity of the New England spirit. Although no love was lost between their husbands, the wives viewed each other with affection and admiration. Martha was in no sense of the word a politician, but she was undeniably the right wife for George Washington during a great moment in history. Mercy Otis Warren, a vigorous propagandist and satirist of the Revolutionary era, wrote to Abigail about Martha Washington, "I think the Complacency of her manner bespeaks at once the benevolence of her heart, and her affability. Candour and gentleness qualify her to soften the hours of private life, or to sweeten the cares of the Hero, and smooth the rugged paths of War."

This was a true assessment of her nature. She was not prepared for war. Her girlhood had been one of riding to hounds and dancing in the ballrooms of Williamsburg. She was small and inclined to be plump, with dark hair and hazel eyes. When Daniel Parke Custis, her first husband and much her senior, died eight years after their marriage, he left her the wealthiest widow in Virginia, so that she was well endowed with property and trust funds for her children when she married George Washington in 1759.

She supervised the management of their estates in Virginia and wintered with her husband at army headquarters when he took command of the Continental Army. She heard the first and last cannon salvos of the Revolutionary War and in the grim winter of 1777–78 rode to Valley Forge on the pillion of the General's charger. Soon she was known as the good Samaritan, spreading comfort and cheer among the troops. She quickly adapted herself to a log cabin, water in a stone jug from a spring, and salt herring and potatoes instead of French cuisine. "The General's apartment is very small," she wrote to Mrs. Warren. "He has had a log cabin built to dine in, which has made our quarters much more tolerable than they were at first."

Martha Washington was never to occupy the White House, but in the temporary capitals of New York and Philadelphia she held court with more formality than the dawning republican spirit approved. She created many precedents followed by later First Ladies, but no successors presented a statelier picture than did General Washington in satin with lace ruffles, diamond buckles and powdered hair, with his small wife in spreading brocades and lace fichus by his side. Proud though she seemed to be as Lady Washington, Martha found her greatest happiness at Mount Vernon, where she pictured herself as being "busy as a bee, cheerful as a cricket, and steady as a clock."

When the President died she wrote, "All is now over. I shall soon follow him. I have no more trials to pass through"—a clue to the difficulties she had weathered. With a final gesture of renunciation she abandoned her own wishes for his place of burial, saying with resignation that, taught by the great example which she had long had before her, "never to oppose my private wishes to the public will—I must consent to the request made by Congress . . . and in doing this I need not—I cannot say what a sacrifice of individual feeling I make to a sense of public duty." This was the disciplined wife bending to public opinion.

As Martha Washington moved into the shadows, Abigail Adams came into full view, but she was already familiar to the American public. Her greatest influence was shown not in the White House but in the years that went before. It was during the days of struggle and while the Constitution was being shaped that she emerged as the authentic ancestor of the emancipated American woman. In this respect she was unique in the impetus she gave to what came to be known in time as women's rights. Today her letters are regarded as classics. They raise the curtain on the role she played, showing time and again how potent her opinions were with her husband, and how politically adept she was in informing and advising him.

Abigail Smith was one of three daughters born in a Weymouth, Massachusetts, parsonage. Her family thought she was stepping down when she married a young lawyer, then the most despised of professions. But Abigail, not yet twenty, had met her match in John Adams. Before long he was telling her that he expected more of her than just being the mother of their four children. Early in their marriage he urged her to take part in the struggle then under way, and Abigail was soon priming him with shrewd analyses of people and events. As early as December, 1773, she suggested civil war as the probable outcome of the conflict of interest between America and Britain. In November, 1775, she was urging total separation from the motherland, and was speculating on the type of government to be adopted when the split came. She favored a republic.

Abigail had a chance to play the straight political game when she, Hannah Winthrop, wife of Professor John Winthrop of Harvard, and Mrs. Warren were selected at Cambridge to examine the Tory women whose sympathies lay with the monarchy rather than with those working for independence. The committee of men appointed by the General Court to examine errant Tories had decided among themselves that the women under investigation might best be questioned and judged by members of their own sex. The special qualifications of Mrs. Adams, Mrs. Winthrop and Mrs. Warren were apparent to all.

Adams was pleased when his wife was selected for this delicate task, and he wrote to her at once: "As you are a politician and now elected into an important office, that of judgess of the Tory ladies, which will give you, naturally, an influence with your sex, I hope you will be instant, in season and out of season, in exhorting them to use their influence with the gentlemen to fortify upon George's Island, Lovell's, Pettick's, Long, or wherever else it is proper."

Abigail became an expert propagandist. She worked with a gentler touch than Mrs. Warren, who had the fierce thrust of the satirist, and she was more astute than Mrs. Winthrop, but together these three women were more potent than many of the elected women of today. The newspapers had called on women to support the economic protests against taxation, and they lent themselves wholeheartedly to this endeavor. It was not a question of woman's role or woman's rights but of political survival. After the Stamp Act was imposed, they boycotted British goods and encouraged American manufactures. Many pledged themselves to refrain from using tea until the tax was repealed. They were as ardent as the peace marchers of the 1960's, and as determined.

The political leaders of the era sometimes discussed their plans with Abigail before consulting her husband, and she never failed to give them shrewd advice. John relied strongly on her judgment but rarely acknowledged it for what it was. He tended to link feminine influence in men's affairs with their degree of education, knowledge and ambition rather than with the traditional virtues of giving comfort, content and balance to the home environment. But he appreciated the happy combination of talents in his own Abigail. In some respects he was ahead of his time, for he astutely expressed doubt about the feminine image that shut out all but personal and domestic concerns. "My opinion of the duties of religion and morality comprehends a very extensive connection with society at large and the great interests of the public . . . public virtues and political qualities, therefore, should be incessantly cherished in our children," he wrote prophetically.

Here was the ground plan of the Adams dynasty—the hard core of Adams philosophy. By chance, or perhaps by inheritance and calculated training, their descendants gave it ample expression and repeatedly showed preoccupation with the role played by women in the destiny of man. Henry Adams singled out Boadicea as a leader of men, and the two women he named as having the greatest influence on the government and civilization of France were the Marquise de Rambouillet, who gathered around her representatives of all the arts, and Ninon de Lenclos, who nurtured bold thinkers like Voltaire, La Rochefoucauld and Condé.

In one of his letters to Abigail, John Adams made the point that most great men, whether generals, statesmen or philosophers, had a mother, wife or sister of superior knowledge and ambition whose precepts, by example or instigation, fostered eminence. Abigail added good cheer to this and wrote to her husband in a dark hour, "I am a mortal enemy to anything but a cheerful countenance and a merry heart, which, Solomon tells us, does good like a medicine."

She was naturally an intellectual and well informed, although she frequently referred to her lack of schooling. The political writings of the day were read by both John and Abigail Adams, and they listened often to the brilliant conversation of Thomas Jefferson, whom Abigail liked and trusted until he and her husband quarreled. After that she became a subtle but effective antagonist. John was not a popular man. His anger flared, and he could be arrogant and unreasonable. He went to extremes in supporting what he believed to be right. Abigail would wait until he had cooled down before projecting an argument. When she found she could not move him, she held her peace. The spirit of acquiescence was soothing to the proud Adams spirit, and in the end her calm judgment was apt to prevail. Abigail was an unseen reporter and courier of genuine status during the Revolution, using her eyes and ears to serve her husband much as Eleanor Roosevelt and Lady Bird Johnson did theirs in the twentieth century. When the hour of crisis arrived she met it boldly and wrote to John from Braintree on October 16, 1774: "And whether the end will be tragical, Heaven alone knows. You cannot be, I know, nor do I wish to see you, an inactive spectator; but if the sword be drawn, I bid adieu to all domestic felicity. . . ."

Soon she was reporting graphically to John in Philadelphia on the warlike preparations on Beacon Hill. Cannon were being mounted and entrenchments dug. "Not a Tory but hides his head," Abigail informed him. In Weymouth bells were ringing, drums were beating, alarm guns were being fired, and she felt that her husband would like to know what the local reaction was to his and other speeches. She was well aware that her letters were loaded with dynamite as she rounded up all the news she could on civil and military affairs.

"I have more particulars from you than from any one else," he wrote to her on April 28, 1776. "Pray keep me constantly informed what ships are in the harbor and what fortifications are going on. Not a moment should be neglected. . . ."

Even in these desperate circumstances the undertones of love were strong in the Adams correspondence. He confessed that he read and reread every line she wrote. Her charming letters, he assured her, served as a substitute for her company and made him wish to take a walk with her in the garden, or to go over to the Common, the plain or the meadow. He was lonely in Philadelphia and longed for his family. "The most agreeable time that I spend here is in writing to you, and conversing with you, when I am alone," he assured her on

December 3, 1775, and the following April he wrote: "The conclusion of your letter made my Heart throb, more than a cannonade would. You bid me burn your Letters. But I must forget you first."

On a May day in 1776 John Adams addressed himself to Abigail in terms that the latter-day feminist might have viewed with dismay. Amid the disappointments and perplexities of his life, he wrote, nothing had helped him as much as the blessing of a wife "whose capacity enabled her to comprehend, and whose pure virtue obliged her to approve the views of her husband." Whatever Abigail may have thought of this she boldly cast a lance for women's independence when the Constitution was being shaped. Her arguments were presented with a prophetic touch, but they did not move the Founding Fathers, if indeed they ever got beyond John Adams. Here she was far ahead of her generation, but she used a light and humorous touch to disarm him. By the way, said Abigail when the new code of laws was drawn up:

I desire you would remember the ladies and be more generous and favorable to them than your ancestors. Do not put such unlimited power into the hands of the husbands. Remember, all men would be tyrants if they could. If particular care and attention is not paid to the ladies, we are determined to foment a rebellion, and will not hold ourselves bound by any laws in which we have no voice or representation. . . . Men of sense in all ages abhor those customs which treat us only as the vassals of your sex; regard us then as being placed by Providence under your protection, and in imitation of the Supreme Being make use of that power only for our happiness.

Abigail's plea went unheeded, and John's answer showed his amusement, as well as some realization of the power exerted by the women of the period. He could only laugh at her extraordinary code of laws, he wrote, and he found her "saucy." He and his colleagues knew better than to repeal the prevailing system, which was more theory than fact in any event. Then he summed up:

We dare not exert our power in its full latitude. We are obliged to go fair and softly, and, in practice, you know we are the subjects. We have only the name of masters, and rather than give up this, which would completely subject us to the despotism of the petticoat, I hope General

Washington and all our brave heroes would fight; I am sure every good politician would plot, as long as he could against despotism, empire, monarchy, aristocracy, oligarchy, or ochlocracy.

Here again Abigail spoke softly and refrained from striking a militant note. She soon took another tack and wrote: "Government of States and Kingdoms, tho' God knows badly enough managed, I am willing should be solely administered by the lords of the creation. I should only contend for Domestic government, and think that best administered by the female."

But in spite of these exchanges, John Adams constantly sought his wife's advice. She cast her vote against his resigning from the Vice-Presidency, a role that he despised. "If I was to consult only my own private satisfaction and pleasure, I should request you to resign it," she wrote. "But alas, that is of small moment when compared to the whole, and I think you qualified and know you disposed to serve your country."

John answered her promptly on May 27, 1776, telling her that she shone as a stateswoman, as well as a "farmeress." "Pray where do you get your maxims of state?" he jested. "They are very apropos. . . . The affairs of America are in so critical a state, such great events are struggling into birth, that I must not quit this station at this time."

By July of that year he was seeking Abigail's advice again, asking her if a confederation should be formed and, if so, how they should vote. Should each colony have one vote, or should votes be apportioned in relation to population, wealth, exports and imports; or should there be a composite ratio of all? And should Congress have authority to limit the dimensions of each colony to prevent any one from becoming so great and powerful as to endanger the rest?

Here were the rudiments of government, and again Abigail came back with an urgent plea on behalf of her sex. This time her cause was education, not political rights. She proposed a more liberal plan for the benefit of the rising generation and suggested that the new constitution encourage learning and virtue. "If we mean to have heroes, statesmen, and philosophers, we should have learned women," she wrote. "The world perhaps would laugh at me and accuse me of vanity, but you, I know, have a mind too enlarged and liberal to disregard the sentiment . . . great benefit must arise from literary accomplishments in women."

During this period the Adams correspondence sharply illumined the birth of the nation in spite of the deep secrecy that cloaked each experimental phase. On July 3, 1776, John wrote triumphantly to Abigail that the anniversary of Independence Day would be the most memorable holiday in the history of America. It would be celebrated "with pomp and parade, with shows, games, sports, guns, balls, bonfires, and illuminations from one end of this continent to the other, from this time forward forevermore."

Abigail listened raptly to the reading of the Proclamation for Independence, along with the rest of the great crowd gathered around the State House in Boston. Bells rang. Privateers fired cannon at the forts and batteries, and she felt quietly triumphant as the King's Arms were taken down. She had truly been part of the birth of a nation.

She was forty years old and in her prime when she sailed for Europe in 1784, the first woman from the United States to represent her country at the French and British courts. Adams was a commissioner in Paris and then the American Minister in London. She fared well at the French court and absorbed the protocol with ease. Her salon at Auteuil was dignified and unostentatious. But she was less at ease in London, where echoes of the war were still close and insistent. The British did not flock to the Adams' house on Grosvenor Square, nor did Abigail easily forget what they had all had to endure in America. Queen Charlotte gave her a chilly reception when she was presented at court, looking grave and unsmiling in a hooped lutestring gown with lilac ribbons and point lace. Her reputation as an active figure in the Revolutionary movement was well known.

Abigail, humane in general, was merciless when Queen Charlotte suffered tortures over the Napoleonic threat to Britain: "Humiliation for Charlotte is no sorrow for me," she wrote. "She richly deserves her full portion for the contempt and scorn which she took pains to discover."

When John Adams was Vice-President, they lived for a time at Richmond Hill, in a mansion overlooking the Hudson. But Abigail found New York a dull city, without any public amusement, not even a public walk like Boston Common. Boston seemed to her to have six dinners to New York's one, and the Senators and their families, living in lodgings, could not entertain in proper fashion. The city was sickly. Servants were witless. There were no levees, and the Vice-President rode in a one-horse chaise while the President had powdered lackeys waiting at his door.

Although Philadelphia was considered a center of culture and fashion at the time, with many clever women circulating in the official set, Abigail did not approve when the government was moved there. Writing to her sister, Mary Cranch, on February 5, 1792, she noted that there were no plays that winter and assemblies were held only once a fortnight. Balls were in private homes, and it was her final judgment that the Philadelphians seemed to be "a strange and impolite people." She longed for her rosebushes, her clover field and the quiet of Quincy. In some respects she was no match for such women as the worldly Anne Willing Bingham, liveliest and most daring hostess of her day, who shocked her guests with her robust language and impressed them with the magnificence of her house on Third Street. Mrs. Bingham was both witty and sharp, and she set up social standards of her own—pretentious ones in the eyes of Thomas Jefferson, who regarded the "aristocratic pomp and court rituals maintained at that time" as a relapse into the despotic ways of the monarchy. Mrs. Bingham encouraged the use of the monster wigs of the French court, the restoration of the deep curtsy, and the announcement by uniformed lackeys of arriving guests. She did not worry about women's rights because she simply assumed them.

Abigail felt more akin to the ways of the distinguished Mrs. John Jay and considered her a brilliant hostess. The Jay family, with a long history of patriotic effort, had been active throughout the Revolution, and John Adams worked with John Jay on the peace treaties that followed the war. Relations with France had reached such a point at the close of the eighteenth century that Abigail was certain of war in the spring of 1798, and it was widely believed that had she been President it would have been declared. She followed all the negotiations closely and saw many of the dispatches from envoys before they were read to Congress. John Adams did not underestimate her judgment in this area any more than he had during the war. When he later appointed William Vans Murray special envoy of the United States to France, he wrote to her: "I have instituted a new mission, which is kept in the dark, but when it comes to be understood it will be approved. Oh, how they lament Mrs. Adams's absence! She is a good counsellor! If she had been here, Murray would never have been named nor his mission instituted. This ought to gratify your vanity enough to cure you."

But Abigail spoke softly, although she had particularly strong feelings about the crisis with France. Her husband's stand was popular at the time, and the covenant signed in 1800 restored the balance in this delicate area. But Abigail had lived through a stormy administration. Strangely enough, she had not been present at her husband's inauguration. His dying mother had needed her at that historic moment, so she missed his famous address and the cheers of the crowd; but she wrote to him on February 8, 1797: "You have this day to declare yourself head of a nation . . . My feelings are not those of pride or ostentation upon the occasion. They are solemnized by a sense of the obligations, the important trusts, and numerous duties connected with it. That you may be enabled to discharge them with honor to yourself, with justice and impartiality to your country and with satisfaction to this great people, shall be the daily prayer of your A.A."

When Abigail moved from the temporary capital in Philadelphia to Washington, she found it to be a wilderness. Her arrival there and her first impressions have contributed historically to the public image of Mrs. John Adams. She found the President's House beautifully situated and the surrounding country romantic, but "George Town" was the "very dirtyest Hole" she had ever seen, and she went through quagmires to do her marketing. However, she made up her mind to hold her peace about the inconveniences.

Mary Cranch in Massachusetts read with interest of the "castle" itself, twice as large as the Meeting House at home and obviously "built for ages to come." But it needed thirty servants and not one room was finished. It had thirteen fireplaces and no logs. Nor was there a single bell in the entire mansion. At this point Mrs. Adams gave posterity an interesting glimpse of hanging her wash in what is now the East Room:

We have not the least fence-yard or other convenience without, and the great unfinished audience-room I make a drying room of, to hang the clothes in . . . there are six chambers made comfortable . . . If they will put up some bells and let me have wood enough to keep fires, I design to be pleased.

John Adams gave the residence his blessing and said in a note addressed to Abigail on November 2, 1800, "I pray heaven to bestow the best of blessings on this house, and on all that shall hereafter inhabit it. May none but honest and wise men ever rule under this roof." His words are inscribed in the White House today.

Abigail was fifty-three and John was sixty-two when he became President. To the public they were Darby and Joan, preferring each other's company to that of anyone else. They were a loving pair, and the President's favorite respite from the cares of office was to drive with his wife among the peach and dogwood blossoms on the banks of the Potomac. Together they simplified the social regime and followed the pomp and formality of the Washingtons with New England austerity. Abigail was a dignified First Lady, but she failed to warm the hearts of the people. One skeptic observed that "notwithstanding she comes from the Eastward many acknowledge her to be superior to her sex."

The fact was that in Washington, as in Philadelphia, she was far from well. She had intermittent attacks of ague and fever, and the damp seriously affected her "rheumatic Constitution." Strong-willed though she was, she could not surmount this condition, even while she deprecated a "groaning, whining, complaining temper." She had to stay indoors much of the time, and it was not until her last winter in Washington that she was able to hold levees and dinners on the grand scale. She longed constantly for the bracing air of Quincy. Her personal sorrows were overwhelming at this time, too, for Abigail had more success as a wife than as a mother. Like Dolley Madison and Eleanor Roosevelt, she suffered over her childen. Abigail had five in all, but one of her two daughters died in infancy. The other, Abby, was a reserved and clever girl who made an unfortunate marriage. Her sons were Thomas Boylston, John Quincy, eventually President like his father, and Charles, a wastrel who died the death of an alcoholic. In spite of her husband's many injunctions about their upbringing and her own rigid standards, John Quincy Adams alone brought further glory to the Adams name.

At the time the children were growing up on the family farm, Abigail was noted for her good management and thrifty ways. She ran the property, kept the accounts, was a "farmeress" from five in the morning until darkness fell. While her husband helped to foment the Revolution, she maintained the status quo on the home front.

Both father and mother worked hard at their parenthood, but the standards set were stiff ones for their children. Abigail assured John in the case of one of their sons that she "would rather he had found his grave in the ocean, or that any untimely death should crop him in his infant years, than see him an immoral, profligate, or graceless child." He proved to be all three, and his mother suffered acutely as he reached his sordid end.

But she had other things to worry her as her husband's administration became stormy and abrasive. Adams and Jefferson were soon in conflict, a situation that distressed Abigail, who admired both men. Each said what he thought, and the President's harsh manner did not help. Abigail used all her tact and diplomacy during this period, and Albert Gallatin called her "Mrs. President, not of the United States, but of a nation." Even his backers, the Federalists, and notably Alexander Hamilton, failed John Adams, and the Jeffersonian Republicans accused him of snobbish leanings toward the rich, the well-born and the able. War taxation, rioting and the Alien and Sedition laws pushed by the Federalists stirred up trouble, and Abigail was in the middle of it. She, too, was considered snobbish because she entertained so little. The feeling was that she was staying aloof because of the treatment her husband was getting.

Abigail scorned this accusation and proudly wrote to her sister: "I wish for the preservation of the Government, and a wise administration of it. . . . The President had frequently comtemplated resigning. I thought it would be best for him to leave to the people to act for themselves and take no responsibility upon himself. I do not regret that he has done so."

This was Abigail's acknowledgment that she had advised her husband to run again for office, unhappy and apprehensive though he was. But she had been equally frank earlier in his administration in expressing her outrage with the Philadelphians for celebrating Washington's birthday after John Adams was in office. She confessed that she had longed to vent her indignation in public, but she warned her sister to say nothing about this impulse. It would merely be labeled pride and mortification, and "I despise them both, as it respects myself, but as it respects the character I hold—I will not knowingly disgrace it."

Abigail left the White House deeply wounded over the defeat of her husband. From 1801 to the time of her death in October, 1818, she remained in Quincy. Now she watched another President in the making, although she did not live for the inauguration of her son, John Quincy Adams. She had been a major influence in his life for years, and had conducted as lively a correspondence with him as with his father. He learned more from his mother's letters than from the newspapers and sometimes even the dispatches. He, in turn, flooded Quincy with comments on politics, people, places and things. "I wrote to my mother and to the Secretary of State," was a frequent entry in his journal.

The crosscurrents of communication were particularly strong during the War of 1812, and she backed her son in his "independence of judgment, his strength to hold his own" when he roused his father's wrath by supporting Jefferson's embargo against Britain. Young John had just become President Monroe's Secretary of State when Abigail died of typhoid fever. His final tribute to her was widely quoted:

Had she lived in the age of the Patriarchs, every day of her life would have been filled with clouds of goodness and of love. There is not a virtue that can abide in the female heart but it was the ornament of hers. She had been fifty-four years the delight of my father's heart, the sweetener of all his toils, the comforter of all his sorrows, the sharer and brightener of all his joys.

John Adams had told his son shortly before her death that "through all the good report and evil report of the world, in all his struggles and in all his sorrows, the affectionate participation and cheering encouragement of his wife had been his never-failing support, without which he was sure he should never have lived through them."

Few women in American history have wielded the power that Abigail did, without benefit of the vote or franchise of any kind. The picture is clear and detailed, thanks to the literary history of the Adams family and their passion for turning their deeds and thoughts into prose.

Chapter 2

The Early Pacemakers

Dolley Madison had a style of her own which made her, where fashion and hospitality were concerned, the most legendary of First Ladies until Jacqueline Kennedy created a fresh and memorable image. Dolley matched her era as Mrs. Kennedy did hers. Her warmth was as pronounced as Jacqueline's reserve; her clothes as flamboyant as her successor's were simple; her cuisine as lavish as Mrs. Kennedy's was knowledgeable.

Using the subtlest kind of power in public affairs, Dolley specialized in kindness, tact and charm. She deserves to be better remembered for the feuds she dispelled and the way she won over her husband's enemies than for her turbans, snuff box and the parties she gave. She was the last of the wives of the Founding Fathers to wield influence based on power and firsthand experience. Together these women were the pacemakers of the period, typifying the feminine influence in the creation of the new republic. If Abigail was the expert politician, Dolley was the master diplomat. She was thirty-three when she made her bow to official Washington, leaning on the arm of Thomas Jefferson, whose wife, Martha, had died nineteen years before he became President. She was eighty-one but still active and vivacious when she bowed her way out as Queen Dolley, this time on the arm of President Polk.

As the daughter of John Payne, a Virginia Quaker, she had been strictly brought up, but tucked under her Quaker kerchief at all times was a tiny bag of jewelry given her by her grandmother. Her first husband, John Todd, died of yellow fever in 1793, when she was only twenty-five. James Madison was seventeen years her senior when he asked Aaron Burr to bring him to call on Dorothea Payne Todd. She was wearing a mulberry satin gown and she captivated the insignificant-looking bachelor with her wit and charm. When she married him he was compared unfavorably with the virile husbands of her predecessors, Martha Washington and Abigail Adams. More than any other President, James Madison suggested the nondescript, the diffident, the inept. His robust colleagues were apt to refer to him pityingly as Poor Jemmy, and Washington Irving commented, "Jemmy Madison. Ah, poor Jemmy! He is but a withered little apple-John." But Dolley viewed him differently. To her he was large as life. "My big little Mr. Madison," she called him, seeing him more as he is regarded today—as a scholar, a man of reserve, of intellect and liberal views, a philosopher who played a leading role in shaping American democracy.

But the public saw only a small, shrinking figure, neatly clad in ecclesiastical black, with a skimpy queue that Dolley herself dressed. Whenever possible she bolstered his ego, tempered the scene around him when he quarreled with others, and talked softly to his enemies to turn away the wrath often directed at this scholarly man. It was evident to all that her opinion carried weight with him, regardless of where they were—in the President's House; in Octagon House, where the Treaty of Ghent was proclaimed; or at Montpellier, where the Madisons entertained lavishly among their tulip trees, silver poplars and willows.

Long before she became First Lady, Dolley was the official hostess for Thomas Jefferson, coping valiantly with his impetuous hospitality, his pell-mell system of seating guests and his own extraordinary personality and attire. He could not be swayed in matters of protocol, and he disavowed the tradition of precedence. His only exception was for Mrs. Madison herself. She was allotted a special seat as his hostess. Her attempts to spruce him up were ignored, and he continued to receive diplomats wearing his scuffed slippers, rumpled woolen stockings, green velveteen breeches and red waistcoat.

When he retired to Monticello in 1809 and Madison became President, it was a simple matter for Dolley to continue what she had begun, but now on her own terms. From the start she was intent on making her husband's administration one that counted, and when she appeared at the inaugural ceremonies in purple velvet and white satin with bird-of-paradise plumes, she was hailed as Queen Dolley. She reverted to some of the pomp of the Washington era that had gone out of style with John Adams and Thomas Jefferson. She seemed showy after Abigail, but the outside world was now viewing America in its new showcase. The most worldly Europeans came and went. French was spoken in the President's House, and Jefferson had introduced French cuisine to its kitchens. Dolley had both authority and experience to aid her in the sixteen years she functioned as the nation's foremost hostess, first with Jefferson, then as First Lady in her own right.

Under her management there was no lack of bells to ring or wood for the open fireplaces. The wear and tear of the Jefferson era was soon amended with new china and glass. Yellow satin upholstery was introduced. Glittering chandeliers and mirrors were installed, and andirons upheld the roaring logs. When her husband became President Dolley drew up some rules of protocol to offset the Jefferson confusion. One skeptic from abroad remarked that Mrs. Madison's table was more like a harvest-home supper than the entertainment of a high official. She good-naturedly pointed out that she considered abundance preferable to elegance. Used to the lavish ways of plantation life, she reminded her critics that profusion arose from the "happy circumstance of the superabundance and prosperity of the country and so she did not hesitate to sacrifice the delicacy of European taste for the more liberal fashion of Virginia."

Dolley's attire was in character. She favored velvet and satin gowns of majestic proportions, Paris turbans, and ermine and ostrich trimmings. It was her custom to brandish large, brightly colored bandanna handkerchiefs and pass around snuff in a lava and platinum box. She was inclined to be portly, and as the years went on she painted and powdered as excessively as the women of the French court. But she was charitable as well as fashionable and spent much time cutting out garments for the children of the capital's orphan asylum.

Her levees were immensely popular, and her most responsive guest was Washington Irving, who wrote of hastily arraying himself in his best "peas blossom and silk stocking attire" to get to Mrs. Madison's within an hour after he had returned from a journey. He basked in the aura of luxury and good living that surrounded her, but some of her Quaker friends were critical of her worldliness. Philip Hone called her a "national treasure," and she charmed, among others, Talleyrand, Chateaubriand, Volney and Joseph and Jerome Bonaparte. Lafayette always gave his friends who visited America letters of introduction to Mrs. Madison.

Dolley installed a piano and guitar in the East Room, and sometimes chose to sail in to a reception with an open book in her hand, immediately focusing the conversation on something she ostensibly had been reading. Everyone knew that she was not an intellectual, like Abigail Adams, but she liked to play up to her husband's literary tastes. Where her predecessor had suffered in the President's House Mrs. Madison gloried in it and enlivened it. She was sympathetic, kind and tolerant, and adapted herself readily to all manner of guests, remembering their names and faces with ease. She made a point of cultivating the wives and daughters of the men in bitter opposition to her husband. In this respect she showed more tact than many of her successors, and was quite consciously a peacemaker, seeking always to lessen the bitterness that divided the Federalists and the Republicans. The Washington feuds were formidable. Feminine gossip raged then as it does today.

Dolley was ever watchful to see where she could help her husband, who was too proud and detached to tangle at close range with his critics. Her Jemmy kept her well informed on political events, and he listened attentively to her shrewd comments. Her late afternoon dinner parties, with staggering menus and vintage wines, were her contribution to the political history of Mr. Madison. Because he had many physical ills he ate abstemiously, but he enjoyed good wines and could be witty with his intimates in a wry way. However, it was Dolley who drew out their guests, listened attentively to their opinions and kept the conversation on a general plane. Popular as she was with men, her diplomacy with members of her own sex was memorable in White House history. When her husband quarreled with Albert Gallatin she immediately asked Mrs. Gallatin to represent her at the drawing rooms. And when William Seaton became editor of the *National Intelligencer* she cultivated his wife with care, foreseeing the influence that the Seatons would have with this powerful paper at their command.

Actually, Mrs. Madison was an early propagandist and much more of a politician than she seemed to be. The thought that she was consciously influencing anyone would have shocked her, or at least that was the pose she took with her adoring husband. "You know I am not much of a politician," she wrote rather sanctimoniously as she begged the President in 1805 to give her information on the war with Spain and the trouble developing with Britain, "but I am extremely anxious to hear (as far as you think proper) what is going forward in the Cabinet. On this subject I believe you would not desire your wife to be the active partisan that our neighbor is, Mrs. L., nor will there be the slightest danger, while she is conscious of her want of talents, and the diffidence in expressing those opinions, always imperfectly understood by her sex."

Dolley needed all her diplomacy during the troubled days of 1812. The politicians who opposed her husband's stand on war stayed away from the President's House, but she reached out in all directions, serving as an able conciliator who listened attentively to differing views and strengthened his position. Not always a realist, she preferred to turn her back on open conflict. "I do not admire contention in any form, either political or civil. . . . I would rather fight with my hands than my tongue" said Dolley, as she calmed the atmosphere around her husband more potently than if she had had direct political power. When she could not win her way she side-stepped and used the technique skillfully applied many years later by Mrs. Theodore Roosevelt and Mrs. Harry Truman—of restraining their husbands from impulsive action or ill-judged speech through a strong air of negation rather than a frontal assault. If the conversation became too controversial Dolley would simply leave the room and return later to find that her guests had taken the hint and settled down. In her own way she rang up a succession of political victories that today's woman, armed with the vote, might envy.

She was the first of the Doves in Washington, but at that time the Doves were all women. Dolley's Dove parties included the wives of Cabinet officers and foreign ministers, and they foregathered happily while their lords and masters ran the country and fought it out. It was a known fact that Dolley's opinion traveled back to the various men involved and that in this bland manner she conducted a courier service on her husband's behalf. She spiced her parties with lotteries, too, for she was worldly in all her instincts.

Dolley is remembered most dramatically for her courage and pertinacity in staying on at the President's House as the British approached until she had rescued Gilbert Stuart's portrait of George Washington. She had already rounded up the public papers and had had them packed in trunks when her eye lit on the painting. Without a moment's hesitation she ordered the few remaining servants to unscrew it from the wall, break the frame with an ax and carefully remove the canvas. The cannons of Bladensburg sounded while this was going on. She had no fear for herself, but she suffered agonies over the safety of her husband. When they were reunited she insisted on going with him to the Virginia shore, and she watched Washington burn from a friend's house two miles beyond Georgetown.

After the destruction of the President's House the Madisons moved into Octagon House, which still stands in the capital, and there the soldiers of the War of 1812 paid honor to Mrs. Madison, their brave Queen Dolley. She entertained brilliantly in the winter of 1815, and Federalists and Democrats, the diplomatic corps and party politicians, plain citizens and visitors from abroad shared in her hospitality and her Irish wit. Her drawing room after the victory at New Orleans was the most brilliant held by a First Lady up to that time.

The Madisons lived at Montpellier until James' death in 1836. In her aging years Dolley returned to Washington, still a figure of consequence. The politicians sought her out and listened to her opinion on many matters. She was always calm and judicious, and she shared her husband's liberal views, although both had seemed conservative in comparison to Jefferson. Dolley was impoverished in her old age, and she suffered endlessly over the profligacy and indifference of her son Payne Todd. He brought her nothing but sorrow. But she went proudly along, living in shabby state, a handsome old lady in worn gowns of ancient vintage. She clung to the short-waisted, puff-sleeved, gored velvet gowns of the days of her magnificence. Her withered throat was encased in a stiff quilling of net, and she was heavily made up. Her dyed hair was always surmounted by a turban of one kind or another. Jessie Frémont, one of her regular visitors, recalled that with all this Mrs. Madison was "handsome, majestic and simply dignified . . . and very agreeable—with a memory and kind words for every one."

On July 4 and New Year's Day people attending the President's receptions would stroll across the square to pay honor to Mrs. Madison. She was still the great hostess, even when crippled with rheumatism. Her husband's manuscripts were bought by Congress as a national work of great value. She had copyright and franking privileges and was voted a seat on the floor of the Senate and House—the only woman to whom such a distinction was accorded. Dolley did not need voting power. She was part of the early history of her country.

A more reserved sophisticate with perfect manners and great poise moved into the President's House after Dolley Madison left it in 1817, but Elizabeth Monroe, who had played a spectacular role in France by helping to save Madame Lafayette from the guillotine, was an invalid during most of her husband's term in office. Washingtonians soon acknowledged that she was one of the stateliest and best gowned of Presidents' wives as she displayed the opulent Empire creations she had brought from France. The Monroes knew how to entertain in the grand manner, but when they revived the stiff protocol of earlier days they were accused of being monarchical in spirit.

During this administration the President's House literally became the White House, for its charred surfaces were painted over and restored. The Monroes introduced a note of elegance, with French furniture and the vermeil bric-à-brac that is treasured today. The mahogany of the Oval Room was gilded, and fringed crimson damask draperies were hung in the public rooms. President Monroe selected much of the vermeil himself, including the gold spoons and the famous glass plateau centerpiece with gold figurines that has been used for the most formal dinners ever since his time. These treasures were as much criticized when they were introduced as they are admired today. The general feeling was that the Monroes were too pretentious for the assorted crowds that flocked through the White House in muddy boots and spurs. But the mansion benefited by twenty-six marble chimney pieces and a hundred and twenty-nine plate-glass windowpanes, as well as the white-and-gold china of the Monroe administration and the vermeil objets d'art.

Like Mrs. Adams, Mrs. Monroe was well trained in the etiquette of foreign courts, but her approach was chilling after Dolley Madison's hearty ways. Her daughter, Eliza Hay, who had attended school in France with Napoleon's stepdaughter, Hortense Beauhamais, stirred up feuds and induced her father to keep the foreign ministers at a distance. This was particularly annoying to John Quincy Adams, who was highly critical of Mrs. Hay, but she took her mother's place with increasing frequency at the formal levees.

Mrs. Monroe was more influential in her husband's counsels before he became President. He served as Minister to France, England and Spain for nearly five years, and his wife was greatly admired in the continental capitals. As the daughter of Hannah Aspinwall and Captain Lawrence Kortwright of the British Army, she fitted harmoniously into the life of London and Paris. When Jefferson became President and the Federalists were in disfavor, he sent Monroe back to France to negotiate the Louisiana Purchase with Talleyrand. Mrs. Monroe, who saw the backwash of the Revolution, was known as La Belle Américaine and had passing fame when she worked adroitly for the freedom of Madame Lafayette, who had been imprisoned by the Terrorists and awaited execution.

Her captors spared the Marquise in order to preserve diplomatic friendship with the Monroes. She went to their home from prison and stayed there until the American Minister got her a passport permitting her to join Lafayette at Olmutz. Although this meant prison, too, she was with her husband and safe from the guillotine. This coup was the work of Mrs. Monroe.

In London Mrs. Monroe had to use her best brand of diplomacy when her husband ran into trouble through his outspoken criticism of the Jay Treaty with England. Relations between the two countries were strained at the time, and Mrs. Monroe steered a careful course until her husband was recalled. She was more tactful than the tall, shy Minister, who was prone to speak his mind and who turned out a pamphlet criticizing his government on his return home. He was the last of the Presidents to have lived through the Revolution, and he was an old friend of Jefferson's and Madison's. Jefferson had said of him that he was a man "whose soul might be turned wrong side outwards without discovering a blemish to the world." After his negotiations for the purchase of Louisiana succeeded, he went to Spain to try to buy the Floridas, but here he failed. Mrs. Monroe played her part on the diplomatic side in each of these capitals and followed with close attention the charting of the Monroe Doctrine, which was cast to the winds in the twentieth century.

Her successor, Mrs. John Quincy Adams, suffered from being in the shade of her powerful mother-in-law, who did not live to see Louisa reign as First Lady. Neither one of the younger Adamses had much influence over the other, but both were regarded as being haughty, literate and reserved. Louisa was an individualist, and neither Abigail nor her husband John could sway her in one direction or another. She had been highly critical of the Russians when her husband was appointed Minister to Russia in 1809, and she had not flourished at the German Embassy, where she went with John after their marriage in London in 1797. She was an American girl, the daughter of a businessman, Joshua Johnson, and she charmed John Quincy Adams as he was recovering from an earlier love for Mary Frazier. He had already served as Minister to the Hague, and he climbed steadily after his marriage until he became President.

The continuation of the Adams dynasty created much interest in Washington, but the White House scene was almost as chilly as in the days of the Monroes. Although Mrs. Adams' background was cosmopolitan and she had coped with society on many fronts, she did not endear herself to the public, as the wife of either the Secretary of State or the President. She was essentially a recluse with the same literary and artistic tastes as her husband. Her books and music, her silkworms and dreams took up much of her time. She had indifferent health and was totally uncommunicative at times. Her husband cared for books, but he also liked to garden, to play billiards, to ride and to swim. He was one of the first Bostonians to take swimming lessons and he sometimes plunged into the Potomac in the buff early in the morning, a habit that drew national attention when Anne Royall, a termagant newspaperwoman, sat on his clothes on the riverbank and refused to stir until the President had promised to give her an interview. Whenever possible he avoided the White House levees, but Louisa did her best to cope with the widening ripples of social interchanges as the country grew. She favored evening receptions with refreshments, an innovation that lapsed with later administrations as the guests became too numerous. It was revived again by the Kennedys, however.

Rachel Donelson Robards Jackson, who was due to follow Mrs. John Quincy Adams in the White House, died mysteriously before her husband's inauguration. She had never wished to see him become President, although she said with resignation when she learned that he had won, "For Mr. Jackson's sake, I'm glad; for my own part, I never wished it." After hearing that she had become a campaign caricature and that her name was infamous she said to her niece, Emily Donelson, "I will be no disadvantage to my husband at the White House, and I wish never to go there and disgrace him. You will go and take care of his home for him, and I will stay here and take care of everything until he comes back."

Rachel was the daughter of Colonel John Donelson, a Virginia surveyor who became one of the founders of Nashville, Tennessee. She married a Kentuckian named Lewis Robards in 1783, divorced him and then in 1791 married Jackson, whom she had known for some time. Later, when doubt was cast on the legality of the divorce, the formalities were observed and Jackson married Rachel for the second time. But by then a storm of scandal surrounded the dark-

haired, silent woman whom Jackson adored, and it burst into flame
when he ran for the Presidency. She was caricatured as a crude and
inarticulate woman who smoked a long reed pipe and had question-
able morals. No other woman in presidential history, with the possible exception of Mrs. Lincoln, caused more uproar, however unwittingly, and she proved to be more formidable dead than alive. Her
influence in the life of the fiery, rough-hewn Jackson, six feet one,
dynamic and always chivalrous to his devoted wife, continued as long
as he lived and stirred up storms in his Cabinet from the start of his
administration.

His wife knew what she would have had to face in Washington.
She had been with him in the capital when he served in the Senate in
the early 1820's and had had a chilly reception. She would have been
totally ostracized but for Mrs. Edward Livingston, the beautiful
Creole from Santo Domingo whose husband had commanded the
Army of the South. The women of the official set were traveled and
worldly wise, and Rachel could find no place among them. But worse
things were in store for her when Jackson ran for the Presidency. His
rivals used the story of the divorce and remarriage as unmercifully as
the enemies of Grover Cleveland sought to besmirch him over an
illegitimate child. Pamphlets were circulated, describing Rachel as
vulgar, disreputable and a dowdy frump. Jackson was so angry that he
decided not to electioneer but to stay close to his Rachel, and she
made her own pronouncement: "I would rather be a doorkeeper in
the House of my God than to dwell in that palace in Washington."

But the palace was looming with frightening closeness when, on
Christmas evening, 1828, she died of what was thought to be a heart
attack. Jackson saw to it that she was buried in white satin with the
kid gloves and slippers that she was to have worn in the White
House. She was sixty-one when she was buried in the Hermitage
garden.

His niece, Mrs. A. J. Donelson, acted as hostess for "Old Hickory,"
and nothing like the inauguration scene had ever been staged in
Washington before. The crowd scrambled, fought, entered and left
through windows, stood on damask chairs in their muddy boots and
broke glass and china. Women fainted and men got bloody noses.

Jackson, on edge over any slur on a woman's name, was soon

defending Peggy Eaton, wife of Major John H. Eaton, whom he had appointed Secretary of War. The other Cabinet wives refused to receive or tolerate the notorious Peggy Eaton, better known as Peggy O'Neale, daughter of an Irish tavern keeper in Washington. Peggy had married a Navy man named John Bowie Timberlake, but had flirted openly with Eaton before marrying him. Rachel Jackson had always considered her an innocent and injured woman, and the President took up the issue and threatened to dismiss any Cabinet members who ostracized her in any way. He made Mrs. Donelson visit her, and he would not drop Major Eaton from his Cabinet. Peggy was completely ignored on Inauguration Day, but Jackson came to the rescue of the graceful, dark-haired girl wearing a pink gown and black plumes. He blamed Henry Clay for much of the gossip, and he collected affidavits testifying to her good character. But Mrs. John Calhoun would not bend an inch, and the other Cabinet wives took the same stand. One walked out of the White House when she learned she would have to sit at the same table as Mrs. Eaton, and several Cabinet members threatened to resign. Jackson reorganized the Cabinet, and the husbands of all the wives who had snubbed Mrs. Eaton were out, but so was Major Eaton. Peggy died at the age of eighty-four after eloping with an Italian dancing master who, in turn, ran off with her granddaughter and her jewelry.

Jessie Frémont, visiting Jackson in the White House and taking note of the wood fires burning, the soft wax lights for illumination, the camellias and laurel banked on the horseshoe dining table and the monster salmon at either end in waves of meat jelly, reflected on the fact that Rachel had never shared in this effect and yet had left so stinging an impression. Jessie's mother, Mrs. Thomas Hart Benton, had made a point of calling on Rachel Jackson when she first came to Washington, even though she did not approve of divorce. She had liked her and had tried to thaw the frost that surrounded her in the capital.

After the Jackson administration things quietened down at the White House until John Tyler married Julia Gardiner of New York. The second Mrs. John Tyler, one of the most influential of First Ladies, reigned only briefly but with direct and discernible power.

She was one of the dazzlers in White House history and controversial, too, since she played politics openly and sometimes dangerously. President Tyler's first wife, Letitia Christian Tyler, had helped his political career with her Virginia fortune. She managed the Christian plantation at Cedar Grove and brought up a large family, but by the time her ambitious husband became President her health was poor and she shrank from social activity. She gave an occasional ball or dinner party, and she was the first President's wife to introduce music on the White House grounds. She died of a stroke in 1842 and lay in state in the East Room. Her daughter, Letitia Tyler Semple, and her daughter-in-law, Priscilla Cooper Tyler, acted as official hostesses until President Tyler married Julia Gardiner in the Church of the Ascension in New York after a somewhat giddy courtship. Julia's father, Senator Gardiner, had been killed by the explosion of a big gun on the battleship *Princeton* when the President was on board. In his efforts to console the beautiful Julia, the President fell in love with her, and she became a potent figure in American politics.

Julia, whose family gave its name to Gardiner's Island in Long Island Sound, was already a somewhat ostentatious belle, who had paraded in the streets of New York modeling French fashions for a dry-goods store. She was known as the Rose of Long Island, and she loved social display even more than Dolley Madison. But her pretensions amused official Washington, particularly her habit of receiving guests while seated in a thronelike armchair on a raised dais, surrounded by twelve white-gowned ladies in waiting popularly known as the Vestal Virgins. Her long-trained purple velvet dress and royal plumes were suggestive of Queen Victoria's court, and she was called the Presidentress.

Julia was tall and striking-looking. She invariably wore a headdress or headband of some sort, most often a crimson Greek cap with tassel, or a band with a heron's plume and diamond star. After her father's death she wore black and white lace and substituted black onyx for the star. She was the first occupant of the White House to employ a press agent, and F. W. Thomas, a friend of Edgar Allan Poe's and an employee of the New York *Herald*, trumpeted her social triumphs during her short term as First Lady. "This winter," she told her mother, "I intend to do something in the way of entertaining that shall be the admiration and talk of the Washington world."

She vowed to make her court interesting with youth and beauty, and the young flocked happily around her and enjoyed her entertainments. Her courier relayed to the public through his paper, the *Herald*, that the Executive Mansion would be thrown open under the auspices of the "most splendid and accomplished lady of the age. . . . Possessed of the highest order of beauty and intellect, and of the most elegant and popular manners, she will draw about her a court circle rivaling in charms of mind and persons, that of Charles II or Louis le Grand."

But Julia was also an intrigante of the first order. She had already traveled and was familiar with the ways of the *beau monde*. Her family was so deeply involved in politics that she was quite at home in government circles. She helped her brothers Alexander and Robert to create a permanent Tyler faction in New York City, and it was soon said that Gardiners walked where Tylers feared to tread. The entire Gardiner family pushed strong pro-Texas annexation resolutions through Tammany Hall, and even Julia tired of Alexander's imperious demands for inside information from the White House. She functioned as intermediary in his correspondence and discussions with the President, and she was guilty of unabashed nepotism. Julia relayed names, jobs and patronage decisions back and forth between New York and the White House, and her own opinion always had weight with President Tyler. She was a dynamo of energy and ambition, and no woman in office today could move as many pawns as Julia did during her period of power. In defending nepotism she said that she wished only to make people happy and to add to her husband's popularity.

When President Tyler drew up his state paper on the proposed annexation of Texas, copies were distributed by the Gardiner and Tyler families, and Julia felt that it created a "prodigious sensation" in Washington. Having vowed to make it a matter of honor to get the support of Associate Justice John McLean, the Ohio Republican who had been Postmaster General during the Monroe administration, she practiced coquetry toward that end.

"There *is* no honor in politics," said John Calhoun, commenting on Julia's intention at her own dinner table.

"We will see," she retorted.

She wrote "Texas and John Tyler" on a slip of paper and handed it to McLean with the request that he propose this toast. He bowed gallantly, raised his glass and said, "For your sake."

Judge McLean, who sought nomination for the Presidency in 1856 and 1860, was one of many men who came under Julia's spell. She amused handsome and aloof John Calhoun. Francis W. Pickens, Richard D. David and Richard Waldorf were among the politicians who danced to her tune. Julia was making good her promise to Alexander that she would win as many friends as she could on the Congressional front. He kept her informed on those who were worth cultivating on her husband's behalf. She was determined that the Texas measure should go through before President Tyler left the White House, so that all the credit would be his. She doubled her efforts on the social front, getting youthful support by popularizing the polka, which was considered a wild and shocking dance. With Julia's help it and the waltz soon became the rage, although a few years earlier Tyler had condemned the waltz as immoral and had forbidden his daughters to dance it. But the young now seized eagerly on sheet music of the *Julia Waltz,* and the more mature took note of the French furniture Mrs. Tyler had installed and the good French wines that had been added to the menus. She tampered also with old established customs and ranged her entourage in a line along the Blue Room wall, putting the President at the head of a formal receiving line instead of leaving him exposed in the center of the room. Her ladies in waiting were commanded to stay in group formation at all times. Julia's gowns invariably excited interest, for she was one of the best-dressed and most beautiful of Presidents' wives.

When the annexation of Texas seemed assured she gave her final ball, resolved that Washington should never forget the Tyler regime. Her farewell went down in history, well publicized by Thomas. A thousand candles shed a flood of light over the East Room. There were beaux enough to staff a dozen balls. Mrs. Tyler wore white satin embroidered with silver and roses, and three ostrich plumes waved from her white satin headdress. Although the Whigs boycotted the ball, the President jested, "They cannot say now that I am a President without a party." But for months afterward clergymen complained about the free use of liquor at Mrs. Tyler's ball, the shameless dancing and the fact that the First Lady had allowed such dissipation within a short time after her father's death. The President was glad to see his beautiful wife referred to in the press as Juno and her party acclaimed as one of the greatest in White House history.

On the last day of his administration Congress passed a joint resolution providing for the admission of Texas, and Julia felt that she had contributed to the future of America. Her husband died in the second year of the Civil War after figuring actively in the abortive negotiations for peace. He was chosen to serve in the Congress of the Confederacy, but did not live to take his seat in that body. Theodore Roosevelt later characterized him as a "politician of monumental littleness," but Julia, who had influenced many of his decisions, remembered him always as the handsome and chivalrous Virginian who had befriended her after her father's death. She lived until 1889 and had financial troubles and involved litigation with members of her family in her later years, but she remained vigorous and attractive to the end. Most Presidential wives have shrunk from drawing attention to their influence, but Julia gloried in hers and boasted of it publicly. In this respect she differed from another young and beautiful White House hostess who had considerable power in the days preceding the Civil War.

Harriet Lane, niece of James Buchanan, was one of the more influential young women in White House history and was a godsend to the only bachelor President because she had tact, good looks and style. Orphaned early in life, she was left well off, and Buchanan, as her guardian, saw to it that she was carefully educated. While attending a convent in Georgetown she spent weekends with him when he was Secretary of State. Listening to the conversation of significant men, she became well versed in political discussion. Harriet also followed the newspapers with more attention than most of her female contemporaries at that time, and she was ready to be her uncle's hostess when he became Minister to Great Britain in 1852.

She was blond, with striking bluish-violet eyes and classically modeled features. In build she was Junoesque, not a disadvantage in her era, and she dressed well but not ostentatiously. After undergoing careful scrutiny she became a pet of Queen Victoria's, and her name was mentioned as a likely wife for the Prince of Wales, later King Edward VII. Harriet kept early hours, exercised vigorously and was pictured as a model of healthy American womanhood. Through attending conferences in Europe with her uncle she had had considerable foreign experience long before she presided at the White House. The press credited her with influencing William Howard Russell, of the *Times* of London, and Lord Lyons, the British Minister, in favor of the Confederacy, and she was a clever propagandist in dealing with visitors from Europe at this crucial time. It was natural for her to play hostess to the Prince of Wales when he visited the United States in 1860, traveling incognito as Baron Renfrew. His visit was significant, for it was the first time that an heir to the British throne had visited America since the loss of the colonies.

All of Harriet's diplomacy was called into play during the early days of secession, while her uncle vacillated between North and South. Wearing the large bertha that she helped to make fashionable, she was one of the garlanded beauties with rosetted slippers and festoons of flowers who danced the nights away as war drew near. With an ingenuous exterior she worked subtly on her uncle's behalf. The President could trust her never to give anything away, or to say the wrong thing at a time when passions had reached the explosive stage. In a sense she tried to be a social solvent in a moment of crisis. Buchanan later said that had she been in elected office, she could not have served him better. The only crack in her bland façade was her deadly feud with Mrs. Stephen A. Douglas, the beautiful Adelaide Cutts, great-niece of Dolley Madison. The wife of the Little Giant had vowed to make all of his enemies her own, and she turned her back in public on Harriet Lane.

The Buchanan dinners and receptions were among the stateliest given in early White House history. After the war Harriet married Henry Elliot Johnston. Little more was heard of her until her death in 1903, but she had played the game of politics with finesse.

Next to Jacqueline Kennedy and Eleanor Roosevelt, Mary Todd Lincoln was the most discussed First Lady in presidential history—and the most assailed. She influenced her husband in many ways but most of all by distracting him with her whims, her tempers, her extravagance, her unreasonable hatred of many of his associates. She brought him happiness, too, for he was proud of the beautiful Kentuckian he had married in 1842, when he was a young lawyer in Springfield, Illinois. She had already been courted by Stephen Douglas and by other men more handsome than the tall, gangling suitor who would find a place for himself among the immortals. But not with Mary's help. Her wayward and impulsive acts were better understood a century after her White House days, when the pattern of her psychosis became clear. Mary could never forgive her son, Robert Todd Lincoln, for committing her to an asylum when her grief over the loss of her husband and her sons brought on a total breakdown.

Long before meeting Lincoln, Mary Todd had predicted that she would be a President's wife. There was nothing about the young lawyer she married to suggest that he would travel that far, however. He himself was not too well balanced emotionally at the time, but Miss Todd's charming ways and clever conversation helped to lift his gloom. There was much interest in this eager First Lady when she reached the White House as the war clouds threatened. The passions of wartime soon affected the public view of her, but there was no concealing her pretentious social ways and her extravagance. The bills she ran up for mantuas and gowns, for scores of pairs of long kid gloves, for furniture and possessions of all kinds, did not endear her to suffering people as the war progressed. She snubbed those she did not like, nagged the President publicly and in private, and embarrassed him in his administrative duties.

The Lincolns had no tastes in common, except their great love for their children and the way in which they spoiled them. Mary became a lively critic of the conduct of the war and the behavior of the generals. She favored General George B. McClellan, who flattered her, but detested General Grant, calling him a butcher and unfit to head the army. The President listened to her opinions with patience and sometimes a jest, as when he told her mildly after her bitterest attack on General Grant, "Well, Mother, supposing that we give you command of the army. No doubt you would do much better than any general that has been tried."

Mrs. Lincoln was even more embarrassing to her husband on the political side, and she waged a ceaseless war against Salmon Portland Chase and his daughter Kate, who outshone Mary in style, looks and intelligence. Repeatedly she shook her husband's confidence in Chase and tried to persuade him that the Secretary of the Treasury was working to unseat him. Although he was always gentle with Mary, the President could not restrain her in moments of desperate rage or prevent her from making scenes in public. She harassed him when he most needed comfort, but after her wild grief over the death of her son Willie in the White House he handled her obsessive melancholy with an understanding touch. She suffered from migraine headaches, and Adam Badeau, General Grant's military secretary, noted that Lincoln bore her rages as "Christ might have done, with an expression of pain and sadness that cut one to the heart."

On one occasion she startled the placid Mrs. Grant by exclaiming, when the General's wife sat down beside her on a sofa, "How dare you?"

It also outraged as well as amused Julia Grant that Mrs. Lincoln should expect her to back out of a room and treat her like royalty. When the two women went together to a military review Mrs. Lincoln became wildly upset when she saw the wife of General Edward Ord riding with the President. Mrs. Ord was a fine horsewoman and an acknowledged beauty, and the President's wife was notoriously jealous.

"What does that woman mean by riding by the side of the President and ahead of me?" Mrs. Lincoln exclaimed. "Does *she* suppose that he wants her by the side of *him*?"

When Mrs. Ord greeted their party Mrs. Lincoln insulted her, called her names in the presence of a crowd of officers, and asked her what she meant by following the President. Mrs. Ord burst into tears and asked what she had done. Mrs. Lincoln ranted on, and Mrs. Grant, who liked Mrs. Ord, stoutly defended her. This infuriated Mary Lincoln further and she said, "I suppose you think you'll get to the White House yourself, don't you?"

Mrs. Grant responded quietly, aware that Mrs. Lincoln had lost all control of herself. She said that she was quite satisfied with the position she had, and it was more than she had ever expected to attain. But Mrs. Lincoln added one more dig: "Oh! you had better take it if you can get it. 'Tis very nice."

That night at dinner Mrs. Lincoln urged her husband to get rid of General Ord, but the President would not be budged. On another occasion she flew into a jealous rage when she learned that the wife of General Charles Griffin, the golden-haired Sallie Carroll whose wedding Lincoln had attended, had obtained a special permit from the President to go with the officers to a recent battlefront while the other women, including Mrs. Grant and Mrs. Lincoln, were ordered to the rear because of active operations.

"Do you mean to say that she saw the President alone?" Mrs. Lincoln asked in a state of high excitement. "Do you know that I never allow the President to see any woman alone?"

She bounced around so vigorously in the carriage that she had to be held down, and she did not quieten until she was informed that it was the Secretary of War and not the President who had given Mrs. Griffin the permit. Later, as Countess Esterhazy, Sallie's social career continued undimmed.

Mrs. Grant's next encounter with the President's wife led to further trouble. Mrs. Lincoln objected to her presence on a riverboat taking them on an excursion to Point of Rocks. Julia got off at the first stop and rambled in the woods to still her agitation. Thereafter there were two boats in use—Mrs. Lincoln's Boat and Mrs. Grant's Boat. It was as a result of these corrosive incidents that General Grant was not in the President's box on the night Lincoln was assassinated, and in later years he often wondered if things might have been different had he been there. His own stalwart presence and a military guard might have deterred John Wilkes Booth, although Grant, too, had been marked for death.

When Mrs. Lincoln invited General Grant and not his wife to the White House on April 13 to celebrate victory and the end of the Civil War, the General would not go, and he and Julia went instead to the home of Edwin M. Stanton, Secretary of War. Next day they were invited to go to Ford's Theater with the Lincolns to see Our

American Cousins, but by this time Mrs. Grant was so incensed that she made an excuse, saying they must get back to their children who were then in Burlington, New Jersey. The General was embarrassed because he had told President Lincoln they would go to the theater. Mrs. Grant also had had one of her premonitory dreams of disaster the night before, and when these occurred she would not budge. Lincoln, too, had earlier had a vision of himself on his own catafalque.

Her husband's assassination was the final blow for Mary. From then on her life became utterly disordered, and a succession of irrational acts caused her son Robert to have her confined. She died in 1882 after a stay abroad and many unhappy incidents. If Mary Lincoln had failed to shake her husband in vital decisions, she had clouded his administration with discord and suspicion and had whipped up endless ill will with the men and women who surrounded him. His biographers have made much of Mrs. Lincoln's eccentricities but have not proved that she affected his course on the conduct of the war, beyond the trouble she stirred up among his generals. But she was profoundly influential on the personal side of his life and at times was an inspiration to him as well as a scourge.

Her successor, Mrs. Ulysses S. Grant, whom Mrs. Lincoln chose to treat with disdain, enjoyed society to the full and knew how to cope with it. She had learned early in life how best to encourage quiet, shy Ulysses Grant, the great war hero, the indifferent President, the beloved national figure. Without Julia Dent it is unlikely that he would ever have been in the White House, although she would have been the first to deny her own influence on his life and character. Bruce Catton has said of her: "I know of no other woman in our history whose influence over her husband has meant so much to the country at large."

Julia was a St. Louis girl of good family, well educated according to the standards of the day, merry and optimistic in spirit, but pretty only in the eyes of young Grant, for she had a severe squint. When he first saw her at the rambling homestead of her father, Colonel Frederick Dent, Grant fell in love with her at once. She had thick, glossy dark hair, a creamy complexion, and a small, delicately fash-

ioned figure. In her later years Mrs. Grant became portly and her
cross-eyed condition was noticeable to all, but to the General she was
never anything but his beloved and beautiful Julia. He proposed to
her when she was thrown into his arms as they crossed a plank bridge
in a buggy. They were married in 1838 after the Mexican War, and
Julia soon had her share of frontier posts. Naturally gregarious, she
adapted herself easily to the life of a garrison wife and enjoyed anything from a rural quilting party to a masquerade. Later, when
Ulysses served at distant army posts, farmed wretchedly at a cabin
outside St. Louis known as Hardscrabble, and drifted from pillar to
post in shiftless fashion, she never failed to encourage him, to send
him loving letters and to do everything she could for their children.
She stood by Ulysses when he gambled and drank. He could do no
wrong in her eyes.

Although used to comfortable surroundings, Julia slaved in their
cabin in the woods while he sold wood and did odd jobs. The
summer of 1859 ended with the Grants almost in despair. At that
point Ulysses went to Galena, Illinois, to work in the family tannery,
and it was there that he responded to Lincoln's call for volunteers.
"History supplies few, if any, examples of equally sudden, brilliant,
and enduring fame," James G. Wilson, one of his favorite aides, later
wrote of the shift in Grant's fortunes at this time. Julia's father tried
hard to persuade Ulysses to join the Confederate forces, but Julia
backed him stoutly in the stand he took. She soon joined him at
Cairo, her first foray into army territory after the Civil War began
but not her last. She became the most regular and important of all
the visiting wives who began to show up at army camps, and she
helped to squash the gossip about the General's intemperance. It was
a legend greatly exaggerated as the years rolled on.

Mrs. Grant regularly bundled up the children in strong boots,
pantaloons, pinafores and kilts, and traveled on the riverboats between St. Louis and Cincinnati. Time and again she raised the General's spirits in depressed moments, and she believed the presence of
the children at headquarters did him good. But on one occasion she
came close to being captured by Van Dorn's troops when she was
visiting her husband at Hot Springs, close to Oxford, his secondary
base of supplies.

She was much more enthusiastic than her husband when she learned that he would soon be President. "I'm afraid I am elected," Ulysses told Julia ruefully after walking up the hill to the old Victorian house in Galena on the night of his victory. She knew that speechmaking would be hard for her silent husband, so she urged him to have Roscoe Conkling write his inaugural address. Grant stubbornly composed his own, economical in words, precise in thought, and when it was finished he turned to Julia, shook hands with her and said, "And now, my dear, I hope you're satisfied."

After the shambles of an inaugural ball in the icy Treasury Building Mrs. Grant settled easily into the role of First Lady. She refurnished the White House in a style that has come to be known as the Grant Steamboat décor. The lace curtains, the crimson brocatel, the gold cornices and frescoed walls and ceilings, the tassels, heavy woods and fringes were described by Ben Perley Poore as a mixture of Doric simplicity and vulgar ostentation.

Mrs. Grant gave elaborate parties with more than twenty courses. She bought handsome, if not chic, clothes for herself, and wildly indulged her children, who romped with much the same freedom as Lincoln's. It was almost impossible to keep Jesse and Nellie in school. Julia practiced nepotism as boldly as her predecessor, Mrs. John Tyler. Her father, Frederick Dent, was a fixture at the White House; all had to pay him honor in the receiving line. At times she showed lapses of memory and observation that were more endearing than irritating to the President. In her malaprop moments she was apt to forget names, confuse Protestants and Catholics, and fail to recognize temperance leaders. Her husband led her on and teased her over these mishaps. But she had special skill and tact with the gold-laced army officers who flocked around him, and in general she was a popular First Lady, kind, warmhearted and tolerant except when someone dared to attack her husband.

She simplified protocol and surrounded herself at receptions with the wives of Cabinet members and Senators. Sometimes she had the added grace of Mrs. Potter Palmer, whose sister, Ida Honoré, had married Frederick Dent Grant, the eldest Grant son. Julia's impulsive loyalty was sometimes embarrassing to Grant. When the Gold Conspiracy crisis that culminated in Black Friday came to a head Abel

Rathbone Corbin, who had married Grant's sister Virginia, was involved through his partnership with Jay Gould and Jim Fisk. When Virginia wrote to the President asking him not to interfere in the gold crisis, Julia whipped off a sharp letter in reply, saying, "My husband is annoyed by your husband's speculations. You must close them as quick as you can."

Corbin backed down and approached Gould to get out of the deal, since the President was angry. It was agreed that Julia's letter should not be mentioned, but Grant moved fast to checkmate the swindlers. The day went down in history as a Wall Street landmark, with thousands ruined. Mrs. Grant's name got a slight dusting of frost, and it was recalled that she had been seen in a box at the Fifth Avenue Theater with Fisk, Gould and the Corbins. In the Congressional investigation that followed the Grant name was cleared, although they stayed on friendly terms with their relatives, the Corbins, who had not weathered the scandal so well.

Julia's influence with her husband was felt in small as well as in large ways. Sometimes when he would refuse to see a caller she would send a card by William H. Crook, the President's bodyguard, with the message "Dear Ulyss—Do please make this appointment. Julia." If the suppliant's request was reasonable, and Julia had sent him, the President usually gave him what he wanted. Crook was of the opinion that Grant considered his wife "absolutely perfect" and that he could not get along without her. Adam Badeau, who had watched both of them under varying circumstances, was equally persuaded of the importance of Julia to her warrior husband. He wrote:

In the first years of my intercourse with Grant I was greatly impressed with the influence of his wife, and the impression deepened until the last. . . . Nobody can understand his character or career who fails to appreciate this; no one who did not know him intimately can ever say how much Mrs. Grant helped him; how she comforted him, and enabled him to perform his task, which, without that help and solace, I sometimes thought might never have been performed. . . . She soothed him when cares oppressed him, she supported him when even he was downcast (though he told so few); she served him and served him at times when he needed all she did for him.

In general, Badeau found that Mrs. Grant advised her husband "simply and strongly to do what he thought right, and perhaps induced him to do it; although he, as little as any man, I believe, required such inducement." No other First Lady in history had been called on to show such faith and trust in her husband as Mrs. Grant in the difficult early days of his career.

Their daughter Nellie was one of the most spectacular of White House brides, an event of 1874 as much discussed then as the later weddings of Alice Longworth and Luci Johnson. The General did not approve of Nellie's husband, Algernon Sartoris, but Mrs. Grant smoothed the troubled waters. She could always mollify Ulysses. Both welcomed little Julia Grant (later Princess Cantacuzène), a granddaughter born in the White House, the child of Mr. and Mrs. Frederick Grant.

No President's wife up to the time of Mrs. Franklin Roosevelt traveled as extensively as Mrs. Grant or was more honored by foreign rulers. In their leisurely two-year trip around the world the Grants were received by dignitaries ranging from Queen Victoria to the Emperor of China. It was a great blow to Julia on their return that her husband, who had been followed by Rutherford Hayes, was not chosen to run again. She could not believe that his party would reject him, but James Garfield swept into power. It was only a matter of weeks until the new President was dead and Chester Arthur had moved smoothly into office. His first state dinner was given in honor of the Grants.

For a time they lived prosperously in New York until the General was ruined in a financial swindle. Before long he was at Mount McGregor, in the foothills of the Adirondacks, racing against time to finish his memoirs and redeem the family fortunes before dying of cancer of the tongue and throat. Julia made a pact before his death that he must be buried only where she could rest beside him. All plans for a national or West Point funeral were abandoned, and she was eventually buried with him in Grant's Tomb on Riverside Drive in New York City. She was too distraught to attend his funeral, one of the most memorable in New York history, and only slowly did she recover from the loss of her beloved Ulysses. At the end she lived quietly in Washington, an honored dowager who received the old soldiers of the Civil War and visitors from all parts of the world.

Although none thought of her as a feminist, Mrs. Grant became a firm supporter of the suffrage movement. She was impelled to take this stand for a characteristic reason—Susan Anthony had backed Ulysses against Horace Greeley for President. Julia never forgot this gesture and had high regard for Miss Anthony. But her power lay far beyond the vote or anything that it could bring. She was always content to take a back seat and let her husband hold the reins. Yet when it came to fundamental issues, hers was the optimistic spirit that served him best in moments of crisis and discouragement.

Mrs. Rutherford B. Hayes, who soon followed Julia Grant in the White House, was also a most influential First Lady, not only where her husband was concerned but as a public image. She was so convincingly linked with the temperance cause that she was widely known as "Lemonade Lucy," but she was not a nonentity in any sense of the word. Her serene looks and modest attire were reassuring to the women of her generation, and she enjoyed the same sort of popularity that Grace Coolidge did many years later. "I have never seen such a face reign in the White House," commented the critical newspaper correspondent, Mary Clemmer. "I wonder what the world of Vanity Fair will do with it."

Worldly vanity was certainly not one of Mrs. Hayes' characteristics, but she exuded femininity of the wholesome, traditional sort. Her large expressive eyes and wide, low brow were framed by a heavy cloud of tidily arranged dark hair. Her gowns were high at the neck and long at the wrist, but she softened them with laces. Neither jewelry nor the puffed and frizzed hair of the period were to Lucy's taste, and she was handsome enough to carry off stark simplicity with some degree of style. With eight children, her domestic life, both when her husband was Governor of Ohio and President of the United States, was a busy one.

Lucy Hayes was the daughter of a North Carolina doctor and was born in Chillicothe, Ohio. Rutherford Hayes met her at Sulphur Springs near Delaware, Ohio. They were married in 1852 two years after he began the practice of law in Cincinnati, and she had considerable experience in official circles before reaching the White House. In Ohio she worked for state charities and had strong church and temperance interests. During the Civil War she nursed wounded soldiers, and her calm face brought serenity into some of the worst wards. Her husband, who had been wounded four times, was elected to Congress before peace was declared.

When Mrs. Hayes took charge at the White House she had no hesitancy about simplifying some of the social pretensions that surrounded it and making it a home for her family. She was the first college graduate among the Presidents' wives, and she enjoyed entertaining former classmates from the Ladies College of Cincinnati and Ohio Wesleyan University. Mrs. Hayes was noted for her tact, and she never gossiped. In many respects, however, she was a free thinker with a healthy, sunny temperament, and she swept through her tasks with some of the efficiency that had been missing in the days of withdrawn and invalid wives. Men jested about her temperance views, and she caused the President some embarrassment in this respect. When the Russian Grand Dukes Alexis and Constantine were being entertained a crisis arose over serving wine. Lucy would not have it. The Secretary of State insisted, and the President compromised for this one occasion. But it was never repeated, although when out of Lucy's hearing Hayes liked to tell of oranges being served with synthetic rum.

Although she was in a sense the new woman, with strong and independent views, Lucy maintained the traditional fiction that she had no influence with the President. The nepotism of the Grant administration was still fresh in the minds of the public, and she vowed that she would never interfere with appointments or consider appeals to use her influence. But when temperance issues were at stake, she was faithful to Frances Willard. When the postmistress of a Pennsylvania town was turned out of office because of her temperance activities, and her Congressman tried to install a man who would not work with temperance organizations, Mrs. Hayes moved fast. Through her husband she engineered a stay of proceedings and saw to it that the postmistress was reinstated by the President's order. Today Lucy would be regarded as the sort of First Lady who "participated" and even without the vote she was an effective and respected force in public life. Her successor from Ohio never had a chance to prove her mettle, for James Garfield's assassination came soon after his inauguration.

A scholarly man with a strong literary sense, Garfield had called his wife "unstampedable." She was strong-willed and could drive her husband into action, but her influence was secondary to that of his mother, Eliza Ballou Garfield. Lucretia, like Eleanor Roosevelt, had to cope with a powerful matriarch in Eliza, who was the first mother of a President to live in the White House. (Ulysses Grant's mother refused even to visit it.) President Garfield was never seen in church without both his wife and his mother, and it was to eighty-year-old Eliza that he first turned after taking the oath on inauguration day.

Lucretia looked meek enough as she presided at the inaugural ball in lavender satin with point lace and a corsage of pansies. She shared her husband's scholarly tastes and tutored their five children herself. The Garfields were old schoolmates from Garrettsville, Ohio, and both had taught before their marriage in 1858. At Hiram College Lucretia was her husband's pupil. Her father, Zebulon Rudolph, was a farmer and one of the founders of the college. When James Garfield went on to Williams College, Lucretia went to Cleveland to teach. Two years afterward Garfield was elected to the State Senate but almost immediately was drawn into combat as Colonel of the Forty-second Ohio Infantry. He was a Campbellite and a preacher as well as a politician, a man of learning and magnetism, and his war experiences were unforgettable. He paid his own tribute to his quiet, serious wife, who passed the war years in Hiram.

I have been singularly fortunate in marrying a woman who has never given me any perplexity about anything she has said. I have never had to explain away words of hers. She has been so prudent that I have never been diverted from my work for one minute to take up any mistakes of hers. When things get worse and there is the most public clamor and the most anger to me and to us, then she is the coolest. Sometimes it looks a little blue before me, but I get courage from her perfect bravery.

One might assume from Garfield's estimate of his wife that tact was one of her assets—a quality that the best, like the worst, of men have valued from time immemorial. Presidents have found it an essential virtue in their wives, and Grover Cleveland, another Ohioan, was doubly blessed in this respect.

Frances Folsom Cleveland was the first bride to be married to a President in the White House. One of its most noted beauties, she was only twenty-two when she was married in 1886 to Grover Cleveland in the Blue Room, which had been converted into a bower of roses and pansies. President Jackson's five-foot candelabra shed a pale radiance as Sousa conducted the Marine Band, playing the wedding march. Church bells chimed throughout the city, and the bride promised "to love, honor, and . . . keep" the man who had been her guardian from her earliest years.

Frances' father, Oscar Folsom, had been Cleveland's law partner and one of his closest friends. When Folsom was killed in an accident, Cleveland became Frances' guardian and saw her through Wells College. When they were married, a scandal that had been used to smear Cleveland during the presidential campaign flared up again. Cleveland was said to have fathered an illegitimate child. Although he always insisted he could not be sure the child was his, he had agreed to provide for it, and the scandal had fallen flat because of his frankness. Now it flared up again to the embarrassment of both Clevelands as the young bride walked into a storm of gossip. Rose Elizabeth Cleveland, Grover's sister, who had been acting as his hostess in the White House, had known for some time that her brother intended to marry his young ward, but the public was taken by surprise, and the marriage on a June day in 1886 became one of the notable events in White House social history.

Frances Folsom was an instant success with the public, and through the two Cleveland administrations was noted for her charm. Her robust and independent husband could stir up a storm, and his second term was turbulent, but Mrs. Cleveland was so popular that one of his political enemies, finding that all superlatives to meet the situation failed, remarked, "I detest him so much that I don't even think his wife is beautiful." Her tastes lay in music, the theater, and social life, and by degrees she quickened his interest in these areas. With wifely tact she discouraged the loud checks he liked to wear, but had no quarrel with his zeal for hunting and fishing. Cleveland had lusty tastes. He chewed tobacco and was thoroughly at home in the saloon and smoke-filled room.

Altogether Mrs. Cleveland, gracefully built and unpretentious in manner, brought a softer touch to the White House than had the President's able sister, Rose Cleveland, a cultivated woman prone to keep the conversation on a literary or historical plane. She and Frances got on well and both understood the vigorous, deliberate nature of the man James Russell Lowell called the most typical American since Lincoln. He readily grew impatient with the social round but was more cheerful in temperament after Frances became his bride and the White House was freshened up with flowers and canaries in the fashion followed years later by Mrs. Calvin Coolidge. He was a hard-working, practical bachelor of forty-seven when he married the girl whose baby carriage he had bought when her father was his law partner. She was radiantly healthy, the opposite of her successor, Mrs. William McKinley, also from Ohio.

By all odds the most memorable of the ailing First Ladies was Ida Saxton McKinley, whose epileptic attacks profoundly affected President McKinley and at times shook his confidence in himself. She was the first businesswoman to serve as the nation's hostess, having been a cashier in her father's bank in Canton, Ohio. Other businesswomen to follow her were Mrs. Harding and Mrs. Johnson. Mrs. McKinley had attended a New York state college but had not graduated. She married the handsome young lawyer of twenty-seven after a brief engagement. Their two daughters died almost at birth, and soon afterward she became a chronic invalid, subject to fainting spells.

Ida had a certain charm of her own. She had thin, aquiline features and quick ways. But she was insistent in her demands for attention from her husband, and he never failed her, no matter how embarrassing the situation might be. She could be querulous and insisted on attending state dinners and receptions when she was not in any condition to appear downstairs. The presence of a noted guest was likely to disturb her equilibrium and cause her to faint. Regardless of traditional form she was invariably seated to the President's right at the dinner table, and when she collapsed, as she frequently did, he quickly threw a handkerchief over her face to protect her from observation until she could be taken to her room. After one attempt was made to observe protocol by seating Mrs. McKinley in the proper place, the experiment was never repeated. Her husband knew better than to cross Ida, in large or small ways. He would walk out of important political meetings to join his wife by the fire, to adjust the shawl around her shoulders or to watch her face for signs of unrest. This did not always contribute to his statesmanship.

Soon after the *Maine* was blown up, H. H. Kohlsaat, a Chicago newspaper publisher, spent an uncomfortable evening at the White House on which he later reported. A piano recital was under way in the Blue Room, and Mrs. McKinley sat close to the pianist, obviously drooping. As McKinley watched her his agitation began to show. With Kohlsaat he moved into the Red Room, flung himself into a chair and buried his head in his hands. "I have been through a trying period," he said. "Mrs. McKinley has been in poorer health than usual. It seems to me I have not slept over three hours a night for over two weeks. Congress is trying to drive us into war with Spain. The Spanish Fleet is in Cuban waters, and we haven't enough ammunition on the Atlantic seacoast to fire a salute."

The President burst into tears and decided he must rejoin Ida at once. He asked Kohlsaat if his agitation showed, and Kohlsaat said that it did, but he advised the President to blow his nose hard as he walked into the Blue Room. This could bring tears to his eyes and account for his look of distress. Although distraught himself, the President joined his wife and sought to comfort her, as he always did. He made a point of listening carefully to what she had to say, and he respected her intuition about the people around him. Mrs. McKinley knew what was demanded of her husband in an official capacity and was ambitious for his career. She insisted on accompanying him when he traveled, regardless of the difficulties involved. She was with him when he was shot in Buffalo. After his death she lived quietly in Canton, Ohio, where Kohlsaat once found her huddling over a register in her old age and moaning, "Why should I linger? Please, God, if it is Thy will, let me go. I want to be with him. I am so tired."

Mrs. McKinley died in the spring of 1907 and the house was filled with roses, her favorite flower, on the day of her funeral. The hymns that her husband had liked were sung, and there was much public interest in the death of this unique First Lady whose invalidism had figured strongly in McKinley's political career. Theirs was one of the strangest romances in White House history, and one of its major love stories. Ida mellowed her husband's life in many ways, even though she was a source of constant anxiety to him. She introduced him to the theater and opera, and brought relaxation into his life at times. Her flair for needlework and flower arrangements was a matter of comment, and she crocheted as persistently as Grace Coolidge and Eleanor Roosevelt knitted. It was public knowledge that the wide black silk ties worn so distinctively by McKinley were crocheted by his wife.

Although fragile in person, her judgments were apt to be razor-sharp and she had the power shared by other Presidents' wives of turning her husband against some of the men around him. Perhaps in no other way have First Ladies been more influential than in their likes and dislikes for the men and women surrounding their husbands. This was particularly true of Mrs. McKinley's successor. As Ida left the White House after the assassination of her husband, a thunderbolt arrived in the person of Theodore Roosevelt. With him came a calm and dignified First Lady, ready to face the fresh challenges of the twentieth century and in her own quiet way to modify some of her husband's boisterous ways.

Chapter 3

A New Era Begins

Two years after the death of his first wife, Alice Lee Roosevelt, Theodore Roosevelt and Edith Kermit Carow were married in London. Mild though she seemed, she became one of the most influential of Presidents' wives, but not in any of the more obvious ways. Several times she shifted her husband's course, and she was frankly less concerned with his political ambitions than with the welfare of their family. None of his critics ever deflated his ego with the skill used by Mrs. Roosevelt, but he worshiped her, and the raging lion would meekly come to heel when she used her restraining hand to subdue his exuberant impulses. Her technique was negative in essence. She never told him what to do, but merely what to avoid.

No President was ever more surrounded by women of strong opinion and influence than Theodore Roosevelt. His wife, his sister and his oldest daughter all loomed large in his political life. Anna Roosevelt Cowles, the sister who was variously known in the family as Bamie or Auntie Bye, was a dynamic force in the fortunes of this powerful dynasty. Alice Roosevelt Longworth once said of her, "If Auntie Bye had been a man, she would have been President." She was tiny, crippled, vital and ambitious. All the dignitaries of the day sought her out and paid more attention to her than they did to the statuesque and dignified Edith Roosevelt.

Early in Theodore Roosevelt's marriage Edith and Bamie began a tug of war that went on for years. Bamie kept urging her brother on to great things in the political world. Edith was essentially the homemaker, the mother, and she hated the rough and tumble of politics. Bamie quickly decided that ever since his second marriage Theodore had been unsuccessfully torn between his political aspirations and his duty—"as he saw it under Edith's influence"—to support his growing family.

Mrs. Franklin D. Roosevelt once said that "Uncle Theodore made no major decision in foreign or domestic policy without first discussing it with Auntie Bye." Auntie Bye herself said that his involvement in the Spanish-American War was the "one decision of his career that he made absolutely alone," and it was also one of the most important political decisions of his life. Bamie did not underestimate his wife's influence, however, and she conceded that Edith, with her cool brown eyes and distant manner, showed better judgment about people than Theodore did. She pictured her sister-in-law sitting mending Quentin's breeches, whereas in reality she was busily forming her own firm opinions as she listened to the conversation of her husband and his associates. Later she would let him know what she thought, and her judgment was apt to be both acute and sardonic. She would dash water on one of his rapid-fire friendships by commenting, "I don't dislike him. I just don't want to live in the same world with him."

"E-die!" he would protest helplessly.

When someone Mrs. Roosevelt disliked was invited to lunch she would plead a headache and stay away. She was as indifferent as Mrs. John F. Kennedy to the game of politics, and no President's wife ever had less desire for power. She refused to be drawn into the melee with Bamie and another strong-willed sister, Corinne Roosevelt Robinson. When she could escape from her household duties and sick children she would drift off to the New York Society Library to pass a few quiet hours reading. She was dead set against Theodore's accepting the challenge to become Mayor of New York in 1894. He was anxious to take it, but in the end deferred to Edith's wishes. Bamie wrote her a scorching letter and Edith replied, "I cannot begin to describe how terribly I feel at having failed him at such an important time. It is just as I said to you he never should have married me, and then would have been free to take his own course quite unbiased. . . . You say that I dislike to give my opinion. This is a lesson that will last my life. . . . It has helped to spoil some years of a life which I would have given my own for."

But Henry Cabot Lodge was already insinuating the thought that Theodore should aim at the Presidency, and Bamie was an ally in this respect. While in London she worked persistently through her powerful political friends on both sides of the Atlantic to help keep diplomatic channels open between Britain and the United States. She was a fascinating hostess in the tradition of Madame Roland, and such men as Lord Bryce listened attentively to what she had to say. Bamie was close to John Hay and, later, to Whitelaw Reid at the Court of St. James's. She had much to do with Theodore's appointment as Assistant Secretary of the Navy in 1897, although Roosevelt himself always gave Lodge credit for that move. Bamie did long-range campaigning from England as America veered toward the Spanish-American War.

Edith was unalterably opposed to her husband's running for the Vice-Presidency at the close of the nineteenth century, although Lodge was pushing hard for it. She always considered the Senator her husband's political Svengali. By that time Bamie had settled in Washington with her husband, Commander William Sheffield Cowles, and she had friends in the Cabinet. Elihu Root and John Hay both liked her, and they all began to think of Theodore as a presidential hope. Senator Lodge tried persuasion with Edith but he could not budge her, and time and again Roosevelt wrote to him, "Edith is against your view. Bamie remained neutral in this."

It seemed to Bamie that Edith was dictating these letters, for Theodore dwelt so much on the family finances. His wife had had an impoverished girlhood. She had worn hand-me-down ball gowns and had stayed in cheap pensions on trips abroad. Much of her resistance to her husband's political ambitions was based on her feeling that their children must be fed, clothed, and educated. For a brief time Edith won the argument and, to the surprise and disgust of Senator

Lodge and Bamie, Theodore gave the press a statement that he had no wish to be Vice-President and would run for re-election as Governor. "Edith bids me say that she hopes you will forgive me," he told Lodge.

Roosevelt was re-elected Governor of New York in 1900. When a politician at a dinner in Albany just before the Republican Convention that year remarked that she would see her husband nominated for the Vice-Presidency in Philadelphia, Edith tapped him with her fan and replied, "I don't *want* to see him nominated for the Vice-Presidency." Had she been the winner in this contest of wills, Theodore Roosevelt might never have become President.

But he actually longed so much for the nomination that he and Lodge cross-checked Edith, who had connived with Nicholas Murray Butler to get Theodore to give out a statement saying that he would not run. Butler drafted it and showed it to Edith for her approval. But her husband sidetracked it, and she sat white and grim-faced in a box while the nomination went through. Lodge said, "Take it," and Roosevelt did, after a long look up at E-die, who had not been able to check him this time. He was forty-one, and the nomination, by a turn of fate, led him straight to the White House.

Mrs. Roosevelt had enjoyed being a governor's wife. She felt that this post suited them both and was right for the children. She blossomed out and became nationally known as a gracious hostess. But when she became First Lady after the assassination of President McKinley, she shrank from the staring crowds and seemed to many to be coldly reserved beside her ebullient husband. However, her well-bred manner was soothing to the Old Guard, who found it difficult at times to approve the President's dashing ways and the unrepressed doings of their children, who threw spitballs at paintings, flew kites on the lawn, used garbage-can lids as shields and tree branches as swords, skated and bicycled in the White House and slid downstairs on tin trays. Their free and happy life at Sagamore made endless copy for the newspapers, and they became the best-known children in White House history—and the rowdiest.

But Mrs. Roosevelt had a problem with her stepchild Alice, the daughter of fragile Alice Hathaway Lee of Boston, who had died when Alice was born. She was fiercely resentful of Edith and spent most of her time with her mother's family in New England. Seventeen years old when her father became President, she emerged as the most spectacular of White House daughters. Alice was game for any skylarking from eating a toadstool to keeping a snake as a pet. She was the *enfant terrible* of her father's administration and was still handing out political advice in the 1960's, the enduring dowager of Washington. In course of time she backed Robert A. Taft, the son of William Howard Taft, her father's traditional enemy, and by 1968 she had bright and approving comments to make on the Democratic Kennedys. Almost alone among her compeers, she predicted that Truman would be re-elected. But in her youth the star of her horizon was her father, even though she often embarrassed him with her poker and gambling, racing interests and smoking, her biting comments and dashing clothes. She made headlines of a spectacular sort when she went to the Orient in 1905 with Mr. Taft and a Congressional delegation. Her romance with Nicholas Longworth developed on this trip, and her marriage some months later made White House history.

Powerful though she was herself in political counsels, Mrs. Longworth, in her eighties, said that she thought few presidential wives had had real political influence. She was inclined to think that Mrs. Johnson had, and "Eleanor had influence, but not political influence . . . she went around doing a job, as other wives do, to help keep the jobs for their husbands." Alice's stepmother had predicted a doleful future for little Eleanor. Looking her over at Sagamore one day she wrote to Bamie: "Poor little soul, she is very plain. Her mouth and teeth seem to have no future, but, as I wrote Theodore, the ugly duckling may turn out to be a swan."

In the end Bamie was the only member of the family who thoroughly approved of Eleanor as a bride for their handsome Franklin. But even the cynical and experienced Mrs. Longworth gave Eleanor high marks as a "sincere do-gooder." However, the White House in the days of the Theodore Roosevelts bore little resemblance to the setting and family ways of the Franklin D. Roosevelts. Theodore Roosevelt decreed that it should be changed from a "shabby likeness to the ground floor of the Astor House into a simple and dignified dwelling for the head of a great republic." His wife took on this task with taste and understanding, directing the architects and selecting the furniture, until it had recovered some of its eighteenth-century tradition. Anything that Edie did seemed right to Theodore, who worshiped her and wrote to a friend, "I do not think my eyes are blinded by affection when I say that she has combined to a degree I have never seen in any other woman the power of being the best of wives and mothers, the wisest manager of the household, and at the same time the ideal great lady and mistress of the White House."

He made no secret of the fact that she acted as his guardian, doling out twenty dollars a day that he never knew how he spent, and in a "tender, gentle and considerate way" pointing out when he was thoughtless, instead of submitting to his whims. "Had she not done this," he wrote to one of their sons, "it would in the end have made her life very much harder, and mine very much less happy."

Mrs. Roosevelt gained stature during her White House days. She became a social success in a quiet way, and she was much loved by the staff. There was nothing fashionable about her. She was apt to be haphazard with her gowns, which she bought from habit at bargain prices; her glossy brown hair was usually adrift; but no one ever discounted her as the power behind the throne. The observant Irwin (Ike) Hoover of the White House staff noted that her "forte was to receive her husband's friends socially and win them over to his point of view by her tact and consideration." She applied the subtly feminine rather than the driving technique, and to good effect. Archibald Butt, aide first to Theodore Roosevelt and later to William Howard Taft, warmed up only slowly to the Tafts because his adoration of both Roosevelts blinded him at first to the virtues of their successors.

The Theodore Roosevelt administration was one of the liveliest in American history, and the guests who flocked to the White House ranged from sheriffs and Rough Riders to big-game hunters, explorers and writers, as well as the usual assortment of diplomats, visiting celebrities and statesmen. It was the era of Henry Adams, John Hay and Henry Cabot Lodge. In her later years Mrs. Longworth recalled the villagelike atmosphere of the capital. Hearing her father and Lodge discuss Jefferson as an obnoxious man, the American Revolution did not seem far away.

Although she had no personal ambition and disliked politics, Mrs. Roosevelt suffered when Teddy's term came to an end. She wept at the dinner table in front of her successor Mrs. Taft on her last night in the White House. Her husband's trip to Africa soon afterward was also something she did not wish him to do. Although Mrs. Roosevelt, Bamie and Corinne Robinson were all antipathetic to the suffrage cause that had begun to have powerful social backing, they were women of political influence in their several ways. Between his ladylike but stubborn wife, his brilliant and independent daughter and his strong-willed sisters, Theodore Roosevelt, the most manly and assertive of Presidents, was subject to more petticoat influence on the home front than any of his predecessors.

The judicious and gregarious William Howard Taft was deeply responsive to the guiding hand of Helen Herron Taft, one of the most ambitious women to share the life of a President. Like Ethel Roosevelt she was a reserved and dignified First Lady, but she had shown great strength and persistence in propelling her husband toward the ultimate goal. It had been a lifelong process and is richly documented in Taft's letters to his wife, since each move she made, each nugget of advice, each damning judgment, emerges in this correspondence.

Ironically enough, two months after inauguration she had a paralytic stroke and was quietly counted out during the Taft administration. Her condition was so well concealed that the public never knew how ill she was, but those closest to the President felt that it impaired his powers and energies and contributed to his unpopularity in office. He was deeply affected by her physical collapse and spent endless hours with her, trying to teach her to enunciate the simplest words. Up to the time of her illness she had shared his political thinking to the full, and he had greatly valued her advice and her judgment about people. He was too judicial to be swayed in his final decisions, but in a discreet way Helen Herron Taft was one of the most influential wives to pass through the White House.

Daughter of John W. Herron, a Cincinnati lawyer, she was an

educated and thoughtful girl, high-strung, nervous, deeply interested in music. The proud Herrons were not well off, and in the early years of her marriage she was a frugal and helpful wife. Big Will Taft found her irresistible. She was small, trim and inclined to be plain, but he always regarded her intellect and spirit with respect. Her advisory power and drive were poured into the years of Taft's rise to fame. She arduously brought up her three children in the way they should walk, and Robert A. Taft in the end was most like her—both in nature and appearance. As a girl of seventeen she had been the guest at the White House of her fellow Ohioans, the Rutherford B. Hayeses, and had thought then that she would like one day to be First Lady. This had been a dream credited to several wives of Presidents, but it was completely true in the case of Nellie Herron, and as Will became a national figure she worked consciously toward that end.

When he was away from home—and he often was in the course of his judicial duties—Taft wrote nearly every day to Nellie, freely discussing his work as well as enlarging on the social scene and the beauties of nature. Unlike the Abigail and John Adams correspondence, few of her replies to him have survived, but his letters disclose how often he sought her opinion and how crisply and clearly she must have responded. Along with his brothers, Charles, Horace and Henry, Nellie pulled the strings when it came to the major decisions of Taft's career, and as in the case of Mrs. Theodore Roosevelt, she was most often influenced by the needs of their children. On three occasions she advised him not to accept a place on the Supreme Court—the spot he most desired in life. She already saw the White House looming in the distance. He was Governor in Manila when word reached him of the assassination of President McKinley. It was not long before Mrs. Taft became the implacable enemy of Theodore Roosevelt, and by degrees her husband's thinking was colored by her attitude.

President Roosevelt was well aware of Mrs. Taft's dislike, even while he was at the full tide of his success in the White House. Taft, who liked and admired Roosevelt greatly, foresaw that the President's impetuosity was likely to get him into trouble. His own rather calm and judicial outlook made no allowance for impulsive behavior in public office. Mrs. Taft's influence with her husband was a paramount factor in projecting him squarely into the presidential picture early in 1906. When President Roosevelt once again offered him a place on the Supreme Court bench, Taft hesitated and Teddy called in Mrs. Taft for consultation, knowing how potent her influence was. She had told Will that he would be making the mistake of his life if he accepted the offer. Such was her conviction that she persuaded the President to let her husband continue as Secretary of War. She felt that he might be more in line for the Presidency in a Cabinet post than if he were sidetracked on the Supreme Court bench.

At this point the President wrote to Taft that of all the men who had appeared on the horizon he was the most likely presidential possibility, and the best man for it. Once this decision was made, the path toward the White House was clearly marked for Taft, although he followed it with reluctance of spirit. All the eagerness lay with his wife and brothers. Later that year the President again called in Mrs. Taft when her husband was away and pointed out to her that Charles Evans Hughes was looming up strongly as a presidential candidate. He wanted Will to show more zest for this high prize.

Elihu Root was present at their conference, and Mrs. Taft was uncomfortable. She could scarcely talk to Root at any time, for she was convinced that he was totally uninterested in her. She quickly saw that Roosevelt was taking a new line and might support Hughes if the tide went with him. She was furious and reported to Will that she had had to restrain herself from saying "Support whom you want, for all I care." But Will, always more benign in spirit than his wife, told Root two weeks later that it would be a great thing for the country if Roosevelt had another term. Mrs. Taft was deeply irritated by her husband's determination to push the cause of Roosevelt, Hughes, Root or of anyone but himself. The President quickly assured him that Mrs. Taft had misunderstood what he had said, and that his real purpose was to encourage Will to work harder for organization support.

The Taft boom was soon in the making, but it was not until July, 1907, that the public could be sure President Roosevelt was actually behind Taft. This was one of many occasions on which Mrs. Taft swayed her husband's decisions. He had high regard for her knowledge of human nature and was inclined to listen to what she had to say, even if he refused to be moved when his own convictions conflicted with her point of view. In addition to the judicial temperament he had a strong will of his own. President Roosevelt was never in any doubt about Mrs. Taft's ambition; in fact she was so intense by nature that she made no secret of her aims. In her autobiography she disavowed any attempt to pose as a woman endowed with special comprehension of "problems that men alone had been trained to handle," but Taft was more realistic. He described his wife as the family politician. Her burning ambition was always discernibly close to the surface. Time and again she urged him to hold out for the greater prize. She believed that Will did not fully realize his potentialities, and by means of her own sincerity and candor she often supplied the touch of skepticism he lacked. To observers she sometimes seemed invincible in her determination to see him get on. But in spite of this relentless drive Mrs. Taft was adored by her husband, respected and loved by her children and admired by the public.

On Inauguration Day she made a point of riding back from the Capitol in the carriage with the President, a decision she had made when she heard that Roosevelt would go straight to the station. She was well aware that she was breaking precedent, and in her *Recollections* she commented, "For me that drive was the proudest and happiest event of Inauguration Day." She professed elation at doing what no woman had done before. Mrs. Roosevelt had driven to the station without going near the Capitol. Her mood was bitter.

It was soon apparent to the White House staff that Mrs. Taft was an initiate in statecraft and that she liked to share in political discussion. Her husband could always rely on her remarkable memory for names and statistics. Archie Butt, the military aide, found her uncompromising where principle was involved. "I cannot but admire Mrs. Taft's honesty and directness," he wrote. But the first time he dined at the White House after President Taft took office he confessed that he missed the "marvelous wit and personality of Roosevelt and the sweet charm of his wife."

Mrs. Taft corrected her husband sharply when he continued to speak of Roosevelt as President.

"You mean the ex-President, Will," she said.

"I suppose I do, dear; but he will always be the President to me, and I can never think of him as anything else."

Although her active period in the White House was brief, Mrs. Taft had the famous cherry trees planted that led to the annual festival. She initiated band concerts outdoors, and the Taft administration was notable for its encouragement of all the arts. A succession of stage stars, musicians, writers and artists dined or performed at the White House. Shakespearean productions were given on the lawn. Mrs. Taft was one of the founders of the Cincinnati Symphony Orchestra, and her deepest outside interests were music and the theater.

In the days of darkness that followed her collapse she was no longer the adviser, the planner, the astute critic. It was Will who helped her through this period as he fumbled with the growing difficulties and storms of his own unhappy administration. The inner sadness of the jovial President was never quite recognized, but intimates felt that it contributed to the disastrous course he followed at times. As her grip on life returned, Helen Taft became his good angel again when he settled happily into the professorial mold, taught, lectured and backed Woodrow Wilson in his war policies. Her illness had stilled her ambitions, and she shared his satisfaction when he finally became Chief Justice. But her powers had failed, and she was never again the driving force, the potent adviser who had helped him in his long climb from a carefree law practice in Cincinnati to the White House. Her own life faded into the shadows after his death, but she watched her two sons rise to fame in their separate ways—Robert to his unique role in the political history of the country; Charles to his humanitarian interests and his tireless fight on political corruption.

The Taft children had traveled the world over. They were sophisticates but were simply brought up and had good manners, good ideals, good education. All were outstanding scholars, a continuing Taft tradition, and the daughter Helen—Mrs. Frederick J. Manning—was one of the significant career women of the early twentieth century, setting her stamp on innumerable college girls and helping the suffrage cause. She was in turn dean, acting president and head of the history department of Bryn Mawr. Early in her teaching career she waved the suffrage banner along with Miss M. Carey Thomas, President of Bryn Mawr. It was a cause deplored by her parents and particularly by her mother, who suffered every time she heard that her daughter was out campaigning and speaking. When finally the amendment was passed, big-hearted Mr. Taft reminded his reluctant wife to go to the polls and vote. After all the furor it would not do to leave this rite to the ignorant, he jested. Always conscientious about her duties, Mrs. Taft on this occasion did as Will told her. But she had wielded plenty of power without the right to vote.

Ellen Axson Wilson, Woodrow Wilson's first wife, died in 1914, twenty-nine years after she married the young scholar in Savannah, Georgia. She was more interested in art, landscape gardening and social service than she was in official entertaining. Her health was frail while she was in the White House, and her three daughters were more in the public eye than she was. But her successor, Edith Bolling Galt Wilson, was suddenly catapulted into the most significant situation a First Lady had ever faced. Her period of regency after the President collapsed with a stroke has been widely cited as a play of power by a woman. Actually she had little interest in politics or politicians until faced with this emergency, but the reserved President had confided in her to an uncommon degree. His sudden marriage soon after his first wife's death fascinated Washington. Norman Galt, Edith's first husband, had been dead for eight years. The Bollings were a well-known Virginia family, but the fact that Galt had been in trade and ran a jewelry shop did not predispose the Cliff Dwellers in her favor.

At forty-three Edith Wilson was dashing, vivacious and built along generous lines. She was interested in travel, books and music, and her life had been spent more among artistic people than politicians. The President wooed her with books and yellow roses, informal dinners and long drives. Early in their friendship he took to asking her for advice. Mrs. Galt was with him on the *Mayflower* the day after he had dispatched his first *Lusitania* note. He was considering dropping William Jennings Bryan as Secretary of the Navy because of his pacifist views.

"What do you think the effect would be?" he asked.

"Good," she said, without a moment's hesitation. "For I hope you can replace him with someone who is able, and who would in himself command respect for the office both at home and abroad."

Her advice counted from the start, but she felt later that she had dismissed "so great a man" too flippantly.

"I doubt if anything I can in honor do will keep us out of war," Wilson told her at the time he proposed marriage.

Colonel E. M. House, the President's closest friend and adviser, turned his face against her from the start, and she never forgave him. But banner headlines proclaimed the event all over the world when the handsome Mrs. Galt, in a plain black velvet gown with orchids at her waist and a velvet toque with feathers, became the bride of Woodrow Wilson on December 18, 1915. She was immediately in the storm center of the drive by Theodore Roosevelt and others to force the President to declare war. So strong were the pressures that she did not think he would be re-elected, but when he won she made an entry in her diary on November 25, 1916: "I helped Woodrow in the study until nearly twelve. He was writing what he says may prove the greatest piece of work of his life. . . ."

It was his last effort to end the war in Europe. He gave Edith a black opal and diamond pendant on the day he finished and dispatched the peace note that brought sharp repercussions from the American public and the British monarch, who thought it pro-German. Roosevelt and Senator Lodge could not be appeased, but William Howard Taft stood by. Mrs. Wilson detested Senator Lodge as much as she did Colonel House. She learned the supersecret code used in the Colonel's dispatches when he headed a mission to France in the fall of 1917, and she devoted no end of time to decoding the dispatches and putting her husband's replies into code. At this juncture she kept up a friendly front with House for her husband's sake, but she never trusted him and thought him a sycophant.

During this period of stress the President, always unwilling to confide freely in his colleagues, discussed the political situation in detail with his wife. They played golf together, went horseback riding and attended a play or vaudeville each week. Wilson had become the man of the hour as the United States entered the war. When the Armistice was signed Mrs. Wilson later recalled, "We did nothing. We just stood there dumbly, knowing the news was true, but *unable to feel it.*"

She was hostess to the major statesmen of the era while in the White House and went abroad with the President for the Peace Conference. They toured the hospitals, reviewed the troops and visited the battlefields. In London Mrs. Wilson would not curtsy to the Queen. President Wilson's shaggy fur coat in juxtaposition with his tall silk hat caused amusement, but Rome gave him the greatest ovation he ever received. Henry White, the United States Ambassador to France (whose wife was Margaret Rutherford), frequently used Mrs. Wilson to convey his views to the President. Ray Stannard Baker briefed the American press, and Mrs. Wilson attended these secret sessions, learning what went on behind the closed doors at the Quai d'Orsay.

She insisted on being present when Wilson presented the draft of the Covenant of the League to a plenary session of the Peace Conference for acceptance as part of the treaty. A firm rule denied access of any unauthorized person to a plenary session, and more particularly a woman. But Edith conspired with Admiral Cary T. Grayson, who also wished to attend. When she set out to see Clemenceau to ask for permission the President remarked, "Wilful woman, your sins be on your own head if the tiger shows his claws."

"Oh, he can't," she replied, "they're always done up in gray cotton gloves."

Clemenceau was acquiescent, and Mrs. Wilson and Admiral Grayson hid in a little antechamber off the Room of the Clock. When her husband began to speak Mrs. Wilson pulled the curtains slightly apart to watch him. They sailed for home, lulled by the belief that the Senate would ratify the treaty. Mrs. Wilson was stunned by Lodge's attack and nearly half a century later commented, "Oh, he was a snake in the grass! Or rather, not in the grass. He was a snake in the open."

"House has given away everything I had won before we left Paris," the President remarked to his wife on their return home. "He has compromised on every side. The League is out of the Treaty. I'll have to start all over again."

Mrs. Wilson regarded this development as the start of his long illness and the collapse of his large-scale plans for his fellow men. Once the treaty was signed he and House never saw each other again. Edith called House a "jellyfish." On the night of August 19, 1919, Wilson told his wife that he must tour the country and lay his case before the people. "Only they can prevail," he said.

The President was tired when he started, and Admiral Grayson, Wilson's physician, predicted that the speaking tour might kill him. After his collapse at Pueblo, Colorado, news of his actual condition was kept from the public, and when he had a more paralyzing stroke a few days after his return to Washington the curtain of secrecy was complete. For the next few weeks Edith Wilson played an extraordinary role, and historians have since disagreed over the amount of influence she actually wielded. Charles Willis Thompson called it "Mrs. Wilson's Regency." Others described her as the "Acting President." George Sylvester Viereck wrote that for six and a half months she was not only Acting President, but also secretary to the President and Secretary of State.

Actually, her "regency" lasted less than two months and was dictated by necessity. Admiral Grayson decided to hush up the true situation while rumors flew about that the President was unconscious, that he was totally paralyzed, that he was a raving madman. Mrs. Wilson and Grayson together kept the truth even from members of the Cabinet and the Senate. When Sir William Wiseman, British secret agent, visited the White House immediately after the President's total collapse, she insisted that he tell her what his mission was and that she would convey its purpose to her husband. She was advised by the President's doctor to channel every message that came in, to weigh its importance and then try to solve it with the suitable department head without consulting the President. Since Wilson was much too ill at this point for thought or action of any sort, Mrs. Wilson tried to follow the doctor's advice. He pointed out that if the President resigned, his will to live would be gone. But Robert Lansing, the Secretary of State, proposed that the Vice-Presi-

dent take over. Joseph Tumulty, Wilson's secretary, was angrily re-
sistant, and Admiral Grayson said he would testify that the President
was competent to perform the duties of his office.

"So began my stewardship," wrote Mrs. Wilson. She was as deeply
in her husband's confidence as Abigail Adams had been in hers. She
was not brilliant, or schooled in politics, but she had an intimate
knowledge of the President's wishes and ideals. Because of his lone-
wolf technique she alone had been party to many of his decisions, and
at times had tipped the balance one way or another. With this special
knowledge at her command she now handled every paper, letter or
document addressed to the President. She referred as much as she
could to special departments, but when a vital issue came up she
made a brief digest and read it to Wilson with explanatory comments. Her answers were also read to him before they went out, but
no one knew if he heard or understood. Instead of writing to the
Cabinet members she usually spoke to them personally.

Washington seethed over this extraordinary situation. Although
Grayson was attending her husband medically, he took no part in the
political decisions. She sometimes consulted Tumulty, although he
did not see the President for six weeks. In effect she carried the
burden singlehanded, but her own description of this interlude in
presidential history reduces her role: "The only decision that was
mine was what was important and what was not; and the very important decision of when to present matters to my husband."

Mrs. Wilson did not dwell on the all-important manner of presentation. Josephus Daniels and Newton D. Baker both were firm allies,
and she sometimes consulted Bernard Baruch. Senator Gilbert M.
Hitchcock was her principal adviser, and Mrs. Wilson pictured her
husband dictating notes to her to send to Hitchcock. David Lawrence
summed up the situation in 1919: "Between the President and the
outside world stands Mrs. Wilson, as devoted and faithful a companion as ever nursed a sick man. . . . It is doubtful if ever a woman
in American history had such a burden. As between the chance to
save a life and answer the numerous attacks that are being made
upon the President, Mrs. Wilson has chosen the course of stoical
silence."

She was indeed a figure of world-wide interest at this time, and the London *Daily Mail* editorialized that although "Washington tongues are wagging vigorously no suggestion is heard that Mrs. Wilson is not proving a capable 'President,'" But as Wilson's condition improved he was able to receive Cabinet members, and then visitors like the King and Queen of Belgium and the Prince of Wales. All the suppressed venom against Mrs. Wilson burst suddenly into the open in the Senate. Was the President's signature on documents his own, or forged? Mrs. Wilson had an answer for this. Two weeks after his stroke, she said, he could sign public documents with help, and he knew what he was doing. Senator Albert Fall visited him and observed at his bedside, "Mr. President, we have all been praying for you."

"Which way?" jested the Presbyterian Woodrow Wilson.

When Senator Hitchcock visited Mrs. Wilson and told her that unless the Democrats accepted the Lodge reservations the treaty would be defeated, she went to her husband and said, "Woodrow, for my sake won't you accept the reservations and get this awful thing settled?"

But he did not weaken. "It is not I who will not accept," he said. "It is the nation's honor that is at stake. Better a thousand times to go down fighting than to dip your colors to dishonorable compromise."

Edith had lost this battle. He confirmed his decision in a letter to Senator Hitchcock and thus signed the death warrant of the treaty. But when he learned on March 19, 1920, that the battle was over and he had lost, he could scarcely accept the news. By April he talked of resigning, but Edith and Grayson worked mightily to dissuade him, feeling that this would be fatal for him and disastrous for the country. From then on Cabinet meetings were held regularly, and Lansing was tactfully ousted. Mrs. Wilson had much to do with this move, since she could not forgive him for trying to unhorse the President. Actually Lansing resigned under pressure, and she was angry with Woodrow for the friendly letter her husband wrote to him.

Mrs. Wilson fell victim to Franklin D. Roosevelt's charm on his first visit to her husband. She underestimated his ability at first, however, and had later to change her mind about his capacities. Both of the Wilsons suffered acutely as Warren Harding rolled into power on a landslide. Edith disliked her successor intensely—her clothes, her manners, her volubility. She was shocked to hear Mrs. Harding shout to the press as they drove away from the White House for the inaugural ceremonies, "They're my boys." Mrs. Wilson felt mortified when Harding jumped from the car and hurried up the Capitol steps, leaving the President alone. But Woodrow Wilson outlived Harding and did not die until 1924.

In spite of the great power she wielded Mrs. Wilson was violently opposed to woman suffrage, and this had its effect on her husband while the suffrage workers battered at the White House gates and harassed him on all sides. As she watched them picketing she described them in her diary as "disgusting creatures," but she sent Ike Hoover out to ask them to come in and warm up, an invitation they refused with disdain. She approved when the picketers were sentenced to sixty days in jail for disturbing the peace. It was inconceivable to her that the well-known lawyer Dudley Field Malone, then married to beautiful Doris Stevens, stood behind them. "Woodrow decided to pardon those devils in the workhouse," Edith reported indignantly in her diary. "Tumulty came over and agreed with me it was a mistake."

Wilson's final capitulation to woman suffrage was none of Edith's doing; in fact, the evidence is that she delayed it. But there was no doubt where Mrs. Harding stood on this issue. It was her proud boast that she had made Warren Harding President. She had little time to show her influence in the White House, but it had been the driving force in Harding's life for many years. Samuel Hopkins Adams has described her as being "more highly energized, more industrious, more ambitious, and more far-seeing than her husband, as well as being definitely the stronger spirit."

Florence Kling Harding had firm principles, a shrewd business sense and a rigid personality, which left those around her cold. Her manner seemed artificial, and she was altogether lacking in the feminine qualities that traditionally are considered an appealing asset in the White House. She had inherited the autocratic spirit of her father, Amos O. Kling of Marion, Ohio, and before her marriage to Warren Harding in 1891 she had divorced Henry De Wolfe. For fourteen years she managed her husband's newspaper, the Marion *Star*, and was a trained business executive long before she became First Lady.

Slim, aquiline in feature and always carefully groomed, Mrs. Harding was stilted in manner and her voice tended to be strident as she moved circumspectly into the limelight. Her silver hair was tightly marcelled; her aging throat was often concealed with a velvet band; her gestures were without grace. But behind her cold and correct exterior, furies burned at times, and she was one of the most ambitious of Presidents' wives. Her husband called her the Duchess, as she catered to the drinking and gambling habits of some of his cronies, who chose to refer to her as the Boss. Spiritualism was a preoccupation with Mrs. Harding, and she spent much time with astrologers and quacks. They had persuaded her that she had a Star of Destiny on her brow, and she had been told by a Madame Marcia that her husband would become President of the United States but would not live to complete his term.

During his days in the Senate Mrs. Harding had taken note of every social slight, and when she reached the White House she paid off these scores from a memorandum book she had kept. At first reluctant to see her husband become President, fearing that incidents in his past might be used against him, she finally gave in to Harry M. Daugherty's persuasion and urged him to go ahead during the month that he took to make up his mind. There was no uncertainty on Mrs. Harding's part of her own capacity to be the nation's leading hostess.

When the primaries were going against Harding he was ready to give up, but his wife took the telephone receiver from his hand and told Daugherty that Warren was in the fight "till hell freezes over." Harding sat down and looked helplessly at his strong-willed wife. He had been on the point of bowing out. Later, when a friend remarked to him that it looked as if he were in the race to stay, he responded, "You mean Mrs. Harding is."

She readily forgot the astrologer's prediction when he won, and exulted in his victory. But her genial husband was depressed. He had been insisting for a long time that he had no wish to be President. Mrs. Harding brightened up the White House after the somber last days of the Wilson administration. Flowers and plants abounded. Bulbs were planted on the lawns and birdhouses hung in the trees. Shades were not drawn, and passersby were invited to gaze at the White House as much as they wished. Although prohibition was the law of the land, poker and drinking parties were held upstairs, and there was considerable revelry by assorted groups of politicians and hangers-on. But Mrs. Harding imposed a number of rules that irked her husband. He was no longer allowed to chew tobacco or to have the wienerwurst and sauerkraut that he had enjoyed in Marion.

Mrs. Longworth viewed Mrs. Harding as a nervous, excitable woman with a strident, high-pitched voice "who kept a little red book for purposes of retaliation." Mrs. Harding thought Alice contemptuous and condescending. These were small social details, but Mrs. Harding made one significant political move that altered her husband's inaugural address on the hottest issue of the day—the League of Nations. A paragraph inferentially committing the United States to eventual entry into the League was in the original version of the address. The text was carefully read by Mrs. Harding, who, according to Daugherty, brandished a blue pencil above the draft and cut out this vital paragraph. There was subsequent bewilderment over the unexpected vacillation that Harding showed that day. William Howard Taft, who had sworn him in, was bitterly disappointed that he had not stood firm for the League.

Mrs. Calvin Coolidge, wife of the Vice-President, soon found her bearings with Mrs. Harding and remained her friend and champion up to the time of the Duchess' death. But Mrs. Harding did not warm to either of the Coolidges and fought a move for an official residence for the nation's second political figure. When Congress was offered Mrs. John B. Henderson's home and grounds for this purpose Mrs. Harding was indignant. The question was discussed at the White House dinner table in the presence of Dr. Nicholas Murray Butler, who was surprised when she "burst into flame and almost shouted: 'Not a bit of it, not a bit of it. I am going to have that bill defeated. Do you think I am going to have those Coolidges living in a house like that? A hotel apartment is plenty good enough for them.'"

The bill was defeated, but "those Coolidges" were soon in residence at the White House itself. Actually, Mrs. Harding was ill during most of her days in Washington, and to many she seemed to be putting up a bold front in a difficult situation. "She was at all times jealous and at most times suspicious of Harding," a family friend told Mark Sullivan. Whatever Calvin Coolidge may have heard or observed of the subterranean scandals that exploded after Harding's death he was too discreet—or secretive—to mention. Although he was the silent participant in Cabinet discussions, he listened attentively and never missed a meeting. But when the corruption of the Harding administration was aired in the early days of his own term in office he stood aloof from it all and never disclosed what he may have thought or heard of the machinations of the men close to Harding.

When the President left for Alaska, Mrs. Harding was already worried about his health. He was depressed, restless, ailing. She was close by when he died, and would not permit an autopsy or the casting of a death mask. Waves of scandal enveloped her, but she went stoically through the burial ceremonies and entombment in his native Marion, directing every detail to the last. When Mrs. Harding died in 1924 she was buried beside her husband. The storms of his administration left their echoes down the years. Although her role was ill-defined, her influence over Harding was never questioned.

Florence Harding's successor brought the kind of womanly charm to her role that has always sat best with the American people. Grace Coolidge shed warmth around the personality of the most aloof and silent of Presidents. Her influence was wholly on Coolidge the man, not Coolidge the politician, for no President's wife was ever kept so completely in the dark about her husband's thoughts and actions. Although it can be said of a number of Presidents that they might not have reached the White House but for the aid and support of their wives early in their careers, it is a safe assumption that Calvin Coolidge, single-minded in his industry and ambition, would have made it on his own, but he did not undervalue his wife and said of her toward the end of his life: "For almost a quarter of a century she has borne with my infirmities and I have rejoiced in her graces." This was a rare tribute, coming from Calvin Coolidge. It summed up the essence of his feeling for the woman he chose as his wife. And in 1926 he said to his friend Bruce Barton, "A man who has the companionship of a lovely and gracious woman enjoys the supreme blessing that life can give. And no citizen of the United States knows the truth of this statement more than I."

Mrs. Coolidge made a smooth transition from her limited role as wife of the Vice-President to that of First Lady. The span from August, 1923, to March, 1929, was a prosperous and lively period in American life. Silent forces soon to explode were at work behind the lurid front of the Jazz Age. The pace was wild; the times were out of joint, but not in the White House. "We New England women cling to the old way," said Mrs. Coolidge early in her husband's term of office, "and being the President's wife isn't going to make me think less about the domestic things I've always loved."

Alice Roosevelt Longworth quickly noted the change from the Harding regime, and observed that the atmosphere had become "as different as a New England front parlor is from a back room in a speakeasy." Mrs. Coolidge had written to her friend Mrs. Dwight Morrow, "We all know Calvin will make good. I have been somewhat doubtful of my own ability but if you say I can come through I know I can."

It was Mrs. Coolidge who showed a particular, if unconscious, genius for striking the right chord on all occasions, and dissipating the chill so easily spread by her husband. Time and again she saved a social situation with her tact and intuition, and never once did she embarrass her husband with a gaucherie in the political field. "The whole union seems cabalistic," said William Allen White of the Coolidges. "She is a vital part of his success, of his life, of his happiness." He found her charming where her husband was silent, quick where he was slow, intuitive where he was logical.

Will Rogers said to her jestingly at a White House dinner, "I wish you would tell me if the President is going to run again."

"You find out if you can, and let me know," said the quick-witted Mrs. Coolidge.

In the end she learned from the press, and not from Calvin, that he had made his famous declaration "I do not choose to run." No one in the country was more surprised than Mrs. Coolidge when this news reached her. But to her Calvin's word was law. She believed in him. She respected him. Moreover, she was deeply aware of the responsibility of her position. When his anger flared she lapsed into total silence but, unlike John Adams and James Madison, he did not veer around as they had done with Abigail and Dolley. Calvin Coolidge was immune to his wife's influence, except that she could charm him at any time, and she was of infinite value to him on the social side. But he would not let her learn to ride, or bob her hair, or drive a car, or fly with Charles A. Lindbergh, or express her views on politics, or in any way step out of character as wife and mother.

The President kept a tight grip on the White House guest list, on the bills, which he paid personally, on the kitchen and even on his wife's mail. He would change the seating list arranged by his aides without qualm and startled Grace by putting the Budget Chief ahead of the Justices of the Supreme Court at a New Year's Day reception. But members of the household considered Mrs. Coolidge 90 per cent of the administration, even though she scarcely knew from hour to hour what she was expected to do. She catered to his liking for official breakfasts. She saw to it that he was served roast beef unostentatiously, regardless of the menu for his guests, and that the sweet part of the ham next to the bone was always saved for him. His favorite pie and muffin recipes were introduced at the White House, and he ate cheese in wedges like pie. Even Grace did not dare to make a social appointment for Mr. Coolidge. He preferred to discuss business at his office.

But Mary Randolph, her social secretary, noted how the President's inscrutable face lit up at the sight of Grace. And although he was parsimonious in all else, she said, "I have never known any man more interested in his wife's clothes than Mr. Coolidge and the handsomer and more elaborate Mrs. Coolidge's dresses were the better he liked it." In their early married days, when they had little money, he would shop around in Boston for a becoming dress for Grace, or a large picture hat with a rose. During her days as First Lady the public viewed her with admiration as she went swinging along the graveled paths, her skirts blowing in the wind, her brown eyes sparkling, while her favorite collie, Rob Roy, dashed ahead.

She saved the day for the President with her tact when Queen Marie of Rumania staged a whirlwind campaign at the White House to get aid for her country. The Queen in all her glory and jewels was quite outmatched by Mrs. Coolidge in plain white satin with red roses but no diamonds. The President's icy resistance to Queen Marie's importunities was mellowed by his tactful wife.

She gave her husband strength and comfort in the bitter days that followed the death from blood poisoning of their son Calvin, Jr. In Calvin's own words the glory had departed from the Presidency with this event, and Mrs. Coolidge's joyous manner was subdued and quiet for a long time afterward. "He really seems to need me," she wrote to Frank Stearns, a family friend, as if this were a remarkable trait in Calvin. But he needed her in so many ways that she was regarded as a real asset to his administration. Mrs. Longworth observed that she "put no feminine finger into affairs of state, made no speeches, gave no interviews," but succeeded in making others happy because she enjoyed life so much herself.

The politicians were her friends and admirers. James J. Davis, Secretary of Labor, told her once that if he could run for the Presidency he would like to have her for his campaign manager. Like Dolley Madison she remembered names and faces. And she got on remarkably well with Cabinet wives and the great variety of women she had to meet in a public capacity. Observers thought that her understanding of the role she must play was a masterly feat in public relations. Publicity and advertising had just begun to blossom in the 1920's. The field was uncharted, but one authority remarked that Mrs. Coolidge "did the front door job" for the Coolidge administration—no small accomplishment when the central character was Silent Cal.

Although not unsympathetic to the women who were breaking some of the old shackles and finding a place for themselves in the working world, she and her husband were impervious to the National

Woman's Party fight for protective legislation for women in industry. In this Grace was following her husband's lead, for in her aging years as a widow she took a much broader view of such matters. The President gave Alice Paul and her followers a chilly rebuff when they petitioned him to help them in their fight. "Women can never escape the responsibility of home and children, and the working woman as a mother and potential mother challenges universal interest," the President commented.

Mrs. Coolidge had no resentment over her isolation in political matters, and in the year after she left the White House she wrote, "I am rather proud of the fact that after nearly a quarter of a century of marriage my husband feels free to make his decisions without consulting me or giving me advance information concerning them." On another occasion she speculated whether he might have confided in her had she been a more serious type. Grace Coolidge was always apt to jest about her own intelligence, and when Boston University gave her an honorary degree she wrote to her Pi Beta Phi friends that she found an LL.D. an overwhelming honor, but that D.D., not for Doctor of Divinity but for Doctor of Domesticity, would have suited her case.

Mrs. Coolidge had the dream—later perfected by Mrs. Kennedy—of collecting authentic colonial treasures for the White House, but the President put the quietus on this plan. With Mrs. Morrow she studied the American wing of the Metropolitan Museum, consulted architects and made a start in restoration, but she did not get beyond collecting some pieces for the Green Parlor. She was interested in the beautification of the buildings in Washington. General Pershing, as chairman of the Commission on Battle Monuments, took the plans for a war memorial to show to the President when he was summering in the Black Hills. Mrs. Coolidge studied them carefully and decided that they were too reminiscent of the guillotine. A new design was drawn up—the Arlington of the future. This was one of the few known instances where she quietly exerted influence in the background. The President kept a watchful eye for any move that might disturb the status quo, for once in a while Mrs. Coolidge was led into innovations through enthusiastic friends.

She worked ardently for the Red Cross and for the deaf, and she was the nation's best-known baseball fan, pulling the President's coattails to make him stay and watch the Senators win a world championship. Actually she took a bright and intelligent interest in the world in which she lived and was a shrewd judge of people, but instead of discussing government and politics with his beloved Grace, Calvin usually discussed family affairs with her, or recalled incidents from his boyhood days in Plymouth, Vermont. Had she shown any particular interest in public affairs, she wrote on one occasion, she "would have been properly put in her place." But she was quick to compliment him when he scored a point in public. She knew when to be silent, and when to speak. Always ready to encourage him to talk, she quickly filled in the gaps when he clammed up in characteristic fashion. When asked, after the fact, what she thought of his decision not to run for re-election Mrs. Coolidge replied, "I have such faith in Mr. Coolidge's judgment that if he told me I would die tomorrow morning at ten o'clock, I would believe him."

This was the kind of trust that helped to give quiet assurance to Calvin Coolidge. William Allen White, who studied both of the Coolidges in their relaxed as well as their official moments, found Grace as "dear as she was wise," and he noted: "To what extent Mrs. Coolidge has influenced her husband's judgment only two persons may testify. One is too silent to say, even if he realized it; and the other too smart! But Mrs. Coolidge has accepted her husband's ideals and striven with him to realize them. . . . But for Mrs. Coolidge, her husband would not have traveled the path he has climbed."

Mrs. Herbert Hoover was perhaps the least known of Presidents' wives, although she was one of the most learned, traveled and accomplished of them all. Since she never let her convictions show in any way, she settled into the gallery of quiet and indeterminate First Ladies, content to be good wives and helpmates. Lou Henry was a native of Waterloo, Iowa, and she was majoring in geology and mining at Stanford University when she met handsome young Herbert Hoover. They were married in 1899, when she was twenty-four, and they sailed at once on a trip around the world, the first of many such journeys. In the years that followed they roved ceaselessly, and Mrs. Hoover became expert at putting together temporary homes in many parts of the world. On their honeymoon they lived through the Boxer Rebellion in China, and Mrs. Hoover nursed the wounded in a temporary hospital in Tientsin, rode through the streets with her husband on a bicycle and had several narrow escapes from the insurgents.

She could rough it at will, but after the birth of two sons her travels were modified to some extent for the sake of their education. When Herbert Hoover's engineering activities took him to remote areas like Ceylon, the Malay Peninsula or Siberia she established herself in the nearest center of civilization. Both preferred houses to hotels, so that they had bungalows in Mandalay and Tokyo, a chalet in the Alps and their famous Red House in Kensington. Wherever they went, hospitality reigned, and this became Mrs. Hoover's conspicuous contribution to White House history. She was the complete cosmopolitan, a true citizen of the world, by the time she became First Lady, and in the desperate days of the Depression she handled the social side of the administration with tact and skill. Like Mrs. Coolidge, Mrs. Hoover was a woman of dignity and reserve, educated, thoughtful and endowed with compassion.

Almost at once Mrs. Hoover had to cope with one of the most famous social feuds in White House history, when Alice Longworth questioned the right of Dolly Gann, sister of Vice-President Charles Curtis, to take precedence over the Speaker's wife at dinner parties. Mrs. Eugene Meyer had let slip the fact that Mrs. Gann would have the place of honor at a party she was giving, and Nicholas Longworth declined to attend. Alice fed the fires, and Mrs. Hoover quietly arranged a series of functions guaranteed to soothe Mrs. Gann's feelings. But soon she had more serious problems as the full weight of the Depression settled on her bewildered husband. The President was so everlastingly busy and harassed as he struggled with disaster on all sides that he rarely talked politics with her. She was well equipped to discuss official matters, but she rarely did. Although scientifically trained, politics was not a dominating interest in her life. Scholarship was. She had helped her husband to translate Georgius Agricola's medieval Latin treatise on metallurgy, De Re Metallica, and she was a full partner in all his scientific interests.

The White House during the Hoover administration took on a tropical appearance reminiscent of Mrs. Taft's regime. Plants and ferns, wicker furniture and grass rugs abounded. Guests poured into the Executive Mansion in great numbers, and the President thought nothing of bringing friends home without any preliminary announcement. Because of their travels the Hoovers' taste in food was exotic, and Mrs. Hoover ordered out-of-season foods with a free hand. She helped her husband in many of the demands made upon him, welcoming delegations to the White House and christening ships and aircraft at a time when the great upsurge of the Depression was casting its blight over his administration. She lent her own prestige to her favorite cause—the Girl Scouts—and she was a symbol for youth at a time when they had little to inspire them.

Mrs. Hoover shared to an excruciating degree the fate of a small number of First Ladies who have heard their husbands assailed and denounced beyond the bounds of reason or common sense. But she lived to see the changing temper of the times, and before she died in 1944 she was conscious of the gradual revival of respect for her controversial husband. She had shared all his humanitarian interests to the full and had stood in the background while honors came his way.

Chapter 4

Power in the White House

The Hoover name was in deep eclipse when Franklin D. Roosevelt swept into office on a great landslide. His wife, Eleanor Roosevelt, will undoubtedly go down in history as the First Lady who created the strongest political image around the world. Her fame is indissolubly linked with that of her husband, and the growth of the Negro movement of the 1960's may be traced back in some measure to the two Roosevelts.

Eleanor was not in any sense of the word a feminist, in spite of the great power she wielded on many fronts. She deplored any emphasis on sex differentiation in the political body. In everything she wrote and everything she said she took care to make the point that she had little influence with her husband in political matters and had never tried to sway him. Yet who could doubt the power she actually wielded through giving him her own findings on the problems of the American people as she traveled far and wide, and in rallying countless numbers to his support through the force of her own personality and the single-mindedness of her aims?

Adlai Stevenson called her a lady for all seasons, leaving a "name to shine on the entablatures of truth—forever." She was the most criticized and also the most revered of First Ladies, and her influence was deep and lasting, he pointed out. For in nearly four score

81

years she had never run out of things that needed doing, and she had worked all her days for the realization of a human city embracing all mankind. "When she died on that gray November day in 1962," he said, "she was the most respected woman of this century. She warmed the cold, beckoned to the lost, and kindled hope where none had ever flamed."

This was one view of her and these were poetic words. Some felt that she was shrewish, interfering, politically too far to the Left, lacking in feminine appeal and generally abrasive. No President's wife, even Mary Lincoln, was subjected to more personal abuse from both sexes, but more often from women than from men. Her voice, her homely features, her attire, her views, her family troubles were held up to scorn. But she weathered it all, chiefly by ignoring it, and became a force to reckon with not only in the United States but around the world.

Mrs. Roosevelt believed that any woman political leader should back other women, although she never liked to be directly identified with avowed feminist clamorings. She was satisfied with the pace at which emancipation was progressing and did not believe in pushing women unless they were well fitted for certain appointments. In her early days she felt that women would never amount to anything in politics, but she is on record as saying in her later years that one day the United States would have a woman President. As a young wife, before her own life stream veered into political channels, she spent her time on charities, her family and the customary social activities. Her first introduction to the other world was through the League of Women Voters and the Women's Trade Union League. She had good health and boundless energy, and first stepped out of the home to teach in a private school.

In time it was apparent, however, that she had an inherited political sense. Corinne Roosevelt Robinson always maintained that Eleanor was Theodore Roosevelt's favorite niece and that she was more like him than any of his own children. But she took to the platform slowly, dismayed by her clammy hands, her high-pitched accent, the uncontrollable giggle that discounted her serious words. She mastered each of these handicaps, taking voice lessons and learning to speak without a text. Before long she turned the role of First Lady into an official national office, and she functioned with speed, dash and individualism. Her trips to coal mines, to the Dust Bowl of the 1930's, to the shacks in the Ozarks, to Negro cabins and city slums, to the irrigation ditches of California, supplied her with firsthand information on the miseries of mankind. She served as eyes and ears for the President as he sat immobilized, directing the country through crucial hours. She went far afield, too—to Puerto Rico and the Virgin Islands, to South America, to Guadalcanal and Great Britain, and to any point at which American troops were stationed.

President Roosevelt thought that one of the problems of his office was the reluctance of people to tell him the straight truth. But this was not the case with his wife. He learned much from her that would never have come to him from any other source. Although he did not always concur in her findings, or act on them, he had the benefit of a wider view of many aspects of national life, particularly on the humanitarian side. He trusted her judgment and impartiality, and in the end made up his own mind. Mrs. Roosevelt was the first to say that she questioned how much she had actually influenced him on major political issues. But few observers doubted her power, pervasive in general, direct at times.

Mrs. Roosevelt was credited with being responsible for the appointment of the first woman member in the Cabinet—Frances Perkins, who headed the Department of Labor. But it was Mary E. Dewson, an indefatigable political worker better known as Molly, whom Mrs. Roosevelt supported at every point, who persuaded President Roosevelt to take this step. Frances Perkins' reputation was already well established through her work for Governor Smith. There is no doubt, however, that Mrs. Roosevelt drew up many lists of potential women employees for key positions. She was deeply involved in all the big causes of her era and was a significant figure in the social revolution of the 1930's, 1940's and 1950's, highlighting racial inequality and social injustice wherever she found them. When she kissed Marian Anderson in public and broke with the Daughters of the American Revolution because they closed Constitution Hall to the Negro singer, she struck a blow for black people, who idolized her. Her influence in this area was profound. She swung millions of black votes into Democratic channels and had no hesitancy about standing pat on controversial issues. Her argument was that since the dark-skinned people outnumbered the white people of the world, survival depended on learning to live at peace together. It was a long step into the future. Mrs. Roosevelt's stand was that one should never turn one's back on life or evade involvement. She never did, but gave fresh meaning to the word before it became mere political jargon. However, she was bitterly and constantly criticized by women who deplored her restlessness, her family misfortunes, her interference in political matters, her liberal views, her personal associations and the cuisine at the White House, down to her scrambled-egg suppers on Sunday nights and the frankfurter picnic for the King and Queen of Great Britain.

Mrs. Roosevelt always traced her political education direct to Louis Howe, the frail asthmatic adviser who loomed so large in her husband's political life. He became part of their household after her husband's disabling illness in 1921 and was with them until his death in 1936. He masterminded Mrs. Roosevelt as he did her husband, and he helped her in her battle with the President's mother, Sara Delano Roosevelt, to keep Franklin from retiring into the protective shell of an invalid at Hyde Park. Mrs. Roosevelt, with Howe's help, was largely responsible for his return to full-scale political activity—a significant act for the future of the world.

As early as 1928 she became an important political link herself when Al Smith and John J. Raskob persuaded her to telephone her husband at Warm Springs and urge him to run for the governorship of New York State. He had been refusing to answer the calls of the politicians, but when Eleanor persuaded him to talk to Governor Smith on the wire, he had taken his first step toward an extraordinary career. She refused to run for any office herself, or to hold an elective position, but as the Governor's wife she visited prisons, hospitals, highway construction jobs, and she became a careful observer and note taker. Before long more of the state's Democratic leaders knew Eleanor than knew Franklin.

She was reluctant to see her husband become President, and a few days before the election of 1932 she said, "If I wanted to be selfish about it, I could hope that Franklin would be defeated next Tuesday." She was quite without personal ambition and saw nothing glorious or even particularly desirable about being the wife of a President. The country was suffering profoundly from the Depression, and her drive to the old army camp outside Washington that her husband had ordered opened for the Bonus marchers was the first step in the twenty years of investigative journeying that followed. It took her to all parts of the country and around the world and into areas never before visited by anyone from the White House.

Her work for the National Youth Administration and as assistant director of Civilian Defense came under heavy fire, and she made individual political moves in the early days that angered people, like backing Caroline O'Day in New York for Congress. This was considered partisan politics, but she gave powerful support to Molly Dewson as head of the Women's Division of the Democratic National Committee, which Mrs. Roosevelt had initiated to expand the role of women in public life.

From the beginning of her husband's administration she was deeply involved in the dynamics of the New Deal, but she was less in evidence with her husband on public occasions than most Presidents' wives, past or present. She seemed always to be absent on missions of one sort or another, or conducting activities of her own. Her syndicated column "My Day," detailing her activities, had a trivial touch not at all illustrative of her big interests and solid accomplishments. She liked James A. Farley and was greatly concerned over the breach that developed between him and her husband. She was something of a peacemaker at the National Convention of 1940 in Chicago. Frances Perkins and others wanted the President to make a personal appearance there. He said his presence would only make matters worse, but he suggested that his wife might substitute for him.

"You know Eleanor always makes people feel right," he told Madam Perkins. "She has a fine way with her. Would you like her to come?"

Mrs. Roosevelt arrived in the middle of a tense situation. Henry

Wallace was under heavy attack. The President had come round to thinking he would make a good Vice-President. "I like him," he told Madam Perkins, who heartily approved of Wallace. "He is the kind of a man I like to have around."

Mrs. Roosevelt took soundings on the spot, and she made a great personal hit on this occasion. "She did sweeten the convention," Madam Perkins noted with approval. "She made friends, shook hands with thousands of people, and made a pleasant, spirited, and high-minded speech which put the political tone where it ought to be—on patriotism and leadership rather than on patronage."

The President complimented her on the work she had done for him on this occasion. He was inclined to call on her when delicate political relationships were at stake, since she had tact and know-how in this field. Moreover, he was aware that his fellow politicians had high regard for her practical approach to problems. Ironically enough, she had no faith in her own political judgment but had endless confidence in her husband's decisions. She believed that he had a perfect sense of timing, something that she lacked, for she was inclined to move impulsively when she saw that something had to be done. Roosevelt, on the other hand, bided his time, gave thought to the right moment, sought advice and then moved with conviction—a course that she often found exasperating.

Mrs. Roosevelt was more disappointed than anyone realized when the President decided to run for a fourth term. She had observed the shattering impact of the war days, and he had given her to understand that he had no intention of running again. Believing this, she had rented a new York apartment larger than she required for herself. Apprehensively she watched him through the closing days of his life, with the future peace of the world at stake. After his sudden death at Warm Springs, Harry Truman asked her what he could do for her. Characteristically Mrs. Roosevelt turned the tables and asked what *she* could do for *him*. When the new President appointed her a delegate to the United Nations Assembly she moved into the international spotlight in a most convincing way. In 1952 she campaigned for Adlai Stevenson, and when she spoke on his behalf at the convention she received the greatest ovation ever given a woman at a national political convention.

When General Eisenhower became President Mrs. Roosevelt resigned as an Assembly delegate and devoted her energies to building up the American Association for the United Nations. This was an organization created to inform the public on the objectives of the parent body. She worked for civil rights and crusaded for assistance to Israel. Much of the money she made from her writings and speeches was turned over to her favorite causes. In addition to her syndicated column she wrote six books, two stories for children, two volumes of autobiography, two collections of essays and a treatise on democracy.

Mrs. Roosevelt also opened the door to the women of the press, an innovation that has profoundly changed and strengthened the role of Presidents' wives in the march of history. She had twelve years in the White House—from March, 1933, until April, 1945—the longest period of anyone since Dolley Madison was hostess, first for Thomas Jefferson and then for her husband. No White House family has ever come under heavier attack. The divorces and financial difficulties of the Roosevelt children became public gossip, but the Roosevelts' only daughter, Mrs. James A. Halsted, the fair-haired Anna of the war years, remembers best the bright light that shone around her spectacular parents. The white stone bench that memorializes Eleanor Roosevelt in the United Nations gardens bears Adlai Stevenson's tribute to her: "She would rather light a candle than curse the darkness and her glow has warmed the world."

Today neither friend nor foe would deny the profound influence Eleanor Roosevelt has had on her times.

She was followed by one of the quietest and least obtrusive of Presidents' wives. Mrs. Truman was so average in all her ways that she settled smoothly into her setting and was a restful image to many after her dynamic predecessor. She never spoke in public, gave interviews, or became involved in a public movement or political cause. Had she not been so well liked, she might have come under fire for her total detachment, but the public viewed her with approval. Few had any conception of the genuine influence she had on her husband's life. President Truman banteringly, but with a measure of truth, called her the Boss. She disliked this colloquialism and firmly put an end to it during the campaign tour of 1948. When they reached Lima, Ohio, Bess told Harry that she had had enough of it.

If Bess in actual fact was the Boss, his daughter Margaret was his joy and pride, and he liked to have both by his side when he campaigned.

Margaret, who later became Mrs. Clifton Daniel and the mother of four sons, was one of the most sprightly and popular of White House daughters. She was as friendly and tactful as her father was blunt and her mother silent. They were an inseparable trio, and family life was warm and unified in the White House during the Truman administration. Bess Wallace and Harry Truman had been first-grade classmates in Independence, Missouri, and their romance developed early in life. She was a slim girl, vivacious and athletic, a good skater and tennis player and a baseball fan. Naturally reserved and unpretentious, she did her own housework, even when Truman was Vice-President. When she became First Lady she cut the White House staff and kept a tight rein on the domestic arrangements.

Mrs. Truman was invariably correctly attired; her hair neatly coiffed, her manner irreproachable if not warm. But she kept a weather eye on her impulsive husband, and her influence, like Edith Roosevelt's, was applied consistently on the negative side. One glance across the room from Bess and the President knew that he was walking on eggs. None but her discreet daughter probably knows how often she tipped the bark one way or another. But one recorded instance is illuminating. When the President found her burning letters he had sent her many years earlier, he protested:

"Bess, you oughtn't to do that."

"Why not? I've read them several times."

"But think of history," the President reminded her.

"I have," said Bess crisply, tossing the last one into the fire.

Nor would she pose for a portrait, and it was not until 1968 that a painting, copied from a photograph, was added to the permanent White House collection. Mrs. Lyndon Johnson had trouble persuading Mrs. Truman to permit even that, and she was not present for the hanging ceremony, though her loyal daughter was.

Margaret considered her mother the least understood member of the family. To her she was a "woman of tremendous character . . . a warm, kind-hearted lady, with a robust sense of humor, a merry, twinkling wit, and a tremendous capacity for enjoying life." Mrs. Truman did not try to dissuade her daughter from becoming a professional singer, although she would have preferred her to have done something less arduous and public. In spite of her habit of warning Harry against impetuous utterances, she could not stop him from sending his famous letter to the Washington music critic who ridiculed Margaret for a performance she gave in the capital. In fact, she had no opportunity to know what he was doing when he slipped out quietly and mailed it himself.

Always ready to play the piano, the President was sympathetic to his daughter's ambition and hard work as well as her good sportsmanship when things did not turn out well. Altogether, her industry, her sparkling nature, her beaux and her devotion to her parents gave the White House a happy family air throughout the Truman years. But both women knew that something vast and troubling was going on while Harry Truman was deciding whether or not to order the atom bomb dropped.

All through her husband's administration Mrs. Truman steered clear of political topics, parried questions and kept on good terms with the official women of Washington. She was a discreet First Lady in a period of extreme tension and anxiety. One of her coups, involving the use of her restraining influence on her husband, might have had more serious repercussions than his letter to the music critic, had it become public knowledge at the time.

The ambassadors of two unfriendly nations had been invited to a White House function. One withdrew when he learned that his enemy would be present. President Truman considered this an affront to his wife, and he asked Dean Acheson, the Secretary of State, to demand the ambassador's recall. It was pointed out to him that the invitations had nothing to do with the Trumans but had come from the protocol division. The President would not relent, and he let off steam until Mr. Acheson found himself in a tight spot. When Mrs. Truman learned what was going on she was so concerned that she called up the Secretary of State and said, "You must not let Harry do what he's going to do." However, the President still did not back down until finally Mr. Acheson quoted Bess's stinging comment on the injudiciousness of her husband's purpose. He had little more to add after hearing what Bess had said. She had had the last word.

Careful as he was not to run counter to Bess's wishes, he rejected her advice at one important moment in his life and lived to regret it. He urged the nomination of Averell Harriman and made a speech opposing Adlai Stevenson at the Democratic Convention of 1956. Later, when Stevenson won, Truman told him, "I don't know why I did it. Bess kept telling me not to."

Certainly Mrs. Truman had no aspiration to be the Boss, in reputation or in fact, but she knew that she had a peppery and impulsive husband. By instinct she took a back seat, but she stayed close to him on public occasions, and her face at times reflected the flow of her thoughts—particularly when he departed from his text and let fly at his enemies. Mrs. Truman unquestionably was a silent force, an unseen influence.

Her successor, Mrs. Dwight D. Eisenhower, was born in Boone, Iowa, and was the mother of two sons, one of whom died in infancy.

Her soft, feminine ways, her bangs and gentle smile, her fragile bearing at the side of her warrior husband, made her an appealing image to the public and spread the feeling that all must be well at home. The General's unfailing gallantry to her, his wish to include her in his public discussions and his solicitude for her well-being were noted on all occasions. Mamie was more in the tradition of the nineteenth-century First Lady. She presided gracefully at social functions, and sometimes launched as many as five charity drives in a week, but her delicate health gave her frequent exemption from public scrutiny. When she appeared, she wore flattering clothes and had a distinctive style of her own.

Yet Mrs. Eisenhower had spirit, too, and in 1968 the public caught a glimpse of this on television when she leaned over and reminded Ike that he had failed to mention Richard M. Nixon in a list he was drawing up for the press of potential candidates for the Presidency. The General hastily added the forgotten name. This came at a time when their grandson David was wooing Julie, the younger Nixon daughter. Since no one had ever known Mrs. Eisenhower to make a public gesture, this spontaneous act caused some talk. It was not characteristic of her to speak out of turn on politics.

In the roster of First Ladies she was pre-eminently one of the homemakers, the attentive wife and mother, constantly at Ike's side during his illnesses and always a bland image to the public. She spent years of her life at army posts, and acquired the bridge-playing tastes of the soldier's lonely wife. She also became expert at Scrabble and liked to play the organ. As the wife of a great soldier, and then of a popular President, she ran the White House smoothly and well. She ignored the whispering gossips of Washington and went into retirement as quietly as she had done everything else in the course of her life. The plans for the Gettysburg farm were drawn up largely by Mrs. Eisenhower.

She was followed by the most exotic and glamorous of Presidents' wives—Mrs. John F. Kennedy, a rare flower who made her mark on her generation, not for the specific political power she exercised, but for her charm and beauty and the spell she cast in the foreign field. Her proud and Spartan demeanor in the hours that followed the death of her husband identified her forever with an unforgettable event in American history. Her stoical acceptance of stark tragedy created a memorable picture of a proud widow with two children, standing in public view in a classic stance. She had much to live up to, much to forget, as her personal history unfolded during the 1960's. In 1968 she married Aristotle Onassis on the Greek island of Skorpios.

Mrs. Kennedy invested the White House with an aura distinctly her own. She disdained the political touch and shrank from the wear and tear of campaigning. Her power lay in other areas, in her instinctive sense of style. Glamour has not been a characteristic of America's First Ladies. The most powerful of all—Eleanor Roosevelt—was the homeliest. But Jackie, as the world knew her, was a sybaritic charmer, accomplished as a linguist, knowing in the arts and well prepared to beguile the rulers of distant lands. Here lay her power, and this was the influential touch she added to her husband's brilliant but ill-starred administration. She was a diplomat who knew how to respond to gallantry, and at all times she was the superb hostess. Underneath the gloss was a shy and sensitive nature.

Born a Bouvier, she grew up the complete cosmopolitan. Her early life swung around New York and Newport. In turn she attended

Chapin School, Vassar, the Sorbonne and George Washington University, then had a brief whirl working as an inquiring reporter-photographer for a Washington newspaper. Not too much was known about her when her husband became President. There had never been anyone like her in the White House, although Alice Longworth had matched her in style and spirit, in the power to attract public attention and to focus interest. But Mrs. Kennedy's image was different. It was devastatingly feminine, and she lacked the sharp wit and political instinct of her famous predecessor. However, as time went on it became apparent that there was tensile strength behind the whispering voice, the wavering smile, the inscrutable eyes. She usually got what she wanted, and her instincts led her to the beautiful and the rare. She has been compared to the Whig hostesses of the eighteenth century, the women who rode and hunted, who ran salons distinguished by men and women of wit and talent, who devised court entertainments of classic proportions.

This feeling was dominant when she took her guests by barge to Mount Vernon in honor of a White House visitor—President Ayub Khan of Pakistan. Government ships ferried the party to George Washington's home; the National Symphony Orchestra played; and a ceremonial regiment in colonial uniforms ran off a military drill. Military trucks brought the cooking equipment, and the menu was discriminatingly chosen. The guests were seated at small tables under a gigantic tent on the historic lawn. This was entertainment in the grand manner, and time and again Mrs. Kennedy showed her preference for functions in which an art gallery or a historic setting served as the background.

The White House cuisine was much commented on by connoisseurs during the Kennedy administration, and although the Jeffersonian emphasis on French customs was restored, it was not done with the lavish touch of Jackie's famous predecessor, Dolley Madison. These two First Ladies had points of similarity, but they were worlds apart in their sense of style and bounty. Each suited her own particular era. Like Dolley, Mrs. Kennedy charmed all the emissaries who visited the White House, and during the first two years of his administration, President Kennedy entertained seventy-four foreign leaders, a dozen more than Franklin D. Roosevelt had welcomed during his twelve years in office. The visiting dignitaries, white or colored, representing huge or tiny territories, were generously exposed to Mrs. Kennedy's winning ways, her knowing sense of fashion, her slow and radiant smile, her well-briefed approach on their countries and their interests. They all wanted to meet her, and a British journalist, after dining with the Kennedys, noted that she had "substituted gaiety, informality, and culture for the traditional stuffed shirt."

But Jackie did not underestimate the importance of protocol when the occasion demanded it, and the simplicity of her gowns and jewels, her simple arrangements of field flowers, her imaginative gifts to visitors were an antidote to the potted-palm effects of the past. The tastes and interests of every visiting dignitary were studied. President Abboud of the Sudan, a Shakespearean scholar, was treated to a program of Shakespearean excerpts by actors from Stratford, Connecticut. These were the first readings of the kind at the White House since President William Howard Taft had a company headed by Charles Coburn give Shakespearean productions on the lawn. The Black Watch Tattoo was run off for Prime Minister Sean Lemass of Eire shortly before the assassination, and there were fireworks for the King and Queen of Afghanistan in 1963. The Pablo Casals recital was one of the most discussed of White House social events, and when the Nobel Prize winners were assembled in 1962 President Kennedy remarked, "I think this is the most extraordinary collection of talent, of human knowledge, that has ever been gathered together at the White House, with the possible exception of when Thomas Jefferson dined alone."

When the President and Mrs. Kennedy went abroad in 1961 she received a welcome that astonished even her dynamic husband. She loomed on the horizon as something better than a good-will ambassador, something more significant than the average First Lady. Eleanor Roosevelt was respected around the world for what she did; Jackie Kennedy for what she was. Storms of laughter and applause greeted the President at the Palais de Chaillot when he said at an official luncheon, "I do not think it entirely inappropriate to introduce myself to this audience. I am the man who accompanied Jacqueline Kennedy to Paris, and I have enjoyed it." This modest disclaimer was wildly cheered.

In London she was mobbed, and when she visited India and Pakistan thousands called her the Amerika Maharani—the Queen of America. Again in 1962 when she went to India and Pakistan by herself, Americans caught novel shots of the horse-loving Jacqueline Kennedy seated precariously in an elephant's howdah. Nikita Khrushchev was fascinated by her in Vienna and she won her way easily with Charles de Gaulle. She journeyed with the President to Canada, France, and Austria, to Venezuela, Colombia, and Mexico, and everywhere she was viewed as a strong national asset. Hers was the old-time combination of feminine charm and worldly assurance, creating its own magical effect and helped along by her strongly photogenic qualities.

On the home front she had critics as severe in their denunciation as those who sought to tear down the image of Eleanor Roosevelt. But all applauded what became her chief claim to fame, apart from the image of tragic widowhood—her restoration of the Executive Mansion. "I want to make the White House the most perfect house in the United States," she told Clark Clifford when the project was first discussed. At that time he was the newly appointed chairman of the Foreign Intelligence Advisory Board.

She had much professional help, and within three years the Executive Mansion had been redecorated and refurnished with impeccable taste. Reproductions were replaced by eighteenth- and nineteenth-century American furniture and paintings. A White House Curator, a Fine Arts Committee and a White House Historical Association solidified this fresh interest in the authentic period touch. Mrs. Kennedy's own understated tour of the White House when the task was finished was viewed by millions on television. This was power and influence of a telling sort in terms of historic continuity.

But it took Mrs. Kennedy a long time to warm up to the role of political campaigner, and the trip south which ended in her husband's assassination was her first positive gesture in this direction. She had much work to do on the home front, for there were critics who deplored her disdain for the commonplace, who failed to admire her haute couture, who noted her lack of interest in women's luncheons, long a White House tradition. The President worried considerably about the public's reaction to his beautiful wife and dreaded her turning up hatless in the wrong place. When he expressed disapproval of a gown she never wore it again. He disliked her in flowered materials and thought brown her most unbecoming color. He advised her on what she should wear on the day they were to spend in Dallas, and the pink suit he approved soon became worldfamous. Oddly enough, John Kennedy and Calvin Coolidge, two New Englanders, were the Presidents who cared most about what their wives wore, and gave the matter careful consideration. Mary Lincoln complained that her husband never noticed how she dressed, except when he thought a gown too décolleté. General Grant would compliment his Julia on her looks, but without really seeing what she was wearing. President McKinley never failed to bolster Ida's ego, making gentle comments on her frail laces and vintage silks. President Taft had to encourage his wife to spend more money on her White House wardrobe.

Mrs. Kennedy was no feminist. Like Mrs. Coolidge her special power lay in her reserved but winning ways. Any show of influence would have seemed as ridiculous to her as to her husband, who did not wholly understand the career type of woman. Jackie specialized in smooth domestic effects, in graceful living, in the chic sports but not in the roughhousing of the Kennedy clan. Perhaps most conspicuously of all she became noted for her devotion to her children. Politics was as alien to her upbringing as it was natural to the Kennedys. She was not a handshaker or a baby kisser, and she steered clear of the ward politics so well understood by her husband's family. Jackie was not afraid to be dashing and avant-garde, yet she maintained the essential conservatism of her upbringing. She avoided crowds when she could and stayed aloof from the din of her husband's world. Instinctively she gravitated to people clever in the arts.

Her delicate health was also a factor in her failure to campaign, but she had just stepped into full action and was being acclaimed by the Texas crowds when the President was shot. From the moment President and Mrs. Kennedy landed at the airport "the crowd applauded the President but it was obvious they had eyes only for her," a newspaper correspondent reported. A Washington paper noted, "First Lady Instant Pro," and predicted that she would be the President's secret weapon in the 1964 campaign.

If Mrs. Kennedy was a sensation before her husband's death, the shattering circumstances under which she watched him die and her unforgettable bearing in the hours and days that followed all burned her image into the public consciousness. She summoned up enough strength to thank personally the sixty-two heads of state who had journeyed to the funeral, and on her final night in the White House she sat up until four-thirty in the morning, writing personal notes of thanks to every member of the staff. Mrs. Kennedy had finished with style.

Even after she left Washington, her potency remained in her careful choice of everything affecting her husband's memory—in the simplicity of his tomb, in various memorials and in her continued push for the arts. Her bloom died hard in the public mind, although even before her marriage to Aristotle Onassis a rising tide of criticism flowed around her when with what seemed an autocratic touch she interfered with William Manchester's book on the death of her husband; when she moved slightly toward the playgirl set in her pursuit of wit and talent; when she made unconventional trips and clearly cared little for what the public said—except as it touched her children.

But none discounted her political importance on the American scene. Her trip to Cambodia in 1967 was a venture to persuade Prince Sihanouk to use his influence to urge the repatriation of prisoners held by the National Liberation front. She was supported by Lord Harlech and Michael Forrestal on this mission—two unofficial diplomats representing British and American interests. Tired and disillusioned, she returned home with nothing accomplished. But her strength in Democratic politics was apparent when she made her first appearance after her husband's death at a fund-raising dinner. Her voice was heard again when she backed Robert Kennedy in his tragically brief try for the Presidency.

No First Lady except Eleanor Roosevelt has ever so impressed herself on the peoples of the world as Mrs. Kennedy, partly because her husband was a national idol—first in his way of living, and then in the manner of his death. But his dynamic nature was complemented by the complex qualities of his wife, and she was influential in a rare new way. She is likely to stand alone in the history of Presidents' wives.

It would have been difficult for any First Lady to follow Mrs. Kennedy. Since there had been so many elements of glamour and popularity about the Kennedy administration, and such high drama at its finish, the family of Lyndon B. Johnson was wide open to unfavorable comparisons, and its members were spared little. But Mrs. Johnson took hold in a practical and effective way, making no secret of the fact that she wished to give her husband direct political aid at every level.

When his announcement that he would not run again took the country by surprise in the spring of 1968, it was slowly learned that his wife was the chief factor in his decision. She had been urging him not to run again for some time, and in spite of his strength of character, Mrs. Johnson was one President's wife who could—and did—influence her husband's decisions, even in such a crucial matter.

In the summer of 1967 she told a visiting politician at the Texas ranch: "If I can prevent it, Lyndon will not run again. It will kill him. He couldn't last another four years. I've got Coolidge and Truman on my side. They withdrew. Lyndon drives himself so hard. He works until midnight every night. I don't think he could last another four years and I am going to make sure he doesn't try it."

The pressures hemming him in grew steadily worse in the months that followed, and Mrs. Johnson, pursuing her official duties without a break, bided her time. She would never admit her power in this direction and has described herself simply as an extension and interpreter of her husband. Actually she is as much of a politician as he and as accomplished in dealing with voters. In 1960 she traveled 35,000 miles in seventy-one days campaigning for Lyndon, and Robert Kennedy credited her with carrying Texas for the Democrats. She seemed to one of the correspondents accompanying her as "indomitable as a Scarlett O'Hara intent on saving Tara from Yankee destruction."

No other First Lady ever appeared so consistently at her husband's side at gatherings of all kinds, and even at press conferences. She was a visible helpmate, always ready to leap into the gap and represent the President with a speech. However pronounced her accent, what she said was always well delivered and carefully thought out, and at times she slipped into spontaneous expression. Only once was she flustered enough to lose her composure, and that was when Eartha Kitt challenged her at a White House luncheon given for discussion of civil rights. Tears came into Mrs. Johnson's eyes as she hesitatingly acknowledged that she had not known such sufferings as Miss Kitt had experienced in her early days.

Stewart Alsop, a correspondent with ample opportunity to observe Mrs. Johnson, has described her as the balance wheel for her moody husband. He appraised her as a woman of great charm and intelligence who played a vital White House role with brilliance and stability, and he wrote of her, "There are some Lyndonologists who believe that his moods get out of hand only when she is away—she was not in the White House, for example, during the Dominican crisis and when she returned, the freewheeling, nonstop press conferences, the plethora of Presidential television appearances and official pronouncements, suddenly ceased." Eric Sevareid has described her as the best of Presidents' wives, influential and considerate.

Mrs. Johnson has attributed her husband's failure to come through convincingly on television to the fact that "he's a human and not a machine man." She reviewed drafts of his speeches and at times helped him give cadence to his words. He took criticism from his wife better than from any of his advisers, and she gave it without hesitation. But it was not caustic or defeating. Her method was to listen to what he had to say on a controversial question, give it careful thought and then comment, "This is what I think about it, and why."

One of the first things that Mrs. Johnson had to learn, and mostly at her husband's prompting, was to smarten up her attire and coiffure. The public observed with interest the growing sophistication of Mrs. Johnson and her daughters, Lynda and Luci. But it took some time for Lady Bird to create a substantial image of her own, and she did it with projects of deep national appeal. When she found herself hostess of the White House at a black moment in American history she felt that she had "stepped on a moving train," and she responded pragmatically to the demands made on her.

Like Eleanor Roosevelt she served as eyes and ears for the President in her travels, but she had more to say in public on specific issues than her predecessor had. Without any hesitation Mrs. Johnson enlarged on her husband's pet program of the moment—on Head Start or federal housing, on the antipoverty crusade or space program. She called herself a weather vane, reacting to things like millions of other people across the country. Not since the time of Mrs. Roosevelt had any President's wife shown such practical concern for the underprivileged, or visited them in their own settings. She made a point of touring the most squalid areas of the capital, of viewing impoverished Appalachia at first hand, of studying the ghettos of New York, the basement slums of Newark and the rural poverty of Lick Branch, Kentucky.

Her beautification program took root from coast to coast, and she drew attention to the wonders and beauties of the United States more effectively than anyone who had preceded her. This was a unique service for a President's wife to perform. She followed it with another experiment in the new way to "Discover America." Forty-four European editors toured the scenic and historic trails in Texas to promote foreign tourism and whip up interest in the San Antonio Fair. During her years in the White House Mrs. Johnson traveled 100,000 miles and visited 125 cities, spreading her own special gospel of national beautification.

Mrs. Johnson was by all odds the most successful organizer among the women who have occupied the White House. She did not need to learn the ways of a political pro, for that was her training from her early days, and she was instinctively helpful, quick-witted and tactful. Innumerable women in business, in the arts and academic life, were invited to her luncheons and teas, and she kept a sharp eye for the rising woman, black or white, in any field. It was in character that she should introduce a fashion show at the White House and thereby give momentum to the fourth largest industry in the country. In the spring of 1968 the first fashion show in White House history was held on the premises, featuring the American touch, from hand-painted "Discover America" scarves to red, white and blue decorations. A runway ran the length of the state dining room on this occasion and slides of America's scenic sites were displayed as backdrops, with mood music. The models changed in the East Room, where Abigail Adams had hung her wash. The wives of the Governors, of Cabinet officers, and a cross section of the fashion industry witnessed this historic display.

Soignée, informed on contemporary developments, an energetic First Lady, Mrs. Johnson was constantly in the presidential picture—not in an obtrusive way but often very usefully. She did not let the public forget that there were Cézannes as well as Copleys in the White House, and Joseph H. Hirshhorn credits her with influencing him to give his art collection to the Smithsonian Institution. "Mrs. Johnson is darling and has completely charmed me," he commented as he made up his mind in this matter. "She is the most perfect wife a President could have." The art of the Southwest and the frontier also drew support from Mrs. Johnson, who believes in viewing the country as a whole. A little stung by the gibes about the Johnson cuisine after the Kennedy distinction in this field, she saw to it that the cordon-bleu touch still prevailed at the White House and that the barbecues were limited to the ranch. The French-Swiss chef who followed the Kennedy entrepreneur made sure that the menus were as far removed from Pedernales chili and enchiladas as possible. Moreover, the service and appointments were impeccable.

From the beginning, Lady Bird played with rare skill the wifely role—that role made implicit in First Lady procedure for all except the invalids who have chosen to shrink in the background and indulge their whims. "The best thing I can do for him," she said of the President, "is to try to create a pleasant little island where he can work—where he likes the food and is not constantly bothered with questions about household and family affairs, or with people who disagree with him on every issue."

Mrs. Johnson is one President's wife who amassed a fortune in her own right, and she was indirectly responsible for her husband's entering the political world. In the year of their marriage she steered his life into the channel that led eventually to the White House, for she gave him a $10,000 inheritance she had from her father. This helped Lyndon when he ran for Congress in 1937. He had proposed to her on their second meeting and had bought her a $2.50 wedding ring for the big occasion. She was twenty-one and Lyndon was twenty-six at the time, and for the next two or three years she had a course in political indoctrination. This continued throughout his thirty years as Congressman, Senator, Majority leader, Vice-President, and President.

As First Lady Mrs. Johnson liked to recall that, like countless other American girls of her generation, she grew up in a country of farm-lands and pine forests; that she walked along country lanes and fished and swam in creeks; that she watched the violets budding in the woods. It became part of her credo that she was the average American woman, reaching out to millions of other average women. She attended a one-room school before going on to college and eventually to the White House. When she graduated from the University of Texas in 1933 with a degree in liberal arts and journalism she headed right into marriage with the future President, and she soon landed in a growing industry—radio and television in a fast-developing community. In course of time these interests, mainly handled by Mrs. Johnson, brought wealth to her family. Under her guidance a floundering Austin radio station became a multimillion-dollar corporation.

On the long climb upward she played the game with considerable skill and impartiality, and was well liked by politicians of both parties and their wives, even when the mudslinging at President Johnson was overwhelming. She became adept at whistle-stop campaigning, at lone ventures into hostile terrain, at mollifying gestures at the White House. With the help of Liz Carpenter, her social secretary, the family image was transformed. It was always picturesque and occasionally controversial. Her daughters made headlines that sometimes dismayed her, and she had to face in *McCall's Magazine* Lynda's account of climbing into her parents' bed like a small child at three in the morning to tell them that she had just promised to marry Marine Captain Charles S. Robb. But Mrs. Johnson coped well with such emergencies, admitting only that she had lived intensely in the White House. "Awareness of this house is like a shot of adrenalin—

intensifying the desire to do the best you can to live up to what this country wants its first family to be," she commented.

Unlike Calvin Coolidge, who kept his wife in the dark when he decided not to run again, Lyndon Johnson let Lady Bird know in advance what was coming—inevitably so, since she had helped him make his decision. Her comment after he had made his historic speech was characteristic: "We have done a lot. There is a lot left to do in the remaining months. Maybe this is the only way to get it done."

With all her tact, Mrs. Johnson was never able to get Mrs. John F. Kennedy back to the White House. But like her predecessor she left the impression of a vital and completely contemporary First Lady. Each brought her own personality to bear on this office, in a fashion undreamed of before the days of television when Presidents' wives were faded figures in the background of their husbands' lives. Mrs. Richard M. Nixon, hard-working and diplomatic, projected the new image in a shy way.

All this does not mean that the First Ladies of yesterday were any less influential than those of today, except as public figures. Their power has been spread in a great many ways over a long span of years, with no consistent pattern emerging in the way they have used it. More often than not their relationship was firmly established long before their husbands rose to political eminence, and it did not change materially when they found themselves mistresses of the White House. A few have been decisive factors in their men's climb to fame, helping them financially when they needed it, like the first Mrs. John Tyler and Mrs. Lyndon B. Johnson. At least two—Mrs. Andrew Johnson and Mrs. Millard Fillmore—helped to educate their husbands. Mrs. Ulysses S. Grant and Mrs. Zachary Taylor contributed notably to the military success of their soldier husbands through strengthening them in the hard days of their campaigning. Mrs. Franklin D. Roosevelt was largely instrumental in preventing her husband from being consigned to an invalid's role after he developed infantile paralysis.

However dim the impressions of the past, when the public merely read of the families of their Presidents, they now see them in startling verisimilitude, and the outlook of the voter is influenced by the visual and animated image of the White House family. It was in the mood of the era that the Johnson daughters should show spirit and independence and that Lynda found employment in the magazine and fashion world. Her switch from George Hamilton to her sturdy marine, Captain Charles Robb, was as much discussed as Luci's conversion to Catholicism and her huge ceremonial wedding to Patrick Nugent in a cathedral, followed by domestic life in Texas.

The presidential campaigns of recent years have brought to the forefront waves of attractive wives, mothers and daughters who have worked openly for their favorite candidates. Seventy-seven-year-old Rose Kennedy was the star of the Robert Kennedy campaign train, and she swung through teas, receptions and luncheons looking her soignée best and rolling up support for the son she was soon to lose. "There are more women than men in this country," she pointed out. "If we can get the women's vote, we're safe. So, we aim at the women." And wholly in the spirit of 1968 she added, "As a mother of a President you have to have a sense of elegance . . . you have to be appropriately dressed."

As the mother of nine and the grandmother of twenty-six children Mrs. Kennedy spoke with some authority and a certain symbolism for the public. She defended her son Robert against charges of ruthlessness and, coming to grips with the criticism of extravagant campaigning, made the down-to-earth observation, "It's our own money and we're free to spend it any way we please. It's part of this campaign business. If you have money you spend it to win. And the more you can afford, the more you'll spend."

There was some dismay in the Kennedy camp over this frank observation, and Mrs. Kennedy was faced with a response that caused her to retreat for the time being from further political comment. But she has frequently said of her family, "All the children were taught that they were to use their lives in some cause for humanity. Their financial resources were not to be used just for having a good time. Although, goodness knows, they've had a good time."

The family dowager has campaigned repeatedly—first for her son Jack, then in 1964 for Robert, when he was running for the Senate.

But she has another cherished cause for which she makes many public appearances—the prevention and cure of mental retardation. This is a matter of deep personal concern to her since one member of her brilliant family has spent most of her life in an institution.

But Rose Kennedy was only one of ten members of the family out campaigning for Bobby in 1968, up to the moment of his assassination. Most remarkable of all was his wife Ethel, already pregnant with her eleventh child. With her easy smile, her tact and kind concern, Ethel was never anything but a political asset to her husband. She ducked public speaking lest she say the unforgettable thing, for by nature she is candid and direct. But in general she was quick with the word that counted and her husband's lieutenants prized her friendly spirit and good sportsmanship. Although she does not express them in public, she has strong views on the issues of the day, and she urged her husband to run for the Presidency long before Eugene McCarthy's success in New Hampshire drew him into the contest.

At forty Mrs. Kennedy is an athletic size eight and wears sport clothes with distinction. She skis, rides, plays touch football, hikes, swims, sails, plays tennis and field hockey and has braved the Grand Canyon rapids in a canoe. Her parties at Hickory Hill during her husband's lifetime were famous, ranging from clever little dinners attended by some of the nation's leading intellectuals and wits to dances around the torchlit outdoor swimming pool, and organized chaos with the young. Mrs. Kennedy closely observed everything written about her husband, and never hesitated to tackle an unfriendly commentator. Although physical courage runs all through the Kennedy family, she suffers agonies over flying. Her parents and one of her brothers lost their lives in air crashes, just as members of her husband's family have figured in flying accidents. Her grit and deep religious feeling showed to an extraordinary degree at the time of her husband's death and in the months that followed. Throwing herself enthusiastically into a series of useful projects, she observed in one of her rare philosophical moments, "We're placed on earth and somehow given a sense of responsibility to give life and love and to help others."

Her husband once said of Ethel, "She's a great supporter for a husband. She always thinks I'm right, and they're wrong." The day he entered the Presidential race she drove to the Senate building with nine of her children, relieved that all doubt about his candidacy was ended. "He heard out all the arguments, then he made up his mind, and did what he thought was right," said Ethel loyally. She agreed with Mrs. Joseph Kennedy that each son and daughter of this dynamic and controversial family shared a "common interest in life and people."

Ethel herself eludes definition. She has little ever to say about her own thoughts and feelings, but concerns herself in a practical way with the welfare of others. This quality has become an essential element in the bearing of candidates' wives, mothers and daughters today, and the Republicans and Democrats are equally concerned about the effect these women have on the voters. Mrs. Robert Kennedy was only one of a group of uncommonly attractive and able wives who figured in the political race of 1968. Except for the most retiring, candidates' wives today are as capable of making political speeches as they are of running their homes, although in general their husbands would just as soon they refrained from being quoted, and project instead the traditional picture of amiable femininity. There are still plenty of women voters—and men too—who view with suspicion a candidate's wife who has been divorced, who is conspicuously intellectual or one who does not fit smoothly into the domestic tradition established by America's earliest First Lady—Martha Washington.

But by 1968 a clear new image had emerged, distinctly modern in feeling and perhaps the result of the terrible immediacy of the issues at stake. After years of smiling sweetly at their husbands' sides, the new generation of candidates' wives shows concern over the problems facing both parties. It would be less than realistic to underestimate the influence of these women when voting day comes around, particularly with members of their own sex. Their husbands regard them as visible assets; so do the professional politicians; and they are weighed in the balance as their men show signs of becoming presidential aspirants. They can wear Dior creations or homemade gowns, but they must be contemporary in feeling and in no way extreme. Obviously they add substantially to the picture if they make a good appearance on television and the platform, if they appeal to the young as well as to the mature, if they are alive to contemporary causes.

The campaign of 1968 involved a great army of eager young neophytes, operating in independent and novel ways to push their candidates. Wit as well as fury was injected into the campaign. From campus meetings and smorgasbords to fashion shows, rock bands, fire trucks and political cabarets, they created excitement and were themselves aflame with the great issue of war and peace. Their costumes, their dolls and baubles, their golden donkeys and pink elephants, their electric guitars and fierce devotion typified the thread of golden youth running through the solid phalanx of party maturity. Susan Anthony's homespun dream of the future found some realization in this psychedelic world, for the girls worked harder and made even more noise than the boys in stirring up their elders. Youth spoke commandingly, and without regard to sex. Under the new dispensation the adult world had to listen.

✺ Chapter 5

Troublemakers and Pioneers

✺ Long before there were Presidents in America, or Presidents' wives, there were women in the new land who figured importantly in the deliberations of the early patriarchs. Their influence was perhaps more personal and profound in the early days of primitive living and churchgoing than ever again. The majority were busy putting together their simple homes, and feeding and clothing their husbands and children. They accepted the fact that their role was to populate and civilize a new country. They adapted themselves to heavy physical toil under Spartan conditions, but they shared the strong convictions that pushed their men into dynamic action. Some came into prominence because of the force or eccentricity of their views, and among the latter were the determined troublemakers who came to be known as the witches.

The individualists were a motley collection of agitators, and the witches, the Magdalens and the religious insurrectionists were all at war with the puritanical authority of the colonies. Piety, modesty and humility were the qualities desired in their women by the early settlers, but in the seventeenth as in the twentieth century there were some who refused to buckle under, and broke away as formidable critics of the Establishment. The most showy, if not the most powerful, were the vain ones who went in for frivolous attire—for tall wigs and tiffany hoods, for silks and jewelry. Vanity was one of the first signs of rebellion as they chafed under the strictures of the puritanical faith. It was inevitable that religion should be the first great cause to draw them out of their homes and into the marketplace. But the long struggle over dogma mellowed into the social causes of the nineteenth century; the humanitarian and charitable drives of the early twentieth century; the fight for woman suffrage that began in 1840 and ended with victory in 1920. Even before the vote was won, however, a larger revolution was in the making, invoked by Freud and spiraling into the total sexual revolution of the 1960's.

From the earliest days the spirit of revolt flashed into view periodically, beginning with Pocahontas, guardian angel of the white strangers who had invaded the land of the red men. The question of equality was raised in the earliest days of the colonies when Anne Hutchinson shook the new land to its foundations and divided its most sacred institution—the religious community. No other woman who came after her wielded such power in America or caused more conflict. Her credo was simple—that men and women were equal in the sight of God. She believed that revelation came from on high and that there was no need for intermediaries. Like some of the modern gurus she argued that love and inner peace were the ideal goals, and she fought the harsh decrees of the Puritans. True holiness was a state of heart, not of good works, said Anne, and nothing that a believer did was past salvation—a *laissez-faire* policy for the rapidly developing town of Boston.

The clergy, the magistrates, the yeomanry and soldiers came under her spell, and children asked their parents if they stood for Anne's Covenant of Grace or the Covenant of Works. The turmoil she stirred up was all part of the Antinomian Controversy. Soon Anne was known as the New England Jezebel, the Notorious Imposter and the She-Gamaliel. Neither a beauty nor a siren, she spurned feminine coquetry but was eloquent and profoundly sincere.

As an English Nonconformist she had watched John Cotton preach at St. Botolph's in Lincolnshire and had followed him zealously when he simplified the service, abandoned the surplice and no longer used the Cross at baptisms. With her mild-tempered husband

William Hutchinson, she followed Cotton to America and settled on what later came to be known as the Old Corner Book Store lot in Boston. Within two years she was the most discussed individual in the Colony. Governor John Winthrop noted her popularity and observed that she was "more resorted to for counsel and advice than any of the ministers."

Although he disliked intellectual women, the Governor was impressed at first by her eloquence and proud bearing. She lived close to his mansion and opened her doors to the women of the community, giving them balms and herbs, and listening to their complaints. Forbidden subjects were aired as she advised them on anything from the propriety of wearing veils when on trial for bearing illegitimate children, to their spiritual state. In addition, Mrs. Hutchinson practiced all the wifely arts. She knitted, spun, made candlewicks and served as midwife. But instead of attending the neighborhood prayer meetings she was soon giving lectures in her home. In the 1630's the settlers had few books and little music; they could not dance or go to the theater, and so discussion was their meat and drink. The hooded women who emerged from Anne's parlors asked questions and listened to their lords and masters with a growing touch of skepticism. Husbands noticed that their wives were becoming strangely disputatious. All too many joined the throngs that attended Anne's meetings. Like all evangelists she had considerable magnetism and was as irresistible to men as to women.

Soon Governor Winthrop was taking a second look at the powerful Mrs. Hutchinson, aware that a revolutionary was at work as she expounded her views before the most experienced and trusted debaters in the Colony. He soon realized that she was stirring up the poor and illiterate against the princes of the Puritan church. With a stark drive that baffled the elders she denounced the offending clergy and defended the Magdalens, giving the first talks on sex offered to American women and in a sense establishing the first woman's club.

She was summoned before the General Court in 1636 and in the following year was tried at Cambridge, with Governor Winthrop and other powerful Bostonians aligned against her. The Governor charged that her opinions "were contrary to the word of God, and had seduced many simple persons who resorted to her." John Cotton, who acted as pacificator for Anne in the early stages of the proceedings, failed her in the end. She was convicted of traducing the ministers after twenty-nine of her "heretical opinions" were argued out in court, with Anne answering with force and eloquence.

The court ordered her banishment. At her second examination she stood before the whole congregation and recanted, conceding faults of temper, speech and conduct; acknowledging that her speeches and revelations were rash and groundless; and asking for the prayers of the church on her behalf. Cotton had helped her to prepare her recantation, hoping to avert her excommunication although he could not undo her banishment. But no sooner had she recanted than she flared out again and listened with defiant pride to the Rev. John Wilson, whom she had bitterly condemned, describe her as a leper who must withdraw herself from the congregation.

Portsmouth and Newport became the new centers of Hutchinson activity as Anne continued to spread her unorthodox views, joining forces with Roger Williams in the Baptist community he founded in Rhode Island. She took many important Bostonians with her, and the mutiny she had sparked led to severe political repercussions among the men of the Colony. Those who had backed Anne, like Sir Harry Vane, fell into disfavor. The Antinomian Controversy was political as well as theological, with Winthrop and Vane vying for top influence in the Colony. Vane had been granted leave by the King to visit the New World for three years, but Winthrop was the actual founder of Boston, and Anne Hutchinson stirred up as much trouble between them as if she had held public office.

Powerful though she had been, her end was catastrophic. She and all of her children except one, who was taken alive, were slain by Indians after she had moved her family to Pelham Bay. Today a statue in front of the State House in Boston commemorates Anne Hutchinson, and a tablet in the First Church of Boston reads: "Anne the Pioneer, Anne the Trouble-Maker, Anne the Martyr."

Although her rebellion was based on religious dogma she opened the way for a succession of pathfinders—or agitators, depending on the point of view—who later battered at the foundations of a man-made world. As the first woman in America whose voice was strongly heard beyond the confines of the home, her eloquence was her great weapon. Down the years this has remained woman's most potent aid in her long fight for what came in time to be known as her "rights." Once Anne had set the example, women bearing such conciliatory names as Faith and Mercy, Prudence and Patience, were defying the restrictive laws of the colonies. Some appeared in public wearing jewelry and fine feathers. Others questioned the canons imposed. The Baptists broke away from the Puritan community, and Quaker women led a long line of dissenting females. They mocked authority and jeered at the magistrates and ministers passing their windows.

Anne Yale questioned the baptism of infants as she followed the teachings of Roger Williams, who considered this rite an inheritance from Rome. She and Lady Deborah Moody, who shared her views, were expelled from the church. Mary Dyer, who had drawn attention to herself by leading Anne Hutchinson from the hall after sentence of excommunication had been pronounced, was the first to die. Like the other "witches" she stood by her convictions and was silent to the end. The hanging of fourteen of these intractable women on Gallows Hill outside Salem stirred up unrest and discontent among the settlers, but it took years for people to recognize the fact that they were women of intelligence and independence. Ann Hibbins swung from the gallows because she had shown flashes of wit and insurrection. Margaret Jones of Charlestown was hanged for flouting the medicine men of the day and treating the sick with herbs and kindness. Things were quieter in Virginia, where heresy was not a bitter issue and the domestic pattern was more firmly based.

But women found their first great cause in the Revolutionary War, and during this period their influence, direct and indirect, was considerable. Soon after the Revolution the Marquis de Condorcet in France made his famous plea for the political rights of women, but Abigail Adams and Mercy Otis Warren had already made themselves heard on the subject in America. Aside from the wives of the Founding Fathers, the generals' wives, and the feminine writers and propagandists, the women of these great days in American history had sundry ways of showing their spirit, independence and influence.

Politicians at heart, they used courage, wiles and ingenuity in outwitting the enemy.

Mrs. John Hancock was sometimes a participant as well as a spectator in the shifting pattern of the war. This leader of taste and fashion, a noted belle, ordered all the stray cows on Boston Common to be milked when her husband brought home more officers for breakfast than she could feed. When Lexington and Concord were under attack she fled with her husband to Woburn. Mrs. Philip Schuyler set fire to her husband's fields of grain rather than let the enemy have them when she heard that they were on their way to Schuylerville to garner the crops. Mrs. Robert Murray detained the British officers with cake, wine, and dancing at her home on Murray Hill to help the maneuvers of General Israel Putnam. Cornelia Beekman was in danger time and again in personal encounters with the enemy. She intimidated a group of Royalists who visited her house when she stared unflinchingly at a musket pointed in her direction.

"Are you not the daughter of that old rebel, Pierre Van Cortlandt?" she was asked.

"I am the daughter of Pierre Van Cortlandt—but it becomes not such as you to call my father a rebel," Mrs. Beekman answered haughtily.

The soldier flinched and lowered his gun.

The story of Molly Pitcher loading her husband's cannon when he was wounded in battle is now folklore, but less is known of Deborah Gannette, who served as a soldier through most of the fighting. Martha Bratton refused to betray her husband, and she blew up a train of powder rather than let the British have it just before the fall of Charlestown. When asked who had done it Mrs. Bratton spoke up proudly, "It was I who did it. Let the consequence be what it will. I glory in having prevented the mischief contemplated by the cruel enemies of my country."

Rebecca Biddle, wife of Colonel Clement Biddle, joined the army with her husband and spent much time at camp during the war. Both were Quakers who were read out of meeting when Colonel Biddle took up arms. Lucy Knox, the wife of Major Henry Knox, followed the army and was a steady support to her husband. She had strong opinions, and he frequently sought her advice. Tart and knowledgeable, she was known as Madam Knox, and she often advised Martha Washington on questions of protocol. When the Knoxes escaped from Boston as the British took occupancy she hid her husband's sword in the quilted lining of her cloak.

Martha Washington reminded Pierre Etienne du Ponceau of a "Roman matron . . . who well deserved to be the companion and friend of the greatest man of the age" as he watched her hold court with her husband in primitive surroundings. Levees and formal soirees were taboo, and so were dancing, card playing and other light amusements. But both men and women gathered in one another's quarters, talked, sang and drank coffee. In mid-morning the women sometimes had oranges and wine. Such women as Catherine Greene, the wife of Nathaniel Greene of Rhode Island, was often at headquarters and was a favorite of General Washington's. Mrs. Samuel Powel, Lady Kitty Alexander and Mrs. Greene gathered around Martha Washington like ladies in waiting. The brilliant Rebecca Franks who later married Sir Henry Johnston and lived in Bath, the beautiful and ill-fated Margaret Shippen (Mrs. Benedict Arnold), Catherine Schuyler, Mary Slocumb and other influential women dined with George Washington and his generals, expressing their opinions frankly to such visitors from abroad as Pulaski and Lafayette, and knowing more of the inner councils of the day than their contemporaries suspected.

Women showed their courage and influence in many ways before the actual fighting began, as well as in the years that followed. They boycotted Tories and British imports wherever they were to be found. They turned their backs on tea, and in some quarters drank raspberry leaves as a substitute. They whirled their spinning wheels with added zest, pledging themselves to buy only domestic products. George Washington's mother Mary worked in her garden at Fredericksburg in the safe haven to which her son had removed her, but she harassed him with complaints and demands for money. She was a familiar sight riding around in her chaise, with a plain straw hat planted on her silvery hair. Talking calmly about her famous son she remarked at the height of his success, "I am not surprised at what George has done, for he was always a very good boy." A century later Hannah Grant, mother of another great soldier and President, was to repeat history by observing when Ulysses stepped up to the Presidency that "he was always a good boy."

Women of letters played a more vital role in the early political history of America than they do today, and their voices were heard. They had no franchise to talk about, no feminine rights to proclaim, but they had the immediate inspiration of a noble cause—freedom and the birth of a nation. The propagandist touch exceeded the literary quality of their work; as poets and satirists their tone was fiercely patriotic and single-minded. They were free spirits in print, if not in person. Patriotism was the constant theme from 1770 to 1795. Just as Anne Hutchinson shook the religious world, Mercy Otis Warren raised havoc on the political front. She was a satirist, a propagandist, a gadfly who stung the hides of the Philistines. She and her friend Abigail Adams made a powerful team, and there were times when Mercy shook up John Adams and fiercely irritated Thomas Jefferson. In her correspondence with John Adams she made it clear that she did not want members of her sex to weaken the resolution of their men about going to war. "Notwithstanding the complicated difficulties that rise before us, there is no receding and I should blush if in any instance the weak passions of my sex should damp the fortitude, the patriotism, and the manly resolution of yours. . . . I cannot wish to see the sword quietly put up in the scabbard, until justice is done to America."

Mercy had uncanny influence and by many was regarded as the most intellectual and powerful woman of the period. Although she favored a republic she confessed to uncertainty about America having reached the proper state of development for a republican government. But whatever her convictions she helped to fan the flame of the Revolution as she turned out mocking political satires and shared in the intrigues going on behind the scenes. She was a freewheeling propagandist in the modern sense of the word, supplying political figures with arguments and the classical allusions in which she specialized.

Her husband, James Warren, was a Plymouth merchant notable in the colony until he lost his reason. For a time he was president of the Provincial Congress of Massachusetts, and he encouraged Mercy to write. Soon she was in correspondence with Samuel and John Adams, Thomas Jefferson, Abigail Adams, General Knox and Martha Washington. General Washington dined with the Warrens at their home in Watertown, and Lafayette charmed her with his "penetrating, active, sensible, and judicious outlook." All of these men took note of Mercy's alert wits, but many of the women feared her sharp appraisal of the political scene. Hannah Winthrop called her Philomela as she turned her satirical eye on the manners and customs of the day. On January 1, 1774, Mercy wrote to Mrs. Winthrop: "Be it known unto Britain even American daughters are politicians and patriots, and will aid the good work with their female efforts."

The Group, Mercy Warren's satirical play in two acts, pinioned the leading Tory characters of the period and was regarded as powerful propaganda, but her history of the American Revolution was her most permanent contribution to the early national literature. As the first woman historian of the new land, she wielded unique influence on the thinking of her time, for she was deeply involved in matters of state policy. John Adams paid heed to her, but was angered by the picture she drew of him. His vanity was touched, and for a time afterward there was coolness between the Warrens and the Adamses; but good feeling was restored when Abigail sent Mercy a ring with her own and her husband's hair. It was Mercy's custom to visit Abigail at Braintree on her trips to and from camp. These two war widows had much in common, besides their interest in political and literary matters. In their bouffant silk dresses with lawn aprons, mobcaps and mittened hands they were formidable matrons.

While Abigail was striking a blow for feminine emancipation in her appeal to John to remember the ladies in shaping the Constitution, Mercy was flaying the Tories with *The Motley Assembly* and *The Blockheads*, two plays printed anonymously. She quoted the soldiers in barracks-room language that has a lurid ring even in the 1960's. When her identity was learned it was difficult to reconcile these farces with the elegant Mercy Otis Warren, who emerged as one of the stateliest dames of the Revolution when painted in blue satin and lace by John Singleton Copley. Although men considered her a true intellectual and women feared her blue-stocking instincts, she was fashionable, too, and when John Adams heard of the coffeehouse murmurings that the public desired an American king he wrote jestingly to Mercy: "Monarchy is the genteelest and most fashionable government, and I don't know why the ladies ought not to consult elegance and fashions," although he personally preferred "virtue and simplicity of manners."

Her long correspondence with Catharine Macaulay, one of the most brilliant political writers of the Whig circle in England, resulted in her own most notable work, *History of the Rise, Progress, and Termination of the American Revolution.* Mrs. Macaulay's *History of England* had not only inspired Mercy Warren but had stirred up Mary Wollstonecraft who, in turn, became a pivotal figure in the suffrage movement. Mercy had had unique experience as an honored adviser from time to time through the administrations of Washington, Adams, Jefferson and Madison. She was as strongly Republican in her sympathies as Abigail was Federalist. She lived to be eighty-seven, but many years of her life were saddened by the madness of her husband. She alone could soothe him, and theirs was one of the strong love stories of the Revolutionary period.

Although she and Abigail towered above the other writers of the period, a number of women contributed in one way or another to the literary and political history of the Revolutionary years. The poetry of Phillis Wheatley, published in 1773 when she was nineteen, made an impression even on Voltaire, who described her as *une Négresse qui fait de très bon vers Anglais.* She was brought to Boston from Africa in 1761 and was sold in the slave market to Mrs. John Wheatley, a merchant's wife. Phillis had an unhappy marriage and died in poverty at the age of thirty-one, leaving three children. One of her treasures was a letter from George Washington in 1776 complimenting her on her poetry.

Anne Bradstreet, who came from Anne Hutchinson's community, was hailed in London as "The Tenth Muse Lately Sprung up in America" when her poems were published there. George Washington, who evidently took serious note of the women pamphleteers who helped the Revolutionary cause, thanked Annie Boudinot Stockton of New Jersey for her patriotic verses on the surrender at Yorktown. Mrs. John Winthrop's letter describing her flight after the Battle of Lexington was widely read, and straight narratives of the Revolution were written by a Pennsylvanian named Sally Wister, by Hannah Drinker of Philadelphia, Margaret Morris of New Jersey, and Mary Gould Almy of Rhode Island. Deborah Logan and Hannah Griffiths were poets of the period, and Elizabeth Graeme Fergusson was a propagandist who retired in confusion when she was charged with aiding the British. In the early days of the Revolution she acted as a medium of communication between Governor Johnson and the American authorities in the hope of bringing about peace. During the war Judith Sargent Murray wrote an essay, not published until 1790, on the disparity of opportunities open to men and women.

In all manner of ways the women of the period made themselves heard. After the war they had a special role in inculcating democratic ideals in their children. Under the new form of government they had to prepare their sons for public office. But first it was their task to restore moral foundations after the ravages of war and to put into practice the principles for which they had fought. Men had died in battle. Restoration and the birth of a new generation were of prime importance as America shed its Old World heritage and created its own image. During this period the woman in the home was perhaps more powerful than at any other time in American history.

Until the republican system was fully shaped the national culture and outlook were mostly derivative, except for the moralistic writings of Cotton Mather. His *Ornaments for the Daughters of Zion*, published in 1692, extolled modesty and humility, and Dr. Benjamin Rush's *Thoughts upon Female Education* stirred up restless yearnings. John Locke's *Some Thoughts Concerning Education*, published in 1693, had reverberations in America, and in 1722 women were fascinated by Benjamin Franklin's *Dogood Papers*, which leaned more to reason than to piety. He gave them a fresh look at their most absorbing preoccupation, the institution of marriage, yet saw to it that his own daughter was educated differently from his son and was exposed only to the feminine arts. Sarah, who married Richard Bache in 1767, combined her vain and worldly interests with strong republicanism.

Thomas Jefferson swung between the feminine arts and scholarship for his daughters. While insisting that they dance three days a week, he besought them to read such works as *The Whole Duty of Man* and *The Young Lady's Library.* Aaron Burr, writing to his wife in 1793, said he hoped that their daughter Theodosia would never become a woman of fashion. He trained her carefully along classical lines and had her reading Greek before she was ten. His aim was to demonstrate through her that women had souls, and if properly educated were capable of genius. The role of women was considered by Enos Hitchcock in his *Discourses on Education,* published in 1785, and this phase merged into the big academic awakening of the nineteenth century.

Like all wars the American revolutionary struggle made women reach beyond the confines of their own homes. The dazzling wit, talent and activity of the eighteenth century had declined after the great efforts put forth during the war, but in their place were the first stirrings toward the humanitarian causes that were shaking Europe. Some were heroic, others were lunatic, but women followed the gleam even more zealously than men, and again New England emerged as a hotbed of this sort of revolt. The quest for full equality with men began early in the nineteenth century. It threaded its way through a succession of allied causes until it stood clear of them all. The two women who did most to project the idea of feminine emancipation at that time were Frances Wright and Margaret Fuller, although Margaret spurned the narrow outlook of the dedicated feminist and had her own neat summation of her views: "What woman needs is not as a woman to act or rule, but as a nature to grow, as an intellect to discern, as a soul to live freely, and unimpeded to unfold such powers as were given her when we left our common home."

It took strong-minded women like these to make others aware of the strange gropings linked to political upheaval and wars, to the seething unrest that had led to the revolution in France and the industrial awakening in Britain. Americans had begun to travel, proud citizens of the new nation, and they saw for themselves that the dazzling exteriors of the European courts had their obverse side in the slums and the limited opportunities of the people at large.

The most disruptive voice listened to by American women for a time was that of Frances Wright, a girl of wealth, background and scholarship who had studied American history at Glasgow University and had been fascinated by the story of the Revolution. She landed in New York in 1818, a stately figure, strong, eloquent and already allied with the philosophical radicals of Britain. She believed that a new society with a fresh culture had been forged in the United States and that the Declaration of Independence was a document without parallel in history. Her interest in the new land led to her close association with Lafayette. She thought that he should adopt her as his legal daughter, but his family objected. However, he continued to address her as "Ma Bien aimée," "Adorée Fanny" and "La tendre fille de mon choix." Fanny and her sister Camille accompanied him on his triumphal visits to American cities and stayed with him as the guests of Jefferson at Monticello. But their presence became so embarrassing to the visiting Marquis in puritanical America that they stayed behind when he returned to France. Through Lafayette, Fanny became involved with Robert Dale Owen, the Scottish reformer.

She was soon committed to the antislavery movement. After visiting plantations and talking to slaves she founded a settlement for race integration at Nashoba, near Memphis. She had already found what she considered "true humanitarianism" in the Rappite communities—Economy in Pennsylvania and New Harmony in Indiana. Like Brook Farm and Oneida, these two settlements aimed at Utopian conditions and attracted scientists, artists, writers and the avant-garde elements of the period. But Fanny's work for exotic communities was disastrous, financially and otherwise. Mrs. Trollope, whom she considered her friend, was scornful of the free-love colony at Nashoba after she had visited it, and she tore it asunder in her *Domestic Manners of the Americans*.

Fanny finally concentrated on oratory, where she was at her best.

Men and women flocked to her lectures, many because of their sensational nature and some because they believed in her radical views. Women were just beginning to be conscious of their potential power on the platform, and she became the advance guard of the endless parade of American women who have backed causes and projected themselves in this fashion. Essentially an intellectual who scorned to talk down to her audiences, she argued logically in musical contralto tones for the better education of women, control by women of their own property, easy divorce, the encouragement of birth control and freedom to engage in sexual relations on the same basis as men—in other words, she preached what has come to pass in the 1960's. But she had little honor and no reputation in the homes of America, as most of the population reacted with horror and concern. Her disciples were regarded in much the same light as the Hippies, the Flower Children or the junkies of today.

She made her first appearance on a New York platform in 1829, and only her coolness prevented a riot. The gas was turned off in Masonic Hall as she spoke, leaving 2,000 listeners in darkness. A fire was started at the door, and shouts echoed through the hall. This scene was repeated in many halls across the country where Fanny, with her hair curled close to her head, her face alight with zeal, was a fashionable as well as an obsessed figure. She was soon recognized as the apostle of free love and agnosticism, and was called "The Whore of Babylon" and the "Great Red Harlot of Infidelity." Although this voluptuous preacher of licentiousness had a Quaker following, she refused to work in tandem with the avowed abolitionists and she was fanatically opposed to every religious influence and movement of her time. Revivalism was in its heyday and she lashed out at the godly until she came to be known as the "Priestess of Beelzebub."

But in spite of her eccentricities Fanny was regarded as the leading and most logical orator of the period, and she dealt so closely with facts that she had more influence over the men in her audience than other women who followed her on the platform. Her interests were strongly political as well as social, and she chose to lecture in the Cincinnati Courthouse with a copy of the Declaration of Independence in her hand. She had a strong appeal for those who felt the growing urge toward full liberty and equality in government, in education, in the relationship of the sexes. Fanny attacked the Bank of the United States and worked against a Whig candidate for President. When Martin Van Buren was elected she took some of the credit for his victory. She said of the Capitol, "While this edifice stands liberty has an anchorage from which the congress of European autocrats cannot unmoor her."

After her name had been linked to a number of notable men, she tried marriage, too, but unsuccessfully. In 1831 she married Guillaume Sylvan Casimir Phiquepal D'Arusmont, in Paris. He was sixteen years her senior and an ardent reformer who had turned from medicine to education and was a follower of Johann Pestalozzi's. Dividing their time between Paris and Cincinnati, they quarreled over Fanny's money and the education of their daughter. He finally went back to France to stay, taking the daughter with him. Fanny divorced him but was never able to recover the custody of her child. Her life slipped gradually into the shadows. Her brilliance and her eloquence declined. She lived with her memories and watched the gradual development of forces she had whipped up. The cause of the workingman, which had once been her chief preoccupation, was being fostered. The feminists were clamoring for women's rights. New voices were being heard where hers had rung out alone when she turned a Baptist church in New York into a Hall of Science, directed lectures, debates and gymnastic classes, and disseminated the views of Tom Paine and Voltaire.

At the end Fanny lived obscurely in Cincinnati until in 1852 a fall on the ice led to a broken hip and her death. She was buried in Spring Grove Cemetery, where other fighters for freedom and the emancipation of the slave would later join her. In all appraisals of the period Frances Wright looms large as a woman of power, with influence on the thinking of her generation. But although she went further than anyone else in her demands for equality with men, she would have nothing to do with the suffrage movement as such, and the only one of the early feminists with whom she had dealings was the strait-laced Lucretia Mott.

Fanny Wright and Margaret Fuller were the true intellectuals of the woman's movement. Both were scholarly, well read and lofty, if eccentric, in their views. Margaret was more discreet in her behavior and less concerned for the welfare of her fellow men. Both had been subjected in their early years to the puritanical disciplines of Scotland and New England, but Frances had been exposed to the French court and to England's most advanced literati and social reformers. This left her uninhibited and a much more scandalous figure than Margaret Fuller. Both took care not to link themselves with the professional abolitionists, but Margaret conceded that Angelina and Sarah Grimké showed "great courage and moral power." In general she side-stepped the more controversial issues of the day, although as a journalist she was quite ready to visit jails and factories at Horace Greeley's prompting, to highlight the abuses women suffered in these institutions.

In essence Margaret Fuller was a literary figure just as truly as Frances Wright was the orator of her day. She was closer to the native American temperament than Fanny and more understandable. Margaret had style as well as intellect, and she contributed more to the advancement of her sex than many of the avowed agitators. Her special genius lay in conversation, and the literati of her time drew inspiration from her famous Conversaziones held in Boston from 1839 to 1844. Julia Ward Howe considered her the most dedicated propagandist of her day, with more genuine power in discussion than in her writings. "Those who recall the enchantment of her conversation always maintain that the same charm is not to be found in the productions of her pen," she commented.

Emerson compared her relationship with her friends "to the wearing of a necklace of social brilliants of the first water." He found "all the art, the thought, and the nobleness in New England related to her, and she to it." Margaret, in turn, valued her place in the Transcendental hierarchy and her influence as editor of the *Dial*. Thomas Carlyle wrote to Emerson that he considered her "very narrow . . . but truly high." Horace Greeley thought her a great asset to the New York *Tribune* but a discordant influence in his picturesque home on the banks of the East River in New York. She was not beguiling in her looks or habits. Margaret was small, with a

fair complexion and coarse, fair hair. Her voice was nasal and dis-
agreeable to those who did not succumb to the enchantment of what
she said. She had tics that involved opening and shutting her eyelids
constantly and looking back over her shoulder. Like many of her
feminine contemporaries she scarcely knew what it was to feel well,
and her whims and headaches distracted the exacting Mr. Greeley.
He attributed her ill-health to her inordinate consumption of strong
tea. It was her belief that she wrote better when ill and that pain
gave tension to her powers, but he thought her self-indulgent and was
exasperated by her slow delivery of copy.

By the time Margaret got round to reviewing a book the "bloom
had been brushed from its cheek" by a rival paper. She caught the
works of Carlyle, the Brownings, Tennyson and Lowell as they first
came out, and she had great power as a critic. Longfellow was one of
her victims; she despised his poetry and any art form that projected
sentimentality. Although Nathaniel Hawthorne knew her only
slightly, she figures in his *Blithedale Romance,* written about Brook
Farm, which she visited but did not approve. Pitching hay was not
Margaret Fuller's forte. She did better in discourse, although she
could be arrogant and dogmatic, and her scholarship was used
unmercifully to strengthen her reputation for satire. Margaret was
fluent in French, Italian and German, and she had a working knowledge of Greek and Latin.

She studied mythology, demonology and French socialism, particularly as it concerned women, and she believed that she had second
sight. This interested rather than displeased Horace Greeley, who
lived in a world where men and women fostered strange causes and
worshiped unhallowed gods. Although basically opposed to woman
suffrage, he beat the drums for such women as Amelia Bloomer, who
taught the American woman to wear trousers, Elizabeth Blackwell,
the first woman doctor, and the Fox sisters, the most discussed
spiritualists of their day. Sundry intellectuals clustered around him,
and the pioneer women were accomplished propagandists, without
benefit of vote. They haunted the right salons and curried favor with
the most influential men. Margaret Fuller was so much admired that
she was constantly in the company of intellectuals, but since she

considered it dangerous to walk half a mile alone at night, and demanded deference from men, Greeley could not see that her "women's rights theories" were anything more than a "logically defensible abstraction."

Harriet Martineau called Margaret's group the "gorgeous pedants," for they were apt to be dressy and have affectations of one kind or another. Margaret used a lorgnette like George Sand, and she considered Joanna Baillie and Madame Roland the best specimens of women of Roman strength and singleness of mind. When she went abroad in 1846 she enlarged her literary horizons by meeting Carlyle, the Brownings, Wordsworth, De Quincey, George Sand, Rachel, Mazzini and other bright stars, political and literary, in the foreign field. She sent back dispatches like many lesser women correspondents of her day. With one shattered romance behind her in America, she fell in love with an illiterate young man, the Marchese Giovanni Angelo Ossoli, and married him to legitimatize her child. It was inevitable that Margaret should become involved with the colony of British and American radicals backing Mazzini. Infused with the Garibaldi spirit, she galloped along the Corso with his lancers, wearing a bright red tunic and Greek cap with plume instead of her usual sedate black mousseline.

Margaret's letters from Rome were as passionate as they were partisan. They traced the downfall of the republican cause in 1848, and it was she who finally persuaded Mazzini to leave Rome when the French troops entered the city. In the spring of 1850 she sailed for America with her husband and small son. Their ship was wrecked on Fire Island beach, and Margaret was last pictured leaning against the foremast in her white nightdress. A steward who snatched her son in his arms heard her murmur, "I see nothing but death before me—I shall never reach the shore." The foremast and deck were washed away when a mountainous wave hit the ship. All three of the Ossolis were drowned.

Eleanor Roosevelt considered Margaret Fuller's *Woman in the Nineteenth Century* an epoch-making book and wrote that her power to impress her personality and her greatness of soul on those around her did more than anything else to show that women had an intellectual and spiritual contribution to make as great as that of men. Margaret stated the case in her own way: "When woman has a fair chance, her work will vie creditably with that of the ages. Don't fear that she will become too masculine. When she learns to use her intellect, she will show that use of it need not absorb or weaken, but rather refine and invigorate her affections."

She lived in the springtime of American letters in the flowering of a great renaissance. The noted men who fed her incandescent spirit were poets, philosophers and politicians. Some of the women who circled around them were writers too—Sophia and Elizabeth Peabody, Lydia Maria Child and the Alcotts. In Europe she met the titans of the literary crop and helped to popularize the Brownings in America. Chopin played for her when she visited George Sand in Paris. On her return home she whipped up interest in Beethoven and Goethe in her native Boston. "My voice excites me; my pen never," said Margaret, but both were used to good effect in enlarging the horizons of her feminine contemporaries.

With greater charm, if less power, Kate Field followed some of the same pathways as Margaret Fuller. She was a correspondent at large, but her interest swung between writing, the theater, music and politics. In manner and dress she was a woman of high fashion; in thought and in speech she was essentially a scholar and social reformer. Like Victoria Woodhull she created a dramatic effect.

Kate was born in St. Louis in 1838, the child of two theatrical figures. At the age of eight her first story appeared in the New Orleans *Picayune*, which her father, Joseph M. Field, had helped to found. She was educated in a New England seminary and then took the first of many trips abroad. In Paris, Rome and Florence she encountered the celebrities of the day and became well known to them as the "charming American Kate Field." Anthony Trollope called her his "most chosen friend." She knew the Brownings and George Eliot well, and Walter Savage Landor taught her Latin. Kate studied opera but a fall from a horse in Italy left permanent injuries, and again she turned to writing. On her return home she joined the circle that surrounded Henry Ward Beecher and Horace Greeley, and took up the causes that were drawing women out of their homes.

The work of Clara Barton on the battlefield, of Elizabeth Blackwell in medicine, of suffrage workers, of poets like Alice and Phoebe Cary, stirred Kate to action, and she began to lecture, like Anna Dickinson, who was a law unto herself. Knowing everyone worth knowing in the arts, Kate became one of the most quoted sophisticates of her day. As she fitted smoothly into the smart and brainy circles of Boston, Newport and New York, she soon showed that in many respects she was far ahead of her time. Her first talk in 1869 was "Women in the Lyceum," in itself a record of enterprise and innovation. She was always fashionably gowned on the platform, with her brown hair held by a Spanish comb, curls cascading down her neck. When she lectured on Dickens in a dance hall in Alaska the miners gave clever Kate a bottle of gold.

She was less successful on the stage, although for years she felt that she drew inspiration from Charlotte Cushman and Adelaide Ristori. Her *Peg Woffington* was a flop in New York, and she made little headway when she played in London as Mary Keemle. Her diction and her voice were as clear and melodious as Margaret Fuller's were abrasive. It always surprised her that she could write better than she could act, and she turned out books, comedies and newspaper articles with the utmost facility. She wrote editorials for the *Times* of London and discussed scientific subjects with Huxley and Herbert Spencer. Her keen interest in the discoveries of her era involved her in a historic moment, for the first time Queen Victoria picked up a telephone receiver it was Kate Field who sang to her over the wire. The Bell Telephone Company gratefully gave her shares that helped her to amass a fortune of $200,000.

As a correspondent and critic Kate made her reputation writing for the New York *Herald*. She was a forerunner of women critics of today—commenting on books, the theater, music and other arts. In 1891 she established *Kate Field's Washington*, a weekly review that was a novel experiment in journalism. She wrote most of it herself in a vivid, fearless style, announcing at the start that since "men and women were eternally equal and eternally different," Washington needed a national weekly edited by a woman. The politicians were interested in her paper, but it was so heavily tinctured with the arts and the occult that it picked up a mixed circulation. Her aim was to mirror the men and events of the time, but she rode her own hobbies hard. Although she often mystified her admirers by the causes she espoused, she never failed to charm them, and she was a favorite guest at diplomatic and social events in the capital.

Magnetic and informed though she was, however, the sparks died almost as fast as she lit the flame. Like many of her contemporaries she was drawn to spiritualism and animal magnetism. Believing herself to be psychic, she wrote *Planchette's Diary*, dealing with mirror writing. Her logic was sometimes less impressive than her passion for reform. She pioneered on cremation and advocated a national marriage law. The preservation of John Brown's farm as a historic site had her support, and other campaigns involved Hawaiian annexation, an international copyright law, a reduced tariff, temperance, civil-service reform and the abolition of polygamy. Returning from one of her European trips and observing the overburdened attire of the American woman she founded the Cooperative Dress Association for dress reform, but it failed, with heavy losses.

Kate Field proved to be a formidable foe of Mormonism. She described Brigham Young as a "vulgar, illogical, wonderful old man" while she urged Congress to outlaw polygamy. When she tackled Grover Cleveland on the subject she reminded him that a good way to influence men was through their wives. As a great concession she was permitted to talk on this provocative issue at the Lowell Institute, sacred to men. Kate gave each of her causes a rapid whirl— immigration, education, labor problems and the betterment of conditions for humanity in general. She worked hard for the arts and proposed a National Conservatory of Music and a National Art Association. Her efforts came to nothing, but she succeeded in having the duties on imported art substantially reduced. President Harrison and President Cleveland listened attentively to Kate on a number of occasions while she outlined her plans to make America more conscious of the arts.

She was a sparkling figure at the Columbian Fair held in Chicago in 1893, and Mrs. Potter Palmer, high priestess of the Woman's Building, welcomed the cosmopolitan Kate, who knew how to wear a hat as well as spark a cause. While she haunted the White City and watched the crowds flow in, she edited her own paper, kept up her weekly syndicated columns and wrote dozens of articles on art, inventions, education and the wonders of the fair. This was the year in which she was finally persuaded of the necessity for the political enfranchisement of women. She had held out for the feminine tradition as she watched the suffrage workers grow more militant, but Lucy Stone drew her in with subtle flattery: "The movement has reached a point now where women like yourself will be wings to it, and this will make parties in power glad to make friends by being just to those who may be valuable allies." Susan Anthony and Elizabeth Cady Stanton added their persuasion, and Kate's support was won, but with reservations. The charmers in general hesitated to plunge into the cold and unpopular world of the feminist. The pattern was drab. Even the seductive Mrs. Frank Leslie, running the publishing empire that her husband had established, was careful not to commit herself and thus antagonize the countless readers who deplored the suffrage movement.

Questing and restless as a butterfly, Kate soon suspended her weekly review and set off for the Hawaiian Islands to inform herself on Oriental immigration and Hawaiian annexation, to visit the leper colony and to foster kindergartens. One of her last acts was to ride over the lava fields. A hurricane blew up and she was thrown from her horse. She developed pneumonia and died in the spring of 1896, having written her own epitaph: "If I am anything I am a Woman of Tomorrow."

Kate Field had made a singular place for herself with her wit and ubiquity. She was one of the more brilliant exponents of personal journalism and was an individualist who gave scope and meaning to the drive for emancipation before it became an organized and moving force in the twentieth century. Such women as Abigail Adams and Mercy Otis Warren, Frances Wright, Margaret Fuller and Kate Field marked out fresh pathways by their own accomplishments and intellectual power. None was a suffrage worker in what came to be the accepted sense of the word; in fact, all side-stepped professional labels. But in their own lives and accomplishments they pushed along the political evolution of women in a personal and effective way. All knew famous men. They brought banned subjects into open discussion. They fostered thought and logic, and were the sibyls of their day. In some respects they were uncannily influential. Except for Abigail Adams and Mercy Warren these pioneers were apt to be found, according to the *Dial*, among the "madmen, madwomen, men with beards, dunkers, muggletonians, Come-Outers, Groaners, Agrarians, Seventh-Day Baptists, Quakers, Abolitionists, Calvinists, Unitarians and Philosophers."

Kate Field had the added touch of fashion. She was more akin to Sarah Josepha Hale, who steered the American woman through the social shoals with such skill in *Godey's Lady's Book*. Left a widow with five children, Mrs. Hale ran up a circulation of 150,000 for her fashion journal and at the same time waged a subtle but tireless battle for the higher education of women, for their entry into the medical and nursing field, for physical education as well as perfect manners. Most American husbands were well aware of the influence that Mrs. Hale exerted in their homes. Her rival, Madame Demorest, queen of the paper pattern and fashion arbiter for a quarter of a century, had Jennie June, one of the most discreet but effective promoters of women's rights, on her staff. Jennie wrote with equal drive and understanding on fashion, love, homemaking or politics. When the Press Club of New York staged a reception for Charles Dickens on his second visit to America, the newspaperwomen of the day were furious about being frozen out. They were important women. They ran magazines and held major editorial jobs. Their husbands were members of the Press Club that took this stand. It was, in effect, what it would mean today if Katharine Graham of the Washington *Post*, Dorothy Schiff of the New York *Post* and Mrs. Norman Chandler of the Los Angeles *Times* were banned from the most important press function of the year.

Jennie June (Mrs. David Goodman Croly) made it clear that if the women writers and editors could ride home in the same hansoms and sleep in the same beds as their lords and masters who belonged to the Press Club, they could also join them in honoring Dickens. She rounded up support and founded Sorosis, the first women's club of importance, at Delmonico's. Here these pioneers showed their influence in a commanding way, since they incubated the movement that eventually made the American woman the most club-conscious in the world. None beat the drums for emancipation; they merely acted the part and so advanced the underlying principles. Fanny Fern (Sara Payson Willis Parton), awash in hearts and roses, was the best seller of her time. Alice and Phoebe Cary were the gentle poets from Cincinnati, and it was Alice who said, as first president of Sorosis, that "they had tipped the teapot." Madame Demorest took care to defer to her husband, William Jennings Demorest, in running her fashion empire, and Mrs. Hale never forgot to be a lady even while she spiced the fare in her magazine with far-out reasoning and an insidious note of rebellion.

But all were women who played it cool to preserve the balance where men were concerned. Married or single, they followed the fashions, had good manners and fetching ways as well as level heads. Jennie June, for instance, was much less abrasive than Margaret Fuller, and she was not as irritating to men as Jane Swisshelm, the first woman to crash the Press Gallery in Washington. The year was 1850 and Mrs. Swisshelm, a termagant correspondent reminiscent of Anne Royall, had decided to set a precedent at the heart of government. "No woman had ever had a place in the Congressional reporter's gallery," she commented. "This door I wanted to open to them." She predicted that the novelty would soon wear off, and that women would work there eventually on a par with men.

Mrs. Swisshelm's particular victim was Daniel Webster, about whom she launched the most shattering charges. Horace Greeley, buying her political letters at five dollars a column, quailed before Jane's fury. He backed down on Webster but gave Jane her head on such assorted subjects as Fourierism, spiritualism, vegetarianism, phonetics, pneumonics, the eight-hour law, abolition and most of the other causes of the day. She was disillusioned on the subject of marriage and liked to cite the fact that in more than twenty years she had been "without the legal right to be alone an hour—to have the exclusive use of one foot of space—to receive an unopened letter, or to preserve a line of manuscript from sharp and sly inspection." All this led her in time to desert her husband and later to sue him over property.

Mrs. Swisshelm crossed the prairies and rode thirty miles a day in an open cutter. She became one of the gadflies of the male hierarchy as she lectured in the Middle West. "That woman shall not have my pantaloons," exclaimed the editor of one big-city daily when she flayed the politicians through the columns of her paper. But Horace Greeley and Nathaniel Parker Willis took her seriously, and *Godey's Lady's Book* and the *Home Journal* thought her effective when she wrote on the married woman's right to hold property. Mrs. Stanton gave her much credit when the Pennsylvania Legislature passed a bill giving married women this right. But Jane scoffed at such "twaddle" as went on at women's conventions, and reserved her most stinging words for men. Women, she maintained, should take one step at a time, get a good foothold and advance carefully. It was her belief that girls should be educated with boys, that their brains should be developed, that their legal disabilities should be removed by degrees.

Jane was a native of Pittsburgh who frequently reminded her listeners that she had been converted at an early age. With the blood of the Convenanters in her veins she became a formidable reformer, with the same fanatical touch as Carry Nation, who broke up saloons with her hatchet. But Jane was opposed to the pledge exacted by the temperance workers, and she was violently anti-Catholic. Since she could find little around her to approve, she determined to set the world to rights, and her nuisance value was formidable. Before her stories and verse began to attract attention in Philadelphia and Pittsburgh papers she had made corsets for Kentucky belles. But she had no personal vanity and attired herself in hideous fashion, arguing that "when a woman starts out in the world on a mission, secular or religious, she should leave her feminine charms at home." In this she differed from Kate Field, Mrs. Leslie, Victoria Woodhull and other protagonists of the feminine cause who majored in charm.

Women spectators drew their skirts aside with horror as Mrs. Swisshelm was presented to President Tyler. When President Lincoln received her Jane remarked, as she shook hands with the gaunt, tired-looking man, "May the Lord have mercy on you, poor man, for the people have none." She wrote so sympathetically about Mary Lincoln that the President's difficult wife approved of Mrs. Swisshelm, and especially so when she visited the army hospitals and campaigned for lemons to check gangrene. After Chancellorsville she paraded through the wards with lemonade for the wounded.

Jane had curious interests. She encouraged women typesetters and gave stimulus to the establishment of small papers, owned and edited by women, in various parts of the country. After a particularly serious train wreck she proposed a red light at the rear of every train, and this became law. She switched political parties with comparative ease in order to support those putting on the strongest antislavery drive. But her early Whig associates never forgave her for the scandal she circulated about Daniel Webster. She despised Congressmen—a group "who sat and loafed with the soles of their boots turned up for the inspection of the ladies in the galleries." In her own eccentric way Mrs. Swisshelm had influence, but it was used more often to destroy than to build.

Two of her contemporaries who had more sophistication and direct power at the seat of government were Grace Greenwood and Gail Hamilton. The latter, a cousin of Mrs. James G. Blaine's, lived with the Blaines and was often thought to act as the Senator's ghost. She wrote his life history shortly before her death. Her stock in trade was satire, and she was described as "a lady, at whose mention stalwart men have been known to tremble, and hide in corners; who 'keeps a private graveyard' for the burial of those whom she has mercilessly slain; who respects neither the spectacles of the judge, nor the surplice of the priest; who holds the mirror of men's failings till they hate their wives merely because they belong to her sex."

Gail Hamilton was a pseudonym for Mary Abigail Dodge, a farmer's daughter of Calvinist stock who grew up in New England and was educated at Ipswich Female Seminary. After teaching for a time she joined the Blaine household as governess, and was soon beguiling the celebrities of the day with her sharp and witty observations. When Blaine was at the height of his power as Secretary of State she was credited with influencing his judgment, and she was courted by political leaders and literary celebrities. She haunted

Congress, as Alice Longworth did later on, and her work appeared in the New York *Tribune*, the New York *World*, and the leading magazines. She understood statecraft better than most politicians, and her articles were informed, if intemperate in tone. She wormed secrets out of the most close-mouthed officials but did nothing to prove that a woman was capable of unbiased reporting. Whether crusading against civil-service reform, backing abolition or attacking Horace Greeley when he ran for the Presidency, Gail delighted clever men with her acid conversation. She was homely but magnetic, dressing in Spartan style for the Press Gallery and in rich raiment at night. She always maintained that "woman was born into the whole world," and with her strong political influence she went far to prove it.

Grace Greenwood belonged more to the school of traveling correspondents, but her influence was considerable in the rising tide of support for feminine emancipation. Like Gail Hamilton she was cosmopolitan and a woman of wit, but although she took an occasional whack at the politicians, in general they liked her. She was a softer type than Gail, who remained a spinster to the end of her days.

Grace actually was Sara Jane Clarke, daughter of a theologian, and she passed her early days in Pompey and Rochester, New York. Before she was twenty she was writing for newspapers and *Godey's Lady's Book*, and had published her *Greenwood Leaves* three years before *Fanny Fern's Leaves* came out with stupefying success. In 1852 she went abroad and once again Dickens, Thackeray and their contemporaries went through their paces for a traveling lady correspondent from America. It was all good business, when the chatty letters appeared in the American papers and helped them to sell their books in this rich market.

On her return from Europe Grace married Leander K. Lippincott of Philadelphia and continued to write, to lecture and to visit the camps and hospitals during the Civil War. Lincoln called her "Grace Greenwood, the Patriot." She ranged across the American continent, informing the stay-at-homes on the growth of their expanding country, and her chitchat was often political as well as social in tone. Countless American women of that period viewed the world at large through the eyes of these busy journalists who could discuss anything from a bassinet to an audience with the Pope. They reported wars and changing social systems as well as Paris fashions or having tea with the Brownings.

Emily Edson Briggs, author of the Olivia letters, who arrived in Washington from Iowa in 1861, was in and out of the Press Gallery and saw government in the making for more than forty years. The correspondents were essayists or commentators until the telegraph came in and speeded up the transmission of news. Mrs. Briggs helped to found the Women's National Press Association in 1882, and she was a vigilant observer of the advances of women on the political front.

Wars and great political movements have always stirred women to write. Harriet Beecher Stowe's *Uncle Tom's Cabin* converted a multitude to the antislavery cause and gave her an international reputation. Mary McCarthy whipped up emotions over the war in Vietnam a century later. Mrs. Warren's broadsides during the Revolutionary period were as evocative of their era as Barbara Tuchman's scholarly interpretation of historical events in the twentieth century. Mrs. E. D. E. N. Southworth, Sarah Orne Jewett, Louisa Alcott, and many others reflected in one way or another the flickering social winds of the nineteenth century. In 1833 Lydia Maria Child wrote the first antislavery book published in the United States, and for seventeen years she fought the suffrage battle by word and pen. For a time she edited her husband's paper, the *National Anti-Slavery Standard*. It angered her that she could not draw up a will without having the signature of her husband, David Lee Child. She resented being officially "dead in the law," a mere chattel, a "femme couverte."

Frances Dana Gage, an Ohio abolitionist known as "Aunt Fanny," reached out to the public with her sympathetic stories about Negroes. Clarina Howard Nichols was an editor who promoted the abolition cause and later worked for suffrage in the West. Matilda Joslyn Gage campaigned in upstate New York and became one of the stars of the suffrage movement. But there were other causes to which the women of the period lent their talents. The voice of Emma Lazarus, "Miss Liberty's Poet," was heard clearly in the 1880's as she campaigned for repatriation of the Jews in Palestine and for industrial training for them in the United States. She became the spokesman for her people, and lines from her sonnet "The New Colossus" are inscribed on the pedestal of the Statue of Liberty.

In the days of the Revolution, women published small papers to push their causes. They were not spectacular personal journals like Anne Royall's *Paul Pry*, *Woodhull and Claflin's Weekly* or *Kate Field's Washington*. But all through the Colonial period papers were published in Williamsburg, Charleston, Salem and Newport by women fostering the monarchy or the republican cause. Female printers staffed dozens of papers established by their own sex during this period of stress. All were propagandist in tone and correspondingly poor in the journalistic sense, but they were influential in their limited way. They spread news and understanding. None essayed the intensely personal journalism of Anne Royall, Victoria Woodhull, or Kate Field. These three were newspaper women only by chance. In essence they were individualists grasping for some striking form of self-expression, and in so doing they influenced men and events through the projection of their far-out views.

Chapter 6

Beauties, Sirens and Spies

Wars have always been of the most profound concern to women, striking at the root of their lives, and in America each successive struggle has led to a period of emancipation, as well as to a high degree of sorrow and turmoil. The Revolutionary War started American women on their road to freedom. They learned to ask questions, to express dissent and to perform valorous and patriotic deeds outside the home. Again, the Civil War drew them away from the hearth and into the world of the wage earner. This involved a new step in their experience and development. Some went to the battlefields and the hospitals, where their acts of mercy and sacrifice softened the horrors of war. All were involved in the age-old rite of binding up wounds and ultimately replenishing the depleted ranks of the population.

The Spanish-American War saw the beginning of a standardized nursing corps and the spread of Red Cross work at the scene of battle. World War I gave women a new place in the world of men. They went abroad, drove ambulances, entertained the troops, ran canteens, chauffeured generals, wore spanking uniforms and found for themselves a new range of action. In a sense the freedom of today began with World War I, when thousands of women learned they could hold down jobs, and function ably in channels hitherto reserved for men.

The Depression hit women hard and enlarged their realization of the need for social welfare and for the role they might play on the large canvas of national life. The rise of totalitarian powers and the horrors of the gas chambers stirred them to mercy for the oppressed. World War II opened many doors for women as the New Deal recognized their usefulness in industry, in making munitions, in holding down jobs vacated by men overseas and in giving women some degree of executive function. This same war also brought the cataclysmic moment when the atomic bomb was dropped and the world changed overnight—for women, as for men. When the space program was developed and nuclear power revolutionized all known areas of science, a new terror shadowed the home, along with fantastic medical promise. Again women were at the heart of the hurricane.

The war in Vietnam stirred up a reaction different from that caused by any other war Americans have lived through, and this time the women did not take it in silence. While the great majority saw their sons and husbands go to battle in the same old way, others became picketers for peace, the outspoken critics of man-made institutions, ready to do battle in the city streets rather than watch the carnage continue in the jungle. Again their influence was powerfully felt as they campaigned against the warmongers and thought in terms of peace and the future of their children.

But the first great quickening in the outlook of American women had come with the Civil War. Their lives were never again on the same simple plane of the domestic arts, to the exclusion of the outside world. The traditional sense of submission to masculine domination lost ground under the long barrage of antislavery campaigning and the rise of the suffrage movement. The war was a sharp stimulus to women who were just beginning to feel the flow of causes that inundated Europe and the United States in the nineteenth century. They learned to make speeches and issue pamphlets. Women like Clara Barton and Mary A. Bickerdyke went independently to the battlefield. Mary Livermore and Mrs. A. H. Hoge of Chicago and Louisa Lee Schuyler and countless others from New York and different parts of the country worked with the Sanitary Commission. Women everywhere functioned as amateur nurses, helped in hospitals, provided comforts, arranged Sanitary Fairs and became organization-conscious.

It was a great awakening, and it was reflected on the lecture platform, where eloquence, an ancient feminine gift, counted. Anna E. Dickinson, the young Quaker from Philadelphia who became known as Queen of the Lyceum, earned $23,000 a year. Lucretia Mott had sponsored her as an abolitionist speaker, and she became a paid campaigner for the Republican Party. She was violently opposed to the Copperheads, and her golden voice harped on the urgent need for emancipation. Early in 1864 she addressed a gathering in the House of Representatives, with President Lincoln present. Anna told him bluntly what she thought was wrong with his conduct of the war. This was power of a heady kind for an unenfranchised woman. But she lacked the staying power of some of the other pioneers of the period, and after a succession of lawsuits Anna faded into obscurity.

The humanitarians, like Dr. Elizabeth Blackwell, who had applied to twenty-nine medical schools before winning her degree as the first woman doctor, and Dorothea Dix, who organized a nursing service during the Civil War and later worked for prison and asylum reform, gave up the shelter of the home for wider opportunities, a trend that grew stronger in the next hundred years and is evident on all sides today. In the 1960's the sparkling media of communications illumines from day to day the commonplace tale of women doctors, lawyers and business executives, of diplomats and political hostesses, of women war correspondents and mighty publishers, not to speak of women's ascendancy in the arts, where they have always had a place. While this germ of freedom was planted with the War of the Revolution, it flowered during the Civil War and came to full estate for women during World War II. Once they had savored the stimulating wine of the larger world, there was no going back to the limitations of narrow domesticity—particularly when women found that both might be encompassed at the same time.

But women of power and beauty have always managed to break the barriers, and during wars their image has become part of the historical picture. From the carefully chronicled Civil War emerge the beauties, sirens and spies who were involved in the councils of the great men of the era. The political hostesses like Mrs. Jay and Mrs. Bingham were deeply committed during the Revolutionary era. The most notable of all was Kate Chase, working ceaselessly to exalt her father, Salmon P. Chase, and lead him to the Presidency. She was a belle of the first water, without peer among American women in the boldness with which she played the political game and worked to undermine her father's enemies. Her drive was directed at men of intellect, and the leaders of both parties listened to her attentively—first as the debutante who played hostess at the age of seventeen for her father when he was Governor of Ohio, and then as Mrs. William Sprague, wife of the Senator from Rhode Island.

Kate had sibylline powers as an adviser of men. Her red hair, hazel eyes, white skin and flawless figure made her striking in any gathering. Worth dressed her, and since she acquired millions in marrying Senator Sprague, she could afford to be luxurious in her attire, her jewels, her homes, her way of entertaining. Her lot was cast in a stirring era, and she held court in queenly fashion, consorting with the top statesmen of her day and maintaining good relations with the women, except for Mrs. Lincoln and a few indignant wives who feared her powers of persuasion.

Although aware of her machinations, President Lincoln liked her and treated her with consideration. Mary Lincoln would not attend her marriage to Senator Sprague, but the President walked alone to the ceremony and kissed the bride even when he knew she and her father were at that very moment plotting to undermine him. After the war Kate focused all her powers on her father's career. When the Democratic Convention was held in New York in 1872 Chase stayed away in lofty silence, but Kate decided to take charge—the boldest convention move ever practiced by an American woman. Her father wrote to her with a warning undertone: "I am afraid, my darling, that you are acting too much the politician. Have a care. Don't do or say anything which may not be proclaimed from the house tops."

Horatio Seymour had been selected to nominate Chase, but the plan failed. Wise as Kate was in the ways of politicians, she had her eyes opened to the behind-the-scenes machinations of a political convention. Always fastidious and disdainful, she was working beyond her depth in this atmosphere of liquor, secret caucuses and vote rigging. Daring and beautiful though she was, she could not invade the smoke-wreathed councils of Tammany Hall, and she had to work through mediators who betrayed her. But the press found her "active and visibly in charge" at the Chase headquarters in the Clarendon Hotel before the convention opened. One reporter wrote that if she could take the floor, her father would win by acclamation. He thought her equipped with "brains of almost masculine fibre," unlike the "foolish Susan B. Anthony," who popped into view with her suffrage petition on this occasion. Kate took care to stay well away from the "female agitators" on the other side of the hall.

But her subtle tactics were no more successful than Susan's noisy bid for attention. Samuel J. Tilden, the sagacious scholar of Gramercy Park, had held his own quiet meeting of the New York delegates which resulted, in the opinion of many, in the downfall of Chase and Kate's humiliation. Until she died she believed that Tilden had maneuvered the Seymour nomination and jockeyed her father out of the picture. Kate was credited with acting on her own responsibility in lending her father's approval to the party platform, while he played croquet calmly in Washington. The outcome was bitter tea for this ambitious daughter who had failed as a President-maker—the dream of her life. Her father was relieved; his own ambition had declined with years and ill health.

No one in the capital, however, underestimated the power that Kate had wielded—as her father's adviser, as a prod to her errant husband and as the intimate of Roscoe Conkling, Senator from New York. James Garfield, Charles Sumner, Horace Greeley, Carl Schurz, William McKinley, John Hay, Chet Arthur, Jay Cooke, Collis P. Huntington, Levi P. Morton, Henry Villard and many other men of affairs had listened attentively to Mrs. Sprague from time to time. Few could have told more of the inner councils of the Civil War period than she, had she ever wished to write her memoirs.

With her strong and imperious nature she moved more political pawns than the public ever knew, and she died without revealing her secrets or leaving papers of any value. Time and the loss of her fortune and reputation chastened but did not change her. At the end she was still proud Kate as she peddled eggs from door to door, wearing soiled white kid gloves, in the Washington where she had reigned like a queen.

She was by all odds the star of the Northern galaxy, but a number of Confederate women kept the political pot stirring with their charm, their influence and their seductive ways. Varina Davis, whose husband, Jefferson Davis, headed the Confederacy, was a politician of stature. Like Kate Chase, she was worldly, knowledgeable, a perfect hostess and a handsome woman. The military men of the day, with few exceptions, respected her judgment, and the statesmen found her witty, thoughtful and astute. Her enemies were as formidable as her friends, for she had a critical temperament and was sharp in her judgments. Throughout her lifetime, and particularly in her later years, she was more liberal in outlook than her husband ever was.

While the war raged, many thought that she interfered unduly in army affairs. "Mrs. Davis rules Jeffy," ran one of the Washington headlines. Her feud with Lydia Johnston, wife of Joseph E. Johnston, one of her husband's generals, was profoundly upsetting on the military front. Mrs. Johnston blamed Mrs. Davis for having her husband sent to command the army in the West. She considered this deliberate exile, and when Vicksburg fell and the President of the Confederacy wrote a fifteen-page letter of reproach to General Johnston, Lydia's ire embraced Varina. She wrote furiously to a friend: "I feel that nothing can ever make me forgive either of them. When I look at my dear old husband's grey head & careworn face, & feel how many of those tokens of trouble that man & woman have planted there, I could almost have asked God to punish them."

Mrs. Johnston was only one of a number of influential Confederate women who sniped at "The Queen." Mrs. Louis T. Wigfall, Mrs. Robert Toombs and the beautiful Mrs. A. C. Myers of New Orleans all feuded openly with Mrs. Davis. In a careless moment Mrs. Myers had commented on Varina's girth, an observation that touched off an explosion in Richmond and led to the displacement of her husband as Quartermaster General. Lydia Johnston and Charlotte Wigfall called her a "coarse Western woman." However, Varina had plenty of support from the top social figures of the

Confederacy—Mary Boykin Chesnut of South Carolina, Mrs. Clement Claiborne Clay of Alabama, Mrs. Roger Pryor and Mrs. Burton Harrison of Virginia, all women of influence in the Southern hierarchy. In a sense Mrs. Chesnut, whose *Diary from Dixie* is one of the truly revealing social chronicles of the Civil War, was a catalyst for the hostile elements that enveloped the President's wife. She could laugh, where the more emotional Varina raged. Both were intellectuals, good talkers and confirmed readers. Both aired their knowledge freely and showed caustic wit in appraising people. Mrs. Chesnut was a hedonist, less serious in purpose than Mrs. Davis, but she never hesitated to toss a lance in political and army affairs. Both were women who counted on the national scene and left echoes down the years.

Mrs. Davis was practicing statesmanship on her own in 1863. She and Judah P. Benjamin, her husband's brilliant favorite, worked in close alliance. Benjamin trusted her implicitly with state papers when he was Secretary of State and used her as an intermediary to convey documents to Rosine Slidell, whose father was Commissioner to France. They used a cipher code, and Varina was allowed to read all the dispatches. In many ways Benjamin, a cosmopolitan of Sephardic ancestry, was the most interesting figure close to Davis. While he was Secretary of War he was deeply involved in the sparring between Davis, Johnston and General Beauregard. Varina was party to all their discussions, and although there is ample evidence that she tried to interfere, Jefferson Davis was a rigid man, not readily susceptible to any influence. Varina herself in her later years wrote of his "radical stand and uncompromising nature."

But where he did not bend easily to the march of events, some practical strain in her induced her to yield to changing currents. Their letters indicate how freely he discussed his generals and state affairs with her, and how he sought her advice, which was always readily given, for Varina was emphatic in her views and dominating by nature. Everyone knew where she stood on all issues, and she was not to be ignored. She was effective with the diplomatic and visiting journalists, all of which was helpful to the Confederacy at the time. Her hauteur in the days of social triumph mellowed to a more

tolerant attitude as sorrow flowed around her like a living stream. She
was as cold to General Beauregard as she was to General Johnston.
She respected General Robert E. Lee, like everyone else; admired
Stonewall Jackson; and had mild affection for Jeb Stuart. None of the
Confederate officers underestimated the influence of Mrs. Davis, any
more than their wives did.

When Richmond fell Varina, who loved her husband deeply,
unwittingly brought him endless pain and humiliation by throwing a
waterproof and her black shawl over him as he attempted to escape
from Union troops at their encampment near Irwinville in Georgia.
This led to the charge that he had disguised himself as a woman in
order to avoid capture, and the cartoons of this incident cut deeply
into the hearts of loyal Southerners. Varina, however, showed her
greatest strength and influence in the years after the war when she
fought Davis' imprisonment, went into exile with him and nursed
him back to health and purpose again. After his death she worked
endlessly to refute what she considered the distorted view of his
actions. She settled in New York and ran a salon where Northerners
and Southerners met and good feeling prevailed. It was her final
boast that she believed she had helped to soften some of the differ-
ences between them.

Although she had been an extraordinarily potent woman in her
own right, Varina never warmed to the suffrage movement. Her
power had been used after the fashion of the women of the Revolutionary era. She said quite frankly, as they did, that she believed in
the mental superiority of men and that married life alone was true
fulfillment for women. Yet she and her husband were credited with
breaking up the romance of their favorite child Winnie, known as
the Daughter of the Confederacy. Winnie had fallen in love with a
Northerner, an untenable thought to her father.

In their separate ways Mary Lincoln and Varina Davis were
women of similar destiny. The sum of their woes was common
ground, and their lives were forced into the ultimate parallel in the
death of young sons while each presided in a presidential mansion.
Both had the gift of love and understanding from the men to whom
they were married. When Mary Lincoln lost this sustaining force, her

life collapsed. Varina, strong, intelligent and more resilient by nature, weathered the storm, and after a peaceful old age in New York was buried beside her husband in Richmond with a military funeral. She had shared in counsels that involved the fate of a nation and may well have helped to shape it.

From time to time her life touched that of Rose O'Neal Greenhow, Confederate agent of no small achievement, who functioned with more finesse than Belle Boyd and other flamboyant spies of the period. This Maryland-born beauty, whose political philosophy was shaped by John C. Calhoun, became one of Washington's most formidable hostesses. As the wife of Robert Greenhow, a Virginia-born scholar who worked for the State Department, Rose made ruthless use of the dispatches that she translated for her husband. She was the confidante of the leading diplomats of the day who haunted her parlors, and when the war began she used all her powers to help the South. Her operations were flagrant, and she was credited with conveying the message to General Beauregard that resulted in the defeat of the Union Army at the first Battle of Bull Run. She warned him of General McClellan's approach and the number of troops he had. One of Allan Pinkerton's men nabbed her as she swallowed an incriminating note, and for a time she was imprisoned in her own house. But such was her influence that she conducted an espionage ring from this shelter, even while under guard. When jailed in Capitol Hill prison with her daughter, little Rose, she compared herself to Marie Antoinette and continued to send military information to General Beauregard.

Exiled to Richmond when the authorities could stand no more of her scenes in prison, she swept out into the Washington sunshine wearing the Confederate flag beneath a torn shawl. Soon afterward she appeared in the ballrooms of London and Paris, seeking support for the Confederacy. She was returning from Europe weighted down with gold to help the Confederacy when her ship was wrecked within two hundred yards of the Confederate guns at Fort Fisher. Rose sank with the heavy load of sovereigns she carried in a bag attached to her person. She had often said that she would gladly die for the Confederacy, and in the end she did.

While she lived, Mrs. Greenhow had exercised considerable power in government circles as a beauty, a wit, a patriot and a spy, and in England she had tried to sway the various statesmen who wrestled at close range with the complications of the Civil War. She talked. She wrote. She lectured. And she advocated the Southern cause with flaming passion. A century later she would have qualified as an effective propagandist. In the period immediately before the war she was close to President Buchanan, urging him to swing to the South. The operations of Rose and other glamorous matrons from the Southern states were described by Colonel Erasmus D. Keyes in *Fifty Years' Observation of Men and Events:* "I found great delight with the Southern damsels, and even with some of the matrons, notwithstanding the incandescence of their treason. . . . Mrs. Greenough [sic], who was reputed to be the most persuasive woman that was ever known in Washington, after expatiating on the injustice of the North, tried to persuade me not to take part in the war. . . ."

These were women of power. Rose, who was related by marriage to another of the influential beauties of the era, turned a chilly front to Adelaide Cutts when she married Stephen A. Douglas. Mrs. Douglas had sworn to make her husband's enemies her own, and Buchanan was one of them. At the time of Adelaide's much-discussed marriage to the Little Giant, Rose was concentrating all her forces on backing Buchanan for the Presidency. She worked quietly for him behind the scenes, while Jessie Benton Frémont, who had learned the political game from her father, Thomas Hart Benton, staged a wide-open campaign for her husband, John C. Frémont. Although Rose Greenhow and Jessie Frémont disliked each other heartily, there were many points of similarity in their life histories. Both were the wives of pathfinders who helped to chart the boundaries of American territories. In time both became involved in land scandals in the West. But their outlook on life was entirely different.

Frémont went down to defeat as a presidential candidate, but he was soon prominent again when Lincoln appointed him to command the Western Division of the army, with headquarters at St. Louis. This was Benton territory, but the Frémonts, fiercely opposed to slavery, found that many of their old friends had swung over to the

Confederacy. The General, always hotheaded, soon got into trouble
in his command by issuing the first emancipation order giving
freedom to the slaves of rebels and putting Missouri under martial
law. Jessie welcomed John Hay when he arrived from Washington
with an appeal from President Lincoln for modification of the order
freeing slaves. Frémont would not budge. He broke with Montgomery and Frank Blair, who were counseling the President, and
Jessie became deeply involved in this breach with her old friends the
Blairs.

As her husband's difficulties became more acute she decided to see
President Lincoln personally. Ushered into the Red Room in Willard's Hotel she was suddenly face to face with the haggard-looking
Lincoln. He did not offer her a seat, she noted, but talked to her
standing up. She saw at once that the interview was to be brief
and that the "President's mind was made up against General Frémont—and decidedly against me."

"You are quite a female politician," the President said.

He then spoke vehemently of Frémont's mistake in converting a
war for the Union into a war against slavery. Jessie said that she had
brought her husband's letter with her to make sure that the President
received it. Lincoln reminded her coldly that Frank Blair would
advise her husband.

The answer that Lincoln said would be forthcoming never arrived,
and Jessie wrote to him again, asking for copies of the charges against
her husband. The Blairs soon circulated a story that Jessie had called
the President "Abraham" and had "threatened and stamped her foot
like a virago." Jessie's supporters were skeptical of this, but in any
event her husband was removed from his command. Almost overnight her hair turned gray. She blamed everything on the Blairs,
believing they favored the South, but her attitude to President
Lincoln changed after he issued the Emancipation Proclamation.
During this period Jessie's parlors, like Kate Chase's, were fountain-
heads of gossip and intrigue as influential politicians came and went
and listened to these fair oracles, both of whom were devoted to the
antislavery cause. Jessie never incurred the enmity of her own sex as
Kate Chase sometimes did, nor did the men through whom she

pulled strings resent her political interference, except for the implacable Blairs.

After watching the triumphant armies march in the victory parade of 1865 the Frémonts settled on an estate on the Hudson. They lived luxuriously, and Frémont bought the Humboldt library after the explorer's death. But trouble developed over their property holdings in California, and they were financially ruined. "I am like a deeply built ship; I drive best under a strong wind," said Jessie, as she broke up their home, sold their books and art objects and turned to writing for a living. Like Kate Chase she had tasted the best and the worst of life, and had exercised her charm and influence under the most primitive conditions in the West, as well as in the most elaborate settings. Many star-chamber meetings were held in her whitewashed adobe house in California, with a grizzly bearskin on the floor, thin planks for a dining table, and Chinese brocade curtains at her windows. Here she served French cuisine as she whisked about in ruffled muslin gowns and spoke mellifluously of large events. Congress allowed her a pension in her old age, and in 1894 Gutzon Borglum did a bust of her. Jessie's writings were widely read, and Bret Harte, visiting her in her Bear Valley home in California, near the Mariposa mines, noted that politics was still meat to Mrs. Frémont. "I sat back and listened to her stories of Benton and the old Washington that were better than a play," he commented.

Her last years were spent in a wheel chair, but she remained something of an oracle to William McKinley, John Hay and other men of note who called on her. She was buried with her husband at Piermont-on-the-Hudson overlooking Tappan Zee and the old stone Frémont mansion. Jessie was one of the Great Ladies of the nineteenth century, known at home and abroad, powerful in the counsels of men, strong in will but not aggressive in manner. Men found her dynamic and charming; women thought her sympathetic. Not until Alice Longworth came along did another woman cast the particular kind of spell in Washington circles that Jessie Frémont did. But her influence went deep, and from time to time she was a profoundly disturbing factor in political affairs. She fought her husband's battles endlessly, and they were not minor in scope. Jessie had watched the antislavery forces grow in strength from the beginning, and she remained militant on the subject all the days of her life. This was a cause that had stirred up women more than anything since the days of the Revolution. It touched their humanitarian instincts and made them vocal and unafraid. When the leading abolitionists met in Philadelphia in 1833 to establish the American Anti-Slavery Society, a few women were allowed to speak from the floor. But they could not join the Society or sign its "Declaration of Sentiments and Principles," so twenty of them met in Philadelphia and formed their own Female Anti-Slavery Society. A mob stormed the building, and at a similar meeting in Boston William Lloyd Garrison, the speaker, had to flee, but he was subsequently dragged through the streets at the end of a rope.

Lucretia Mott was their presiding goddess, and Angelina and Sarah Grimké, two sisters from a slaveholding family in the Carolinas, joined the Quakers and kept up constant agitation on behalf of the Negro. They were regarded as unwomanly and unchristian, but they picked up intelligent support and strengthened their cause when they linked it to woman's place in society. At first the antislavery and suffrage forces interlocked at every point.

"To me it is perfectly clear that whatsoever is morally right for a man to do, is morally right for a woman to do," said Angelina who, along with many of her fellow workers, viewed the issue as a moral rather than a political one. Theodore Weld, who later married the beautiful Angelina, and John Greenleaf Whittier upheld the women but disapproved of their mingling the two causes. Angelina's eloquence made her a public figure, and she dared to speak for the abolitionists at hearings held by the Massachusetts State Legislature in 1838. She was the first woman in America to make a stand of this sort, and she almost fainted with trepidation, but instead continued eloquently for two hours, backed by Lydia Maria Child, author and orator who worked for the abolitionist cause for seventeen years.

Sarah, the plain Grimké sister, had never forgotten the sight of a slave girl being beaten. She was only five at the time, and as the years went on she developed a keen sense of justice. Both girls were carefully nurtured in the Southern style, receiving tuition from the best masters in Charleston. But shedding their worldly training, they became symbolic of the educated women who stepped out of their homes to help this cause and agitate for legislation. The Grimké sisters gave great encouragement to the Underground Railroad that involved the feats of many women who harbored fleeing slaves and hid them in cellars and attics. Some drove Negroes hidden in wagons to safer stations along the Underground.

Several black women lectured, wrote and helped the fugitives on their way. Harriet Tubman and Sojourner Truth became famous for their bold and selfless operations. Harriet, a turbaned figure five feet tall with piercing eyes and a scar on her skull that had been inflicted by a plantation overseer, made nineteen journeys in ten years into slave territory as a conductor on the Underground Railroad. She brought back more than three hundred men, women and children, and although there was a price on her head she was never caught. Sojourner Truth was an illiterate slave who had been flogged by her master and forced to marry the man he approved, rather than the man she loved. She bore thirteen children, most of whom were sold into slavery.

Anna Mae Douglass, the wife of Frederick Douglass, the Negro who ran for the Vice-Presidency with Victoria Woodhull, was another ardent worker for the slaves. Many of the writers of the period pled the cause of Woodhull and Douglass. The humanitarians like Lucy Stone, Antoinette Brown and Dorothea Dix campaigned for them, and the civil-rights movement of today goes back to this period when women shared with men a tough fight for the rights of blacks. In actual fact, a social revolution was in the making as the downtrodden, the slaves, the poor, the unemployed, the insane and the criminal were studied from the humanitarian point of view, but the two major drives were for abolition and woman suffrage. These beginnings set up a wide canvas for the reforms of the next hundred years. And the Civil War itself opened the doors to jobs.

President Lincoln gave women a helping hand by having a few of them installed in government departments, although it was not until 1870 that they were officially welcomed into federal service, starting the long chain that enlivens government circles today. Until then government service had been solely a man's world, except for a few women employed in the postal service in the pre-Revolutionary days. As early as 1773 Baltimore had a woman postmaster named Mary K. Goddard, and Elizabeth Cresswell was handling the mail at Charlestown, Maryland, in 1786. But it was not until Clara Barton became a copyist in the Patent Office in 1855 that women were known as government workers. Clara functioned in this capacity between 1855 and 1857, and again between 1860 and 1865 when she was not visiting the battlefields and helping the wounded. These substitute war workers made such an impression that in 1868 one of the Treasury supervisors said that "female clerks are more attentive, diligent, and efficient than males, and make better clerks."

From then on women found some sort of place in the working world and felt the intoxication of making a little money on their own. It also gave the suffrage-minded the feeling that they had established a foothold, however precarious, in the great outside working world where men flourished. Other benefits had come their way, too, in the sewing machine, gaslight, plumbing, canning and new kitchen tools. There was no slipping back to the more primitive ways of life that preceded the Civil War. Like all wars, this one had shaken up the settled background of people's lives and had led to stimulating developments. The metamorphosis was much greater for women than for men. Since they had known so little of freedom before, it was a giant step toward their ultimate emancipation.

One of their great benefactors was Jane Addams, who turned the tide for the working woman and laid a deep foundation for the social concern that infuses the American scene today. Considered a radical and a rebel in her time, she shook up both the political and social structure, and she rates as one of the more influential women in American history. In many respects she was ahead of her generation. She stood for peace, for the brotherhood of man and for help to children, to the ill, to the peoples of all races. Her zeal for trade unionism and her pacifism in time of war led her into deep waters, but after she was awarded the Nobel Peace Prize in 1931 the clouds of criticism drifted away in worldwide recognition of a great pioneer.

Hull House, which she opened in 1889, became a training ground

tha Washington, though she did not in the White House, set many preces for future First Ladies who were to de there. (Library of Congress)

Mrs. John Adams, the popular Abigail, exercised considerable political power in a wifely way during the Revolutionary period and was an early advocate of the rights of women. (Painting by Gilbert Stuart, National Gallery of Art)

y Madison was one of the most ar and successful First Ladies in ican history. Her influence in ington continued until her death age of eighty-one. (Library of Con-

Mrs. John Tyler, an influential and interfering First Lady, was also a charmer who actively promoted her husband's policies. (Library of Congress)

Mrs. James Monroe, called by the French *La Belle Américaine*, gave the White House a new look with French furniture and vermeil bric-à-brac. (Miniature by Lemée. Prints Division, New York Public Library)

Mrs. Ulysses S. Grant exercised great influence over her soldier husband before and during the Civil War, and backed him during his less happy days in the White House. (Library of Congress)

Mary Todd Lincoln, one the most discussed of President's wives, consta stirred up trouble du Abraham Lincoln's admi tration. (Library of Cong

Mrs. Grover Cleveland, one of the best loved of Presidents' wives, whose tact and adroitness smoothed the way for her forthright husband. (Library of Congress)

Mrs. Theodore Roosevelt, a discreet and popular First Lady, who often restrained her impetuous husband. (Library of Congress)

Mrs. Woodrow Wilson and President Wilson with King Albert (right) and Queen Elizabeth (left) of Belgium at the Palace in Brussels, June 19, 1919. Mrs. Wilson was credited with running a regency after the President's breakdown. (UPI)

Mrs. William Howard Taft, intelligent and ambitious, was a strong influence in her husband's career from his days as a young lawyer through his Presidency and years as Chief Justice. (Library of Congress)

Mrs. Franklin D. Roosevelt, photographed in the White House on June 19, 1940, beneath a portrait of her grandfather, the first Theodore Roosevelt. (Courtesy Bradford Bachrach and The Franklin D. Roosevelt Library, Hyde Park)

Mrs. John F. Kennedy with André Malraux, French Minister of Culture, and Mme. Malraux in the National Gallery of Art in 1962. Behind them is a John Singleton Copley painting of himself and his family. (UPI)

Mrs. Lyndon B. Johnson and Mary Lasker, who share an interest in beautification, display a picture of flowers planted on New York City's Park Avenue. (UPI)

Margaret Fuller, writer, reformer, and brilliant conversationalist, was America's most noted woman of letters in the nineteenth century. (Bettmann Archive)

Kate Field, roving correspondent, edito critic, actress, and humanitarian, ha both political and social influence.

Mercy Otis Warren, a political satirist and effective propagandist, whose advice and help were sought by such men as John Adams, Samuel Adams, and Thomas Jefferson. (Painting by John Singleton Copley, Museum of Fine Arts, Boston)

Mrs. Jefferson Davis, a woman of commanding presence, figured significantly in the counsels of the Confederate leaders during the Civil War. (Courtesy of Mrs. John W. Stewart)

Jessie Benton Frémont, author and famous hostess, played a strong role in the checkered career of her explorer-politician husband, John C. Frémont. (Bettmann Archive)

Kate Chase Sprague, the most ambitious political hostess in American history, used her outward charm and inner ruthlessness in a fruitless attempt to help her father, Salmon Portland Chase, gain the presidential nomination. (From *Queens of American Society* by Elizabeth F. Ellet)

Monument in the Capitol to Elizabeth Cady Stanton, Susan B. Anthony, and Lucretia Mott, three great suffrage pioneers, by Adelaide Johnson, also a suffrage worker. (Library of Congress)

The women of Cheyenne, Wyoming, cast ballots in a local election as early as 1869. (Wide World)

Victoria Woodhull, one of three American women who ran for the Presidency, asserting her right to vote. (Sketch by H. Balling)

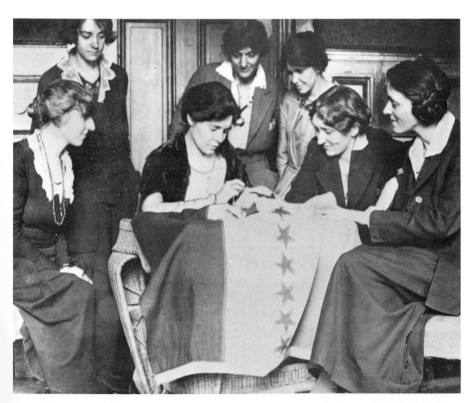

Alice Paul, founder of the National Woman's Party and a militant suffragist, stitches the thirty-sixth star on her party banner in 1920 when Tennessee ratified the suffrage amendment. With her are women who picketed the White House, some of whom went to prison in their fight for women's rights. (Wide World)

Lucy Stone, who by refusing to take her husband's name set a precedent for professional women, was another of the great suffrage leaders of the nineteenth century. (Library of Congress)

Jane Addams, pioneer social service worker who founded Hull House in Chicago, was awarded the Nobel Peace Prize jointly with Dr. Nicholas Murray Butler. (Library of Congress)

Carrie Chapman Catt, noted leader in the suffrage movement, shown with some of the treasures from her collection. (UPI)

Virginia C. Gildersleeve (right), dean emeritus of Barnard College, with Millicent C. McIntosh, her successor, at the unveiling of a bust of Miss Gildersleeve in 1949. (Wide World)

Margaret Sanger, founder of the birth-control movement in the United States, before a Senate judiciary subcommittee in 1932. (UPI)

Frances Perkins, first woman to serve in the Cabinet, was Secretary of Labor from 1933 to 1945. (UPI)

Oveta Culp Hobby, editor and publisher of the Houston *Post*, was Minister of Health, Education and Welfare in the Eisenhower Cabinet. She had organized and directed the Women's Army Auxiliary Corps during World War II.

Senator Margaret Chase Smith, Republican from Maine and one of the women who have run for nomination the Presidency. (UPI)

Alice Roosevelt Longworth, daughter of Theodore Roosevelt, and one of the nation's most admired political hostesses, with Wendell L. Willkie at the time he ran for the Presidency in 1940. (UPI)

Clare Boothe Luce, former Republican Congresswoman and Ambassador to Italy, a writer and public speaker. (UPI)

Marietta Tree, shown as delegate-at-large to the United Nations, is active in the liberal wing of the Democratic Party. (UPI)

Mrs. J. Borden Harriman, Ambassador to Norway during World War II, receiving a citation of merit for public service from President Kennedy in 1963. (Wide World)

Anna M. Rosenberg, expert in labor problems, being sworn in as Assistant Secretary of Defense in 1950. With her are George C. Marshall, Secretary of Defense, and Robert A. Lovett, deputy Secretary. Felix Larkin (left), general counsel, administers the oath. (Wide World)

Dorothy Schiff, editor-in-chief and publisher of the New York *Post*, when she independently resumed publication of her paper on March 4th, 1963, during the 87-day printers' strike. (UPI)

Katharine Graham, publisher of the Washington *Post* and *Newsweek*, and owner of TV stations and wire services, with (right) British Ambassador David Ormsby Gore, now Lord Harlech, and his wife and British Labor Party leader, later Prime Minister, Harold Wilson. (UPI)

Constance Baker Motley, Borough President of Manhattan, with President Johnson after he nominated her for the bench of the U.S. District Court for the Southern District of New York in 1966. (UPI)

Frances P. Bolton, Republican Congresswoman from Ohio, 1940 to 1968, was a specialist in foreign affairs. The African wood sculpture was collected on a 20,000-mile journey through Africa. (UPI)

for neophytes who spread her philosophy far and wide. She worked directly in the ghetto, feeding the hungry, clothing the ill-clad, bringing medical care into their lives, improving their homes and educating them in arts and crafts. Nearly three-quarters of Chicago's population of a million were foreign-born at the time. The fifty thousand inhabitants of Ward Nineteen where she had her settlement were mostly immigrants ignorant of the language. The streets were inexpressibly dirty. The number of schools was inadequate. Sanitary legislation was not enforced. Street lighting was meager, and the back alleys resembled the worst ghettos of today.

Soon the politicians were aware of the quiet, insistent tones of Miss Addams demanding fair play for the poor as she cut across ward politics and lobbied for new legislation. Well educated herself, she decided at the start to emphasize recreational pursuits rather than scholarship. The first public building added to Hull House was an art gallery. This was followed by a music school and little theater. Soon her "Cathedral of Humanity," as she liked to regard it, had forty different activities, from college extension courses and summer schools to a Lincoln Club and an Eight-Hour Club to encourage women to hold out for an eight-hour working day.

In 1892 the first public playground in Chicago was established by Miss Addams, and the Mary Crane Nursery for the children of working mothers became a model for the future. The Jane Club was the first vital link in the chain forged to organize women through labor unions. Soon shirtmakers, cloakmakers and other sweatshop workers were banding together through Hull House, and in 1904 Miss Addams became vice-president of the National Women's Trade Union League.

During the Pullman strike of 1894 Hull House maintained avenues of intercourse with both sides, and she was sent as an arbitrator to talk to Pullman employees. But negotiations failed, and when she returned to Chicago she found federal troops in Halsted Street. She regarded George Pullman as a figure of tragedy and prepared a pamphlet *A Modern King Lear*, which he resented. Both sides in the argument disliked it. Eugene Debs called it an attempt to put out a fire with rosewater. But when it appeared in a magazine and was widely read, it focused attention on Miss Addams as a national figure, expressing a fresh philosophy of social progress.

Within a decade she had become a leader, speaking at schools and conventions, women's clubs and businessmen's luncheons, before legislative committees and labor unions. At times men listened to her more attentively than women, for she was skilled in the pragmatic approach. The problems she faced in the Chicago slums were the problems of today. She worked on juvenile delinquency, and of her nine books the one she liked best was *The Spirit of Youth and the City Streets*. She fought child labor for fourteen years and corrupt politics for as long as she presided at Hull House. In course of time she was called a "great statesman without a portfolio."

Miss Addams stirred up a good many women of wealth to civic action, and among them was Mrs. Potter Palmer, the leading hostess of the Middle West. When she worked for the Civic Federation Mrs. Palmer had much to do with Hull House, and she was a familiar sight at the settlement, attending meetings or organizing crusades. She admired Miss Addams, and Jane in turn influenced Mrs. Palmer's social thinking. At the Columbian Exposition of 1893 Mrs. Palmer demanded that "artisan diplomas" be awarded in recognition of the skill of craftsmen, and she accepted the cooperation of the Chicago labor unions in enforcing her demand. She also saw to it that Miss Addams was appointed over the opposition of the French directors at the Paris Exposition of 1900 to an important post on the award jury.

Jane was reluctant to align herself with any special group. She always said that she would neither be subsidized by millionaires nor bullied by workingmen. She had a remarkable number of friends at both ends of the social scale, and she would tramp about in rubbers on the sunniest day at Bar Harbor, sneezing madly from hay fever but never desisting in her efforts to raise money for her settlement.

Although she gave social service a mighty thrust forward, it was her work for peace that made her an international celebrity. All through the years of World War I and the decade that followed she was a controversial figure, first attending a Congress of Women at The Hague in 1915, then planning for a woman's peace conference in

1919 to run parallel to the Peace Conference in Paris. Sixteen countries were represented at this Congress, with many of the best-known women in Europe assembled to talk peace. She went into Germany at the invitation of the American Friends Service Committee after touring the battlefields and finding the grave of her nephew, who had been blown to pieces three weeks before the Armistice was signed. When she sought food for German children on her return she was accused of being pro-German. Her name, which had brought storms of applause in lecture halls in 1912, had become unmentionable by 1920, except for abuse. It took another decade to bring her back into prominence.

Although practical, Miss Addams was a mystic. "You utter instinctively the truth we others vainly seek," William James said to her. She was tolerant of those who opposed her and fluid in her appraisal of all sides of a question. In some respects she had the negative stubbornness of Gandhi. Like many of the women pioneers, she had a history of nervous and physical ills and had had spinal trouble until she was operated on at the age of twenty-five. For a year she was in a metal strait jacket. It was not until her thirties that she developed as a woman of strength and purpose, but all her life sadness was imprinted on her face. She inherited her austerity from her father, a prosperous miller of Quaker ancestry who lived in Cedarville and was a Senator in the Illinois State Assembly for sixteen years and a personal friend of Abraham Lincoln's. He died when Jane was twenty, and for the next eight years she drifted aimlessly, ill much of the time and without any definite purpose in life. After attending Rockford College she went to Philadelphia in 1881 to study medicine, but stayed only seven months. Two years later she went abroad and in the East End of London had her first close view of the miseries of the slums. She studied the work of Toynbee Hall and came to know Sidney and Beatrice Webb. Although she was drawn into the Marxian circle in London, she found little inspiration in Fabianism or the economics of Marx. Her settlement house and the development of trade unionism for women engaged her interest fully on her return home, and life took on new meaning for her. The industrial life of today was being shaped as immigrants poured into the country and

were rapidly absorbed in the general population. Nineteen national-
ities were represented in her district.

But from the 1920's until the time of her death in 1935 at the age
of seventy-five Miss Addams was the leading figure in the Women's
International League, presiding at congresses in Vienna, Washington, Dublin and Prague. She resigned in 1929 and was elected
honorary president for life. The League stood for united effort by the
women of all countries to oppose every kind of war, exploitation and
oppression. Miss Addams was often misunderstood and was a focus
of hate for many years of her life. Even the unionists condemned her
at times. "I am a very simple person," she said on one occasion, but if
she was simple it was strictly in the sense that she was unique. Her
advice was sought by presidents and prime ministers, but she was
never a member of any political party or elected to any public office.
Yet few women in American history have been more influential
politically. When it was suggested in 1912 by the leaders of a
woman's suffrage group that they announce her as their candidate for
President, Miss Addams laughed. She said that women could take a
joke, but men could not.

🦋 **Chapter 7**

A Cause Takes Root

🦋 The Daughters of Eve and the Sons of Adam broke ranks when the long suffrage battle began at Seneca Falls in 1848. It was scarcely a primrose path that the rebels followed. Seventy-two years of enterprise and soul-searing effort were needed to win the vote. A few militants think that the ultimate has yet to be obtained, but the phrase "equal rights" has an anachronistic ring in an age when women are firmly embedded, if still a minority, in the business and professional worlds; when they have a qualified say in government; when they reign supreme on the domestic front; when they are still the mothers of men and at last can also control the size of their families.

Early visitors to America detected the incipient power of the American woman. It was self-evident during the days of the Revolution. In the eighteenth century the Duc de la Rochefoucauld noted that America was a land where woman was queen and that single young women enjoyed the same degree of liberty that married women did in France. Alexis de Tocqueville in the nineteenth century observed in his study of political and social institutions in the United States: "If I were asked . . . to what the singular prosperity and growing strength of that people ought mainly to be attributed, I should reply: 'To the superiority of their women.'" Jacques Offenbach found that ninety out of a hundred American women were ravishing. Matthew Arnold considered their unusual measure of feminine charm an authentic touch of civilization in an otherwise uncivilized country.

The fact that American women were spoiled and petted was noted by many, and Henry James focused attention on the more deadly side of their freedom and independence in *Daisy Miller*. As knowing a historian as James Bryce found that "in no country are women, and especially young women, made so much of. The world is at their feet. Society seems organized for the purpose of providing enjoyment for them."

But these observers were looking mostly at the Beautiful People of the era—the courtly ladies in brocade who were painted by John Singleton Copley; the wives and daughters well-off enough to do the Grand Tour of Europe. The early feminists saw the other side of the picture. To them the women of the growing young country lacked education, personal freedom, property rights, voting rights, marital equality or any kind of legal redress on the basic issues of life, however vivacious, charming, spoiled and ravishing they might seem to visitors from abroad.

The feminists moved strongly into the forefront at a time when strange causes—some imported, some home-grown—were shaking up the social body. A few had been leading figures in the strong anti-slavery movement that preceded the Civil War. But once engaged, their battle for the franchise that raged until 1920 was violent and bitter, abrasive, dangerous and upsetting to the social order. Darkened halls, rotten eggs, broken windows, hosing and slander did not weaken the spirit of the pioneers who had picked up the torch in a small church in Seneca Falls when Elizabeth Cady Stanton, wife of State Senator Henry Stanton, read her Declaration of Principles, paraphrased from the Declaration of Independence. This significant document set forth that the history of mankind involved the absolute tyranny of man over woman, with repeated injuries and usurpations of power. Mrs. Stanton continued:

In entering upon the great work before us, we anticipate no small amount of misconception, misrepresentation, and ridicule; but we shall use every instrumentality within our power to effect our object. We shall employ agents, circulate tracts, petition the State and national legislatures, and endeavor to enlist the pulpit and the press on our behalf.

Senator Stanton decided to leave town when Elizabeth showed him the vital line in her resolution—"that it is the duty of the women of this country to secure for themselves their sacred right to the elective franchise." But James Mott, husband of the stately Quaker, Lucretia, braved the gathering, although Mrs. Mott warned him that they should move carefully lest they become objects of ridicule.

Men as well as women made up the audience of nearly three hundred that arrived in rigs, wagons and on foot to listen to Elizabeth Cady Stanton, with her bobbing ringlets and braided crinoline, give a scholarly and logical address. Sixty-eight women and thirty-two men signed her Declaration of Principles, and her own Henry, in course of time, caved in as the tornado roared around him. When she reached out for the vote Elizabeth had already been married for eight years to Stanton, who was an abolitionist well used to stormy meetings and unpopular causes. They lived in Seneca Falls. Elizabeth was discontented with domestic drudgery and the limited aims of her life. Although she ended up with seven children, her active mind ranged over the larger needs of humanity.

At heart Mrs. Stanton was a parliamentarian and her oratory and legal training were to serve as bulwarks for the suffrage movement. She knew her Blackstone, and her first breakthrough was on the property rights of married women. Mrs. Stanton and Mrs. Mott, daughter of the captain of a Nantucket whaling ship, had joined forces as early as 1840 when both attended an international anti-slavery convention in London and were told that only men in the American delegation would be seated. They tramped the London streets together and made significant plans for the future. Mrs. Mott was already well known as founder of the first Female Anti-Slavery Society. Her home was an underground station for fleeing slaves, and she had talked often on the subject in her quiet, dignified manner.

Suffrage and abolition were interlocking causes as the movement got under way, and the women who pioneered for the vote were the political strategists of the era. Some used direct methods; others veered into dangerous channels like the abolitionist and free-love colonies founded by Frances Wright. They had many causes to champion, aside from the need of the franchise. Even at antislavery meetings they often had to sit behind curtains and could not raise their voices. They had few working opportunities. Teaching was the only profession open to them before the Civil War. Divorce was beyond the pale, and husbands could legally beat their wives or commit them if they were troublesome. Their property, their clothes, their persons, their children were wholly subject to masculine control.

The women who had been clamoring for education, abolition and the vote expanded their aims by 1850, the year in which a suffrage convention was held in Worcester, Massachusetts. Paulina Wright Davis of Rhode Island organized this gathering, which brought women of means and social position into the movement. Among them was Miss Delia Torrey, who liked to think that she helped to run the country when her nephew, William Howard Taft, became President. For the next decade these conventions were held regularly until the public became as aware of the "cackling hens" and "she-hyenas" as it is today of the Hippies. The press was in full cry, and women's rights were held up to scorn. But while others jeered, Horace Greeley, well used to advanced thinkers and feminine neophytes, took up the cause with interest and gave space in the New York *Tribune* to the new breed of women.

In spite of the herculean efforts of the pioneers, however, women as a whole clung to submissive femininity and refused to back up the women fighting in their behalf. Men took the suffrage movement in their stride, treating it with contempt, skepticism, good nature, humor, ridicule or downright cruelty, as the spirit moved them. It was a new experience to have their women talk back to them on public issues and stray away from the fireside, to trudge along country byways, make speeches, ring doorbells and tackle legislators. Only the men of larger vision were impressed by their fortitude and intelligence. And one, appropriately enough Abigail's son, John Quincy Adams, was bold enough to say, "The mere departure of women from the duties of the domestic circle, far from being a reproach to her, is a virtue of the highest order, when it is done from purity of motive, by appropriate means, and the purpose good."

Today men have little to complain of when their wives dash off to the polls or to attend a public meeting. The home does not fall apart in their absence. The deep freeze is stocked with food. The electric washer takes care of the laundry. The children are driven to school in cars and buses. Husbands can relax and even take pride in the accomplishments of their busy wives; many feel that the home benefits from their pay envelopes, too. But it took the better part of a century for women to accept the results or approve the ways of the feminists. The Victorian curtain lay heavy on the land when the pioneers were at work, and the average woman in the home sank back against the antimacassars with disapproval and disdain. At no time in their history have American women been as spiritless as in the mid-nineteenth century—smothered in burdensome clothes, tightly laced and crowned with false hair. Sunk in the depths of ineffective domesticity, with too many pregnancies, too much ill health, they drew away from the extremists, the agitators, the exhibitionists, the shakers of the status quo.

Yet the workers for women's rights were not the unnatural freaks pictured by the cartoons and news stories of the day. Most of them were happily married. They had large families and made no attempt to shed the warm image of their femininity. Many were women of substance, some learning, good family and a certain degree of economic independence. On the whole they were not a stern spinsterhood, in spite of the stark demeanor of Susan B. Anthony, the most noted organizer and persistent fighter. Her coworker, Mrs. Stanton, was a plump and pink-faced mother of seven, with an aureole of curls, a benignant air and frilled collars. None of the American feminists, however, matched the fragile looks and iron will of Mrs. Emmeline Pankhurst, the English suffragist with the face of a saint who could aim a telling kick at a policeman with her slender legs swathed in lace-ruffled petticoats.

Mrs. Stanton was no believer in planned parenthood, and her repeated pregnancies were of much concern to her suffrage friends. It was never good to have her *hors de combat*—her touch was needed constantly on the legislative end. Elizabeth was the daughter of a judge, and her logic was one of the great weapons of the suffrage fight. On one occasion she wrote apologetically to Susan Anthony: "Courage, Susan—this is my last baby." Susan believed that the wicked Sons of Adam deliberately used this method to slow up the suffrage fight. As a spinster she could devote all her time to the cause, but Mrs. Stanton, Mrs. Mott and the learned Lucy Stone had effective home lives of their own.

It took hedonists like Frances Wright, preaching free love, and Victoria Woodhull, an advanced exponent of every sex cause that shakes up the social order today, to stir the feminine population into a wave of fierce opposition to the outlandish behavior of the extremists. With some cause the aura of sexual license had attached itself to the suffrage movement. Mrs. Woodhull, who had seemed an impressive figure on the horizon and had dared even to run for the Presidency, soon lost ground when she exploited sex and brought Dr. Henry Ward Beecher into the courts as the seducer of one of his parishioners. In the midst of all the uproar Julia Ward Howe preserved a bland approach, convinced though she was of the need for reform. Another dissembler was Mrs. Frank Leslie, the least vocal of the hedonists yet the one who wielded the most power, first as the wife of Frank Leslie, then as the editor of all his publications.

One of the earliest testing grounds was the bloomer costume, designed by Elizabeth Smith Miller and modeled attractively by Amelia Bloomer, who without intention gave it her name. This proved to be one of the most disastrous moves made by the feminists, for it cut to the root of the feminine image and brought waves of ridicule and opposition from both sexes. Mrs. Stanton abandoned the costume when she saw that it was doing the suffrage cause no good, and she warned Susan Anthony, who looked like a ridiculous scarecrow in her Turkish trousers, to give it up. "We put the dress on for greater freedom, but what is physical freedom compared with mental bondage?" Elizabeth wrote. "It is not wise, Susan, to use up so much energy and feeling that way. You can put them to better use. I speak from experience."

Some wore the costume for comfort and convenience; others as a gesture of revolt, but wherever the bloomer appeared there were jeers from street loafers, small boys and even from men of substance. Women in general were equally revolted. The feminists quailed and gave up, but not Dr. Mary Walker, who wore men's clothes throughout her lifetime and successfully practiced medicine in top hat and frock coat. The dress reformers tried other tacks and campaigned against tight lacing, too many burdensome petticoats, the distortion of the feminine form and the use of too much false hair. The tendency to swoon, have nosebleeds and hysteria was blamed on fashion excesses, but it was not until well into the twentieth century that freedom of movement was achieved. It took the sexy and feminine 1960's to bring trousers of all kinds into full estate, and to have women of every strata wearing them in the ballroom, bedroom or on the street. Amelia's garb was modest and enveloping compared with the city pants and silhouetted Levi's of 1968. Yet it did as much to antagonize men and chill women as any aspect of the fight for freedom. Bloomers never attained the chic attached to trousers a century later, and quickly fell into disuse, but not before the costume had strengthened the picture of Amazonian women fighting their way into the world of men. The dissolution of the home and the downgrading of motherhood were freely predicted by many who saw nothing but chaos in a senseless battle between men and women.

Equality for women made headway in the West long before it did in the more sophisticated East. Because of the frontier tradition women had been more on a par with men all along. They had done manual work and had raised large families under primitive conditions. They had owned property and managed farms and mines. The western men were more disposed to listen to the views of their women, and they flocked to the lectures given by the women orators who traveled West to spread the suffrage message. The first women in the country to vote legally were in the Wyoming territory, and the year was 1869. Esther Morris, six feet tall and as craggy in appearance as Susan Anthony, invited a group of political leaders to a tea party at her home and made a businesslike appeal to them for the vote. Mrs. Morris quoted Miss Anthony, whom she had heard speak in Illinois. The message reached her small audience, and at the next territorial election the bill was passed, with some hilarity. The Governor had early memories of being impressed by women's conventions in Salem, Ohio, and he signed it promptly. Joke or no joke, it became law.

Abigail Scott Duniway dominated the fight for woman suffrage in the Northwest and wrote the suffrage proclamation for Oregon, sixty years after her arrival in that territory. She published the *New Northwest* in Portland until 1887 and traveled by river boat, sleigh and stagecoach to address meetings under the most primitive conditions. Sex played a strong part in the early victory the suffrage workers won in Utah. Polygamy had become a national issue with the Cullom Bill in 1869–70 designed to outlaw multiple marriage. The Mormons seized the opportunity to enlist the help of their women on this issue by giving them a voice in territorial affairs. But when plural marriage was revoked in 1887, one clause in the bill disenfranchised women again, and it was 1896 before they regained the vote after the Mormon Church renounced plural marriage and Utah was admitted to statehood. Its constitution provided for woman suffrage. Such women as Kate Field had fought this battle stoutly.

As small victories were registered here and there throughout the country the suffrage workers gained momentum and a measure of prestige. They could no longer be brushed off as cranks and eccentrics. Gallantry was added to vituperation as Congressmen and public speakers laced their attacks on the feminists with bursts of oratory on the time-honored functions of women. But some serious thinking was done in the home late in the nineteenth century, and wives did not always accept the dictum of their men that politics was too rowdy a field for women, an unfit setting for their gentle natures. There were times, too, when women slapped back with some of the old weapons that had been used on them. At a meeting held in Salem, Ohio, men were not allowed to speak, and if they uttered one word they were ruled out of order. The Sorosis Club pursued the same technique when its members invited the men of the New York Press Club to tea but would not let them speak. The good humor and wit, as well as the endurance of the feminists, all contributed to the ultimate capitulation. More bantering went on than the history of the suffrage movement suggests.

But the three great pioneers, Susan Anthony, Elizabeth Stanton and Lucy Stone, could neither be flattered nor cajoled into compromise. They met argument with argument, and their steady purpose and lofty principles had a profound influence on men. The pressure was withdrawn during the Civil War, but the freedom given women during this period contributed to the strong drive of the 1870's and 1880's, which ripened steadily into action. It took fifty-two years of ceaseless campaigning to remove the word "male" in effect from the Constitution. Their campaigns ran through many channels.

Nineteen were directed at as many successive Congresses. Thirty were staged to get presidential nominating conventions to include woman suffrage planks in their platforms. Forty-seven were required to stir state conventions to include woman suffrage in their constitutions. And 480 big drives were needed to persuade legislatures to submit suffrage amendments to the voters. All this represented a fabulous amount of individual effort by countless women across the country.

In New York State Mrs. Stanton argued the property rights before the Legislature with all the assurance of a trained lawyer and the added conviction of a torchbearer. A bill was finally passed that enabled women to collect and invest wages without the legal interference of their husbands, to make contracts in their own right, to sue and be sued, to have joint guardianship of their children and the same property rights as their husbands. Mrs. Stanton followed this at the Woman's Rights Convention of 1860 with resolutions on divorce, arguing that "any constitution, compact, or covenant between human beings, that failed to produce or promote human happiness, could not in the nature of things, be of any force or authority, and it would be not only a right, but a duty to abolish it."

This greatly strengthened the influence of women in the married state, but it caused less furor than the vote cast by Susan Anthony in the national election of 1872. She threw her support to Ulysses S. Grant against Horace Greeley, a choice that made Mrs. Grant her undying friend and a supporter of the suffrage cause. "Well, I have been and gone and done it!" Susan wrote jubilantly to Elizabeth Stanton. "Positively voted the Republican ticket . . . fifteen other women followed suit in this ward. Twenty or thirty other women tried to register but all save two were refused. Not a jeer, not a word, not a look disrespectful has met a single woman." It mattered not to Susan that her moment of triumph was followed by her arrest and the payment of a fine. She would not pay it, insisting that "taxation without representation is tyranny."

The first measure demanding the suffrage amendment was introduced into Congress in 1878 by A. A. Sargent of California, and it was always linked to Susan Anthony, who wrote it. Word for word it became the nineteenth amendment that was added to the Constitution forty-five years later, and it read: "The right of citizens of the United States to vote shall not be denied or abridged by the United States or by any State on account of sex." It was introduced in each succeeding Congress until it passed. In 1887 it first came to a vote in the Senate, and the women took their medicine, although a few friendly masculine voices were heard orating on their behalf. They were beginning to chip at the marble block of indifference, and repercussions were being felt in the home. Mrs. Stanton was preaching open militancy, urging women not to carpet churches or hold fairs to raise money for stained-glass windows; to let their babies go without baths, their husbands' shirts without buttons and their homes without care until the Sons of Adam gave in. Women had been too benevolent to the churches and to their men, and the time had come to attend to their own interests, said Mrs. Stanton, with an added threat in her tones: "When they find their comfort depends on allowing us the ballot, they will wheel into line and give it to us. We are going to vote, peaceably if we can, but with war if we must."

The militant spirit was readily absorbed by the suffrage pioneers, and attempts to vote were accompanied by refusal to pay taxes. "No taxation without representation," said such women as Dr. Harriot K. Hunt, an able doctor in Massachusetts who was as insistent on refusing to pay taxes as Vivian Kellems of Connecticut in the 1950's. Abby Kelly Foster's house in Worcester was sold for taxes, and Julia and Abby Smith of Glastonbury, Connecticut, fought the tax collectors for years. But the core of the battle was the vote itself, with a long parade of self-sacrificing women leaving their traces in the march of

American history. Each was remarkable for some special quality, but the dynamic partnership of Elizabeth Stanton and Susan Anthony, and the strong, scholarly persistence of Lucy Stone wore away the roadblocks, one by one. Droves of women contributed in countless ways to the ultimate effect. They represented a wide range of education, background and viewpoint. Victoria Woodhull could scarcely read or write, but by using two men as ghosts she soon had the aura of literary achievement, in addition to her authentic power on the platform. Abigail Adams bemoaned the fact that she had had no formal schooling at all, and she could not spell; yet she left a rich heritage of letters to the American people. But most of these pioneers were at least well read, and in the year of the Seneca Falls convention, the American Academy of Arts and Sciences elected to membership Maria Mitchell, the astronomer who discovered the comet bearing her name and later inspired a generation of Vassar girls to earnest contemplation of the heavens.

As time went on the leaders of the movement tried to dissociate it from the more eccentric causes that abounded in the mid-nineteenth century. Mrs. Stanton was skeptical of the bands of temperance workers, of the prayers, hymns and revivalist spirit of the 1870's. Although she approved of the temperance movement in essence, she was convinced that women could do nothing to help this or any other cause without voting power as a base. "You can never talk down or sing down or pray down an institution which is voted into existence," she observed with cool conviction. However, in her later years Mrs. Stanton became enmeshed herself in causes to which Susan Anthony did not warm.

In spite of the great power and drive of Frances Willard's temperance crusade, Miss Anthony stayed aloof from it. She admired its invincible leader but in 1896 urged Miss Willard to refrain from holding her W.C.T.U. convention in California, as planned, lest it affect the state referendum on woman suffrage. Miss Willard agreed but was constantly on guard for small snipings from the suffrage leaders. The movement had great appeal for wives, and Frances was one of the wonder women of the era. She built up a strong and flexible organization that affected the lives of the white and black people of the land. Like Billy Graham at a later time she toured the world and was an international figure. The suffrage leaders were obscure by comparison.

Miss Willard was as temperate as her contemporary Carry Nation was ferocious. Carry's saloon-smashing tactics made her one of the most discussed characters of her day, and her hatcheteering zeal had its own effect on the temperance laws. But Susan Anthony, a fighter too, found it hard to countenance Carry. There was valiant blood in Susan, and she liked consistency in others. Her family were Quakers. She was born in Adams, Massachusetts, and later moved to a farm near Rochester. Her father had run a small textile business but had failed before turning to the land. Her mother had danced on the night before Susan was born. Because of her rural upbringing she was trained in the domestic arts and could churn or orate with equal facility. Her apple tapioca pudding was well advertised by free-thinking wives intent on persuading their skeptical husbands that the vote and good cooking were not incompatible. And she was Mrs. Stanton's most skilled baby-sitter when the occasion arose.

Susan had taught, and had disliked the classroom intensely, before she met Mrs. Stanton when she was thirty-one years old. From then on she was the tall, gaunt beacon of the suffrage cause, winning a place eventually in the Hall of Fame and a memorial in the Capitol. She had risen above the abuse, the cartoons, the sticks and stones, the threatening pistol she had faced in Syracuse and the widely held opinion that she was a harridan with a nutcracker face and false teeth who dared to tell wives and mothers that they should have equal rights with their men. But impartial observers, including a great many men, in time detected the energy, intelligence and purpose that illumined her craggy face. She bore some resemblance to Lucretia Mott, who was equally inflexible in purpose and who typified the moral force of the movement.

These Quaker dames and the women from small towns and villages who rallied to the cause became used to being spat at, to having doors banged in their faces, to encountering obstacles at every turn. But they could always turn to their powerful leaders for inspiration. Susan and Elizabeth never met without issuing a pronunciamento on some question, Susan the researcher coming up with the facts and statistics, Elizabeth the philosopher molding them together and turning them into telling prose. They wrote for the *Lily*, the *Una*, the *Liberator* and the *Standard*, and urged men to remember their claims as well as those of the slaves. Although many of the suffrage workers had been ardent abolitionists, Susan held out strongly for total concentration on the one cause. The crosshatching of interests during the nineteenth century presented additional difficulties, and the ablest leaders clung to their own crusades, except where suffrage and abolition overlapped, as they constantly did. Miss Willard backed away from the antislavery issue until Lincoln signed the Emancipation Proclamation, and the educator Mary Lyon warned Lucy Stone to refrain from leaving copies of the antislavery paper, the *Liberator*, in the students' reading room.

Susan, beyond all others, suffered in the long siege for the franchise. She performed fantastic feats of physical endurance as she traveled from place to place with her leaflets and her message. Storms did not stay her as she pushed her way through snowdrifts and arrived at her destination with frostbitten feet but ready to organize on the spot. She was always where Mrs. Stanton wished her to be, the wheel horse of the movement who held local meetings, raised money, foraged for publicity and scattered leaflets and posters. Elizabeth had to stay at home with her small children, but Susan was free to roam. For twenty years they worked together and, as Mrs. Stanton recalled their association,

Whenever I saw that stately Quaker girl coming across my lawn, I knew that some happy convocation of the Sons of Adam was to be set by the ears, by one of our appeals or resolutions. The little portmanteau, stuffed with facts, was opened and there we had . . . false interpretations of Bible texts, the statistics of women robbed of their property, shut out of some college, half paid for their work, the reports of some disgraceful trial: injustice enough to turn any woman's thoughts from stockings and puddings.

The two suffragists often quarreled about religion and temperance, and Susan was appalled when Elizabeth veered down alien channels in her later years and produced *The Woman's Bible*. Both were honored when the International Council of Women met in Washington in 1888 under the auspices of the National Suffrage Association. Fifty-three countries were represented, and Susan, wearing her red shawl over a black dress, made the opening speech. This time the suffrage advocates reaped praise instead of ridicule from the press. The President received them, and Senators and Congressmen smiled affably on the women who had questioned their authority. Congressional hearings were granted and permanent national and international councils were formed. This gathering linked the suffrage workers of America with the most advanced women's groups in other lands. Clara Barton, well known around the world as founder and head of the American Chapter of the International Red Cross, was official hostess. Beyond question, she and Susan Anthony had influenced men, women and the future of the world.

The most scholarly and, in some respects, the most womanly of the suffrage workers was Lucy Stone, a tough-minded girl with the outward serenity of a saint. She neither wilted nor quailed as she stood up to savage abuse. Like Julia Ward Howe, she preserved a ladylike and reserved demeanor under all forms of attack, yet Lucy went further than any of her peers by refusing to share the name of her husband, Henry B. Blackwell. The Lucy Stone tradition of today, strong in business and professional circles, goes back to this determined New Englander. It was sharply revived in the 1920's by Doris Fleischman, the wife of Edward Bernays of advertising fame; Ruth Hale, the wife of Heywood Broun; and Jane Grant, then the wife of Harold Ross, who founded the *New Yorker*. Miss Grant later shepherded the movement along as president of the Lucy Stone League. None of the pioneers wished to travel on their husbands' passports; to sign their married names on hotel registers; to be recognized in any way with the prefix "Mrs." Today's women swing back and forth, using their maiden names professionally but sinking into happy acceptance of the benefits of their husbands' names in private life. However, a succession of divorces is apt to send them back to the name they assumed at birth.

Lucy Stone went through the most curious of marriage ceremonies with Henry Blackwell, beside a tea table in her New England home.

They joined hands and read aloud a statement protesting the inequality of the law which gave a husband control over his wife's property, person and children. The word "obey" was dropped, and both agreed that Lucy should keep her maiden name. She had asked Antoinette Brown, the first woman to have been ordained a minister in America, to officiate, but this was contrary to Massachusetts law, so the broad-minded Thomas Wentworth Higginson conducted the ceremony and paved the way for the endless army of career women who now live interchangeably by their maiden and married names. Lucy abandoned her Turkish trousers to wear ashes-of-roses silk for her wedding. Henry Blackwell considered pants on women a "monstrous invention" until he saw them on Miss Stone. Then they became a matter of common sense. There was never any doubt about which was the master voice in the Blackwell home.

Actually, Lucy Stone was one of the more engaging members of the suffrage movement. Her calm, wide-eyed face with its smooth planes and neatly coiffed dark hair carried no suggestion of turmoil or fight. But she had watched her mother suffer from bearing and nurturing too many children and had developed strong views on what women might do with their lives. "There was only one will in our house, and that was my father's," said Lucy, who grew up on a farm in western Massachusetts. Her mother had milked eight cows the night before Lucy was born because the field hands had been summoned to protect the hay from a thunderstorm, and the hay crop mattered more than a wife in labor. Lucy herself knew what it was to drive the cows barefoot through the dewy grass before sunrise, to do the family laundry and cope with every household emergency. At sixteen she was teaching to pay her way through college, and she was the first Massachusetts woman to earn a college degree. Antoinette Brown, who became her sister-in-law when she married Samuel Blackwell, was her friend at Oberlin, although she had been warned to avoid Lucy as a dangerous girl of advanced thinking.

After she married Samuel Blackwell, Antoinette played the woman's role to the hilt, when she was not preaching or spreading the suffrage message along with the gospel. Susan Anthony warned her as she did Elizabeth Stanton that she must not let the nursery slow her course in pushing woman's rights. "Now Nette, not another baby, is my peremptory command," Susan wrote chidingly to the prolific Antoinette. "Two will solve the problem," she said, "whether a woman can do anything more than be a wife and mother. I do feel that it is so foolish for her to put herself in the position of maid-of-all-work and baby tender."

But in spite of the single-minded feminist's threat, Antoinette went ahead and had six babies, losing only one in childhood. She wrote nine books, lived to be ninety-six and preached her last sermon at the age of ninety. Nor did she ever cease to work for the advancement of women. Lucy and Henry Blackwell had one child—born in 1857. Her parents gave her their joint names, Alice Stone Blackwell. She was to combine many of their qualities in her own personality and to push forward the cause of women with all the strength of her forceful nature. Lucy's last words to her daughter as she died of cancer in 1893 were, "Make the world better." Alice took up the challenge in the way she knew her mother would have approved—by working ardently for the suffrage cause. When her father, who was described as the only man who ever really devoted himself wholly to the cause of woman suffrage, died at the age of eighty-four, Alice took over the editorship of the *Woman's Journal*, which had long recorded the advances of the feminist army. Although never as famous as Lucy, she carried on the family tradition until blindness overtook her in her old age. She lived until 1950 and so was the only one among the original group to celebrate their victory in 1920.

Lucy Stone's career had been meteoric and somehow different from those of all her colleagues. Her judgment and steady purpose kept her from making some of the impulsive mistakes of less disciplined enthusiasts. Her melodic voice was extraordinarily persuasive on the platform, and her arguments were clear-cut and decisive. Although she knew how to paint a house, milk a cow, make choice preserves, dry her own beef and make candles, her great contribution to the woman's cause was her honeyed eloquence on the platform. Under all circumstances she had the bearing of what was once euphemistically known as a lady. Both she and Julia Ward Howe were careful to preserve this image. They kept themselves aloof from the crackpot characters and in a sense were the snobs of the movement.

Oddly enough, Lucy would have nothing to do with trade unionism, and she avoided such side issues as divorce or the social evils exploited by some of her colleagues. The proprieties were also strictly observed by Mrs. Howe, who was upset by Mrs. Stanton's frank handling of birth control and infanticide. She did not feel that these were subjects fit for public discussion by civilized people. Sophisticated and advanced though she was, Mrs. Howe lagged behind many of the sisterhood in shaking off the Victorian shackles, and it pained her to know that Dr. Elizabeth Blackwell was giving sex talks in a New York chapel. Nevertheless, Julia formed a valuable bridge between the feminists and the nation's women as a whole. The breach was wide until the close of the nineteenth century, when the zealots modified their ways and proceeded with more decorum. After the high-flying tactics of such women as Victoria Woodhull and Frances Wright, they gave some thought to their influence with men, some of whom were beginning to view them with respect and even to listen to their arguments.

Their status had improved with party organization. The National Woman Suffrage Association, started by Elizabeth Stanton and Susan Anthony in 1869, worked aggressively, cutting across party lines in order to back the suffrage interests. Its object was to achieve a federal amendment, and its organizers swung their ablest lieutenants into the game of lobbying. In the same year the American Woman Suffrage Association was founded, specifically to work for the vote in state after state. After years of rivalry the two organizations merged in 1890 to become the National American Woman Suffrage Association.

All was not smooth sailing when the two organizations functioned separately. Victoria Woodhull, who had charmed Congress in 1871 with her shapely figure and her plea for women's rights, tried to take over the National Woman Suffrage Association to further her own political aspirations. She was neatly foiled by Susan Anthony, who had considered her an asset to the cause until she became notorious. When Victoria tried to have the National Equal Rights Party, with its motley membership of Communists, spiritualists, free thinkers and suffragists, convene jointly with Susan's organization in Steinway Hall, Miss Anthony rejected the idea. Vicky then cheerfully swung her followers over to Apollo Hall, where her own nomination for President took place. She had done much to publicize the suffrage movement, if she had not added to its prestige. Men took notice, since she and her sister, Tennessee Claflin, were known as the lady brokers of Wall Street who had Cornelius Vanderbilt and other financiers eating out of their hands.

But aside from the more sensational aspects of the endless campaign, work was diligently pursued across the nation. The leaflets, magazines and oratory reaching the homes of America were slowly influencing the most laggardly of women, and many men. The Civil War had opened the eyes of many to woman's capacities outside the home. The wide sweep of industrial activity had brought them into the working world. They had become more articulate and demanding. The wine of independence was potent, and they found the experience exhilarating. Their pay was negligible, but they grasped at the chance for freedom. As workers they thought more frequently and concretely about their rights. Women could scarcely close their ears to the constant barrage of oratory that reached them from the largest halls in New York and Boston to barns and small frame churches across the land.

The spread of clubs, such as the Sorosis in New York, the New England Woman's Club in Boston, the Fortnightly in Chicago and the Century Club in San Francisco, touched their social instincts and whipped up community interests. By 1890 there were enough well-established clubs to form the General Federation of Women's Clubs, which by the 1960's was an international body with membership in fifty countries. In the United States alone 15,500 clubs with nearly a million members represented a mighty show of feminine power by that time.

Three expositions gave their work a showcase, and Susan rained broadsides on the Centennial of 1876 in Philadelphia. She led five women to the platform on Independence Day and handed Senator Thomas W. Ferry a declaration of her own while the guest of honor, the Emperor of Brazil, looked on in amazement. The pickets and placards of 1968 were for love, love, love—and peace. The pickets and placards of 1876 were for votes. But so accustomed had the public become to the troublesome suffragists that the Woman's Declaration of 1876 went almost unheeded. A greater fuss was made about Mrs. Howe's more womanly presentation at the World's Fair of 1883–84 in New Orleans. With her daughter Maud she ran the woman's department and had to arbitrate the question of whether the work of women should be shown separately or in the general exhibits of their states. Carpenters from two United States warships in the harbor built an all-woman's gallery, partitioned off in brightly decorated alcoves. Julia was particularly proud of a heavy iron chain made by a woman blacksmith and fine jewelry fashioned by women. The black people had their own art gallery on this occasion, and they all sang Julia's "Battle Hymn of the Republic."

But a sharp change in viewpoint dated from the Columbian Exposition held in Chicago in 1893, with Mrs. Potter Palmer in supreme command of the Woman's Building and the suffrage organizations in full flower. It had now become fashionable as well as tactful to speak up for women's rights, and everything from Mary Cassatt's mural in the Woman's Building to Saint-Gaudens' Diana, of Madison Square Garden fame, proclaimed the new femininity. There had been some hesitancy about installing the winged goddess on Mrs. Palmer's building lest the country visitors find it shocking. "What nonsense!" said Chicago's distinguished hostess and champion of women's rights. But caution prevailed, and in the end it adorned the Agriculture Building.

Without benefit of vote, Mrs. Palmer helped notably to fill the coffers of the fair and bewitch the celebrities who came to the White City on Lake Michigan. It was a fruitful but not altogether happy time for the suffragists, who spread their message widely from the Woman's Building, fighting sundry battles along the way and not always worshiping at the shrine of Mrs. Palmer, the golden goddess. The party stalwarts were not too pleased to see society stepping into their Spartan field and snatching some of the glory.

This, too, was the year in which Lucy Stone died, shortly after she, Elizabeth Stanton and Susan Anthony were greeted with storms of applause at the meeting of the National American Woman Suffrage Association in Washington. Elizabeth retired after that but continued to lecture and write. In 1902, at the age of eighty-seven, she wrote to President Theodore Roosevelt urging him to immortalize himself by effecting the complete emancipation of his countrywomen. Her work was done. Next day she died in her chair. Antoinette Brown Blackwell, Phoebe Hanaford and Moncure D. Conway conducted her funeral services. "I am too crushed to speak," said Susan. "If I had died first she would have found beautiful phrases to describe our friendship, but I cannot put it into words."

Together they had stirred up a social revolution that is close to total fulfillment today.

Chapter 8

The Hard Road

Women's rights, a shifting goal depending on the eye of the beholder, became a fashionable cause just as Queen Victoria's reign came to an end. By the beginning of the twentieth century the suffrage drive was shaking off the blight of social disapproval and was picking up style. Mrs. Potter Palmer had set the stage at the Columbian Exposition in Chicago. Mrs. J. Borden Harriman gave it impetus in New York when she led a suffrage parade up Fifth Avenue. Smart young matrons and aging dowagers, with large fortunes at their command, were swinging into line. Colleges were a live recruiting ground. The freshly minted interest in sports, the drift to the arts, the growing sophistication of women, all gave pizzazz to a Spartan cause.

Fashionable mothers corralled young men with petitions for them to sign and tickets to buy. Their daughters were sneaky allies as this game was played. The bright creatures in the home had begun to score a point or two. The Gibson Girl had the look of one who might be trusted at the polls. With the *beau monde* swiveling in this direction the satirists of *Life, Judge* and *Harper's* gave a merry twist to their cartoons. They pictured the vote-hungry girls invading men's sacred retreats; bathing with them at Newport; demanding money for clothes and trips to Europe; cutting off their view of the stage with monster hats; hogging Delmonico's; even beating them at tennis. Somehow the movement lost the grim touch it had had in the nineteenth century. Girls in society lacked little but the vote at this time. They were part of an opulent era, and their curvaceous forms were enfolded in lace, feathers, silken petticoats and jeweled stockings. Quite often their men were gourmets with yachts and country estates, shooting boxes in Scotland and villas on the Riviera. Calisthenics and barbells were cutting into the picture, and Mrs. Frank Leslie did her exercises regularly to keep her sixteen-inch waist in trim. However, slim women got no encouragement from their men, who prized the bounteous armful of the 1890's. The age of Twiggy had not yet arrived.

But conservatives still argued that no nice woman would go to the polls and vote. They thought it unwomanly to fight for their "rights," or even to talk about these shadowy ghosts. John Hay's daughter, Mrs. James Wadsworth, was president of the National Society Opposed to Woman Suffrage, and she had Mrs. William Howard Taft and Mrs. Elihu Root on her side. When Mr. Taft (whose mother and aunt, Louise and Delia Torrey, had been taken captive early in life by the feminist pioneers), agreed to lecture against suffrage at the Cosmopolitan Club in New York, Katrina Ely Tiffany, an old family friend, was horrified. "You, the most logical and honest-minded of men!" she protested, signing herself "Your dumb-founded admirer."

Mrs. Root warned Mr. Taft that the mere sight of the committee of suffragettes who were going to present him with a petition would make him run or look the other way. He wrote back blandly that while he thought better of her sex's capacity for government than she did, he would wait until the "best women and all the women" had agreed that they ought to have the ballot.

The issue became acute when Woodrow Wilson decided to haul down the flag of resistance, a piece of news that seemed to interlock with the startling announcement that he was about to marry Mrs. Galt. Another four years would pass, however, and pickets would storm the White House and be hauled off to jail before either man capitulated completely to the suffrage forces. Mr. Taft was finally won over by the evidence he gathered on his travels that women stood for peace and had the best right in the world to an equal voice in efforts to prevent war.

The old image of the suffrage harridan conjured up by Mrs. Root lost ground in the twentieth century with such gifted beauties as Inez Milholland, Doris Stevens and Edna St. Vincent Millay waving their banners. The *grandes dames* of the period were already in full action, and among them was Mrs. Christopher Temple Emmet, ninety-five years old in 1968. She had much to look back on from the time she made her debut in 1892 at the ball of the original Four Hundred given by her great-aunt Mrs. William B. Astor. Elida Emmet was a poet as well as a suffragist, and two of her books were published while she was busy campaigning for the vote between 1907 and 1918.

In the West Mrs. Leland Stanford and Mrs. William Randolph Hearst gave powerful financial support to the suffrage cause, and in the East Mrs. J. Borden Harriman, Mrs. O. H. P. Belmont, Miss Anne Morgan, Mrs. Henry Morgenthau, Mrs. Norman Whitehouse, Mrs. Frank Vanderlip, Mrs. James Lees Laidlaw, Mrs. Ogden Reid and many others worked effectively for emancipation. Before she died in 1967 at the age of ninety-seven Daisy Harriman said, "I am not a militant. I always regretted the picketing," but she did it with considerable verve at the time. In 1917 she marched past the White House with a delegation from New York led by Mrs. Whitehouse, but she wrenched a banner inscribed "Kaiser Wilson" from an overzealous marcher who had raised it. She had supported Woodrow Wilson for the Presidency and he had named her the only woman member of the Federal Industrial Relations Commission.

Daisy Harriman, born Florence Jaffray Hurst, was an early crusader for social rights, and her interests took her into politics, diplomacy and the battles of the day. The social conscience stirred early in this child of wealth who had been brought up severely. Her mother died when she was three, and her father, Francis W. J. Hurst, a retired British army officer, had her riding when she was three and swimming at four. She attended her first school in J. P. Morgan's house along with Juliet and Anne Morgan. Clara Spence was their elocution teacher. The family fortune came from railroads, and Daisy early in life was hunting with the Meadowbrook Hounds and sailing on the favored yachts. She attended her first ball at Delmonico's in 1888 and was nineteen when she married Harriman. A tall girl with proud bearing and bright blue eyes, she was restless and ambitious, and soon after her marriage she plunged into social service.

Political blood ran in her veins. Her grandfather, Edward S. Jaffray, had proposed the electoral commission that settled the Hayes-Tilden dispute over which candidate had won the Presidency. When she became involved in labor relations she toured the country with her fellow commissioners and argued it out with labor representatives. They went from city to city, concentrating on special strike areas, tracing the history of the I.W.W., investigating the world of the child worker and talking to mine owners, bishops, settlement workers and blacksmiths. Mrs. Harriman surveyed the results of the tent-colony fire at Ludlow in 1914 and in the same year took soundings on the Colorado strike.

Anne Morgan and Daisy Harriman were soon committed to poking into all manner of labor abuses, as seen through the plutocratic tele-scope. Daisy campaigned against child labor and for certified milk. Charles Evans Hughes named her manager of the New York State Reformatory for Women in Bedford. When World War I broke out Samuel Gompers made her chairman of the Women in Industry Committee of the A.F. of L. Henry P. Davison sent her to France in charge of the Red Cross Motor Corps. She toured munitions plants and hospitals in France and England, reporting back on conditions to Gompers. She visited Lady Astor at Cliveden, and entertained in Paris at the time of the Peace Conference. She was back in the French capital for the signing of the Peace Treaty and watched the scene in the Hall of Mirrors. Guns were fired, fountains played, air-planes buzzed overhead—it all seemed to Daisy like the "jeweled palace in the fairy tales."

As Minister to Norway she directed delicate negotiations when Germany was exerting pressure on Norway to stay neutral. But gut-tural voices on the telephone and motorcyles racing through the streets informed her one morning in 1940 that her cause was lost. She got through to the American Legation in Stockholm, thereby notifying the world that the Nazis had invaded Norway. With the American flag covering the top of her car, she followed the fleeing Norwegian government over slippery roads already half blocked with Nazi machine guns. She crossed into Sweden with Crown Princess Martha and her children. It had taken her four days to reach the Swedish border, dodging German bombers along the way by hiding in the woods. She was then sixty-nine years old and a grandmother. From Stockholm she helped to evacuate American citizens from Norway, and eventually she returned home on an American warship with the Princess and her children. Mrs. Harriman journeyed to Oslo in 1947 to be decorated by the King. In 1963 President Kennedy chose her as the first person to receive the Citation of Merit for Distinguished Service.

Always an enthusiastic worker for the Democratic Party, she founded the Women's National Democratic Club as well as the Colony Club in New York, the latter a joint venture with Miss Anne Morgan. She was national committeewoman for the District of Columbia for years, and was one of the powerful women of her generation who helped to create a strong image abroad of the dominant American matron.

The suffrage drive in the first two decades of the twentieth century was threefold, involving the hard-core professional workers, the affluent society women who backed them up, and the academic community. The growth of women's colleges and of increased educational opportunities drove the movement forward like an irresistible tide. The great pioneers and the fantastic lengths they went to in reaching for their goal faded into a more assured picture of women at last convinced that they were close to victory. With Virginia Gildersleeve at Barnard College, Mary E. Woolley at Mount Holyoke and M. Carey Thomas at Bryn Mawr, the college drive was strong. When Miss Thomas went to Germany in 1879 to work for her doctorate she was regarded as a disgrace to her conservative family and her name was rarely mentioned.

Incensed by this fallacious reasoning she rounded up the suffrage groups from the college campuses of fifteen states in 1908 to form the National College Women's Equal Suffrage League. Faculty members from Barnard, Bryn Mawr, Radcliffe, Smith, Mount Holyoke and the Universities of Wisconsin, California and Chicago teamed up and heard Miss Thomas say: "Women are one-half of the world, but until a century ago women lived a twilight female half life apart, but looked out and saw men as shadows walking. It was a man's world. The laws were men's laws, the government a man's government, the country a man's country."

From 1894 to 1922 Miss Thomas was a significant force on the educational horizon, emphasizing academic excellence and high purpose in life. She lectured on suffrage at every opportunity, often taking Helen Manning, the daughter of William Howard Taft, along with her. Miss Thomas influenced the outlook of a great many young women who passed through Bryn Mawr, which was founded in 1885 by a group of Quakers. Not the least of Carey Thomas' graduates was her niece, Millicent Thomas, who in course of time became Mrs. Rustin McIntosh, headmistress of the Brearley School and later president of Barnard College. Brilliant though she was, she was not wholly in the Bryn Mawr blue-stocking tradition. As the mother of five children, including twins, she was equally adept at Greek translation, chamber music or baby care, and she preserved the feminine image under all circumstances. Mrs. McIntosh was no Lucy Stoner and retired at the height of her career because the time had come for her husband, a noted pediatrician, to retire. She preferred not to be called Dr. McIntosh, although she had a right to be. In her estimation there was only one doctor in the family, and that was Dr. Rustin McIntosh. But she was always impressive to men of affairs, many of whose daughters she had helped to educate.

The college leader who influenced politics, as well as men, was Virginia Gildersleeve, Dean of Barnard from 1911 until her retirement in 1947 and, after that, dean emeritus. She was sympathetic to the suffrage cause, which gave some of her students' mothers deep concern. One approached her to beg the Dean to keep the students from marching in a suffrage parade. This particular parent said that it would be a shameful thing for them to do and would damage the reputation of the college. But a few years later the Barnard unit of the Women's Land Army marched in a great war parade on Fifth

Avenue, wearing breeches and being heartily applauded. Freda Kirch-wey, later editor of the *Nation*, startled the students and professors by arriving at Barnard bareheaded. This kind of far-out behavior was compounded in 1951 when the students appeared barefooted for their annual spring festival, the Greek Games.

Dean Gildersleeve was called on to assemble at Barnard the repre-sentatives of fifteen women's colleges and coeducational universities to organize the Women's Army and Navy Reserve during World War II. Mildred McAfee, president of Wellesley, was selected to head the Waves. The Dean of Barnard took a review herself at Hunter College. She had studied the Wrens and Wafs in Britain and had been received by the Queen. Eighty per cent of the American student body engaged in war work of one kind or another.

Because of the war Dean Gildersleeve became involved in politics. She attacked isolationists and concentrated on international coopera-tion among the university women of the world. The British govern-ment invited her to fly to England in 1943 to see and hear what was happening there. President Roosevelt chose her in the following year to serve as a member of the American delegation at the International Conference held in San Francisco, where the United Nations Char-ter took shape. She argued with Senator Arthur Vandenberg to have the word "education" included in the Charter as one of the areas of international cooperation. He was against it, but the Dean stood her ground until he finally said, "Oh, have it your own way, Dean; put in education or anything you want."

When chosen to run the committee meeting that shaped the scope of the Economic and Social Council Dean Gildersleeve functioned as if she were presiding at a faculty gathering, with an imposing bat-talion of advisers and experts. She later commented: "I thought how disappointed all these men must be to have a lone woman speaking for them in the councils of the world, and I tried to cheer them a bit." She was surprised to find women delegates at San Francisco voicing the old militant feminism that she thought had become passé. "There was really not very much for the militant feminists to do," she remarked. "The position of women so far as the Charter was concerned was definitely established by the words which occur often in various articles. Human rights and fundamental freedoms for all, without distinction as to race, sex, language or religion."

Dean Gildersleeve was the only woman at the banquet given by the Secretary of State in San Francisco for President Truman, who led her into the room. In 1946 she and Mildred McAfee Horton visited Guam, Pearl Harbor, Tokyo and other points as the guests of General Douglas MacArthur and the Japanese Ministry of Education. While becoming an internationally known figure Dean Gildersleeve worked steadily to raise the standards at Barnard. She was thirty-three when she became dean, and she remembered that as a student there some years earlier she had been shy and snobbish. Her childhood had had Victorian flavor. She sprang from a family of dissenters who had come to America from East Anglia in 1635. Her father was a judge, and she attended the Brearley School before attending Barnard. As dean she inherited the tradition set by Jacob H. Schiff, who was treasurer when the college was organized but pulled out because he had no faith in its future. "You can't force a woman's college down the throats of the people of New York City," he said. "They don't want it, and they won't support it."

But the Dean had three vigorous and progressive women from the world of journalism on her board of trustees—Mrs. Arthur Hays Sulzberger, Mrs. Ogden Reid and Mrs. Eugene Meyer. They backed her in her efforts to have women admitted to the medical, law, engineering, architectural and business schools of Columbia. After Pearl Harbor many of the girls took engineering courses, and they were soon given full status. Romances flourished on the campus, but they did not involve the serious disciplinary problem the incoming President, Miss Martha Peterson, faced in 1968. When Linda Le-Clair told the world she was sharing an off-campus apartment with a Columbia student, she set a precedent for a women's college and touched off an explosion at a stormy moment in the university's history. Miss Peterson was forced to concede her right to remain.

Dean Gildersleeve had seen it coming. She said in her later years that women were worse off than thirty or forty years earlier. "Professionally and emotionally they are not going onward and upward," she said. "I attribute this partly to over-emphasis on sex. It tends to make women interested only in getting married." While she was dean it was her practice to advise her seniors to give up all thought of careers for five or ten years after marriage in order to have children and get them started in school. But she expected them to work usefully beyond the boundaries of their homes. Although she herself never married, her life was an extraordinarily full one. She lived to be eighty-seven and she wrote, lectured and was a public figure for more than half a century. She was twice president of the International Federation of University Women and for more than thirty years was president of the board of trustees of the American College for Girls in Istanbul, later Robert College.

Both Carey Thomas and Virginia Gildersleeve were carrying on a tradition fostered by such women as Emma Willard, Mary Lyon, Catharine Beecher and other pioneers in education. If Anne Hutchinson beat the timbrels and Abigail lit the way, it was in the nineteenth century that the drive for emancipation and education waxed strong. All the amateur interests, the dilettantish courses in painting, music and dancing, the reading circles and lyceum lectures tightened into more concentrated education as the colleges opened up. Mount Holyoke was founded as a seminary in 1837 and became a college in 1888. Vassar stirred up excitement in 1861. Smith was founded in 1871 and the Society for the College Instruction of Women in 1882, three years after the first class for women was held at Harvard. Bryn Mawr got under way in 1885 and Radcliffe in 1893. Smith was endowed by a Massachusetts woman, Sophia Smith, and when Jennie June visited it in the early 1880's she decided it was the only women's college where "women were treated as rationally as men and were allowed the same freedom." It was neither a nursery nor a nunnery.

By degrees some of the larger universities became coeducational—Boston University and Swarthmore in 1869, Cornell in 1874. Yale was responsive to the idea in 1968, but when Vassar decided to stick to its own famous campus instead of transferring to New Haven, the step was delayed, but women were accepted by Yale for 1969. Wesleyan University admitted women undergraduates in 1968 in order to become a "more realistic reflection of the larger society," and Princeton for the first time granted professional tenure to a woman professor and became coeducational in 1969. Oberlin, founded in 1833, was the first to open its door to all, regardless of race, color or sex. And all of the colleges were admitting more black women by the late 1960's. Only thirty had received college degrees by 1890. There were hundreds in 1968.

It was not until after the Civil War that girls made any headway in getting into secondary schools, but the opening of academies and seminaries in New York, Boston, Philadelphia and other cities paved the way for the college era, and contributed substantially to the final drive for suffrage in the twentieth century. Carrie Chapman Catt, a farm girl from Wisconsin who studied law and taught in a high school, brought the long campaign to fruition. She gave thirty-three years of her life to suffrage and built up an organization of two million women. The picturesque and flamboyant attributes of her predecessors were missing from Mrs. Catt's professional way of doing things.

She picked up the suffrage torch from Lucy Stone, inspired by the speeches she had heard her make at conventions. Leo Chapman, the Iowa editor to whom she was married, trained her in editorial and printing techniques. After his death she lectured on suffrage and great women in history. When the two wings of the suffrage movement joined forces in 1890 and she made her first appearance among the tough-minded reformers, she observed tall, angular Alice Stone Blackwell, the portly and eloquent Dr. Anna Howard Shaw and the practical Mary Garrett Hay of Indiana. Mrs. Stanton was stepping down, and a new leader was needed. Susan Anthony welcomed Mrs. Catt into the suffrage establishment as a "constructive genius of the first order" when Mrs. Catt was chosen at the national suffrage convention to succeed her. Four years earlier Mrs. Catt had made her presence felt at the Democratic convention remembered best because of William Jennings Bryan's Cross of Gold speech. She demanded a suffrage plank in the party platform then, but without success, for Bryan would not endorse it. When ill health caused Mrs. Catt to give up her leadership after four years she went to work building up the International Woman Suffrage Alliance. She toured the world just before World War I and everywhere she went she found women restless or in revolt.

After the death of Mrs. Catt's second husband, George Catt, she settled in New York and worked with Miss Hay along parliamentary lines. Mrs. O. H. P. Belmont had become a spectacular suffrage worker, but she and Dr. Shaw were at loggerheads. Through this feuding and fussing, Mrs. Catt went smoothly on her way, the stateswoman of the movement, although she was not beloved like Miss Anthony and Mrs. Stanton. The old professionals were disposed to underrate their society colleagues who had come recently into the field with dash and diamonds.

In 1915 Mrs. Catt directed the campaign for the first New York referendum on woman suffrage, staging a lively campaign with torchlight parades, soapbox oratory, county fairs, night meetings in war plants and a great parade up Fifth Avenue, with five thousand school teachers carrying blackboards inscribed with slogans. Long skirts, cartwheel hats, clumsy boots did not stay their course, and great camaraderie between rich and poor distinguished this unique parade. Since the Social Register was so strikingly represented alongside the factory girls, businessmen took note and began to view the movement more seriously. Headquarters were opened in Washington, and Mrs. Leslie's jewels were displayed; in fact, in a jocular moment Mrs. Catt was crowned with one of her tiaras. By this time the Leslie inheritance was financing the *Woman's Journal*, edited by Alice Stone Blackwell, as well as paying for promotion and educational work. When America entered the war Mrs. Catt and Dr. Shaw were appointed to the Council for National Defense. Although a pacifist and disapproving of the war Mrs. Catt took the stand that it had to be fought. She put suffrage first and war second.

Alice Paul, who headed a separate and more militant body, the National Woman's Party, was quite different from Carrie Chapman Catt. Miss Paul brought fire and brimstone into the suffrage movement and quickened the pace all round. She was antiwar, except for her own, but she fought fiercely for suffrage. A delicate figure with hazel eyes, shadowy hair and a melodic voice, she was a Quaker with a degree from Swarthmore. Before she cut loose in America she had been arrested in Britain and had gone on hunger strikes there. As a settlement worker in London she had worked with the Pankhurst forces. Her style was not Mrs. Catt's, but each contributed in her own way to the ultimate victory.

Miss Paul had a picturesque following, including Mary Beard and Crystal Eastman, Inez Milholland and Doris Stevens among her many other spirited disciples. Mrs. Milholland was a beauty who had ridden a white horse in the great suffrage demonstration of 1913 just before Woodrow Wilson's inauguration. Troops had been called out to preserve order as the parade started from the Capitol and passed the White House through the crowds assembling for next day's inauguration. When Woodrow Wilson asked where all the people were as he drove from the station through empty streets he was told, "Over on the Avenue watching the suffrage parade."

Alice's army never looked drab. Her followers wore purple and white with gold surplices, and across the country she organized small, active groups with plenty of dash. When the Suffrage Special set out from Washington on a tour of twelve states, buglers sounded the farewell and a crowd of five thousand gathered at Union Station to see them off. Decorations floated from the train windows as they traveled west, and even the Sons of Adam saw that a fresh and powerful force was loose among them. "Here come the Suffragettes!" people shouted as the train pulled in. Alice's legions sang their campaign songs, "The March of the Women" and "The Song of the Free Women." They were bright, noisy and defiant, with Miss Paul, tough-spirited, moving delicately among them. Mrs. Stanton's daughter, Harriot Stanton Blatch, was one of Alice's allies. She had come over from England to help.

This junket of the suffrage special made the entire country aware of the Woman's Party, and after it they moved to larger quarters and proceeded to plague Woodrow Wilson and to lobby at the Capitol. While Mrs. Catt worked in a quiet, orderly fashion, disapproving of their flamboyant tactics, Miss Paul stirred up a whirlwind. Envoys elected at a convention in Salt Lake City during the cross-country tour brought their resolutions to Washington, where Miss Paul staged a pageant for them at the Capitol. They marched up the steps through an aisle of girls wearing the party colors and linked together with ribbons.

When Theodore Roosevelt at last succumbed to their wiles they went to the Progressive Convention in 1916, and the delegates gratefully endorsed woman suffrage. For the first time the Democrats and Republicans chose to introduce woman suffrage in their party planks. Although Miss Paul tried all her powers of persuasion on Charles Evans Hughes, he failed to mention their cause when he was nominated for the Presidency. But he, too, finally came around, and Wilson, addressing his first suffrage meeting that year—1916— boosted their spirits by saying that the "war in Europe has forever set at rest the notion that nations depend in time of stress wholly upon their men." But when nothing happened, they adopted a new slogan "He kept us out of Suffrage" to match the popular jingle "He kept us out of War."

Members of the National Woman's Party began to picket the White House in January, 1917, and continued for a year and a half. More than a thousand women took turns flaunting their purple, white and gold banners at the White House gates or in front of the Capitol. It was done with imagination. Various states celebrated their own special day on the picket line. Labor had its day, and so did office and factory workers. Susan Anthony's birthday was celebrated in rain and snow. On Inauguration Day a thousand pickets circled the White House to band music. Vida Milholland, Inez's sister, headed the line with a gold banner bearing her sister's last words for suffrage: "Mr. President, how long must women wait for liberty?"

Inez had died in 1916, presumably worn out from campaigning in the Western states. Miss Paul shook up Congress by insisting on a memorial service for her in Statuary Hall at the Capitol. Early in 1917 arrests began. The pickets had become disorderly as they hid banners under their sweaters, hats and skirts, and fought in the streets. Alice was carted off to jail, and immediately new followers joined the picket line. "Resistance to Tyranny is obedience to God," said their banners. The suffrage prisoners all went on a hunger strike. Alice was forcibly fed and was finally moved to the psychiatric ward of a hospital, where she was treated as a maniac.

By 1919 President Wilson had a "perpetual delegation" of twelve women in purple, white and gold at the West Gate and six at the East Gate of the White House. They made a point of burning his written words, and finally they set fire to an effigy of the President himself. They staged a demonstration in Boston when he returned from the Peace Conference. When he spoke at the Metropolitan Opera House in New York before returning to France Miss Paul staged a demonstration with disastrous results. The pickets were clubbed and she and Doris Stevens were thrown into jail for disorderly conduct.

But state by state the returns were coming in, and Mrs. Catt gave President Wilson credit for ensuring the last vote needed, while he was still in France. On May 21, 1919, the House passed the nineteenth amendment by a majority of 304 to 90. The Senate passed it 66 to 30, and it was proclaimed on August 26, 1920. The long hard fight was over, and the honors were even. After signing the official proclamation Secretary of State Bainbridge Colby invited Mrs. Catt to the State Department to see it. True to form, she showed no excitement. Governor Smith greeted her on her return to New York, and an army band played "Hail the Conquering Hero Comes." She led a suffrage parade up Fifth Avenue—the last.

Miss Paul's nuisance tactics, her boundless persistence, her vivid campaigning had helped to beat down resistance. When the fight was won neither she nor Mrs. Catt sought office, however, and in England it was not Mrs. Pankhurst, the master strategist, who took the first seat in the House of Commons but Lady Astor from Virginia. When she visited America in 1923 Lady Astor said: "It is a strange thing that England's first woman Member of Parliament should have come from England's first colony. . . . I can conceive of nothing worse than a man-governed world except a woman-governed world. I feel men have a greater sense of justice, and we of mercy. They must borrow our mercy and we must use their justice. We realize that no one sex can govern alone."

🕊 **Chapter 9**

The Feminine Establishment

🕊 American women have by no means scaled the heights politically. They have shown their particular genius in the working world, where they have been highly successful, productive and attractive. In philanthropy and social service they make up a mighty army. They are soundly based in the professions and are an indispensable factor in the business world. They are well represented in all the arts, although few rank among the greats. But in politics they have shared less in high office than the women of Britain or even of tiny Finland. They have failed to show effective leadership and have had to win most of their battles by indirection.

In practical terms it is evident that they have not succeeded in steering the ship of state along a better course, nor are they yet enough a part of government to win or defeat a major cause, except perhaps by the traditional use of the vote. No woman has come within sight of the Presidency. The Cabinet, the Supreme Court and the top-echelon jobs in government elude them, with few exceptions. The two women who have held Cabinet rank did not seek the honor. It came to them chiefly as a sop to the women voters. Neither ever seemed completely at ease in office although both were credited grudgingly with doing effective work. Will today's young, telling their elders, both men and women, that the older generation has failed, do better? Will the daughters of the atomic age build effectively on the foundations laid by the pioneers?

America's first woman Cabinet member passed muster creditably although she had one of the most difficult portfolios in the most troubled of times. When Franklin D. Roosevelt appointed Frances Perkins his Secretary of Labor in 1933 the world came to know the stern-faced lady in the tricorne hat who had to stand up to John L. Lewis through the steel strikes and the first sit-in strikes. But neither threats nor leers dismayed low-voiced Madam Perkins, and she held the post longer than anyone who came before or after her.

Dark-haired, prim-looking, she kept sewing needles and thread in a drawer next to presidential memoranda. She was said to be a colorless woman who talked as if she had swallowed a press release. Her failure to establish spontaneous relations with the press did not help her image across the country, but her thoughts were focused first on the business of the day and not on the fact that she was a woman doing what was considered strictly a man's job. She was the wife of Paul Caldwell Wilson, a financial statistician who died in 1952, but she chose to use her maiden name in the Lucy Stone fashion and preferred to be known as Madam Perkins.

No one disputed her qualifications for the post she held, but she was never popular and she took massive punishment, sometimes even from the President, who leaned heavily on her judgment in labor issues. She already had a long record in the labor field and had worked harmoniously with Governor Alfred E. Smith in New York State. After graduation from Mount Holyoke she taught, then did social service work at Hull House. The Triangle shirtwaist fire in New York in 1911 that took the lives of 145 workers brought her into the labor field, and she headed Governor Smith's State Industrial Board and was appointed State Industrial Commissioner by Governor Franklin Roosevelt, steppingstones to her Cabinet post.

The unemployment score was fifteen million when she took office, and industry was practically at a standstill. She stood her ground through the Depression and World War II—a period of fierce infighting in the labor ranks as Lewis shaped the C.I.O. Both labor and industry recognized her as a tough executive who had pushed through a fifty-four-hour work week for women in industry in the state legislature and worked for wider objectives on the national level. She became a major factor in planning Social Security and unemployment insurance, and she helped to enlarge the scope of the public-works program. Her constant drive was to get management, labor, economists and engineers working with the government. For twelve tempestuous years Madam Perkins was a front-page figure, pictured at times as being "befuddled, rattlebrained, unreliable and in awe of John L. Lewis," who indeed became more awesome by the month during her term of office.

Madam Perkins was a quiet woman, although a determined one. She did not believe in talking unless she had something specific to say. At her first Cabinet meeting President Roosevelt drew her out as she sat silent after a spate of talk from her colleagues. Her statement was brief. In a low voice she told them that she had already called a conference of labor leaders and expected to draft recommendations for the relief of unemployment with a program of public works as the first step.

Although unmercifully assailed in the outside world, Madam Perkins was treated as an equal in the Cabinet. "As far as Roosevelt was concerned, I was one of the team," she later wrote. "There was no special deference beyond the ordinary daily amenities, because I was a woman. Nor was there any suggestion of a patronizing note." She found the President a "firm, supporting friend" in times of crisis, although he knew that she had to be the spearhead. On her first appearance before a committee of Congress he asked if she minded having Mrs. Roosevelt attend. He wanted to get Eleanor's reaction to her performance and to fortify her with his wife's support.

Hugh Johnson, the fiery chief of N.R.A., thought her the "best man in the Cabinet" as she helped him fight some of his battles with his colleagues. On more than one occasion she threw her weight to force him to go along with the President's wishes. When Harold Ickes was chosen to run the public-works program Johnson balked. Madam Perkins hustled him out a side door of the White House and away from the press, drove him to the Tidal Basin and reasoned with him to be a good soldier and cooperate with the harassed President. He finally agreed, and a crisis was averted, but there were times when Madam Perkins expected the N.R.A. to blow up from internal combustion.

She found that the sit-down strikes, which began in Akron in 1935 and spread like wildfire, bewildered the President. To her they seemed unwise and demoralizing, and she frequently sought advice from such men as Averell Harriman, Walter Teagle of Standard Oil, Myron Taylor of United States Steel and Gerard Swope of General Electric when the problem was to get employers to start collective bargaining. A memorable crisis in her career was the day she brought some of the steel magnates face to face with William Green, of the A.F. of L. When they backed away from the labor leader Madam Perkins, a correctly brought up New Englander, described it as the most embarrassing social experience of her life. On their way out she scolded them like the school teacher she was originally, telling her millionaire consultants that they had acted like eleven-year-old boys at their first party rather than as men running the most important industry in the country.

Madam Perkins made a point of visiting the homes of the steel-workers as well as the plants. She found that President Roosevelt had little interest in the internal politics of the labor unions, although he considered the rivalry between the C.I.O. and the A.F. of L. stimulating. It seemed to her that he was not a good negotiator in a labor dispute because he was too imaginative and in too much of a hurry. His concern was not for the economics of a situation but for improvement in peoples' lives. He would always ask Madam Perkins to give him the human part of the story—how workers absorbed silicone while polishing dials on clock faces; how girls got radium poisoning by pointing fine brushes with their lips. "He used us all as eyes and ears," she commented. "He wanted to see the country through our eyes. He liked to get vivid descriptions of places, people, events—not long-drawn-out encyclopedic reports, but the high spots."

Since Madam Perkins saw more working people than any other Cabinet officer he would listen enthralled to what went on in the union halls she visited, feeling that they gave him a picture of the worker's life. He was also keenly aware of the power and influence of the woman's vote, and he was responsive to the work done by Molly Dewson in "making the women of America politically conscious." It was part of Madam Perkins' job to attend women's meetings of all kinds and to view a cross section of the women of America. They did not all approve of her, but the President said, "I notice that we haven't lost the labor vote or the women's vote on your account."

He admired Wendell Willkie but noticed that when the protagonist of One World said he would appoint his Secretary of Labor straight from the ranks of organized labor, and "it will not be a woman either," even the Republican women were pained and insulted. "That was a boner Willkie pulled," the President remarked to Madam Perkins. "Why did he have to insult every woman in the United States? It will make them mad, it will lose him votes." But later he said to her: "You know, he is a very good fellow. . . . Willkie would have made a good Democrat. Too bad we lost him."

He decided to offer Willkie a government post, and Madam Perkins suggested him as chairman of the Defense Labor Board, but Willkie declined. He preferred not to take on anything so controversial, he told Madam Perkins when she telephoned to ask him if he was interested. After that the President sent him to England as his personal representative.

"Make it simple enough for the women to understand, and then the men will understand it," he used to say to Madam Perkins. Once when she wrote the phrase "We are trying to construct a more inclusive society," he changed it to what seemed to her magical simplicity: "We are going to make a country in which no one is left out." She found that if a member of the Cabinet chose to go out on a limb for some theory the President would never say no, but he reserved the right not to rescue the culprit if he got into trouble. "Say what you please," he would tell them. "Use your own judgment. But if it turns out wrong, the blame be on your own head." Madam Perkins sometimes found that it was.

She would drive about with him in his little car at Hyde Park and discuss John L. Lewis or Harry Bridges, whom he called her "mandolin player," and ask for his advice. He patted her on the back and told her not to worry when J. Parnell Thomas of New Jersey sought to have her impeached for failing to deport Bridges. When John Lewis failed him in January, 1937, the President was deeply shocked, since he took it for granted that all the labor people were on his side. A year earlier he had had the same sort of blow when Al Smith deserted his camp. Madam Perkins continued to see Smith, and the two men surprised her at times by speaking affectionately of each other, deep though the breach between them was. But there was no reconciliation.

She was locked up in a New York club, dictating a report to her secretary, when she was summoned suddenly to the White House on Pearl Harbor day. This was one of the few occasions in her contact with President Roosevelt when he could neither smile nor give her his usual personal greeting. "You all know what's happened," he began in a low voice. "The attack began at one o'clock. We don't know very much else." Frank Knox then told the story, with interpolations from Cordell Hull, Henry Stimson and the President.

After that Madam Perkins noticed a great change in Roosevelt. He seemed to her to touch bottom at the time of the Battle of the Bulge. Just before his fourth inauguration she renewed her attempts to retire from the Cabinet. He had told her earlier that it would not have been good politically for her to step down, but as she became insistent, he agreed that Inauguration Day would be the time to make the announcement. When the moment came he had a change of heart and appealed to her to stay. "Frances, you can't go now," he said. "You mustn't put this on me now. I just can't be bothered now. I can't think of anybody else, and I can't get used to anybody else. Not now! Do stay there and don't say anything. You are all right . . . you have done awfully well. I know what you have been through. I know what you have accomplished. Thank you."

There were tears in the President's eyes and also in hers. She had never seen him so distraught, and she felt alarmed. But he braced up for the Inauguration next day and made a ringing speech. Then he went to Yalta. After that she saw him a number of times before he went to Warm Springs, and she talked to him at some length the day before he left. When President Truman took office he appointed Madam Perkins to the Civil Service Commission and she dropped from the Cabinet without regret, but with the all-inclusive admission, "I'm grateful to God to have lived in these times." Her record of her service to Roosevelt and the nation appeared in *The Roosevelt I Knew*, published in 1946. When she died in New York in 1965 at the age of eighty-three she was still conducting seminars, and was lecturing on political science and labor relations at Cornell. Her name remains a significant one in the history of social progress in the United States, but her record was doubly belabored because she happened to be a woman.

When President Eisenhower appointed Oveta Culp Hobby, of Texas, Secretary of Health, Education and Welfare, a different type of woman stepped into view on the national scene. Better known today as a newspaper publisher than as a politician, Mrs. Hobby is an accomplished member of the feminine hierarchy who have shown capacity in different fields. She was the efficient head of the Women's Army Corps during World War II, and although she had seen little of General Eisenhower during her army days she became a national leader in the Citizens for Eisenhower organization when he ran for the Presidency. In 1952 he asked her to head the Federal Security Agency, which she reorganized into the Department of Health, Education and Welfare. As in the case of Madam Perkins the old argument that a woman in command upsets the works clouded some of her days in office, but the men who have followed her in the same spot have not found it a bed of roses. Mrs. Hobby was the first to hold this freshly created Cabinet portfolio, which has since become one of the most controversial in the government. Her appointment was significant in terms of woman's power in politics. It also had meaning for the future, since she broadened the base of Social Security to include the self-employed and others not then covered. Her department handled old-age funds for sixty-seven million Americans, with a combined pension and welfare outlay of $4 billion a year.

Mrs. Hobby weathered a fierce storm over polio vaccinations in 1955, when she was caught in the crossfire of Republican and Democratic politics. Hubert H. Humphrey, Wayne Morse and Estes Kefauver led the fight in Congress over her handling of the Jonas

Salk vaccine inoculation program. Mrs. Hobby had sharp questions fired at her as the impression spread that the vaccine was not safe. Why was it licensed in the first place if there was any doubt about its harmlessness? How much advance planning and testing had been done on the program as a whole? Why was a plan for systematic, controlled distribution not prepared in advance? Who was to blame?

The mothers of America studied Mrs. Hobby with deep-rooted interest at that time, since the health and lives of their children were involved. Many parents across the country, alarmed by a rising tide of doubt, refused to sanction shots. Houston had had many summer outbreaks of polio, and the Secretary's own children lived there, so she knew how the mothers felt. The problem she faced was whether the vaccine should be held back until there was an adequate supply for all children to be inoculated simultaneously, or whether it should be used as soon as possible to protect the greatest number. Tales of doctors inoculating adult patients when there was not enough vaccine for all the children fed the fires of controversy. Mrs. Hobby stood firm, but the issue was so serious and the demand for federal control so insistent that she referred the matter to the White House for decision. President Eisenhower backed her up. At one point the vaccine was withdrawn from the market until a volunteer arrangement had been worked out with the Surgeon General to make sure that there was fair and even distribution.

In her Cabinet role Mrs. Hobby worked six days a week, lunching at her desk, taking time off on Saturdays only to have her hair done. The most decorative touch in the eight-room apartment she kept in Washington while in office was Mrs. Secretary herself, in gold sandals and Valentina gown, receiving guests against a background of Matisses and Morandis. Her children came and went, and her husband, former Governor William P. Hobby, came up from Texas for weekends. When Lyndon B. Johnson was Minority Leader he said of his fellow Texan: "She's the type of woman you'd like to have for a daughter or a sister, a wife or a mother, or the trustee of your estate."

The serious illness of her husband led to her retirement after two years in office. Mrs. Hobby has always denied that the vaccine controversy had anything to do with her giving up her Cabinet post.

When she left, President Eisenhower remarked that she had done a "mighty magnificent job and was highly efficient." He had watched her in action in an earlier and most demanding role. Unique though her Cabinet post was, she will be best remembered as the woman who headed the Women's Army Auxiliary Corps during World War II. General George C. Marshall and Secretary of War Henry Stimson, anticipating a manpower shortage, asked her to recommend a commander for a woman's corps. Mrs. Hobby submitted seven names, all of which they rejected. They urged her to take the post herself. She was then thirty-six years old, with a seven-year-old daughter, Jessica, and an eleven-year-old son, William Hobby, Jr. Her husband urged her to respond to the challenge as a patriotic duty.

She had to start from scratch, with no precedents to guide her. It was important to move fast and not make tactical blunders. Before long the public became familiar with the picture of military efficiency and feminine charm projected by Mrs. Hobby as she moved about briskly in the Pentagon in her trim uniform with the famous visored "Hobby Hat" poised on her prematurely silver hair. The Corps insignia was Pallas Athena, but the problems she faced were by no means classical in their nature. In the early days of recruiting she traveled in the only Wac uniform then in existence, taking along an electric fan and an iron for a daily laundering of the heavy cotton outfit. Many times, during the first year of organization, she worked all day and all night, went home, showered and returned to her office to face another day. Her impish sense of humor came to the fore at times as tall generals towered over her, voicing sundry opinions on the Wacs. From 1942 to 1943 her title was director of the Women's Army Auxiliary Corps. From 1943 to 1945 she was colonel of the Women's Army Corps.

Pink lingerie floating on barracks clotheslines was a challenge to army decorum, so she ordered khaki underwear to assuage the disapproving army brass. Special diets were worked out since the Wacs had to be neat and trim. Their marching pace was adjusted to shorter steps than their fellow soldiers, and Mrs. Hobby drew up complicated rules for leaves, recreation and inspections. In course of time Congress conceded that women were capable of doing fifty-four different army jobs, but Mrs. Hobby quietly enlarged the score to 239—in short, to nearly all noncombatant military duties. By 1944 the services of the Wacs were in demand around the world, and Mrs. Hobby's name was internationally known. She flew to England with Mrs. Roosevelt to study the war work of the British women.

When she resigned in 1945, the Wacs had become a full-fledged branch of the United States Army. Worn out from her incessant labors, Mrs. Hobby had a physical collapse, common enough among the men and women who bore heavy wartime responsibilities. She returned to Houston to continue her work for the family paper, and among her trophies was the Distinguished Service Medal. Mrs. Hobby was the first woman to receive this honor.

Her life history in review suggests that she was destined for fame from her earliest days. She feels that she has been lucky and often says, "Everything that ever happened to me simply fell in my lap, and I could never have done any of the things I have done without the Governor." She was born in tiny Killeen, Texas, with a population of 1,750, and was the second of seven children. Her name is Indian for "forget," but her memory was always good and before she was thirteen she had read the Bible all the way through three times and could quote from it at length.

She was a solemn child, reluctant to waste time on films or automobile drives if there were books to be read. When her father, a rugged lawyer with a taste for horses as well as politics, went to Austin in 1919 to sit in the legislature, Oveta was with him. Although this meant missing weeks of school, she graduated from Temple High School and entered Mary Hardin Baylor College. When her father was returned to office in 1923 she spent much of her time in Austin, sometimes auditing law classes at the University of Texas, but also learning a great deal about government.

At the age of twenty the Speaker of the House asked her to act as parliamentarian during a special session. In 1928 she codified the state banking laws when working as a legal clerk in the state banking department. At this point she stepped into the profession best guaranteed to keep her in touch with public affairs. Through a friend she was offered a job on the Houston *Post-Dispatch* (later the *Post*).

Ross Sterling owned the paper at the time, and former Governor Hobby was the publisher. Between 1931 and 1952 she worked as research editor, literary editor, assistant editor, vice-president, and editor and finally, in 1952, she became editor and publisher.

She was on the paper for more than a year before Hobby was aware of her presence there, although he had been a friend of her family's all her life. He fell in love with the clever and attractive Oveta, and they were married in 1931 when he was a widower of fifty-three and she was twenty-six. The Governor bought the paper eventually, and they worked together to strengthen it. They reorganized the business department and Oveta, like Mrs. Lyndon Johnson, built up the paper's radio station. Her soft contralto voice soon became influential in Texas politics. She has been listed for years as an independent and has voted both the Democratic and Republican tickets on state and national levels. The Houston *Post* is an independent newspaper.

During this period, when the Hobbys were becoming nationally known as an able newspaper team, Oveta was seriously injured when thrown from her horse, and she also survived a plane crash. But her newspaper interests continued without interruption. Life broadened out for her in many ways after her Washington experience. She turned her energies to public service and engaged in civic and philanthropic enterprises. Her interest in politics continued as president of the Texas League of Women Voters. She was much in demand as a speaker, and in the late 1950's she became active in economic development, employment of the physically handicapped, graduate education, educational television and the international exchange of students and scholars.

Mrs. Hobby presides over a twenty-seven room Georgian mansion in Houston and nurtures the arts. She is a member of the board of the Houston Symphony Orchestra, the Museum of Fine Arts and the Community Chest. Among the many honors that have come her way she is particularly proud of the fact that the library of the new college in Killeen is named after her. President Johnson attended the opening ceremonies. A scholar at heart, she received the Publisher of the Year Award from the Headliners Club in 1960, and the Living History Award from the Research Institute of America. While awaiting the birth of Jessica who, like her son, was born on Oveta's birthday, she finished a book on parliamentary law, called *Mr. Chairman*, which was adopted as a textbook in Texas and Louisiana.

Mrs. Hobby is one of the few contemporary American women who may be said to have shown real power in areas usually restricted to men. As editor, businesswoman and politician, she has shown quality, but she disowns the feminist label and prides herself on working harmoniously with the members of both sexes. In assuming her Cabinet office she announced that she wished to be known as Mrs. Secretary. Frances Perkins had lived to regret her "Call me Madam" fiat on her first day in office.

Titles and labels can work adversely for women in politics, as Betty Furness discovered when President Johnson appointed her special assistant on consumer affairs. As successor to the practical and experienced Esther Peterson, and with new and topical functions added to the role, Miss Furness' appointment was greeted with skepticism. All America knew her well as the clever pitch girl on television who had been opening refrigerator doors for years and had even sparked up the political conventions with her vivacious expertise. Betty, definitely a knowledgeable member of the Feminine Establishment, played it in low key at first, studying the field before emerging as the most energetic champion of consumer interests to appear on the national scene. She stirred the men on the Hill to action as she put effective pressure on Congress for tougher packaging legislation. In challenging the powerful meat lobby on the protection of consumers from tainted meat she dramatically demanded a stronger meat inspection bill than had been agreed to by the industry, or than Secretary of Agriculture Orville Freeman had favored. In 1968 the House passed a landmark consumers' bill that gave her satisfaction.

Miss Furness took a tough stand on rising prices in slum areas, on unsolicited credit cards and consumer frustrations over repairs and inferior goods. She measured toasters and let women know some of the ways in which they were being cheated. She proposed repair shops in shopping centers to make life easier for the housewife. As one with expert knowledge of the inside and outside of kitchen appliances she told the Association of National Advertisers late in 1967,

"I am a spokesman for American consumers—all two hundred million of them. My job is to find out what is in the consumer's mind and then to see that the voice of the consumer is heard—loud and clear."

To make this stick she ran a three-way campaign on behalf of the consumer—education on his rights, persuasion of the seller to mend his ways on a voluntary basis, and support of legislation to make control mandatory when the consumer showed no drive in this direction. Miss Furness, who had easy access to President Johnson, has always been slightly unorthodox in her ways and did not feel hampered by the bureaucratic tradition. She was apt to move first and tell the President about it afterward. And she had no qualms about being a real glamour girl in her $26,000-a-year job. Her office was done in red, white and blue, her mini dresses were as likely as not to be designed by Rudi Gernreich, and she looked dashing in her tall black boots. In private life she is Mrs. Leslie Midgley and has a married daughter by the first of her three marriages. Her husband is a television producer whom she married after seventeen years of widowhood, and their home is in Hartsdale, New York. She prepared for Congressional committee hearings, until her resignation in 1969, as she would for an oral college exam. Miss Furness was "with it" in the contemporary sense of the phrase, the New Woman in the Feminine Establishment, her green eyes alert to the prevailing mood. Mrs. Patricia Reilly Hitt, a Californian appointed by President Nixon to serve as assistant secretary for community and field services in the Department of Health, Education and Welfare, succeeded Miss Furness as the government expert on consumer activities.

Aside from the Cabinet and independent appointments, women have not been a scorching success, nor have they been numerous, in the Capitol itself. Two women who have stayed the course with distinction have been Senator Margaret Chase Smith of Maine and Representative Frances P. Bolton of Ohio. They have influenced men and legislation, and have charmed and angered their colleagues at various times, but the men who sit in Congress have had to acknowledge that the exceptional woman can work harmoniously at their side.

Mrs. Smith has brought stern conviction to her role. Her forthright manner has left none in doubt of where she stands. She ran for the Presidency, not in the spirit of Victoria Woodhull for self-aggrandizement, but to prove a point. Her campaign was quiet and dignified. She had no money behind her, and she rolled up only a few thousand votes—but she came out of the campaign more respected than before. Many Republicans view her as radical because of her opinions. She made one of the boldest moves in American legislative history when she tackled Senator Joseph McCarthy in 1950 with her withering Declaration of Conscience, signed by six of her Republican colleagues.

The controversial Senator sat close to her, his face reddening with fury, as Mrs. Smith announced that she did not covet a Republican victory that November if it were to ride in on the "four horsemen of calumny—fear, ignorance, bigotry and smear." As a woman she wondered how the mothers, wives, sisters and daughters felt about the way in which members of their families had been "politically mangled in Senate debate." Mrs. Smith went on in stern, even tones:

I am not proud of the way we smear outsiders from the Floor of the Senate and hide behind the cloak of congressional immunity and still place ourselves beyond criticism. . . . As an American, I condemn a Republican "Fascist" just as much as I condemn a Democrat "Communist." I condemn a Democrat "Fascist" just as much as I condemn a Republican "Communist." They are equally dangerous to you and me and to our country. As an American I want to see our nation recapture the strength and unity it once had when we fought the enemy instead of ourselves.

The smoldering feeling against McCarthy burst into flame with Mrs. Smith's pronouncement that Americans were sick and tired of seeing innocent people smeared and the guilty whitewashed. She pointed out that the basic principles of Americanism were the right to criticize, the right to hold unpopular belief, the right to protest, the right of independent thought. "It is high time that we all stopped being tools and victims of totalitarian techniques—techniques that, if continued here unchecked, will surely end what we have come to cherish as the American way of life," she finished.

Mrs. Smith had been warned not to make this attack, and her

speech was a bombshell when it came. She had waited in vain for her fellow Senators to move against McCarthy, and her strong Maine face was tense when she finally stood before them in an aquamarine silk suit with the customary rose on her lapel and made her stinging speech. Senator McCarthy rose when she had finished and left the Capitol without a word. Senator Millard Tydings of Maryland called her speech one of "statesmanship," and Stuart Symington said that she represented all that was best in American public life, even though she was a Republican.

Finally Senator McCarthy issued a sarcastic statement referring to her and the Senators who had signed her declaration as "Snow White and the Six Dwarfs." She was dropped from the subcommittee investigating the State Department. She lost her place on the Republican Policy Committee, but served ultimately on the Senate subcommittee that investigated McCarthy and led to his censure by the Senate in 1954. Her Declaration of Conscience was finally inserted in the Congressional Record when McCarthy attacked General George C. Marshall. She sued Jack Lait and Lee Mortimer for a million dollars for linking her with the Communist conspiracy in the United States. There was a settlement out of court.

Mrs. Smith has never hesitated to tilt at the champions when she thought they were wrong. She challenged Senator Robert A. Taft's campaign statement that linked the C.I.O. with Communism. She had not always supported his policies, but she had helped with the Taft-Hartley Act. The Senator said of her: "Margaret Smith is the Joan of Arc of the Republican Party, who may well lead us out of the morass of defeat." She was often a thorn in his flesh, but when she served on his Policy Committee her convictions were so obviously sincere that contention did not dim their mutual respect. After his death she walked over to his old desk in the Senate and placed her rose on it. In 1955 when she and Frances Bolton introduced a bill in Congress suggesting that the rose be made the national flower, *Red Star* denounced her as a "military Amazon who hides behind bouquets of roses." Moscow had bracketed her with the American Right when she introduced the first bill in the Senate to outlaw the Communist Party in the United States.

The rose has become a personal symbol with Senator Smith. When she first ran for her seat a friend gave her one in a vial of water. She immediately made the rose the daily accessory to her costume, and she has a standing order for three red roses to be delivered twice a week. Behind her office desk is a giant mock rose given her by the National Women's Press Club. Her fellow legislators view this feminine gesture with approval. If her spirits are low after a grueling session, she likes to wear red. Her silver hair and keen blue eyes are as reassuring as her Maine tones and steady judgment. The Senator's private life is as efficiently run as her political career. She rises before seven, exercises, watches the birds as she takes a simple breakfast in her Silver Spring home, then drives twelve miles to her office. She lunches in the Senate dining room and usually leaves her office around seven, taking letters and papers home with her. If she does not have an evening engagement she prepares her own dinner, listens to the late news, then falls asleep.

When Mrs. Smith entertains she likes to have lobster flown in from Maine. She thinks nothing of turning down invitations to cocktail parties or big dinners, and she has even been known to refuse a White House bid. One of the few embarrassments she has experienced on the social side has been her lack, as a widow, of an official escort for social functions. As an unmarried woman Senator no one ever thought of inviting an escort to accompany her until President and Mrs. Kennedy included in their invitations any man of her own choosing. When she was a Congresswoman she was invited to the Veterans of Foreign Wars Salute to Members of Congress. They hastily withdrew the invitation when they learned that Senator Smith was a woman. It was a stag affair. Later this organization abolished the policy of discrimination against women members of Congress.

Mrs. Smith's legislative assistant is William C. Lewis, an Air Force Reserve colonel, who has been of immense help to her in her official duties. But she is so independent in her opinions that she is never afraid to act as she sees fit. She served as her own campaign manager when she ran for the Presidency, touring Maine with a red hatbox stuffed with "Vote for Margaret Smith" buttons and leaflets. She writes blistering notes when correspondents annoy her, and she feuded with May Craig, the spirited correspondent from her own state to whom Presidents have kowtowed at various times.

The Senator was in office for more than a year before she made a speech, and it lasted only seventy-three seconds, an unprecedented performance in the halls of oratory. Like Calvin Coolidge she speaks only when she has something to say, but she can be eloquent when the occasion demands. She has held the Senate voting record for many years, and went so far as to cut short her own campaign for the Presidency in order to be present for an important vote. Her first miss came in the autumn of 1968 and was due to illness. During filibusters she has been known to camp in her office, having had it stocked beforehand with necessities, and to sleep under a blue and gold afghan knitted by a Maine woman, until the quorum bell rang. She always emerged looking rested and blooming in a fresh dress, even if she had to change three times a day.

Mrs. Smith is the only woman who has served in both the House and Senate, and the only woman ever sent to Congress from the State of Maine. She had varied experience before reaching Washington, having taught, worked for a telephone company, been an executive in a woolen mill and circulation manager of a newspaper, the *Independent Reporter*, published by her husband, Clyde Smith. In 1936 he became a Congressman and Mrs. Smith helped him with his speeches. When he had a second heart attack in 1940 his doctor urged Maggie to take her husband's place. He had another attack and died right after announcing that she would complete his term in Congress. World War II was raging when she took her seat in 1940. From the beginning she followed a free and independent course, but always with strength and sincerity. It gives her no satisfaction to be called a liberal. "I'm an independent," she says, "and I think that's what my record really shows." Her own party suffered at times from her attacks as much as did the Democrats.

When sworn in to the Senate in 1949 she was an object of great interest as the one woman to join what is customarily known in masculine circles as the most exclusive gentlemen's club in the world. She was fifty-one and was considered unpredictable in her views. Among other things she had voted for Lend-Lease to Britain in the teeth of opposition from the Maine delegation. She had backed universal training and had weathered the opposition of power companies, railroads and many large corporations. She favored reciprocal trade agreements and voted against further appropriations for the House Un-American Activities Committee. She shaped the bill that created the Waves, and she has an honorary degree from Smith College, where they were trained. In 1944 she introduced a bill permitting Waves to serve in hospitals and offices overseas. She was the first woman to ride on an American destroyer in wartime and in 1957 she was the first of her sex to break the sound barrier on a flight in a supersonic jet.

Mrs. Smith is better informed than most of her colleagues on armaments and power. During the war she inspected the Pacific bases and in 1947 she was assigned by the Armed Services Committee to make an inspection tour of European countries. This was followed in 1955 by a world tour. She met the leading figures in every country she visited and was always viewed with special interest as the Woman Senator from what some assumed to be a woman-run country. On the home front she has been deluged with honors over the years, and in polls is rated among the top ten Senators. The intractable press gives her a high credit rating as seventh, although she has never been known to kiss babies, swing the skillet or wear an Indian headdress for the camera. But she has gone far out on welfare measures and keeps a watchful eye on matters involving women and children.

To the amazement of her fellow Senators their Maggie burst into tears when they passed a resolution in 1967 honoring her a few minutes after she cast her two thousandth vote without a single miss. Their laudatory speeches overwhelmed the woman whom Khrushchev said had decided to beat all records for savagery in her hatred of everything new and progressive. His outburst followed her attack on President Kennedy at the time of the Bay of Pigs for not backing up the strong words he had used over the Cuban crisis. Another side of her nature was revealed at a Manhattan dinner in that same year, when she raised a warning finger and said that Americans yearned for the safe world of Dwight D. Eisenhower. Mrs. Smith spoke firmly in her most down-to-earth manner:

One of America's greatest needs is for more people who are square. . . . There has been too much glorification of the angle players, the corner cutters, and the goof-offs. . . . The square deal was an honest deal. A square meal was a full and good meal. It was the square shooter rather than the sharpshooter who was admired. What is a square deal? He's the fellow who never learned to get away with it, who gets choked up when the flag unfurls. . . .

The Lady from Maine was speaking in a campaign year, but obviously from the depths of her conviction. Government agencies and public figures are prone to listen when a call comes through from Senator Smith. Whatever members of her own sex think of her—and conservative Republicans are disposed to watch her with a wary eye—she projects a steadfast image and is genuinely influential with her colleagues in the Senate. In 1960 she welcomed Maurine Neuberger of Oregon as her Democratic opposite number, but Mrs. Neuberger soon deserted the fold.

Senator Smith and Mrs. Bolton, both veterans at the Capitol, have done much to show that women politicians can work together in harmony and make substantial contributions to Congressional deliberations, however far apart their political views. When Mrs. Bolton ran for office in 1940 after the death of her husband, Chester C. Bolton, she was reminded that politics was man's business. With a strong political inheritance in her blood, this was a judgment that she refused to take seriously. The Bolton name is nearly as well known in Ohio as that of the Tafts. It is identified with the Hanna coal and steel interests that helped to build Cleveland. One of her grandfathers was a United States Senator. Another was a member of the Cleveland city council. Her great-grandfather was a judge, and Mrs. Bolton herself helped write a constitution for the Ohio State Committee.

Once her own mind was made up to run for office she campaigned with zeal and dash. She was finally defeated in 1968 after twenty-eight years in Congress. Although in the House she was a quiet, thoughtful force rather than a fire-eater, on the campaign trail she could indulge in oratorical flourishes and has been known to dance with truck drivers and engage in other gambits to roll up votes.

Almost as soon as she took office Mrs. Bolton landed in one of the Congressional hot spots—though one of vast importance—as a member of the Foreign Relations Committee. Her major interests up to that time had been nursing, education and philanthropy, but she quickly buried herself in State Department documents and by degrees her outlook shifted from isolationism to the broader view of the internationalist. Today she is one of the best-informed women in the country on problems involving Africa and the Near East. It was she who persuaded the other members of the Foreign Relations Committee to specialize in various areas, and she took the Near East for her own province. When President Eisenhower appointed her a delegate to the United Nations Assembly in 1953 she was the first woman to represent the United States in that capacity. She was soon outlining to the delegates the way in which Puerto Rico's independence was established, and was urging the United Nations to help the African people attain their aspirations for self-government. On a November day in 1953 she spoke up boldly and clearly:

We Americans are a libertarian people. I think we would all of us still prefer, as our forefathers did, the terrors of the sea and the wilderness to the loss of our liberties. We cannot help but have a sense of brotherhood for all people who share our own belief in the fundamental and primary importance of individual human dignity. . . . People are not expendable as far as we are concerned, nor do we hold that Congress has the right to decide the uses of another man's life.

At times Mrs. Bolton found her essential independence at war with her party loyalty. She was rated a conservative, and went all out for a bold stand on various occasions but was not afraid to change her mind when persuaded of her error. She opposed Lend-Lease in 1941 but supported it when war was declared. Two of her four children were in the Army—Oliver and Kenyon—and she experienced the fall of buzz bombs in London during 1944. In 1955 she was the ranking Republican member of a Special Study Mission to Africa and visited twenty-four countries. Two years later she was a delegate to the Ghana independence ceremonies. Mrs. Bolton became almost as well known in deepest Africa as on home ground.

Oddly enough, she and Senator Smith were much involved in the most difficult and dangerous areas of Congressional conflict—policies of war and peace, of armaments and the rising tide of independence around the world. Neither one could say that she had been frozen out from the inner parleys, or been patronized in any way. Mrs. Bolton helped to draft the foreign-policy plank of the Republican platform in 1944, and she was one of the women invited to Denver to help plan General Eisenhower's campaign. She has been a successful vote getter and came up smiling, and with her Congressional seat intact, after the Roosevelt and Truman landslides. Her own background of wealth, social prominence and private education has not minimized her belief in the faceless fellow who came to be known as the Common Man in the days of the New Deal.

From first to last Mrs. Bolton has been a worker. Politicking with her could go on from 6 A.M. to 10 P.M. She made five hundred calls during her first winter as a Congressional wife, and her work came first to the very end. At the time of the 1968 Republican Convention she was eighty-three and still committed to Yoga, which she has practiced for years. She can stand on her head with ease, although she now does fewer somersaults, realizing that she must make a few concessions to age. Her perennial youthfulness and energy were marveled at by many of her more sluggardly colleagues in the House. When her friend, Helen Gahagan Douglas, was under attack for her liberal views, Mrs. Bolton used to urge her to do daily nip-ups to raise her spirits.

Physical fitness is inherent in her training. During World War I she was instrumental in persuading Newton D. Baker, Secretary of War, to organize the Army School of Nursing, and in 1967 she introduced a bill in Congress to permit male nurses to receive commissions in the Army and Air Force Nurse Corps, making it a two-way street for men and women. Today Mrs. Bolton has sixteen honorary degrees and she does not feel that being a woman has kept her in any way from fulfilling her political destiny.

Her family life has been rich and strenuous, too. Of her four children her only daughter died in infancy. In 1928 her eldest son Charles broke his back in a swimming accident, and for four years she worked tirelessly, teaching him to use one set of muscles after another until he was well enough to manage two dairy farms. When another son, Oliver P. Bolton, joined her in the House in a much publicized Mother and Son combination, they split on their first vote and disagreed on important bills. Mrs. Bolton was more pleased than dismayed by this expression of independent opinion. But she was amused when Oliver, offering a toast at a women's gathering, quipped: "Here's to the ladies; once our superiors, now our equals."

More than a third of the women who have served in Congress were elected to succeed husbands who died, but this has not always worked out in their favor. Edith Nourse Rogers of Massachusetts, elected in 1925 after her husband's death, was one of the exceptions and became widely known as the soldiers' friend. During the Coolidge and Hoover administrations she had much to do with the establishment and construction of veterans' hospitals, and she served as chairman of the House Veterans Affairs Committee. She introduced the bill creating the Women's Army Auxiliary Corps, paving the way for Oveta Culp Hobby to become a nationally known figure. Mrs. Rogers' reign was less stormy than that of Congresswoman Mary Norton, a liberal Democrat sponsored by Mayor Frank Hague of Jersey City. "Battling Mary," a title she bore with satisfaction, fought pugnaciously. Before civil rights was a big issue she backed better opportunities for the Negro, and her work for the Wage and Hour bill enhanced her popularity in labor circles. The quiet parliamentarians of her own sex studied Mary's tactics with surprise, but sometimes found that they worked magic. For a decade she was a ceaseless focus of controversy, but she asked no quarter. When a fellow Congressman referred to her patronizingly as "the lady," Mrs. Norton stared him down and reminded him that she was not "the lady" but a member of Congress who expected the same consideration given any other member.

Mrs. Norton was a Jersey City housewife in her forties when she ran successfully for Congress, and she had been a Wall Street secretary before her marriage. She organized the Democratic women of New Jersey for Mayor Hague. In Congress she presented a lively image, wearing her most becoming dresses and pinning an orchid on her shoulder when she knew a fight was coming up. Labor issues took up much of her time, and she served on many committees.

Administrative changes have stayed the advancement of many appointees. Since Jeannette Rankin was first elected to Congress in

1916 only sixty-six women have followed her in the lower House and two in the Senate. "It takes so long before you're recognized in Congress," said Edna F. Kelly, a Brooklyn Democrat who used to ride a bicycle around the Capitol grounds. She is a liberal Democrat who backed bills involving the minimum wage, the Peace Corps, income-tax deductions for higher education and working mothers. Mrs. Kelly, a lawyer married to a lawyer, was appointed by President Kennedy to the United States delegation on the United Nations, and she was still doing battle in political circles at the Democratic Convention of 1968.

The pioneer Congresswoman, Miss Rankin, reappeared in 1968 when she led a peace march to Capitol Hill demanding the removal of American troops from Vietnam. Mrs. Martin Luther King, Jr., was in the Rankin brigade. It seemed like the echo of an old tune, for when Miss Rankin was first in Congress she reminded the nation that she was a woman by bursting into tears as she cast her solitary vote against the nation's entry into World War I. She had run for Congress in order to vote against participation in the war. Theodore Roosevelt had invited her to Oyster Bay to try to dissuade her.

When she failed to get the Republican nomination for the Senate in 1918 she bought a farm in Georgia and raised pecans. She ran again for Congress in 1940, and in December, 1941, she was the only member of the House to vote against war. By then she was as closely identified with Georgia as with Montana. Miss Rankin was never a segregationist, and she backed civil rights at every opportunity. In 1958 John F. Kennedy named her one of his "Three Women of Courage" in an article in *McCall's*. The other two were Anne Hutchinson and Prudence Crandall. Miss Rankin headed the women of Montana in their successful fight for suffrage in 1914, but while she was in Congress she felt squeezed between the two warring factions led by Mrs. Catt and Miss Paul. Hattie Caraway of Arkansas shared honors with Miss Rankin as one of the pioneer Congresswomen. Another landmark was reached in 1969 when Shirley Chisholm of Brooklyn became the first black woman member of Congress, and Elizabeth Duncan Koontz, also a Negro, was appointed director of the Women's Bureau of the Labor Department.

Helen Gahagan Douglas was catapulted into politics after being asked in a Vienna coffeehouse in 1937 if she was pure Aryan. On the spot she tore up her contract to sing with the Vienna State Opera and returned to America, fully committed to fighting the racist viewpoint. She and her actor husband, Melvyn Douglas, rounded up volunteers to organize relief for the Okies, but they pulled out when they found that some of their helpers were spreading Communist doctrines. At the Democratic National Convention of 1940 Mrs. Douglas, present as her husband's alternate delegate, sang the anthem and was elected national committeewoman for California. That year she made 168 speeches and became a controversial figure. In 1944 she was elected to Congress and served on the House Committee on Foreign Affairs. In 1946 President Truman appointed her an alternate delegate to the United Nations Assembly. When she ran for the Senate in 1950 the conservatives in her own party helped to unseat her, and she was defeated by Richard M. Nixon after a vituperative contest.

Although they have made so little impression at the Capitol, women have moved ahead as members of state legislatures and as convention delegates. They became country clerks, tax assessors and collectors, treasurers, recorders and clerks of the court. A total of 286 women were serving in state legislatures by 1953, a steady climb from twenty-nine in 1920, the year in which they won the vote. Vermont and New Hampshire, Connecticut and Arizona were in the front line in giving women important public office. Five have served as Secretary of State for Connecticut, including the gifted Alice K. Leopold, who finally resigned to head the Women's Bureau of the Department of Labor in Washington. Mrs. Leopold was one of the women summoned to Denver to help map out the Eisenhower campaign after a long history as an able Republican worker in Connecticut. She concentrated on matters directly affecting mothers and homemakers, the schools, church, health drives and P.T.A. activities.

The path was set by such early workers as Ruth Pratt, who carried the Republican banner in New York State for many years and by Katharine St. George, who was elected to Congress in 1946. Both were women of wealth and social background, and they challenged the tyranny of old-fashioned ward politics. Mrs. Pratt often defied Tammany Hall, and when she served on the Board of Aldermen she accused Mayor James J. Walker of carelessness, indifference, bungling and inefficiency. She seconded Herbert Hoover's nomination in 1932, and she battled with Heywood Broun, who was running on the Socialist ticket, when she was re-elected to Congress in 1930.

The attitude of the President has been significant in top appointments for women. All have come to recognize the importance of giving them political status, and the women's organizations have put on considerable pressure toward this end. Calvin Coolidge was skeptical of giving the inferior creatures too much leeway, although he never forgot the power of the woman's vote. Women were important in a quiet way in the Hoover administration, but it was not until 1933 when Molly Dewson took hold of the Women's Division of the Democratic National Committee and became the leading woman in the national party organization, that appointments came thick and fast. Mrs. Roosevelt was at hand to make them stick. President Eisenhower plumbed all the good Republican areas for talented women to fill posts and serve on committees. President Truman remembered them in a substantial way. President Kennedy had no real understanding of the woman with political ambitions but, good politician that he was, he saw to it that they got office and worked for administration causes. President Johnson claimed to have appointed 265 women to top-level government positions, as ambassadors and commissioners, and also to have promoted 818 women to posts paying more than $10,000 a year.

Molly Dewson, who originally sparked this trend, was a Yankee spinster with a keen sense of humor who decided to shake women "out of the tea-party routine and put ginger into them." She believed that women should share equal representation at national, state, county and precinct levels. Molly was indifferent about holding office herself but watched with satisfaction while scores of women were given local and federal jobs. One of her coups was to get a woman alternate for every man on the Platform Committee at the Democratic National Convention in 1936. She has been credited with being responsible for the appointment of Frances Perkins as Secretary of Labor, former Governor Nellie Tayloe Ross as Director of the Mint, Ruth Bryan Owen as Minister to Denmark, and Judge Florence E. Allen to the United States Circuit Court of Appeals. Each was the first of her sex to hold her respective rank.

Women sometimes help women in public life, but not always. However, the Democratic women in the 1936 campaign were responsible for 80 per cent of the printed material distributed. They peppered the land with eighty-three million Rainbow Fliers, colored leaflets amusingly illustrated by professional cartoonists. But clever promotion gimmicks are now the order of the day in campaign circles and have never been more ingenious than in 1968, with the youthful touch in the ascendant.

India Edwards, a Chicago newspaperwoman who lost her aviator son in World War II, walked into the picture in 1944 as a volunteer and became closely identified with government affairs. Immediately before the death of President Roosevelt she became executive secretary of the Women's Division of the Democratic National Committee. She flourished during the Truman administration and, like Molly Dewson before her, proposed a number of women for major jobs. Mrs. Edwards chanced to be one of the few persons in the country who felt sure that President Truman would be re-elected, but she declined the chairmanship of the National Committee when he offered it to her. She figured prominently again in the party deliberations of 1968. Women have shown more durability as top party workers than in elective office. Men have had to reckon with them as hard workers and astute politicians.

It was President Truman who gave a woman the highest rank in the military establishment attained by any member of her sex in American history. Anna M. Rosenberg, tiny and dynamic, became Assistant Secretary of Defense in 1950, the third woman to serve in the "Little Cabinet." Mabel Walker Willebrandt had fought the prohibition battle, futilely and unhappily, as Assistant Attorney General in the 1920's, and Josephine Roche, a Colorado coal-mine operator, had served as Assistant Secretary of the Treasury in the late 1930's.

George C. Marshall had asked for Anna Rosenberg, already known as a specialist in labor relations and a prominent Democrat. President Roosevelt had sent her to Europe during World War II to report on the morale of the fighting men. She had eaten G.I. rations, slept on the ground, talked to soldiers about their families. On her return she made long-distance calls to four hundred families about their soldier sons and fathers. President Truman sent her back to the war theater in 1945 to study the needs of the troops, and she reported realistically on what the men thought of their weapons, clothing and food. With this background in military affairs she was soon called before the Senate Armed Services Committee, which had approved her appointment but had come to think that she was Communist in her sympathies. Mrs. Rosenberg dismissed this charge with scorn, pointing out that there were forty-six Anna Rosenbergs in New York and that a grave mistake had been made in her case. For a time her path was thorny, but she fought it out, and General Eisenhower gave her the first Medal of Freedom awarded to a civilian.

Mrs. Rosenberg was introduced to politics by a powerful mentor— Belle Moskowitz, who had been Al Smith's adviser on political and social legislation. Mrs. Moskowitz was one of the inscrutables who could be brusque and uncommunicative with her colleagues. The women's organizations were not her field, and she trained Mrs. Rosenberg in the realistic school of the district club. Anna worked like a whirlwind and held a succession of state and city posts. Eventually she became one of the highest-paid labor-relations experts in the country, but much of her work was done on the volunteer basis. She is now the wife of Paul Hoffman, once a Republican presidential dark horse.

Within six months of his inauguration President Eisenhower had appointed twenty-seven women to high policy posts in his administration, including Ivy Baker Priest as Director of the Mint. Mrs. Priest, who came from Utah, worked as a telephone operator as a girl, then in a Salt Lake City department store, meanwhile teaching American history and citizenship in a night school. She learned to distribute campaign fliers before she was old enough to vote, and she joined the Young Republicans during the Coolidge administration. She made an unsuccessful bid for Congress in 1950. Mrs. Priest was a popular appointee, and the feeling grew in government circles that women gave style to the Mint.

When Mrs. Priest became Treasurer of the United States, capable Bertha S. Adkins succeeded her on the Republican National Committee, and the dynamic Mary Pillsbury Lord was appointed American member of the United Nations Human Rights Commission. All told, at least 407 women received top recognition during Eisenhower's two administrations. They ranged from the singer Marian Anderson, a member of the advisory committee on the arts, to the versatile and gifted Dr. Leona Baumgartner, with a long record of public-health work, including being Health Commissioner of New York City and doing international studies for the United Nations and the State Department. In 1968 Dr. Baumgartner was appointed director of the Medical Care and Education Foundation, a regional medical program designed to reach all social classes in New Hampshire, Massachusetts and Rhode Island. At the same time she continued her work as visiting professor of social medicine at Harvard Medical School. Scholarly, brilliant and humane, a woman who can run a home as well as she can draft a covenant, Dr. Baumgartner's career has been singularly free of conflict. She has twelve honorary degrees and is a woman with international prestige in the field of public health.

Each President has gone one step further than his predecessor in drawing on women for both volunteer and professional help, with all the voters down the line to remember. "A woman's place is not only in the home, but in the House, the Senate and throughout Government service," said President Johnson benignly to his early appointees—Mrs. Edwards, Rose McKee and Mary Keyserling.

"It's a good time to be a woman," says Kate Louchheim, who was rated by President Johnson "one of America's best women doers." In 1962 she became the outstanding woman in the State Department and in 1966 assumed the post of Deputy Assistant Secretary of State for Educational and Cultural Affairs. Before leaving office the President gave her the personal rank of ambassador. A poet, an experienced politician and a clever hostess, Mrs. Louchheim advises women on the political front to keep their aims high and their voices down.

She is one of the expert lobbyists who does her work over the dinner table or in the drawing room. Her relations with Congress are exceptionally good, and she is well primed on international affairs and personalities. Mrs. Louchheim likes music, skating, tennis and well-scrambled guest lists, never hesitating to invite the outcast as well as the man of the hour.

Katie, as she is best known, plays the feminine role and insists that her husband, an investment counselor, tells her what to do, but everyone on the Hill knows that she has plenty of her own expertise to guide her. She is an experienced hand at the political game and floats about Washington with instinctive assurance. Her job involves a $46-million budget and hundreds of programs and agencies, including those that send scholars, artists, entertainers, athletes and labor leaders in and out of the United States. Her collection of poems is entitled *With or Without Roses*. In Mrs. Louchheim's case it is usually *with* roses. She represents the high-powered American woman of the Feminine Establishment, with husband, children, artistic leanings and political power.

Mayors' wives are of growing importance on the American scene, but women mayors have been rare. Dorothy McCullough Lee became Mayor of Portland, Oregon, in 1948 but was defeated four years later because she was thought to have "done too good a job and to have gone too damned far." Known as "No Sin Lee," she had been in office for twenty-three years as chairman of the Oregon Crime Commission, as a municipal judge and as a member of the City Council. She was twenty-five when she first ran for office on the Republican ticket, and she fought corruption all along the line.

In 1967 Antonina P. Uccello became Hartford's first Republican mayor in twenty years and its first woman mayor. In an upset decision she won in the home of the state and national Democratic chairman, John M. Bailey. She was an executive in the city's biggest department store when she benefited by a party split. But if women mayors are few and far between, mayors' wives have become something like the wives of presidential candidates—brightly reassuring symbols, smartly attired, coping well with home and platform, working in the background to keep the peace. The shining example in

1968 was Mrs. John V. Lindsay of New York, who fitted into the picture with grace after a few preliminary fumbles traceable to her candid manner. She does not electioneer, but at times she helps the Mayor with his proclamations. She has firm political views of her own but she confesses: "I go along with John on most of his policies, mainly because he knows so much more than I do. . . . I feel very strongly about a woman being feminine. . . . You have to be tough as nails sometimes . . . but still, my first job is being right here."

Mrs. Lindsay superintended the doing over of Gracie Mansion and the social side of life in the Mayor's home is individualistic. She handles the mail, pays the bills and devotes herself entirely to John and her children after four in the afternoon. She was more dismayed than the Mayor when one of their daughters decided to model clothes. But she has bowed to the trend of the times and shows up at the smart restaurants and at fashion showings with the other town sophisticates. She admits that her clothing bills have tripled since her husband became mayor. This, however, is not Mary Lindsay's essential nature. Until she was needled to smarten up her wardrobe, she was the well-bred matron in casual clothes. She is a reader and likes opera, the ballet and prowling in museums. Up at six, she cooks her husband's breakfast, sees her children off to school at eight and zooms off in her pale-blue station wagon for the day's engagements, mostly official. Her parties at Gracie Mansion take in a wide range of guests and require some skilled hostessing.

Mrs. Lindsay represents a growing number of wives who stand behind their men in office with grace and aptitude, shedding some of the stiffness of the past. They are attuned to their era and are apt to be clever in their own right. Mrs. Lindsay happens to be independent, a smart New Englander with a breezy, cooperative manner. Her predecessor, Mrs. Robert Wagner, was gentle and unassuming. Mrs. Fiorello La Guardia was strongly political in her own right and has remained a respected figure in city affairs.

When seeking his last term in Congress, handsome John Lindsay was opposed in the so-called Silk Stocking district by one of the most resilient of women politicians. Eleanor Clark French staged a lively campaign and lost with good spirit. She is used to being on the losing side and reacts buoyantly to defeat. She lost a bid for the State Senate in 1956. In 1968 she worked for Eugene McCarthy with her customary verve and was a delegate at the Democratic Convention. She had met Senator McCarthy fifteen years earlier at a political meeting in New York and on that occasion had said to him: "Someday you ought to run for President of the United States." It was Mrs. French who led three hundred McCarthy supporters out of the Commodore Hotel when the Democratic State Committee allotted them a disproportionately small number of delegates-at-large for the convention. In a dramatic speech she said: "This day will go down in the history of the Democratic Party as a day of perfidy."

"Politics beats housework," says Mrs. French, who was born and bred a Republican but has shown maverick tendencies in backing men in whom she believes. Her father was a banker, and her early years were spent in the traditional fashion of the well-to-do. She and her cousin, Mary Todhunter Clark, the first Mrs. Nelson Rockefeller, studied music together in Paris after attending boarding school. When the Depression came along, Eleanor's life changed radically. She considers this the best thing that happened to her along the way, since it brought her face to face with realities. Since then she has taken a firm liberal stand on public issues and has always been ready to play a lone hand for her convictions. Because she is original, independent and practical, men listen to her with respect, but the party politician regards her with a wary eye and her efforts have not been crowned with success.

Mrs. French tried philanthropy and journalism before stepping into politics. She soon became noticeable as a hard worker, prone to use original methods in picking up votes. Her husband, John French, is a Wall Street lawyer, and she has three stepchildren. Like many other women politicians of vintage 1968 she grows roses at her summer place, does needlework and can turn out a successful cheese soufflé. Most women running for political office today let the public know that they are skilled in the domestic arts.

Three women have served as governors, with varying degrees of success. The most sensational, Miriam Amanda Ferguson, won by a majority of 80,000 in 1924 over Felix D. Robertson, who was endorsed by the Ku Klux Klan. Her rule was stormy, and she became more famous as the foe of the Klan in Texas than as one of the two American women who first administered the affairs of sovereign states. She was pitchforked into office when her farmer husband, former Governor James Ferguson, was impeached on charges of mishandling state funds. When the courts refused to let him run again, his wife announced: "Well, *I* will."

When she learned that she was the winner she said, "I am to be the Governor and I shall be Governor in every sense of the word."

"And I shall be the handy man about the house," said Jim with a grin. "I will cut the wood and bring in the water."

All through the red-hot campaign he had been his wife's chief advocate. "Elect Miriam, give her your votes, friends, but I'll be the Governor," he shouted. While "Ma Ferguson" fed her two thousand white leghorn chickens on their ranch, he was hailed by delirious crowds. "Me for Ma" and "Two Fergusons for the Price of One" became statewide battle cries. But the bucolic picture was overdone, and Mrs. Ferguson finally announced that they were making a fool of her by playing up her mules, chickens and the rustic life. Actually the Fergusons lived with considerable style and in comfortable houses.

It was all part of the madness of the 1920's, and Mrs. Ferguson became a national character. Nothing she did fell into the traditional pattern. She refused to shake hands, to bow and scrape, or to receive guests at the Governor's mansion. She would not have an ashtray in the house, and she was a stern prohibitionist, one of the planks on which she had run. She was considered the friend of the poor and the foe of the privileged, and during her first term of office she granted pardons to 1,500 prison inmates in Texas. In the eyes of her critics her clemency reached "scandalous proportions," and in 1926 she was forced to defend her position.

"Ma Ferguson" was a woman who gave an impression of harshness rather than of charm. She was big-boned and broad-shouldered, with heavy lids drooping over hazel eyes. She came from a well-to-do family, was a college graduate, and gave her husband great help in the early days of their marriage. He was a handsome, robust man who had been a laborer, miner, teamster, builder, farmer, real estate dealer and finally a banker. Since he had served a term as governor Mrs. Ferguson was quite familiar with her role when she took office in 1925. The fact that she had a strong family inheritance and much Texas tradition commended her to the public, but in the end the Fergusons' rule covered two decades of constant battling. Though their opponents scorched them with open charges, legislative action, court decisions and ridicule, the Fergusons survived. They had a forum in their own paper, and Mrs. Ferguson wrote a syndicated column that was not greatly admired. She had a strain of native humor, and her combative spirit enlivened her manner when something moved her.

But she was plagued by asthma, and when her husband told her that she must campaign a second time she wept for three nights. She was not a politician at heart, and her two terms of office brought her little happiness. She had stayed at home as much as possible, continuing her domestic duties, canning and preserving, and insisting that woman's place was in the home. Meanwhile, her husband sat behind her desk while Texans said, "Ma signs the papers but Farmer Jim's the Governor." The power play between them was self-evident in 1925 when she signed a bill restoring Jim's rights as a citizen, which had been forfeited in the course of his impeachment.

Both of the Fergusons were opposed to woman suffrage. Jim had fought it in 1918 when a bill was rushed through, giving Texas women the vote. But in the end Mrs. Ferguson and Mrs. Catt exchanged pledges to work for the good of womankind. Ferguson died in 1944 and his widow lived on alone in their house overlooking the Capitol at Austin until her death in 1961 at the age of eighty-six.

Women governors, like women in general, are apt to outlive their husbands, and Nellie Tayloe Ross moved into office as Governor of Wyoming, succeeding her deceased husband, almost at the same moment that Mrs. Ferguson became Governor of Texas. Each claimed to be first, but although they were elected on the same day, Mrs. Ross was installed a few days before Mrs. Ferguson. She caused much less furor and moved at first with caution. She was serene and good-looking, quiet and discreet in her widow's attire, and was different in all respects from her luridly advertised colleague in the

South. Her regime was not dynamic, but the public approved of her dignified ways, and during the boisterous 1920's she was regarded as the number-one woman politician in the country.

However, she soon had to fight some tough battles on the prohibition question, and she went personally into Buffalo Bill's county and mounted the bench of the crowded courthouse at Cody to enforce the Volstead Act against an errant sheriff. A huge basket of carnations by her side was the one concession to the fact that for the first time a woman was presiding in a notoriously rowdy courtroom. The trial lasted for a week, and the sheriff was removed for misconduct in office. But Governor Ross was not forgiven locally. She lost that county in the next election and was accused of being prejudiced and unjust in her findings. Many took occasion to say that justice could not be expected from a woman governor. She further aggravated the sportsminded among her constituents by enforcing the Wyoming law against professional prize fighting, stepping in without a moment's hesitation when she learned that a professional prize fight for large stakes was pending.

But her national image in general was rose water and decorum, and in later years she regretted that she had not answered accusations and protested strongly the slights she suffered when the battle cry was "We need a man" to bring greater economy and efficiency. When she ran for re-election her opponent toured the state insisting that it was not Governor Ross but her advisers who were running Wyoming. She always insisted that although she asked the local politicians for recommendations, she was never swayed against her own better judgment, and she firmly dislodged one of her husband's henchmen, who later fought her in the courts. Governor Ross was a stickler for law and order, and not more than a dozen persons condemned to death were pardoned during her term of office. Governor Ferguson at this time was freeing prisoners by the hundreds. The techniques of the two lady governors in this respect invited comment.

Although she ran for re-election and scooped up seven-eighths of the normal Republican vote in Wyoming, Governor Ross lost and was bitterly disappointed to have met defeat after one term in office. The applause for her administration had far outweighed the criticism, but she was not a tough fighter, and the lusty forces of the

Prohibition era were all around her. With a harder shell she might have become one of the abler representatives of her sex in politics. It might be said of Nellie Ross that her femininity helped to defeat her. She was better adjusted in her later role as Director of the Mint.

In the decades that followed the administrations of Mrs. Ferguson and Mrs. Ross there were great changes in the South, and where Ma Ferguson had fought the Klan, Governor Lurleen Wallace of Alabama dared a federal court in the 1960's to enforce a desegregation order. She charged that intellectuals were out of touch with the people and were on a collision course with public officials. Mrs. Wallace was the third woman governor in the United States, but her reign was brief for she died of cancer in the spring of 1968, after two years in office. Most of the time she was ill, and her husband, the controversial George C. Wallace, ran state affairs much as Jim Ferguson did for his wife in Texas.

Mrs. Wallace, a quiet type who had risen from an impoverished youth to the governor's mansion, sat beneath the crystal chandeliers of the State Capitol in Montgomery while her husband shaped policy and pushed through measures. She handled ceremonial affairs with skill and promised that her programs would be administered "from the standpoint of how they affect the family." Mrs. Wallace showed that she could hold her own when she refused to retain in office an official held over from her husband's administration of whom she disapproved. And quite on her own she pushed through an appropriation for improving conditions in the mental institutions of the state after she had visited them and observed their wretched condition.

Mrs. Wallace had run for office because her husband could not have a third term. Since she had never made a speech in her life, the voters were first incredulous and then intrigued. But she soon made an impression of her own. She was poised and self-assured without the bombast of her husband. Her own best speeches were nonpolitical, and she left it to her husband to answer attacks. It was her custom to refer to herself as a wife and mother as well as governor, and she projected the family picture, taking pains to emphasize the old-fashioned virtues.

Since the public viewpoint about women in office had mellowed in thirty years, Mrs. Wallace suffered less than Mrs. Ferguson from gibes about a woman holding such an imposing public office. But in acknowledgment of the jests and quips about the Husband and Wife hierarchy, she gave Wallace a frilly apron for Christmas, and kept a rolling pin on her desk inscribed, "To be used with judiciousness, and without discrimination, and complete authority."

In general the women governors proved that even when endowed with full political power they leaned heavily on their husbands' advice. Mrs. Wallace was too ill to cope alone with her responsibilities. Mrs. Ferguson was in a difficult situation because of her husband's own political history. Mrs. Ross had a sound record on her own, but all three are remembered more for the novelty of their appointments than as solid members of the political establishment.

Chapter 10

Charm School

The political scene is spiced today with elements symbolic of the incredible 1960's. High fashion and worldly understanding invest the once-shabby world of politics. The idealistic intensity of the young sparks up the battleground, and a strain of elegance permeates the councils of the political camps. With beautiful wives, daughters and mothers in the background, the old image of windy rhetoric is now laced with the fashionable, the feminine, the involved.

Millions of critical eyes focus on the woman in public life and, more significantly, on the woman behind the man in public life, so that the candidate's wife and the woman politician tend alike to be platform-conscious, television-conscious and crowd-conscious. They need to be if they are to survive in the raucous jungle and register as appealing helpmates for their husbands, or as worthy performers on their own account.

The scoffers who feel that things should be done in the same old way are simply out of touch with the present reality, for the psychedelic world is in the ascendant, and the feeling reaches right down to the grass roots. Candidates' wives are on the firing line and can profoundly affect their husbands' fates. A breach of taste, a hasty malapropism, a dash of snobbishness or a show of ignorance invite discussion from coast to coast. The attractive, tactful wife, the well-ordered children, the general atmosphere of sound family life count heavily on the political scene, as they always have, except that all these qualities are now more visible to the voting public and therefore more significant to the man seeking office. Never were women more influential in the fate of their husbands, whether or not they go to the voting booth. Even in 1968, after a half century of eligibility for public service, most women were still proving to be more effective in their natural setting than in holding office on their own. And those in office tended to build up the home image, to make people aware of their children and to hand out their favorite recipes as a propaganda sop. This domestic emphasis has lost some of its meaning in a world of supermarkets and frozen foods, but it's a time-honored gag and is part of the two-edged game played today before the cameras.

The blue-stocking image is out, and Mrs. Eugene McCarthy had to play down her scholarly attributes. The fashionable and all-feminine image is in, with renewed strength. Even today's counterpart of the early feminist, grasping for power and office, thinks of her clothes, her looks, her feminine charm. She dare not be less than well turned out for television and the platform. The tumbling psyche knot, the wrong-length skirt, the offbeat hat, the lack of a sense of style, have faded before the searching beam of television lights. The Mad Hatter effects of the early gatherings of women, dignified and noble in purpose though many of them were, have been supplanted by fashionable assemblages of women spankingly smart and up to the minute, even in the matter of mini skirts. The quick propulsion by jet from point to point has diffused the fashion picture, so that campaigning women in designers' clothes no longer feel the need to turn their diamond rings around when they move from the club luncheon to a slum area. The women who crossed the country in 1916 on Charles Evans Hughes' campaign train practiced what the *New York Times* described in a headline as "Rings In, Rings Out."

But the women of 1968 were not apologetic for their Cartier or Kenneth Lane jewels. Diors and Norells showed up amid the placards, and Kenneth curls and Gucci shoes were not amiss. They were there to be looked at, to make an impression on the camera, catching a national audience as well as the one on the spot. It all adds up to what the public expects today of its leading women, as of its leading men. It's the first lesson that Presidents' wives have to learn, as Mrs. Johnson quickly admitted. The bevy of attractive relatives must help their men at this visual level, where their influence is considerable. It's an ancient instinct in any event. Even lofty-minded Dr. Elizabeth Blackwell, penniless as she graduated from Hobart College, borrowed money for a new black silk dress for the occasion. And Abigail Adams wore high-heeled shoes with her quilted petticoats and short cloaks— "everything of the best," she insisted, "but nothing different from the modest attire of other citizens."

Politics is no longer the game of the spinster, the Whoops Sisters, or the dowdy, monster-hatted matron of the cartoons. The great hostesses of the Revolutionary era, the political sirens of the Civil War, all have their counterparts in the salons of today, which flourish in Washington, New York, Boston, Chicago, Philadelphia and Detroit, in San Francisco, Dallas and other large cities. They are masterminded by rich and worldly-minded women, who play the traditional game of pushing their political convictions and backing their candidates by bringing together a mélange of bright wits, avant-garde thinkers and steady-minded citizens. The early American women absorbed their political convictions at first hand from the Founding Fathers. Today's women help to shape the political picture on their own. They function in their drawing rooms, at the fashionable resorts, in the cocktail lounges and hotel lobbies. They give great parties in exotic settings and, imaginatively costumed, run the charity balls swathed in the extremes of fashion or fantasy and wearing the most smashing of jewels, real or false.

Much of the wealth of the land is in their hands, and they are potent in many areas, for they push the arts, are strongly culture conscious and take heed of the young. If they are not far out to the left they are apt to be far out to the right, and both work hard to maneuver the men they want into office. They represent a small but powerful segment of pace setters and opinion shapers. The great majority of American women still live with respect for the Godhead, man-made laws and established traditions. They practice quiet diplomacy, centered in the home, and few think in terms of $38,000 sable coats, $5,500 silver sequin gowns, $250 jeweled evening slippers and earrings costing $10,000, as some of the more noted political hostesses have been known to do.

Glamorous women have always been disposed to attach themselves to men of political power, and the magnetic, handsome and rich candidates of the 1960's have drawn a special following. Quite often it is the woman of charm who moves at the root of government, and today it has become a cult with smart women—even a patriotic duty—to know what government is about, to talk to the candidates, to study and distribute their leaflets, to organize support for them. They show up with political buttons at the races, at the discothèque and ballet, loaded with arguments and "in" talk on the issues. The endless dialogue goes on in the smartest lunching places, where the Beautiful People and the Political People crisscross and sometimes are one. The country club set as well as the urban hostess is in action. The all-powerful younger generation has declared itself on the college campus, and the slum dweller has the message dinned into his ear, as he is wooed by millionaires and their smiling wives.

These restless figures bespeak good works at every turn. They plead for the retarded child, for the beautification of town and country, for urban housing and better schools, for integration and medical care. They work for charity or the spread of the arts, for all good causes that match the times. Above all, they must feel involved, even when they are beautiful moths wheeling around Truman Capote or Norman Mailer. They adorn their homes with far-out décor or revive the stateliness of the past. They dress with wit and originality. They buy and collect and make flashing use of their own and their husbands' fortunes. They build fabulous homes in unexpected places and would rather be dead than be ignorant of political issues. Their modus operandi differs from that of Dolley Madison, Anne Bingham, Kate Chase and Mrs. Astor, for they are the new, new women, touching shoulders at times with the Teeny Boppers and the Flower Children. They are a fresh power to be reckoned with on the political horizon, like the earnest-minded students on the campuses, or the youthful exhibitionists who twine themselves around the political cabarets, to catch a moment of the limelight. Hollywood sets its own swift pace, with Shirley Temple Black putting on her spunky but fruitless drive for office, and other stars from the hierarchy of stage, television and screen squandering their political opinions and financial support in all directions with the generous and uninhibited instincts of their calling.

As money raisers the new breed of women dabbling in top-level politics is respected by the most hard-boiled politicians. Some have already taken their politics in depth, like Alice Roosevelt, a focal figure in the picture for the last half century, or like Marietta Tree, dynamic in the immediate present. Washington has its own powerful home guard, changing with each administration, but it has been unprecedently brilliant and clothes-conscious since the days of the Kennedys. Some of the magnificent political hostesses of the 1960's now outclass the great ladies of Embassy Row, who have always led the social field in Washington. Here and there a Senator's wife, like Mrs. John Sherman Cooper, gives dinners of distinction and dares to spoof the spendthrift charity ball by running a No Ball for her favorite cause.

The irreplaceable Alice Longworth, though glad to have had a taste of the Edwardian world, likes the present. "It's exciting," she says, at the age of eighty-three. A White House debutante in 1902, a White House bride in 1906, she has lived the political life to the full and has always added her own quotient in an individualistic way. She voted for Lyndon Johnson in 1964 and is fond of the Kennedys. Although she now insists that her only accomplishment has been to have lived to such a ripe age, actually her quick, astringent deductions have sparked the political scene since the beginning of the century. She has frequently been the consultant and critic of men of affairs, and long before women could vote Alice was pulling strings and sharpening her wits on the endless procession of celebrated men who crossed her path. The fact that she liked to play poker, gamble and smoke, before smoking was an accepted custom in the feminine world, gave emphasis to her heady ways. And she has never hesitated to think and do what she liked, a refreshing change of pace from the women behind the scenes in Washington who have had to major in discretion. The official wives move circumspectly in the political jungle.

James Reston, of the New York Times, who has closely observed the significant hostesses and the simpler wives of many of the Senators and Congressmen, says of the latter: "The chief charm of women in official Washington—aside, of course, from their reckless beauty—is that they are essentially more honest than their menfolk. . . . Except in rare instances they are not surrounded by droves of bureaucratic drones and press agents. They are not protected and puffed up by official aides and are therefore not so likely to confuse themselves with power. . . . The Government officials' wives are not as a rule at ease in the big official limousines, the endless receiving line, and the big crystal-chandelier dining room."

Many of them come from simple backgrounds. They have regional tastes and prejudices and are used to saying what they think in a friendly setting. The bite and sting of the political center is not their natural milieu, but their men carry them along when they fumble, and sometimes it is up to them to carry their men along. Such women as Mrs. Truman and Mrs. Humphrey made a point of cooking at home for their husbands when they were Senators—a not uncommon state of affairs in a world where dyspepsia flourishes and servants are scarce. In general the wives do their work behind the scenes when it comes to criticizing the administration.

But in no area is discretion more imperative than in the Diplomatic Corps. The wives of United States ambassadors today play even more important roles than in the time of Abigail Adams, when they were an untried novelty at the European courts. In an era of fallen monarchies and shifting politics, they must exercise understanding of a new order. From the stately days of Mrs. Whitelaw Reid fulfilling the Edwardian tradition at the Court of St. James's to Mrs. Angier Biddle Duke in the 1960's organizing a fashion show in the Embassy at Madrid and hanging paintings lent by American museums, the emphasis has changed. A model, a scholar, a famous surgeon's daughter, a journalist, an artist, an Irish matriarch named Rose Kennedy, have livened the ambassadorial picture around the world. Their influence has been considerable in shaping the feeling surrounding their husbands. The women who now hold sway in the American embassies tend to play down the snob appeal that traditionally attaches itself to diplomatic life. Most of them are contemporary in feeling. Some are outstanding in the world of fashion, the arts and philanthropy. They are all aware of social injustice and are doubly alert now to the unpopularity of the United States in foreign countries.

But their role is secondary to the richest political plum likely to fall to a woman today—an appointment as an ambassador. American women have fared well in this field, from Clare Boothe Luce to Patricia Roberts Harris, the Negro beauty appointed to the Luxembourg post in 1967. Presidents have given them some play in this appropriate milieu. Perle Mesta might be taken as the symbol of them all, but in addition she is one of America's most discussed hostesses. The world at large is apt to think of her as the original of *Call Me Madam*, but American politicians respect her political acumen and cherish her parties. Her quips have entertained kings and presidents, although they left the Kennedys cold. Friendly Perle was chilled by Jacqueline. But her great good nature and sense of bounty were again in evidence at the Democratic convention of 1968, tempered to some extent by the rigors of the times and the monstrous events she viewed in Chicago.

She may lack the quiet distinction of some of the great political hostesses of the past, but Mrs. Mesta has drive and political prescience. She has been invincible in her efforts to include the greatest number of people in the aura of her flamboyant generosity. Besides, her fame has spread in the bright beam of present-day publicity. She is a law unto herself, and many notable politicians have used Mrs. Mesta's dinner table as a testing place for their ambitions. Her great days were in the time of the Trumans. She was chairman of the inaugural ball and immediately showed her skill at raising large sums of money from her friends for party purposes. During that administration she was so much a part of the family that she used the back stairs of the White House and proved herself to be a clever politician behind the scenes. Although she had her favorites, she knew all the Presidents back to William Howard Taft, and from the 1940's on she entertained them in the lavish fashion of Dolley Madison.

Suitably enough, since her own fortune was founded on steel, Mrs.

Mesta was appointed Ambassador to Luxembourg by President Truman. She felt at home in this steel-producing country and was soon on friendly terms with the miners as well as with the Grand Duchess. She welcomed hordes of American tourists and helped to put this little country on the map. Her parties for the G.I.'s stationed in Germany became legendary, an image sharply focused by Ethel Merman in *Call Me Madam*. Mrs. Mesta began with seventy-five soldiers but wound up giving a ball for 1,200. General Eisenhower, whom she had known as a lieutenant at West Point, headed straight for her kitchen and gave her a lesson in how to feed his soldiers when he called at the Embassy. She had been giving them elaborate dinners which they did not seem to enjoy. "Give 'em hamburgers, hot dogs and potato salad," he told Mrs. Mesta, and he showed her how to make his own brand of potato salad.

She always had music for the General on his visits because he liked to sing. She also set up bridge tables, knowing his devotion to cards. When he took office as President she resigned but continued to travel, to throw parties at every opportunity, and to strengthen her image as a personality with public appeal. Her hospitality took on more of the philanthropic touch, in the mood of the times.

Ruth Bryan Owen, daughter of William Jennings Bryan, was the first woman to head an American Legation in a foreign capital. After serving two terms in Congress she was appointed Minister to Denmark in 1933. Mrs. Owen was brilliant, enterprising and highly successful in her post. In 1936 she resigned to marry Börge Rohde, and she later served in the American delegation of the United Nations. Another American woman, Eugenie M. Anderson of Minnesota, followed her in 1949 as Ambassador to Denmark. She worked on tariff problems and in 1951 signed a treaty of "friendship, commerce and navigation." This was the first time a woman's signature had appeared on a treaty between the United States and another nation.

Mrs. Anderson was the daughter of a clergyman in Red Wing, and she had hoped for a career in music, but while attending Carleton College she met John Pierce Anderson, heir to the puffed-rice fortune. They were soon married and she became prominent in Democratic politics. She arrived in Copenhagen at a time when Denmark had been persuaded to abandon its neutral attitude and join in a military alliance to protect Western Europe from the Soviet Union. Mrs. Anderson learned enough Danish to use it on the air, and she bicycled along the highways like her neighbors, a slender, brown-haired woman with gray eyes and an engaging smile.

She resigned after the Republican victory of 1952 but was given another diplomatic post by President Kennedy in 1962, this time to go behind the Iron Curtain as minister to Bulgaria, a novel assignment for a woman. The Bulgarians liked her and called her "Grandmother." Her house in Sofia was known as "The White House," and she boldly flew the American flag on the Legation and on her automobile. She refused to close the display windows of the Legation when the Communist government demanded that she do so. When four hundred African and Communist students stoned the Legation to protest the Belgian–United States hostage rescue operation in the Congo, she demanded—and received—an apology from the government.

Her husband, an artist and expert in three-dimensional photography, carried on his work wherever his wife went and helped her in a series of cultural exchanges. She resigned when President Johnson took office. The Andersons have two children, and while their son and daughter were growing up, and before Mrs. Anderson became active in politics, they lived on the family farm at Red Wing. She was a founder of the Americans for Democratic Action and in 1948 she became a Democratic National Committeewoman. Ambassador Arthur Goldberg chose her to serve on the Trusteeship Council at the United Nations, and in the spring of 1968 she succeeded Angie Brooks of Liberia as Council president.

Denmark again welcomed a woman ambassador from the United States when Katharine White was appointed to the post by President Johnson in 1964. A Vassar graduate with many interests, Mrs. White had a long political career behind her when she moved into the big league. She summed up her political philosophy in one crisp sentence: "I believe in good, Yankee common sense."

But the cream of the ambassadorial crop, from the point of view of international interest, was Clare Boothe Luce—a diplomat, but much else besides. Perhaps no American woman has shown more breadth in her career, yet none has incurred more ill will from members of her own sex. She has been an ambassador, a Congresswoman, lecturer, writer, playwright and noted beauty. She first stirred up antagonism with *The Women*, a play that was as much discussed in the 1930's as *The Group*, Mary McCarthy's novel, in the 1960's. At this stage in her life she had a cool, ruthless approach, but her attitude changed when, after the death of her only daughter in an automobile accident, she became a Roman Catholic.

Mrs. Luce has been the most discussed, if not necessarily the most significant, woman politician. Her congressional career, which began in 1943, was undistinguished, but in 1944 she gave the keynote speech at the Republican National Convention, the first major speech delivered by a woman at a convention since 1892. It became known as her G.I. Joe speech, and it was considered a masterpiece of persuasion or invective, depending on one's point of view. Like Anna Dickinson and Fanny Wright, Mrs. Luce was eloquent, silvery of voice and arresting to look at as she swung her audience with her. She seconded Barry Goldwater for the presidential nomination at the Republican Convention of 1964, and she was Congresswoman from Connecticut, and Ambassador to Italy, during the Eisenhower administration. In 1959 she was confirmed as Ambassador to Brazil, but battled so furiously with Senator Wayne Morse that she withdrew from the contest. Similarly, she backed down on her decision to run against Senator Kenneth B. Keating in 1964.

As the wife of Henry Luce, she was in double jeopardy from Wayne Morse. Time and again she had to pay for the sins committed by his lively magazines. But her husband's easy contacts with world celebrities often paved the way for her, too. And sometimes she made him her courier to carry messages straight to the President instead of channeling them through the State Department. As a prima donna by nature and experience she resented not being consulted more about policy, and when she backed Arthur Vandenberg for the Presidency at the Philadelphia convention, Foster Dulles and Thomas Dewey both gave her the cold shoulder. Touring the European theater of war in the early 1940's she reaped a harvest of publicity, to the chagrin of her fellow Congressmen, but she did not shine in the Congressional setting at home. When she stepped down in 1947 she was better known for her looks and style than for positive accomplishment.

Her political career was only beginning, however. She figured importantly in the Eisenhower campaign, and after the General's election she was sent to Italy as United States Ambassador. High drama surrounded her in this setting, and she was popular and effective in her role until her health made it necessary for her to come home. Nauseated, nervous, fatigued and numb, she finally decided that she was being poisoned by arsenate fumes from flakings drifting down from the ceiling of her rose-embellished bedroom in the Villa Taverna.

Marriage to two rich men helped Mrs. Luce on her climb to the upper echelons of government. She was twenty when she married George Brokaw and became one of the much publicized sophisticates of the 1920's. After their divorce in 1929 she satirized the czars of the *beau monde* for *Vanity Fair*. They were all stuffed shirts to Clare. When she and some fellow wits from the magazine decided to organize a new political party, Frank Kent, Arthur Krock and Mark Sullivan persuaded her that this would be madness. But when she sat in Mrs. Woodrow Wilson's box at the Democratic Convention of 1932 the die was cast for her to become a practicing politician. She studied international politics and applied her bright wits to the issues of war and peace, isolation or intervention.

Before long she was a confirmed internationalist, and in 1940 she backed Wendell Willkie. Her first political speech was made on his behalf. After a furious debate with Dorothy Thompson, the noted correspondent who was strongly pro-Roosevelt at the time, they were compared to two blond Valkyries rampant on the prows of opposing ships of state. Other women of literary stature were involved, for Marcia Davenport and her husband, Russell Davenport, were campaigning strenuously for Willkie.

The years and her sorrows softened Mrs. Luce and made her more tolerant of her fellow women, but she has always chosen to play a lone hand and to stay aloof from the feminine establishment, whose members are inclined to be wary of the author of The Women. Too, she seems unassailable in her own calm isolation. In the years before the death of Henry Luce they lived quietly in Fairfield, Connecticut, at Phoenix, Arizona, and in the Hawaiian Islands, where she returned to build another house in 1968. They floated in their swimming pools and talked politics and news. It was her husband's custom to read to her by the hour while she painted freak animals or made Christmas tree baubles with velvets and jewels.

As a practical politician Mrs. Luce has always shown up best in debate, with her well-reasoned views expressed in clear tones. She is optimistic about the role women might play in the political world if they were given equal opportunity at top, policy-making levels. No woman is qualified to be Vice-President, let alone President, in Mrs. Luce's opinion, but she favors a second Vice-President—preferably a woman—to mastermind the social end of the administration.

The suffrage militants failed to get help from her when Doris Stevens, of the Woman's Party, urged an Equal Rights for Women plank in the Republican platform of 1940. Yet she deplores the fact that in 1962 there were only nineteen women in Congress, their highest point, and that in 1965 the number had dwindled to twelve. None seems to her to have reached a high degree of distinction, and she cites the fact that out of 2,181 Time covers, only 177 women were found to be notable in a man's world. Fifteen had won the Pulitzer Prize in this century, but only one American woman—Pearl Buck— had rated the Nobel Prize for literature.

If women have not done well, or even fairly well, in politics, Mrs. Luce concedes their success as writers and in the other arts. Her own list of the major American women writers includes Margaret Fuller, Harriet Beecher Stowe, Louisa May Alcott, Emily Dickinson, Edna St. Vincent Millay, Edith Wharton, Ellen Glasgow, Amy Lowell, Gertrude Stein, Willa Cather, Elinor Wylie, Edna Ferber, Katherine Anne Porter, Susan Glaspell, Kay Boyle, Mary McCarthy and Rachel Carson. In the several worlds of art, sculpture, music, ballet and fashion she gives women top marks and wryly adds: "A woman can produce what no man can: a child."

Strong on the political horizon today is another fragile blonde of iron will with her own combination of beauty, worldliness, wealth and political prescience. Marietta Tree is tall and honey-haired and has topaz eyes and an infallible sense of style. Her political influence is by no means minor, although it is not always visible at surface level. She runs a twentieth-century salon in the eighteenth-century tradition. The brainy and the witty, the dedicated but not the naïve, circulate around her. Her guests range from Arthur Schlesinger, Jr., to Truman Capote, and the princes of the press, television, law and politics are at her beck and call. "I have a New Englander's elasticity," she says, a natural inheritance since she is the daughter of Mrs. Malcolm E. Peabody, who cheerfully went to jail at the age of seventy-two for joining in a civil-rights demonstration in Florida. An aging Boston Brahmin who climbs mountains and runs one house in Cambridge and another in Maine, Mary Parkman Peabody is the fiercely independent daughter-in-law of the Rev. Endicott Peabody, founder of the Groton School, the wife of a Bishop and the mother of a former Governor of Massachusetts.

The strong will and decisive spirit of her mother spark Mrs. Tree's political understanding. She is frankly scornful of frilled femininity in politics. When appointed a United States Ambassador to the United Nations, she remarked: "My job means lots of hard work. Contrary to some people's impressions, one doesn't go around tapping ambassadors on the arm with a fan." She is direct and businesslike when there is a job to be done, and she never hesitates to engage in the spadework herself. She prefers not to be one of the so-called Beautiful People, although she shows up in their orbit inevitably as she pursues her interest in art, the theater and fashion. Now in her early fifties, she edged her way into politics during World War II working for Nelson A. Rockefeller when he was Coordinator of Inter-American Affairs. A brief period as a researcher for *Life* stirred up an interest in journalism. She headed the Volunteers for Stevenson Committee in New York in 1956, and four years later was deputy chairman of the Citizens Committee for John F. Kennedy. In 1961 President Kennedy appointed her United States representative to the Human Rights Commission of the United Nations. She valued her

$24,500 salary check, believing that it made her a professional and gave her more authority in her job.

Mrs. Tree was working closely with Adlai Stevenson at this time, and was walking in a London street with him, not far from the United States Embassy, when he dropped dead at her side. Next day all the world had heard about Marietta Tree. In 1967 she became a delegate-at-large to the United Nations. The liberal wing of the Democratic Party, civil-rights activities and other volunteer causes command her interest. As a member of the New York State Constitutional Convention in 1967 her attention was focused on urban renewal problems and she began a serious study of city planning. She lectures on foreign policy, the United Nations, human rights, the role of women and kindred subjects.

Mrs. Tree has not found that being the wife of a millionaire and having impressive homes in Manhattan, Palm Beach and Barbados has interfered in any way with the pursuit of her dazzling political career. Her husband, Arthur Ronald Lambert Field Tree, grandson of Marshall Field, appreciates her, and she takes a keen interest in the hotel he opened in Barbados, the botanical garden he started, the orchids he cultivates and his work for Planned Parenthood and the Council of the University of the West Indies.

Their daughter Penelope is both romantic and amusing in her ways, and she interrupted her freshman year at Sarah Lawrence College to become a model. In no time she became a headline character, an Alice in Wonderland circa 1968. Marietta's elder daughter, Frances FitzGerald, the child of her earlier marriage to Desmond FitzGerald of the C.I.A., is witty and worldly, with a magna cum laude degree from Radcliffe behind her. She writes for *Vogue* and has done a book about her experiences as a war correspondent in Vietnam.

Mrs. Tree concedes that this is the day of the young, although she is frankly glad to be in the senior ranks herself, finding life "more relaxed, enjoyable, concentrated and fascinating after thirty-five." She believes that the man of today has a better understanding of women because of coeducation, and that women have more in common with men because they are better educated in the contemporary world. Mrs. Tree shares her daughters' appreciation of the fact that the young have suddenly become leaders in all manner of fields, and that they are more open-minded than their elders toward things in general.

Since World War I each President in turn has gone a little further in finding suitable political appointments for women, but the Ladies Without Portfolio function with eighteenth-century power. They are a revived breed of political hostess, with extensive influence of their own. They are liberal in their point of view and are keen participants in the world of today. The fact that some of them are immensely rich, philanthropic, fashionable and worldly ensures them constant attention in the press. Mrs. Tree is representative of this trend, and Mary Lasker, a supporter of Democratic causes and a friend of the Johnsons, is another. She is one of the treasured hostesses whose politics and philanthropy overlap. There are others like her from Texas to San Francisco, but Mrs. Lasker's fame is national and is closely related to medical research and the adornment of cities.

Long before Mrs. Johnson started her beautification campaign Mrs. Lasker had decked Park Avenue with tulips, lilies and other seasonal flowers, sparking a trend to restore to the city the feeling of trees, gardens and greenery that New York had had in its early days before it became an arid city of skyscrapers. In remembrance of her friend, Susan Wagner, the Mayor's wife, Mrs. Lasker had forty flowering cherry trees planted on Park Avenue after Mrs. Wagner's death from cancer. When the United Nations garden needed enlivening she ordered forty thousand daffodils and many cherry trees to add to its seasonal interest. Her magnolias and other trees may now be found in many parts of the city, and in response to Mrs. Johnson's campaign, she added 10,300 azalea bushes and 150 dogwood trees to the visible beauties of Washington's springtime. She advocates vast new nurseries and mass plantings across the country.

Flowers, in Mrs. Lasker's estimation, are therapy for a disordered and troubled world. "I am mainly interested in medical research," she says. "The flowers are just a little thing to keep me from being depressed until a cure is found for diseases like cancer and arteriosclerosis." Her husband, Albert D. Lasker, the Chicagoan who headed the advertising firm of Lord & Thomas, died of cancer in 1952. Since then his widow has worked tirelessly in this field and has

thrown money and influence into medical research. The Albert and
Mary Lasker Foundation gives awards and scholarships, and sends
around loan exhibits from the Lasker art collection to benefit the
American Cancer Society, of which Mrs. Lasker is honorary chairman.

Daughter of a Wisconsin banker, Mrs. Lasker majored in art history at Radcliffe, then attended Oxford briefly. Her interest in art
became a lifelong taste, and after she married Lasker in 1940 they
collected art, and particularly the French Impressionists. Her town
house on Beekman Place in New York, all white indoors, is hung
with the works of Monet, Picasso, Matisse, Van Gogh and Renoir.
Her archaeological finds, Chinese porcelains and lavish flower arrangements are familiar to the doers, thinkers and unpretentious citizens
that she likes to entertain there. Her hospitality has a wide range,
from her country estate near Amenia, New York, to her villa at Cap-
Ferrat on the Riviera.

American women of assorted heritage have been notably influential
in steering family riches to the public good. They have often turned
their fathers' and husbands' interest in specific directions, and when
they inherit family fortunes they are disposed to channel their
philanthropy to medicine, education or the arts. Such names as
Rockefeller, Harkness, Duke, Ford, Warburg, Schiff, Guggenheim,
Lehmann, Vanderbilt, Astor and Whitney have figured repeatedly in
the charmed circle of the givers.

Music, art and philanthropy are frequently tied together nowadays,
with or without political association, and among the various society
women who spread their influence in these areas are Mrs. Lytle Hull,
the musicians' good angel; Mrs. Paul Mellon, whose taste in land-
scaping art was applied to the White House Rose Garden and the
John F. Kennedy Memorial at Arlington; Mrs. Merriweather Post,
whose cereal millions have helped the underprivileged around the
world; and Mrs. Whitney Payson, sister of John A. Whitney. Like
Mrs. Lasker, Mrs. Payson is dedicated to medical philanthropy. In
addition, she uniquely adds to her horse-racing interests the ownership of the New York baseball team, the Mets. Most of these women
in one way or another are drawn into the political circle today, and

Mrs. Vincent Astor was one of Governor Nelson A. Rockefeller's backers in the presidential campaign of 1968. Out of the running at ninety, Mrs. August Belmont was still the *grande dame* of opera in 1969, founder of the Opera Guild and fund raiser for many good causes. Bernard Shaw wrote *Major Barbara* for Mrs. Belmont, when she was Eleanor Robson, the actress.

Another hostess of experience and sophisticated wit is Mrs. Averell Harriman, who smashes protocol with dash. "I love a country house in the middle of a city and not having to move on weekends," she says, liking Washington as much as Mrs. Jacob Javits, another well-known politician's wife, detests it. The capital is well aware of Mrs. Harriman, of her dinners and her teas, of her taste for bridge parties, dogs, Scrabble and canasta. As wife of one of America's most imposing conciliators, she is equally at home in New York, Washington, at their country home at Sands Point, Long Island, at Hobe Sound or abroad. When her husband was Governor of New York between 1955 and 1958 she injected life into the big Victorian executive mansion at Albany, and hung Copley and Gilbert Stuart portraits with Walt Kuhns.

Mrs. Harriman has special interest in art. She ran her own gallery and dealt in Impressionists at one time. Members of the Jet Set cultivate her today, and the Kennedys are her close friends. When she made her debut she was regarded as one of the best-looking girls in New York society, known for her gentian eyes and witty ways. Today she is the experienced matron who speaks her mind and refuses to be squelched at board meetings. She was with Harriman in Paris when he worked for the Marshall Plan and again in 1968 for the Vietnam peace negotiations. After Pearl Harbor she busied herself with the Welfare and Recreation Service of the United States Navy. Her grandson calls her a swinger, and Peter Duchin, whom she brought up after his mother's death, calls her Ma. She and Mr. Harriman have five children between them. In no sense of the word would she call herself a political hostess, but she is another Harriman who rates power, if not in the fashion of Daisy, at least in her own image.

Chapter 11

View from the Summit

The successful career woman is an American tradition, and in this blue heaven she glitters like a star, dismays her domestic sisters, influences men and in general is a dynamic factor in the social picture. She is apt to be an irresistible force when she reaches the summit, and legends gather around her like garlands. She is photographed, quoted, pampered and copied. But spectacular though she may be, she cannot be viewed as typical of the millions of average women who not only influence public affairs by casting their vote but now have added sexual emancipation to their show of power.

If women have not been smashingly successful in the political world they have found their own Eden in top-flight jobs, chiefly in advertising, fashion, communications, interior decoration, cosmetics and big business of one kind or another. Here they operate on a high plane of achievement and gain. Here they have found their deepest satisfaction, particularly when they can combine their jobs with marriage and motherhood—as they often do. Those who link professional success with domestic harmony are regarded as winners in the sweepstakes.

They come in all shapes and sizes, young and old, jeweled or unadorned, fashionable or indifferent, intellectual or hedonistic, beautiful or homely as the case may be. They are deep in the arts.

They design clothes or write about them. They run sensational advertising campaigns and edit magazines. They mastermind the beauty business and are brokers on Wall Street. They remodel houses and design striking interiors. They publicize themselves and others, making headlines that catch the eye. They are editors, columnists, commentators and the silken ladies of television to whom world celebrities and top politicians give heed. They are a new breed, a powerful breed, but nowhere are they more potent today than as Ladies of the Press— not in the old Nellie Bly tradition but as newspaper owners and editors, competing successfully with the most seasoned men in the field. They are contemporary in spirit, worldly, wealthy and fashionable in their attire.

Katharine Graham, publisher of the Washington *Post* and *Newsweek*, and owner of TV stations and wire services, inherited some of her newspaper instinct from her famous parents, Agnes and Eugene Meyer, philanthropists as well as editors. It was sharpened during her years as the wife of the brilliant Philip Graham, and then his death brought her into the forefront of the picture by inheritance. She runs her various worlds—press, political and social—with marked success.

Dorothy Schiff has survived newspaper mergers, strikes and drastic shake-ups and has carried the New York *Post* from the doldrums to success as the one afternoon newspaper in the metropolis. Her credo is "independent, liberal thought and ideas in the Press," and her keen business instincts are inherited from her grandfather, Jacob Schiff, noted banker and philanthropist. A more recent entry in the field is Mrs. Norman Chandler, the famous "Buffy," vice-president of the Los Angeles *Times-Mirror*, guardian angel of the Music Center, and czarina of a new type of woman's page in the family paper. Mrs. Chandler works with her husband and son, Norman and Otis Chandler, but Mrs. Graham and Mrs. Schiff go it alone. Mary King Patterson, widow of Joseph Patterson, was a power behind the throne at the New York *Daily News* until her retirement in 1969, and his daughter Alicia, with her husband Harry Guggenheim, made *Newsday* sensationally successful. Oveta Culp Hobby is a veteran newspaper publisher who knows the political field as well as she does the inner workings of the Houston *Post*.

Executive power for women in journalism is not a new tradition,
but it has never been practiced on a more effective scale. Phoebe
Apperson Hearst was influential in her husband's newspaper empire
as well as being an early suffragist. As owner of the Washington
Herald, Cissie Patterson was one of the capital's most dazzling
personalities who did not hesitate to feud openly with Mrs. Longworth from her front-page vantage point. There is much invisible
feminine influence in the incandescent world of journalism. Iphigene
Sulzberger, daughter of Adolph Ochs and wife of the late Arthur Hays
Sulzberger, has been in the inner councils of the New York Times for
a lifetime but without the slightest inclination to interfere. One
daughter, Ruth Golden, is publisher of the Chattanooga Times and
Evening Post, and another, Marian, is the wife of Andrew Heiskill,
chairman of the board of Life and Time.

Mrs. Clifton Daniel would be the last person in the world to
concede that her marriage to the managing editor of the New York
Times has given her any special influence in the world of the press.
Even in her White House years she majored in discretion and, like
her mother, she leans strongly to keeping woman's place in the home.
But she stepped out in the summer of 1968 to campaign discreetly for
Hubert Humphrey. This was her father's idea, and when she discussed it with her husband he told her it was her own business, as
long as it did not interfere with things at home. They have four sons,
and when the time came to announce her co-chairmanship of
Women for Humphrey she did not throw open her apartment to the
press but was interviewed at political headquarters. Mrs. Daniel has a
strong sense of privacy, perhaps because she is so knowledgeable
about the power of the press. She is candid and natural on radio and
television, and still hankers for the stage, but she has settled harmoniously into the domestic pattern of the wife who is more likely to
accept the decisions of her husband than to attempt to influence
him.

On the whole, however, petticoat rule is more marked in newspaper circles today than it has ever been as these powerful women
entertain the politicians, attend the most flashing parties, foster the
arts and charities, and dictate some of the editorials that sway politi-

cal opinion. They are more obvious in their operations than was the brilliant, soft-voiced Helen Rogers Reid, who persuasively scattered memos throughout all departments of the family paper in the golden days of the New York *Herald Tribune*. But even today's great Ladies of the Press make it seem as if they work through men, a seasoned tradition that has not been lost in the swinging world of the 1960's. Any talk of equal power for these women would be nothing short of absurd. They have it. They use it. They are decorative, too. All have been married and are chic and worldly. Men work for them ungrudgingly and sometimes—if not always—with admiration. None is assertive in manner.

The press is an old playground for ambitious women, but the new trinity of fashion, politics and society gives them added strength. They are constantly involved with the men and women close to the White House, with the most potent figures in the State Department, and with other government agencies. They are familiars along Embassy Row, for while not forgetting Dubuque, they are concerned with the world at large. The magazines welcome these sophisticates and reflect their influence in a thousand ways—as department heads, as writers, critics and researchers. The empresses of fashion down the years, from Sarah Josepha Hale and Madame Demorest to Diana Vreeland and Eugenia Sheppard, have gathered power along the way. They have new fields to cultivate today—the young, young generation, and here Enid Haupt leads the parade on the ownership level as publisher of *Seventeen*. Where women do not actually own the home and fashion magazines they are the top executives, the inspired policy makers, the gadabouts who tie in with the lush world of advertising, who stay close to the designers, both male and female.

They help to shape taste, to inform the consumer and delight the manufacturer at the same time; to push the far-out arts as well as the traditional; to illumine the swiftly changing social scene. They are firmly entrenched in the meshing activities of the publishing and magazine worlds. As foreign correspondents they have the widest range in their entire journalistic history, from jungle warfare to interviews behind the Iron Curtain. As commentators and critics of books, the theater, cinema, television and the various arts they have unlimited power and reach millions of people where Margaret Fuller was read by meager thousands. Their power and influence have grown. They are the queen bees on television and radio, and their faces, voices and views invade the American home from morning to night.

As publicists and advisers on etiquette, morals and the woman's role in general, they are a mighty power, affecting men, women, children and the home. In medicine, law, architecture and science American women have found new horizons, and some have achieved distinction, although numerically they are not strong in the professions traditionally identified with men.

But on all fronts it is self-evident in the 1960's that women on the whole have derived more satisfaction from their work in the outside world than from their political gains. Their influence on men has been much more strongly felt in business and professional circles than in the world of politics. Here they are as indispensable as wives and often better treated. When their mere jobs flower into careers they feel themselves doubly blessed, and some of the richest plums fall their way in advertising. Not all can play the game on the scale of witty Jane Trahey, who writes novels, runs her own agency and sometimes strikes an acid note along the Madison Avenue freeways. "Accomplishment," says Miss Trahey, "is getting where you want to and having a ball." She knows all the angles and plays for big stakes. Male colleagues expect to hear the truth from Miss Trahey, conveyed in a voice less soft and mellifluous than that of Mary Wells, an Ohio girl with two adopted daughters, one divorce behind her, and a much publicized marriage in 1967 to an advertising client, Harding Lawrence, president of Braniff Airways. It was Miss Wells' dashing idea to have the Braniff airplanes tinted in rainbow colors, to have Pucci design special costumes for the hostesses and to scoop up as much creative talent as she could lure from other agencies.

With a duplex penthouse, a home in Dallas, a pied-à-terre in Acapulco and a ranch near Phoenix, Miss Wells might be taken as symbolic of the American girl who has made it to the top in a spectacular way. She had her indoctrination at Macy's, then worked for McCann-Erickson and Doyle Dane Bernbach, before establishing her own advertising firm of Wells, Rich, Greene, well fortified with past experience and future promise. All the way she had a thrilling climb, boosting Alka-Seltzer sales by $13.3 million and stepping up Bristol-Myers, American Motors, Western Union, Benson & Hedges cigarettes and an assortment of razor blades, candy, oil and other products.

Miss Wells is blonde, delicately fashioned and, like all extremely successful career women, is assumed to be made of steel behind a velvety exterior. Power is exercised in subtle ways by these lambent beauties who have hit the top, often merely by using their good brains and working hard. If they are ruthless the signs usually are not self-evident. They all recognize the fact that it is in their own interest to maintain good relations with the men around them. The tug of war is more likely to be behind the scenes, and with members of their own sex. The American man does not complain. He is apt to be proud of the brilliant women in his organization, unless they mow him down, which does not often happen since there are too few women in the upper echelons of business to shift the balance materially. This is still man's domain, and the petticoat influence that has invaded it on the executive side is more provocative than threatening. Moreover, the American male is invincibly convinced of the superiority of the American female to all other women in the world. And he regards with more interest than alarm the wonder girls who make sensational headway in his own particular preserve. Nor does he undervalue the priceless Girl Friday who may have contributed substantially to his own success.

Women millionaires are usually so by inheritance. They are credited with owning from 70 to 85 per cent of the nation's inherited wealth, although their money is often controlled by men. *Fortune*, in listing the great fortunes of 1968, found that thirteen women had more than $150,000,000. As large moneymakers on their own their numbers are not impressive. About five thousand have attained imposing stature among the top quarter-of-a-million financiers. In New York Stock Exchange reports the market value of the shares held individually by women is 20 per cent of the total held by men. Women are prized investors, and it is an actuarial fact that they live much longer than men.

Potent though they are today in the market, Wall Street has never had a match for Hetty Green, who was born an heiress in 1835 and died in 1916, a friendless eccentric leaving more than $150,000,000 to her son and daughter and nothing to charity. In the intervening years she established herself as the most remarkable miser of the nineteenth century, in addition to being America's all-time leading woman financier. Money was her god, her lifework, her hobby and her obsession. She became one of the prized legends of Wall Street, controlling large investments across the country, juggling real-estate mortgage deals, supervising railroad interests and making huge loans.

Hetty's influence over men was awesome. Bankers, brokers and corporation heads came to this shabby woman in a stream during the panic. She regarded them with cold gray eyes, remembering the yachts, the art collections, the elaborate parties on which they had spent their money while she had been roughing it (with miserly satisfaction) in a forty-dollar-a-month flat in Hoboken. She spent most of her life in wretched quarters, moving from place to place to avoid tax collectors. Her clothes were shabby, her children were denied good food and medical attention and she fought an endless series of battles in court. But Hetty had the Midas touch and rarely lost money, even in periods of panic. She bought when everyone wanted to sell and sold when everyone wanted to buy. Henry Clews called her "one among a million of her sex," and Collis P. Huntington described her as nothing more than a "glorified pawnbroker." Without blinking an eye Hetty gave the State of Texas $6,000,000 during the panic of 1907.

She had all the instincts of the militant feminist. Although she could not be said to favor her own sex, she waged an endless battle with men. Growing philosophical in her old age she drew a picture that had little relation to her own life history. "A woman need not lose her femininity because she has a good business head on her shoulders," said Hetty. "Some of the most charming and feminine women I know have well-balanced brains which would easily fit them to cope with the business world should the necessity arise."

In 1968 a likely candidate came along in Muriel Siebert, who crashed the New York Stock Exchange, the first woman member in its 175-year history. She paid $445,000 for her seat but decided to stay off the floor and use traders instead. It took "Mickie" Siebert only thirteen years to hit the top on Wall Street after coming to New York in quest of an "interesting job." A Cleveland girl who majored in business and economics at Western Reserve University, she moved from firm to firm, working mostly as an analyst and researcher until she opened her own office. Miss Siebert bears no resemblance to Hetty Green as she goes to work in a leopard coat and shiny black boots, with a cream-colored Mercedes-Benz to convey her. She enjoys bridge, golf, travel, theater, opera and the beach.

Although Miss Siebert considers the stock business an open field for women now, it took time for them to be accepted even as speculators in stock. During the Depression they were considered bad losers, and they gave the brokerage houses considerable trouble. With unlimited funds to invest, however, women are now catered to more zealously than they were when Mary G. Roebling moved into the banking field with great authority in the 1950's. In course of time Mrs. Roebling became chairman of the Board of the Trenton Trust Company. Her interests are broad and philanthropical, and she has led the way in a field that has been slow to welcome women, except as investors, secretaries, researchers and clerks. Now banking, the Stock Exchange and real estate are among the most inviting avenues open to women.

In general, the orchidaceous career girls are few and far between, and from end to end of the country complaints are heard from women who feel that they are passed over time and again for executive positions, that they are paid less for equal work, that they are discriminated against both in business and the professions. In 1962 the last legal barrier to full equality of opportunity for women in the federal service was removed by President Kennedy, but things did not change overnight. Esther Peterson, Assistant Secretary of Labor, soon found that although much of the discrimination that had slowed women's advance had been wiped out, equal pay for equal work was still largely a dream of the future.

The feeling lingers on that the top job will always go to a man in a given department, and usually it does. The girls who reach the executive suite generally have luck—or magic—on their side. Fewer than 2 per cent have attained the summit level, and those who have made it all the way do not emphasize discrimination. In their fight for the prize they have learned discretion. Thoughtful employers, discussing the small number of women who control large interests, are disposed to fall back on the old biological arguments—that a woman is always a woman; that she can ruffle office decorum by her charm; that love and home always matter more to her than the office; that she has more health problems as well as emotional disorders; that she would rather take orders than give them; that she does not often seek, because she does not often want, the ultimate responsibility of running a large organization. A few will concede that there are still men who refuse to work for a woman in top authority.

A study made in 1965 by a Harvard Business School team showed that 35 per cent of the men questioned were favorable to women in management, 41 per cent were against them. The rest were simply "indifferent." But only 11 per cent agreed that women in their particular firms had "equal opportunity." When big executive jobs are advertised the quest almost invariably is for a man, and the male and female differentiation in classified ads is now a point of contention with the avowed feminists of 1968. It has become a picketing issue, like war and race discrimination, but they won in the case of the *New York Times*.

Universities and business firms are finding new ways to train women for top-level management jobs. In a study made in 1961 by President Kennedy's Commission on the Status of Women, directed by the anthropologist Margaret Mead, it was found that at comparable high levels women differed only slightly from men in length of service, reliability and job turnover. Skeptics find that in the old suffrage days women stood together better than they do in the competitive world of today, and that considerable clawing goes on in the upper reaches of professional work. But millions of women would deny this man-made charge and would point to unity of purpose and loyalty to their sex.

Surveys, rich in the ambivalence that all such studies show, suggest that the college graduate is not likely to do as well as the high-school girl in making a swift ascent to the top. The secretarial pad and pencil are still the surest way to the glamour jobs. Counsellors like Alice Gore King, director of the Alumnae Advisory Center, a New York counseling center for college graduates, always reminds them that they must have something more concrete to offer than distinction in English literature—preferably stenography or a background in statistics.

The highest salaries are earned by statisticians, mathematicians, research workers and editors, copywriters and reporters. Only 4 per cent of the college graduates of 1967 became secretaries; 60 per cent went straight into teaching, 6 per cent into nursing, and the others turned to professional jobs of one kind or another, with many dropouts after six months for marriage and other reasons. One survey of 15,000 college women taken three years after graduation showed that "taking care of a home" was the winning factor, with 75 per cent subscribing to the traditional role. Only 28 per cent voted a career or work of any kind as being of importance, and 27 per cent listed personal hobbies as a way of life.

But these statistics merely skim the surface of the great labor market, where 46 per cent of all American women between the ages of eighteen and sixty-four are earning a living in the world outside their homes. There are now 28,000,000 women in this massive army, and approximately 15,000,000 are working wives. These are not the women who powder their noses in the executive suite. Half of those working in the general labor market today earn less than $4,000, as compared with a $7,000 level for men. More than 3,000,000 women are engaged in technical and professional work and another 6,000,000 work intermittently. Most of the remaining number hold clerical, factory or domestic jobs. The largest concentration of workers is in the clerical field, but the new trends in occupation were illustrated in the 1960 census, which showed 431 geologists and geophysicists at work. The space age has opened the door to such work for women as radio astronomy, aerospace technology and chemical research. They are a living force today in the world of biochemistry, working on a par with men. But comparison with Russian statistics show American women to be less deeply involved than Russian women in occupations once considered open only to men. The United States has

6,000 women engineers as compared with 379,000 in Russia. The legal profession has 7,434 women in practice to Russia's 204,974 and in medicine the ratio is 15,513 to 213,413. In 1960 only 765 of America's 29,496 architects were women.

There are 307 women in the Foreign Service. Their work is exciting, and they steer through the shoals of foreign policy with some of the sense of adventure common to journalists abroad. Although they rarely get the top jobs, they are advanced on the lower levels as rapidly as men. But war conditions have swept the ground from under the feet of many in recent years. They have had to make rapid exits, to return home at a moment's notice or be reassigned to other areas. Frequent changes in their background limit the marriage range in the diplomatic service, and only 17 per cent of the regular foreign officers are married.

Women lawyers, however, are a rising power on the political scene in America. As often as not they are also the wives of lawyers, from Mrs. Abe Fortas, wife of a Supreme Court Justice, to the newest graduates from the nation's law schools. Carolyn Aggers Fortas, who is a specialist in tax law, is by no means typical of women lawyers, but she is conspicuous among them, and doubly so since President Johnson raised a storm by proposing her husband to succeed Earl Warren as Chief Justice.

Mrs. Fortas ranked second in the 1925 class at the Yale Law School. She was in Adlai Stevenson's law firm until 1960 when she joined her husband's firm as head of the tax division. "She doesn't do anything unless she does it superbly," he says of her. And those who visit her pale yellow house in Georgetown or their country place at Westport, Connecticut, agree that she shares the best of both worlds —the woman in the home and the woman who is highly successful in the complex field of law.

Mrs. Fortas is a tiny, compact dynamo, with a relaxed view of women battling earnestly for what they deem to be their rights. "I believe in feminism," she says, "but I don't know what I do about it other than keep my maiden name for professional purposes." Everything about her is contradictory. She is casual but precise, relaxed but highly efficient. She prefers to wear hat and gloves, pointing out that she grew up at a time when "no young lady was seen without them," but since she gave up smoking two packages of cigarettes a day more than a decade ago she has smoked cigars. She swims, skis, and is an inspired gardener. Liberal causes and the protection of animals engage her interest. She can cope with any sort of domestic crisis in the two households she runs—and she is equally at home in a setting of Victorian or Chinese furniture. Both houses at times are flooded with the music of a string quartet, for her husband plays the violin. There is much talk of law and of the judiciary around their dinner table, and Mrs. Fortas has decisive views.

It is significant that three hundred of the nation's 8,748 judges in 1965 were women, but only three were federal appointees. It was one of the latter, Sarah T. Hughes of Dallas, who swore President Johnson into office ninety-nine minutes after the death of John F. Kennedy. The women lawyers now deeply embedded in public affairs are apt to be married, to have children and to run their homes as well as their offices. Doris Lipson Sassower, who headed the New York Women's Bar Association in 1968, makes the point that "the law is not incompatible with feminine goals."

"I don't think brains have any sex," said slender, vivacious Margaret Mary Mangan, of the New York State Supreme Court, the second woman to sit on the state's high court bench. (The first was Birdie Amsterdam.) Miss Mangan's grandfather was a friend of Thomas Parnell's in Ireland. Her father worked at the Metropolitan Museum and became a curator at the Cloisters. Mayor Wagner appointed her a Justice of the Municipal Court. Governor Harriman appointed her to the City Court of New York, where she ran as the candidate of the Democratic, Liberal and Republican parties, and in 1962 she reached the New York Supreme Court to serve a fourteen-year term.

Reddish-haired, with an Irish wit, Miss Mangan firmly believes in the inequality of the sexes and the supremacy of the male. "A woman has one advantage in law . . . everyone in the court will remember her because she's a woman," she observes. Matrimonial problems are constantly presented for her consideration, and she drew attention with a ruling that a man on relief could not collect alimony from his estranged wife, even though she was working and he was unemployable. As with men, there seems to be a special link between the law and politics, and many of the women landing good political appointments are lawyers. Mrs. Virginia Mae Brown, appointed chairman of the Interstate Commerce Commission for 1969, is a lawyer, and the first woman to head an independent administrative agency of the federal government.

The traditional resistance to women lawyers was broken down by Calvin Coolidge in 1928 when he appointed Genevieve R. Cline to the United States Customs Court in New York. Next on the horizon was a vigorous suffragist, Florence E. Allen of the United States Circuit Court of Appeals. President Roosevelt promoted her from the Ohio Supreme Court to the United States Court of Appeals in 1934, and she eventually became chief judge of the United States Sixth Circuit, the highest federal judgeship ever attained by a woman.

But the most publicized of all female judges was Reva Beck Bosone, a red-haired Democrat with a breezy Western manner. She was the first Utah woman ever elected to Congress, but after two terms she was defeated in the Eisenhower landslide. As a municipal judge in Salt Lake City she won national fame with her program for dealing with alcoholism and cutting the number of traffic deaths. When Alcoholics Anonymous was organized in Salt Lake City she induced its members to sit in court with her and to take the hopeless drunks into her chambers for quick therapy. She was so tough with traffic offenders and fined them so heavily that the roadways of Utah became more safe.

Mrs. Bosone was a teacher before being admitted to the Utah State Bar in 1930. She married a classmate and campaigned with her baby daughter in one arm and leaflets in the other. She called on every voter in her district and invaded the miners' cabins in the tradition of Susan Anthony. She backed all legislation beneficial to women and children and was one of four sponsors of the bill that laid the groundwork for many of Utah's water-control projects. Women voters were enthusiastic backers of Mrs. Bosone's unorthodox methods, and it was a local joke that none of the lawyers dared to vote against her because their wives would not speak to them if they did.

Politics and the practice of law interlock constantly, and the Portias of today have become a formidable body with a fresh image. It is now fashionable for the graduates of the prominent women's colleges to go to law school. The purpose is twofold. It has been found to be an admirable marriage market, but to many it is also a steppingstone to social service and a first-rate career. Sometimes it is both. The nation's courtrooms now harbor glamorous young women, some white, some black, all carefully coiffed and fashionably gowned. "The law offers a great many options," says Mary Bunting, head of Radcliffe College. "A woman can be the kind of lawyer she wants to be." "Mothers are awfully good lawyers," says James J. White, professor at the University of Michigan Law School.

Many women choose to work in the international field or in areas involving the poverty laws and the social ills of the era. Top Wall Street law firms, which have raised their starting salaries to $15,000 a year, are disposed to take one or more women lawyers on their staffs, and many of the candidates choose public service. It is estimated now that 3½ per cent of the nation's lawyers are women. Sixteen Vassar girls of the class of 1967 turned to law compared to one in 1955. Twenty law schools sent scouts to the Smith College campus to recruit applicants, a new development. Black women lawyers are becoming more numerous, and Gabrielle Kirk, one of two women lawyers who work for the national headquarters of the N.A.A.C.P., thinks there are good opportunities in this field.

Of ten civil-rights cases argued before the United States Supreme Court, Constance B. Motley won nine. Mrs. Motley, a gentle-mannered Negro with a firm touch in court, became a federal judge after twelve years in the New York State Senate. She was the first black woman to sit in the New York Senate, the first to become a federal judge, the first to serve as Borough President of Manhattan. She is the wife of Joel Motley, a real estate operator.

In Chicago another black woman who presides on the bench with skill and compassion is Judge Edith Sampson, who has four honorary doctorates and has known four Presidents. After serving as Assistant Corporation Counsel of Chicago she was nominated by the Democratic Party in 1962 to fill a circuit-court vacancy and in 1964 was elected by an overwhelming vote for a six-year term. Judge Sampson presides in Chicago's new Civic Center over landlord-tenant cases, and innumerable other disputes that pass through the Circuit Court. She functions with informality; her manner is direct and kindly.

One of eight children born in Pittsburgh to a cleaning employee, she worked in a fish market to help her family, while her mother made hat frames. In Chicago she worked her way through college and law school. In 1949 she touched wider horizons when she went round the world on a radio tour, and in the following year President Truman appointed her a member of the U.S. delegation to the United Nations. Today she lectures and projects a moderate point of view. "Color never bothered me very much," she says. "I know what I am, and a blonde I am not."

Fully 75 per cent of the cases she hears involve Negroes. Deeply conscious of the hardships the poor experience from crowded calendars and long delays, she disposes of cases at a swift pace—sometimes a hundred in a morning. She knows her people well and feels that since they cannot afford to appeal their cases, they must get justice on the lower court level or lose out altogether.

In 1967 when Ersa Poston was appointed president of the New York State Civil Service Commission by Governor Rockefeller at an annual salary of $32,265, she had reached the highest appointive office ever held by a black woman in New York State. She was with the New York City Youth Board for four years until the Governor appointed her head of the Office of Economic Opportunity at $18,000, and this led to her Civil Service appointment. Mrs. Poston is of mixed Negro and Indian ancestry. Her great-grandmother was a wiry little squaw and her grandmother ran a soup kitchen for black and white people during the Depression. Mrs. Poston was graduated from the University of Kentucky in 1942 and took her master's degree in social work at the University of Atlanta. She knows the South as well as the North. Her career represents a strong new trend in the political advancement of able black women.

Bennetta Bullock Washington, head of the Women's Job Corps, is a Negro who came from Washington's toughest precinct, attended segregated schools and took degrees at Howard University and Catholic University. She taught in Cardozo High School for emotionally disturbed boys and wrote a book, *Youth in Conflict,* about her experiences there. Her husband is the Mayor of Washington.

The problem of the aging, as well as of the young citizen, looms significantly in the 1960's, and here women are somewhat less well off than men. They are apt to live longer, to suffer from more physical ills and to have fewer resources to fall back on in their declining years. Although 40 per cent of the population is now under twenty-one, at the other end of the scale the tide is rising fast, with women now living to be eighty and not infrequently reaching the ninety mark. Yet because of living conditions today few families seem to have grandmothers, aunts or spinster cousins at hand who can take over the household duties of the working mother.

In 1940 married women made up less than a third of the total work force, but by 1962 the proportion had reached one-half. Since one marriage in three goes on the rocks today, and the number of divorced women rose from 273,000 in 1920 to 1,708,000 in 1960, the care of the young is deeply involved, and the latchkey child is a reality. Day care is a vital issue in determining the modern woman's role and how much she has benefited from political emancipation. It was not until the industrial revolution that women left their homes in numbers to work in factories and domestic service. In 1967 the Office of Economic Opportunity provided $70,000,000 worth of day care for 54,000 children. New York City seeks to combine family day care with job training for mothers on welfare. The city has ninety-three publicly supported day centers, many of them in housing projects. Because of the shortage of help, the need for day care affects the affluent home as well as the slum family. Innumerable women quietly give up their ambition to work outside the home because they know that the care of their children is at stake. Almost 2,500,000 children were in kindergarten in 1964.

The big breakthrough in employment came during World War II when married women were drawn out of their homes in vast numbers to do war work. At that time the barrier against employing the well-off disappeared dramatically. The late 1940's, 1950's and 1960's were rich in working opportunities for all kinds of women. The drop in man power, the planned spacing of children, the spread of technology, the magic aids to housekeeping, the new scope and variation in jobs, all tended to free women for work outside their homes. The change was felt both in the blue- and white-collar areas as women learned to drive fork-lift trucks, service automobiles, run heavy factory machinery or deliver mail. The in-depth perception, manual dexterity and eye and hand coordination of women were found in many instances to excel that of men.

White-collar women move into place more slowly. The proportion of working women classified as professional and technical had fallen from 45 per cent in 1940 to 37 per cent in 1967. The G.I.'s have moved into many of the niches women filled. But in relation to the total work force women moved up 10 per cent during this period. And the increasing use of contraceptives is helping to keep them longer on the job. Employers who once considered women poor risks because of marriage and pregnancies are now more willing to employ them in large numbers. But women are still faced with lack of mobility and of having to stay where their families are. In 1967 John W. Gardner, then Secretary of Health, Education and Welfare, established the Professional and Executive Corps—a talent pool of highly trained women to work part time in his department. The group of twenty-two included a city planner, a mathematician, educators, writers, editors and a college dean of social work. At the same time Mr. Gardner pointed out that the "underutilization of American women" was one of the tragedies of the times.

The need to work comes at both ends of the social spectrum, but most pressingly among the poor. Never in history have so many American women been at work outside the home, and in 1967 the working mothers numbered eight million. In 1940 only one out of ten mothers of children under eighteen held jobs outside the home, but today the ratio is one out of three. Many work because they must. Others seek to raise the family standards, to pay for their children's education, to help their husbands through college or to fulfill some need or ambition of their own. A survey made by the Women's Bureau of the Labor Department showed that more than half of a group of 6,000 women who graduated from college in 1957 were still employed in 1964. Among them 83 per cent were, or had been, married, and 66 per cent were mothers.

College girls tend to marry around twenty-two, or two years later than the national average. More men than women graduate from college and more girls than boys from high school. In 1930 women took 40 per cent of all the baccalaureate degrees. In 1960 they received the same number of B.A.'s but slipped from 40 per cent to 30 per cent at the master's level, and from 15 per cent to 10 per cent in doctorates. The ardor of the career-minded woman of the 1920's and 1930's, tasting the first fruits of emancipation, is dimming slightly in the love-befuddled 1960's, when women are playing up femininity and the home and are reluctant to put in the long, arduous years of scholarship for their Ph.D's. There is a swing away from the blue-stocking conception of education. More than 90 per cent of all college girls are now coeds, with the last bastions among the prestigious colleges weakening.

Marriage is the central preoccupation. The birth rate has taken a marked drop since the Pill and other efficient contraceptives have been so widely distributed. The white population is close to the stabilizing level where births balance deaths, but the birth rate of the black population is dropping, too. A total of 3.5 million babies were born in the United States in 1967, a decline of 19 per cent in five years. Many factors enter into this, but the dissemination of birth-control information is already linked to the diminishing birth rate. Infant mortality rates are high in the aseptic United States—thirteenth in the world. The score in 1967 was one to every thousand live births.

The changing civilization is significantly illustrated with a drop in 46 per cent of the number of women working on farms in America. There are 3.4 million women trade unionists, constituting 18 per cent of the total union membership. Women have had a long, hard fight on the industrial end but have won substantial victories in the last half century. The unions for factory workers picked up strength early in the twentieth century. From 1903 to 1917 women were organized in the clothing industry in New York, Philadelphia and Chicago. The earliest locals of today's powerful International Ladies

Garment Workers Union date back to the turn of the century. There were many strikes along the way, but even as late as 1945 the Women's Bureau found that discrimination in the industrial field was still overwhelming where women were concerned.

The Women's Trade Union League was represented on every picket line around 1905, and this organization figured in the garment strikes of 1910 and 1911, the strikes of the collar starchers in Troy, the textile workers in Lawrence and Fall River, the brewery employees in Milwaukee, the corset makers in Bridgeport, the telephone operators in Boston and the laundry workers in New York. Such social leaders as Mrs. O. H. P. Belmont, Daisy Harriman, Anne Morgan and Mrs. Henry Morgenthau joined forces with women like Lillian Wald, of the Henry Street Settlement, Ida M. Tarbell, a militant journalist, and Mary Simkovitch, a social worker, to protest the treatment given strikers by the courts.

In another half century they had learned to picket for other and more inclusive causes—not alone for pay and better working conditions, but for civil rights, for race equality, for better housing, for peace, for improved education—for a complex of causes, good, bad and indifferent, depending on the point of view. But Jane Addams of Hull House in Chicago, Lillian Wald of the Henry Street Settlement in New York, Rose Schneiderman, the trade-union organizer, and other social-service workers contributed richly to the lives of the industrial workers and their families during the period of sharp strife early in the century.

Events moved swiftly in the next fifty years, and in 1968 the vote of the organized working woman was a mighty one. She was being wooed by all the politicians reaching for the Presidency as ardently as was the more leisured woman in the home. The 1960's was preeminently the decade of the picketer, with some raucous female voices shouting defiance along with the more restrained tones of other outraged women protesting various injustices involving their homes and the lives and education of their families. Leading the din was Youth Incarnate—bouncy, noisy, untidy and belligerent or earnest, eager and dedicated. Here there was no disparity between the aims of boys and girls. They played it fifty-fifty.

Today more women than men work as dietitians, librarians, stenographers, typists, telephone operators and in all forms of social service. They are more numerous in personnel administration, in libraries and archives, as statisticians, as accountants and in all forms of clerical service. Teachers and nurses—the traditional roles for women—are in desperate demand, but opportunities for women in the higher academic posts are shrinking. Men are apt to preside at women's colleges and other institutions of higher learning, and women do not abound on the boards of trustees. The constant drive to raise funds, involving tussles with politicians and rich men, is considered a man's game. Not every suppliant could match Millicent McIntosh's coup when she persuaded John D. Rockefeller, Jr., to give a million dollars for Barnard scholarships.

Although the employment of women dates back to before the Civil War it was not until 1883 that women were allowed to compete in civil-service examinations on the same basis as men. World War II was the opening wedge to nearly all forms of government service, from economists and research scientists to lighthouse keepers and park archaeologists. However, jobs rating $7,000 or more a year are still largely man's preserve in government circles, and women have much to complain about in that area. They feel they are being by-passed constantly for the post that counts. Half stay in grades three or four, and a quarter in grades five and six, with a top salary of $7,430 a year. Above that figure the girls are few and far between except in highly specialized work. There are all manner of ways of frustrating the ambitious upstarts, mostly by giving them inferior ratings.

Research institutes have choice jobs for some women, but here again specialization counts. Fear of nepotism at the college level may keep a professor's wife from being employed, and here and there even the woman of the 1960's runs into the old-time prejudice against visible pregnancy in an office. The mothers of young children who go out to work must weather considerable criticism from both sexes. In big business as well as in small firms husband-and-wife teams are becoming more common, particularly in high fashion. In journalism this is an old tradition. Some of the finest small papers in the country are owned by husbands and wives—the most notable case being that of the *Vineyard Gazette*, lifework of Henry Beetle Hough and the late Elizabeth Howie Hough, and since 1968 the property of James and Sally Reston.

Mrs. Louchheim has pointed out that the influence of women resembles an iceberg—much more of it is below the surface than shows above. Women constitute more than half the population. They make up one-third of the labor force. Their longevity exceeds that of men. A woman's life expectancy in 1900 was forty-eight years; today it is seventy-three. Women have traveled far and won their spurs in many fields, although a strain of feminine timidity, a lack of self-confidence or a sense of caution, at times has kept them from reaching for the ultimate rewards. But in no area, outside of their wifely and motherly functions, have women been more profoundly influential than in the work they do, and the place they hold in the outside world. Here many have found deep and abiding satisfaction, and excel as useful citizens.

꧁ **Chapter 12**

The Vote That Counts

꧁ The electrifying issues of 1968 tended to draw more women to the voting booths than ever before, but the victory of 1920, which was presumed to give them full equality with men, took a long time to bear visible fruit. Once the battle was won women did not grasp at the chance to influence government. In fact, their relationship with men on the political level was at a standstill, while they moved briskly into the more personal world of jobs and careers. They scarcely stirred when action was needed at the polls. A study made by a Columbia University sociologist in 1950 showed that only one wife in twenty-two admitted to having voted differently from her husband. Even as late as 1960, four decades after they were enfranchised, an estimated twenty million women of voting age did nothing about it.

The Gallup polls which in the past have indicated only the smallest percentage of variation between the voting record of men and women, except for a slight swing by women to the reassuring image of General Eisenhower, are showing new trends today. The Vietnam war has finally energized them. Recent polls suggest that the number of so-called doves is growing, with 49 per cent of the nation's women so identified compared with 33 per cent of its men. The deeper truth, aside from public findings might strengthen this disparity. In 1968, a year of turmoil and deep feminine "involve-ment" (the key word of the era), women of all ages were more openly engaged in political discussion than at any time since the vote was won. A sense of impending doom had got through to them, and this time they meant business.

American women as a whole were not profoundly stirred by the feminist struggle, and their indifference affected to some extent the thinking of their daughters and granddaughters. It took the quick-ening influence of World War II and the raging issues of the 1960's to sharpen their awareness of their role in government. Perhaps for the first time since women won the vote, the very young among them were moved by the principles involved in 1968. In addition, they responded to the good looks, magnetism and television image of the candidates of that year of excitement. In the past, polls have shown that sons and daughters have been disposed to vote for the party of their parents, but this no longer holds true. The revolt of the youthful in this respect has been as strong as in all else. The most staid of mothers have watched their sons and daughters stampeding the college campuses for what they deem to be strange ideology. The mothers of the 1960's demonstrably have much less influence over their offspring than the voteless women of Abigail Adams' day.

While there has been little direct evidence in the last twelve years of independent thinking on the part of older women, this may result in part from the fact that they are inclined to vote according to their educational background, their financial standing and the region in which they live. Richard Nixon, having fallen heir to President Eisenhower's fatherly image, won 52 per cent of the woman's vote in 1960 against 48 per cent for John F. Kennedy. Divorce or scandal in a candidate's background chills women today as much as it did in the days of Andrew Jackson, and both Adlai Stevenson and Nelson A. Rockefeller were made to feel this prejudice. It has been well established that women are less likely to vote for a woman candi-date in any area than for a man. All surveys show that men go to the polls more regularly than their wives, and the feeling persists—al-though statistics are elusive on this point—that they are still disposed to vote the same ticket that they did in the beginning. Women find all manner of excuses to stay away from the polls. Some still feel that it is enough to have the man of the house cast his vote. Bad weather, lack of transportation, the care of their children easily divert them from committing themselves to the vote that counts. The well-off obviously find it easier to get to the polls than the poor, and surveys show that the people in the ghettos, or immigrants who have trouble with the language, shy away from this ordeal. Farm women in general have more trouble getting out to vote than their urban sisters, and today younger women show more enthusiasm for casting their vote than the more mature.

Although three wars have intervened and humanity has moved into the nuclear age since the suffrage question was settled, it was not until the campaign of 1968 that women developed this deep sense of urgency about their political power. But startling elements involving the home, education and the future of their children were at stake, and many turned out to campaign, to protest, to picket, perhaps to vote. Moreover, it is somewhat chic now to be vote-conscious as well as socially conscious. The worldly and sophisticated, the Beautiful People and the eggheads, make a point of casting their votes unless they are stranded on one of their isles of escape at election time and have forgotten what is at stake.

The political conventions are now gathering grounds for the "name" people of press and television. In their smartest attire, with spangled glasses and fetching coiffures, prominent women liven up the traditional scene and lend support to their favorite candidates. Long before women had the vote the relatives of candidates liked to pack the galleries, and Alice Longworth was as much a part of each convention scene as the veteran politician. Their participation was a slow but progressive development. They were seen and heard at both the Republican and Democratic conventions of recent years. They called the roll in 1968 with strong affirmation. Some made seconding speeches, and black and white women voiced their opinions freely into the microphone, aware that they had an audience of millions. Candidates' wives and daughters smiled and clapped and tried to look responsive at difficult moments. They now have stellar billing on the political scene. The cameras seek them out while the entire country looks on in a proprietary and critical way.

Women made their first official appearance at the Republican National Convention in Minneapolis in 1892. They succeeded in getting the first "Equal Rights for Women" plank into the platform, but the five feminine delegates and nine alternates took a back seat and were scarcely noticed. Their presence could not be wholly ignored in 1920, the victory year for the suffrage workers. Twenty-seven delegates and 129 alternates were present, and for the first time men gave them some official duties at the convention in recognition of their new status. By 1932 the representation was climbing, with eighty-seven women delegates and 305 alternates. This time a woman broke ice by serving on the Resolutions Committee. Clare Boothe Luce lent glamour as well as bite in 1944 by making the first formal address to be delivered by a woman at a Republican National Convention since 1892. Eleanor Roosevelt rocked the Democratic Convention of 1940 and won her husband's accolade for the smart politicking she did on his behalf. Betty Furness, glittering with paillettes, enlivened the Democratic Convention of 1968 with a brisk talk in the contemporary idiom.

Chain belts, mini skirts and sombrero hats showed up at the Democratic Convention that year, which mustered 917 women delegates and alternates, including thirty-five black women delegates and twenty-five black alternates. At Miami the Republicans had 224 women delegates and 335 alternates, including three black women delegates and twelve alternates. The feminine bloc has become an increasingly significant part of the convention picture. It has been a slow progression, covering nearly seventy years and with many steps along the way. Here women function more nearly on a par with men at the base of government, and in all the uproar they are not wholly ignored. Their presence has become an accepted fact in the dizzying world of politics.

Margaret Mead reported to President Kennedy in 1963 through the Government Commission on the Status of Women that party recognition of women as practicing politicians was developing and that at some levels in party hierarchies it extended to the inner councils where central decisions were made. But in the main it remained ceremonial, with women sitting on platforms at campaign rallies and lending their glamorous persons to party fund-raising dinners. For some time, national committeemen had been matched by national committeewomen, men chairmen by women vice-chairmen on committees below the national level and at the national party headquarters. The report continued:

Few women have been elected or appointed to state executive offices of cabinet rank; Secretary of State, Treasurer, and Auditor are the posts most commonly held. In some states, appointments of women in public office have clustered in certain fields regarded as "women's areas"; those dealing with juveniles, school affairs, health, welfare, libraries.

Men have not been slow to recognize the place of women in the all-over picture and its effect on public thinking, but in the final clinches of party decision they have not yet given women a chance to pull their weight. They are still apt to be left outside the closed door of the caucus room. Only the few women who sit on the Senate and Congressional committees are in at the forging of legislation. Yet who would dare to assess their hidden power at the polls? The picture is by no means clear, for one of the major elements in it is the quiet voice in the home that sometimes shapes the thinking of the husband—if one is to accept the world-wide opinion that the American woman is a dominating personality reaching into all areas of her husband's life.

Where women have lagged most is in backing their own sex. The three women who have run for the Presidency—Victoria Woodhull in 1872, a lawyer named Belva Lockwood in 1884 and 1888, and Margaret Chase Smith in 1964—had little support from women. Of the three Mrs. Smith alone could be considered a candidate of serious intent, and she ran a dignified campaign without funds or official backing of any kind. A vote for Mrs. Smith would have been a wasted vote since the idea of a woman as President is not a popular conception at any level. One poll taken on this question showed that one-third of the men interviewed were definitely opposed to the thought; another third said they would rather not vote for a woman; and the remainder conceded that they might vote for a woman to fill this role if she were the extraordinary, rather than the ordinary, woman.

A magazine study done in 1968 to determine what various women in public life might do with the Presidency, provided they hankered for this impossible goal, resulted in mixed and provocative opinions. Margaret Chase Smith, who at least had made a try, said that the first thing she would do would be to make an effort to stop the war in Vietnam, although she supported President Johnson in his policies. She added that she would encourage women to play a more active role in public life and not be afraid to assume positions of authority in government. She had never asked for quarter, nor received any, and she did not feel that she had been discriminated against as a woman in the Senate. "I believe in equal rights," said Mrs. Smith. "But, by the same token, I do not believe in special privileges for women." She would abolish the electoral college, and have films classified so as to protect children from spectacles of violence and sex. And she would work to restore the national sense of moral and spiritual values.

Maurine Neuberger, former Democratic Senator from Oregon, said that she would limit the ceremonial functions that drain the President's energies. Mrs. Clifton Daniel, who had experienced life in the White House, expressed the view that a woman looked at life too sentimentally to function well as President. Personally she preferred to take orders from her husband, as she had once done from her father—a President with strong opinions of his own. Mary Lasker said without any hesitation that under no circumstances could she conceive of bearing such a terrible responsibility. But if she had presidential powers she would press for more funds for medicine, for re-creation of the cities, for decent housing, for trees and flowers and parks. She would make family planning available to everyone, and back centers for advanced studies. Furthermore, she would explore all possible means of getting along with the Communist countries.

Of the sixteen persons questioned by *Harper's Bazaar*, including poets, critics, writers, Senators, singers, seers and philanthropists, nearly all took the matter seriously, although some found it merely amusing. Practically everyone acknowledged that it was a job she would turn down if it were offered to her. Marya Mannes, author, lecturer and television personality, wryly observed that her Vice-President would have to be a man.

The question did not seem as strange in 1968 as it might have been half a century earlier when suffrage was still in the balance. All the accepted rules showed signs of crumbling in that year when women of steady background, such as teachers, nurses and responsible homemakers, picketed ardently and persistently for peace, for racial equality, for better schools and housing, for higher wages, for shorter hours, for a new deal all round. It was a form of expression they had not used since the early suffrage days. The hazard of dangerous rioting had been added, and the demonstrators showed a tendency to lie down in the streets and obstruct traffic, to whack and be whacked by policemen and generally stir up trouble.

This tangential view of the American woman, however, is only a small part of the total picture. It has set her in melodramatic juxtaposition to the restless mood of the nation at all levels. Most American women, whether or not they vote, are still not too unlike their God-fearing ancestors, and clear across the country there are monuments to their efforts in the form of new schools, clean water, consolidated libraries, improved city charters, better lighting, more usable voting machines and acres set aside for parks and recreation.

Although they did not rush to the polls when they won the vote, neither was home life wrecked, as the prophets had predicted. Many went quietly to work in their own communities, and bit by bit over the years they have helped to shape public opinion on local issues. The work at the grass-roots level increasingly is done by women who stuff envelopes and ring doorbells, as in the days of Susan Anthony, and shake hands with voters on the village green or the college campus, as in the epoch-making campaigns of Robert Kennedy and Eugene McCarthy. But their influence is most strongly felt on school boards and town councils, and in this area their husbands are inclined to follow their lead. They are the homemakers, and therefore they campaign hard for their children's safety, for urban planning and causes close to the home. They fight war, as women have done from time immemorial, but more determinedly now than at any time in history.

Early in the twentieth century two American families out of five lived on farms or in small towns in rural areas. They had lamplight, drew water from the well and had outdoor plumbing. But in the 1960's fewer than one family in ten lives on a farm. Most farm houses have electricity and indoor plumbing and are equipped in many instances as well as those of the city dweller. This leaves farm families with considerable time for the old-fashioned art of politicking. Still more involved is the suburban population, which has become a mighty factor in the world of politics. Women are drawn into community interests more readily in their suburban homes than in the city. With their husbands at work in town it has fallen to them to do much of the political canvassing. In some suburban areas the women political workers outnumber men five to one, and they are called on to perform many tasks from baby-sitting to sweeping floors. Many of the old methods are still pristine today. The candidates of 1968 found that getting close to people in the street is still good usage, and the telephone is particularly effective in their hands as a last-minute reminder to vote—and for the right candidate. Thousands of women volunteers raised almost $200,000 in 1960 in one-dollar contributions from a mammoth door-to-door drive.

The National Conference of Commissions on the Status of Women, initiated by President Kennedy and now continued from year to year through state commissions appointed by the governors, has a blue-ribbon membership of educators, businesswomen and community leaders, who function as private citizens. Grandmothers who can remember being pelted with rotten eggs and tomatoes in the days of the suffrage fight now seek full equality for their sex where once they tried to cushion their lives through protective legislation in the labor field. Since the state commissions started their work in 1962 they have helped to improve state laws involving minimum wage levels, equal pay and equal employment opportunities. In Alabama they have helped to enact laws permitting women to serve on state juries. In California and Florida they have worked for more guidance shelters for girls and education programs for older women. They are sometimes asked by institutions to help look for women presidents, but as one of the commission members put it, "You always have to look at the second level of administrators to find qualified women. They're seldom on top."

Few women need to be ignorant of political affairs today if they are in the mainstream of living. Various organizations educate, inform and encourage them, but it has taken years to interest them at all social levels in the technicalities of government. Television has spread the message in a more direct and penetrating way. But the constant flow of immigrants into the United States requires renewed effort year by year, and many cling to the faith of their fathers that women should leave political issues to their husbands.

Perhaps the League of Women Voters has done more than any other organization to stir up women to the need for voting and to educate them in public affairs. Its members are political strategists, free of partisan interests and dedicated to presenting plain facts. They dispense a subtle form of education, without any emphasis on militancy. The League members first educate themselves on issues, then they educate the voters and sometimes they end up educating the legislators, too. They are expert lobbyists, majoring in tact rather than in aggression.

The League is the watchdog of individual performances in Congress and state legislatures. The lawmakers do not like to stir up their wrath. When the League, during its annual breakfast coffee on the Hill, pinned daisies on the Senators and Representatives who attended, those who were absent sent staff members to pick up their flowers. It would have been disastrous to have been left unpinned by the ladies of the League.

Although the first rule of the organization is to be nonpartisan, increasingly the members take up public issues with considerable force, and in 1967 the League of Women Voters of New York State campaigned for the defeat of the proposed constitution. Although they had been insistent in their demands that a new one be drawn up, they turned thumbs down on it when they found they disliked its provisions. And in May, 1968, the National League of Women Voters, meeting in convention in Chicago, threw its weight in a qualified way on the side of open housing. For several years this had been a matter of debate in the national organization, and the vote was a significant step in the history of the National League.

Members are urged to work as individuals in the political party of their choice, but board members or others prominently identified with the organization are not supposed to show their party preference. The League was created in the first place "to promote political responsibility through informed and active participation of citizens in government." It grew out of the National American Woman Suffrage Association when the vote was won, and by the 1960's there were 1,250 Leagues in the United States, with a membership topping 150,000. The members make up a strong army of volunteer workers. Eighty-five per cent of them are married, and most of them have children. They are women of education and substance in the community. Since their activities are compatible with the well-run home, they usually have the solid backing of their husbands. Men in general approve of their work, for it is direct, practical and affirmative. The League members study election laws, fiscal policy, home rule, foreign policy, regional planning, higher education and urban improvement. The structure of government is examined exhaustively, and a study of the electoral college was under way in 1968.

The Leaguers testify at hearings and can be tough in backing a worthy bill. At election time they reduce voting procedure to its simplest terms for the uninformed person. They have been a strong force in getting people out to vote and in showing them how to cast their ballots. In the election of 1968 their drive to educate non-English-speaking voters was strongly felt in ghetto regions where the use of the ballot was little understood.

By dint of hard plugging over the years, and by widening their horizons with each election, the League by radio, television, press, lobbying and public relations has spread its message that every eligible voter should turn up at the polls. Their Practical Politics Workshops map out techniques for public speaking, discussion sessions and the use of films and other visual aids. Their handbook *Choosing the President* was distributed by the Book-of-the-Month Club in 1968 *pro bono publico*. Millions of copies of the League's *Facts for Voters* circulate, giving the pros and cons of election issues in different languages. Few Americans need be ignorant today of the causes for which they vote, but many still are.

Prima donnas are discouraged in the network of centers the League maintains across the country, not as a federation, but as a single unit with many groups. In one year 546 local Leagues worked on planning and zoning, 483 on public schools and education, 266 on recreation and parks, and 206 on public-health problems. They have made a specialty of conservation and the development of water resources, nationally, locally and regionally. Their activities have ranged from a study of potato pollution in Maine to irrigation in Oregon. In various areas they have worked to meet specific local and regional crises.

Membership in the organization has encouraged a number of women to move on to elective office, and most of the women prominent in party councils have belonged at one time or another to the League of Women Voters. A number of notables have worked in the ranks, and Lucretia Mott's great-granddaughter, Anna Lord Strauss, president from 1944 to 1950, was reflecting the spirit of her famous ancestor when she urged Leaguers in the 1940's to reach the unorganized, the unconvinced, the less informed, and impress on them the importance of the United Nations. "It is absolutely essential that the imagination and intelligence of millions of individual citizens shall be deeply stirred," said Miss Strauss. The League hammered home the message "Yours is the Power" as the United Nations came into being.

In the years that followed it gave its support to many international measures and sidestepped others. It backed the bill that led to the Atomic Energy Act of 1946, putting atomic energy under civilian control. In 1949 it gave reluctant approval to NATO. Leaguers worked for the Kellogg-Briand Pact as well as for the Trade Agreements program. It supported the Lend-Lease bill and repeal of the Neutrality Act. From 1946 to 1948 it pushed legislation to provide for the admission of displaced persons. In 1968 it stood behind the efforts to make peace in Vietnam.

On the domestic front the Leagues have worked for the inclusion of a maternal and child health program in the Social Security Act, and for modernization of the 1906 Pure Food and Drug Act. But it is their fixed policy to avoid entangling alliances with other organizations and to stand apart from pressure groups. They take credit for sending out the first questionnaires asking candidates of all parties how they stood on issues; for conducting the first get-out-the-vote campaign aimed at women as well as at men; for arranging meetings where candidates from opposing parties were heard together; and for first circulating the records of candidates' votes on specific questions.

The League's campaigns on state and local politics have made it a recognized educational force in America, respected by men and women of different parties and organizations. It has its critics, too. The organization's nonpartisan attitude at times annoys politicians eager to push their causes. The air of amateur effort surrounds it in some areas in spite of its strong and effective organization. An aura of upper-crust conservatism tinges its reputation in a few communities. Regional interests and prejudices cloud the gleaming mirror from time to time.

The League's discreet ways and lack of showmanship in the age of political gimmicks are countered by solid effort and scholarly enterprise. It bears small resemblance to its progenitor, the National American Woman Suffrage Association, which went in for a madcap round of parades, pickets and posters. When Mrs. Catt called for a League of Women Voters "to help make our democracy safe for the nation and for the world" she turned over an inheritance left by Mrs. Frank Leslie to finance an education fund. Mrs. Leslie, one of the *grandes dames* of the late nineteenth century, had never actively joined the ranks of the suffrage workers or indicated in any way that she admired them. "When I come to die," she said to Mrs. Catt on one occasion, "you will find that like yourself I am interested in woman's advancement." In the end she left her entire fortune of two million dollars to Mrs. Catt, but so much litigation followed that the inheritance dwindled seriously before it could be used.

The fashionable women who had joined the suffrage movement during the two decades before the vote was won moved smoothly into the practical work of the League, and in some instances they passed on the torch to their daughters. In 1944, when Mrs. Dana C. Backus, a convinced Leaguer, flew to Tonga in the South Pacific to attend a conference, she took with her one of the banners used by her mother, Mrs. James Lees Laidlaw, who had taught her to aim paper darts with the "Votes for Women" message at farmers' doorsteps as they drove through the countryside when she was ten.

Mrs. Backus was pinning up the old suffrage poster on a wall when the Queen of Tonga, looking it over, let her know that she was already well informed on the suffrage movement in America. In fact, the Queen had given voting rights to the women of Tonga four years earlier. The message of Mrs. Pankhurst, Mrs. Stanton, Susan Anthony and Lucy Stone had traveled far in a century.

Chapter 13

The Tree of Knowledge

The Daughters of Eve were designed to please the Sons of Adam, according to Rousseau and other oracles of the past, but the world at large sees America today as the country where the man must please the woman. Cool observers insist that he surrenders to her will in many areas of his life. Not only does she pass judgment on their joint interests, such as the choice of homes, cars and vacations, but she often helps him choose his clothes and sometimes even his candidate for political office. Only in his working life does he get credit for controlling the springs of initiative, and even there he is exposed to the influence of that all-pervasive creature, the American woman holding down a responsible job.

Although recently it has become highly fashionable once again to play the feminine role to the limit, with gourmet cooking, sex maneuvers and provocative attire, a glance beneath the surface shows that woman's wish to have her way has not been assuaged by political equality. Paradoxically the Pill and the frank sexuality of the era have given her a more convincing form of power. "The Pill makes woman a Bomb," says Marshall McLuhan. "Watch for traditions to fall."

Mr. McLuhan sees romantic love, the florescence of the Middle Ages, as the likely loser, with effective contraception qualifying as the most significant discovery in the history of women—an aid that has freed them more conclusively from the ancient bondage of their womanhood than the vote itself. The sex revolution, sudden, overwhelming, has shifted the balance of power for the older as well as the younger generation, the prudish as well as the informed. The power of decision is now at woman's command—the only thing she lacked.

Though in the use of sex techniques and the pampering of men the American woman still lags behind the international parade, her resistance to the submissive role is evidenced in the fact that she is the most emancipated, the most self-assured, the most demanding of women. "Whatever Lola wants, Lola gets," is no mere empty jingle. She is ablaze with energy and independence. She has great flexibility of movement. She exudes glamour, real or artificial. She likes to make herself heard, and her role in the strikes and picketing of the 1960's shows how articulate and belligerent she can be in terms of mass effects. In this respect she is not unlike the women of the French Revolution, the followers of Emmeline Pankhurst in England, or the early advocates of the suffrage movement in the United States, critical though she may be of the tough tactics her ancestors used. The word "feminist" today makes her shudder, and she shrinks from being called a career woman.

Stung by the gibes of outsiders that she cracks the whip on the domestic scene, more often than not she takes care to accentuate her femininity and to tell the world that her husband is master in the home. She has become sensitive on the subject, since she not only gets it from abroad but also at home, with the magazines, papers and airways treating her status from all manner of provocative angles. She is a *cause célèbre* as the woman who has everything, yet is the most restless, the most dissatisfied, the most neurotic, the most divorced of her sex in the world.

But this universal view of her is both magnified and distorted, since the United States has a diversified population, representing the ethics and morals of nearly every other civilization. If there is a great leveling off through the vivid young generation now in the ascendant, it is equally true that the deeper roots still hold and help to stem the tide that engulfs the young of every land. The age of restraint and austerity that John and Abigail Adams knew may be worlds away from this period of uninhibited youth, but the underlying principles have not been lost to Americans as a whole.

Each century has had its own outbreak of the robust spirit, and each period of repression has been followed by one of excess. Although the Puritans rode herd on the Magdalens in the community and had tight and repressive rules, they did not foreswear love, and some of the most flagrant sinners moved in godly circles. Boston was thought to have few prudes in the 1740's, and bundling, the strange courting custom which involved a boy and girl sharing the same bed under parental supervision, flourished at the time of the Revolution. In 1721 Harvard students were debating "whether it be fornication to lye with one's sweetheart before marriage," a custom that was not unfashionable in 1968.

The bawdy spirit prevailed in the eighteenth century, and the Regency gowns were seductive variations of the revealing fashions of today. But American women were temperate in their imitation of the more extreme French fashions, insisting on chemisettes to veil their bosoms. It was not until the 1960's that sheer blouses, near-topless gowns and total nudity on the stage took the edge off all concealment. With their Puritan inheritance Americans were profoundly affected by the taboos of the Victorian era, except for the individualists who in any generation find a way to be as racy as they choose. Homes, attire and novels attested to the sentimentality of the period.

But toward the close of the nineteenth century the image emerged of strong, fearless girls as well as of clever wives who no longer jumped when Father spoke. As great fortunes were amassed women came to be cherished objects who radiated charm when decked with jewels and fine raiment. The woman in the home was on a pedestal; the woman who chose the unconventional life had a standing of her own. But the authoritarian spirit lost some of its force as college women coolly took soundings on their status; as sports enlivened their physical lives; as the automobile, the cinema and the telephone gave them wider vistas; as the suffrage message began to penetrate.

Then came Sigmund Freud to shake them out of their inherited conceptions of the relationship of men and women, of parent and child. Sex became a matter of open discussion and debate, a trend that developed rapidly in the 1960's. By the time the Freudian theories had influenced a new generation, World War I had been fought, and the flappers of the Jazz Age were prepared to put the theories into practice. This, too, was heralded as a period of sexual revolution before the shorn Charleston hoppers settled down and became the grandmothers of the long-haired, idealistic and earnest girls of today—as well as of the Hippies and the Flower Children.

"We have moved from Puritanism to lust," says Dr. Mead, the thrice-married anthropologist. "The only marked development . . . is that when infidelity occurs it is less likely today to break up a marriage. The couple is more likely to sit down and explore psychologically what is wrong with their relationship."

World War I and the 1920's marked the line of division and the birth of the New Woman. She had won the vote. Good jobs were hers to command. She went to college. She played all manner of games. Her hair was short. She smoked and wore knee-length skirts. Authority in the home lost ground. "Momism" became a catchword with the publication of Philip Wylie's *A Generation of Vipers*. And by the 1950's Hendrik de Leeuw in *Woman: The Dominant Sex, From Bloomers to Bikinis*, expressed the view that Momism, like an infectious disease, had permeated all forms of American culture. The war had opened the emancipated woman's eyes to new possibilities, and she became keenly conscious of her power over men. Or at least she talked about it more, and not because she had won the vote, but because of her fresh understanding of men.

If the young of the 1920's were known as Flaming Youth, the young of the 1930's were the deprived children of the Depression. In the 1940's it was war again, and in the 1950's the world changed after the atomic bomb was dropped. The flood of technology that flowed from the nuclear breakthrough tended to swamp the ways and customs of past generations. In the 1960's the Vietnam war stirred up the young to unprecedented resistance on the college campuses of the United States. Higher education in itself had removed many of the inherited barriers. Students had learned to question the absolute view of right and wrong. The ancient dread of venereal disease, of unwanted pregnancy and of ostracism for unconventional behavior flickered out, leaving the young free of binding strings although far from happy.

The number of young Americans who still lack sex experience at the time they marry is rapidly declining, a group of doctors agreed in a series of articles published in the *New York State Journal of Medicine*. They found in general that American youth was undergoing a total revolution in its attitude to sex, life and decorous behavior. Dr. Graham B. Blaine, chief of psychiatry at Harvard University Health Service, reported that one out of every eighteen babies born in the United States today is illegitimate, in spite of improved techniques in birth control. Many professors perforce admit the promiscuity, drug taking and general freedom of spirit on the campus. Statistics in this field vary from college to college, and a countdown on chastity and virginity rarely touches the truth. The most searching questionnaires on the sex life of the young are riddled with deception and error, but Oberlin, in a 1968 college poll, reported that 40 per cent of its students had engaged in sexual intercourse, a figure that has widespread support.

Dr. Joseph Katz, of the Stanford Institute for the Study of Human Problems, reported after a four-year study of the subject that the popular stereotype of widespread sexual promiscuity was not confirmed by his findings. Dr. Seymour Halleck, a psychiatrist at the University of Wisconsin, said in 1967 that despite the much-publicized sexual revolution on the campus, "the incidence of premarital relations has not changed much in the last half-century." Virginity is still the norm, and "the double standard is still with us," he reported in the *Journal of the American Medical Association*. But, "make love: not war," he added, has great appeal for the young and is an effective argument for sexual permissiveness.

The California woman does not compete with the male, says Dr. George R. Bach, founder of the Institute of Group Psychotherapy in Los Angeles. "She is the first really free woman in history; the equal of the male in every respect. She can make her own living. She is politically free; above all—and newest of all—she is sexually free.

She is no longer the passive object of chivalry or conquest as in the past. She is as privileged as any man to take the initiative in sexual conduct."

With Freud, Kinsey and Timothy Leary to explain them to themselves, the young have come up with strange conclusions and the most massive resistance to authority in the history of the ages. Scientific courses in anthropology, psychology and related subjects give them early briefing. Surveys add provocative understanding to their sex drives. Sex education and easy access to the most explicit books leave few in darkness. On top of this flows a rising tide of suggestion and stimulation from the screen, from television, the theater and advertising. And through the back channels runs a dark strain of pornography in art, in paperbacks, in the written word and flaunted message.

Even in the psychiatric world, which first opened the door to this development, there are specialists who feel that too much knowledge does more damage than the old-time combination of ignorance and innocence. In *The Unfinished Society* Dr. Alexander Reid Martin, a New York psychiatrist, observes: "I am absolutely sure that all the prissiness of the Victorian era, with the children whispering among themselves and sneaking the home medical book for consultation and parents blushing and coughing at embarrassing questions did more to invest sex with the delicacy that belongs to it than our clinical frankness."

Be that as it may, it was novel for American boys and girls, brought up in the Puritanical tradition, to thread their way through the streets, embracing and kissing in the spontaneous fashion of the Left Bank. It was novel for them to wear beads, bells and bangles as they gathered barefoot in parks to talk love and peace and amity, to make strange music and offer marigolds to passersby. The clergy viewed them benignly. Their parents gasped for air and tried to bridge what came to be known as the "generation gap." But somewhere along the way the power of communication had been lost, confronting parents with the most deadly problems they had ever faced. Freedom lost its glow as it edged too close to drug addiction, violence and general degradation and homelessness. The infusion of drugs into the lives of their young had given a new and sinister turn to what historically has passed as experience. They found their sons and daughters running away from them instead of fighting them. Total escape was their goal, and even parents who had given their children careful upbringing, the finest education, the best medical care and every opportunity faced the bitter moment when they learned that a cherished son or daughter was dead in a bohemian dive, or in the trunk of a car.

Mothers, more than fathers, have had to bear the onus for the strange conduct of their young. But the Flower Children, the Hippies and the more sinister junkies represent only a small, although highly publicized, percentage of a young generation militantly on the move, eager for a better world and not afraid to involve itself in the struggle to get it. A new generation with strong political feeling is in the making, different from any America has known and with girls more strongly entrenched than at any time in history. The rights they talk of now are not alone their own rights, but the rights of mankind at large. A Gallup poll taken in 1968 showed that the young voters were "more hip than hippy" and that most young people were in the main stream of political life, without necessarily being drawn to radical appeals for change.

Beyond doubt the sex revolution of the 1960's has upset the balance between the sexes as well as widening the gap between the young and their parents. The moralities have found new levels, affecting both the young and their elders. Dr. Mary Calderone, director of the Sex Information and Education Council of the U.S., has pointed out that women find it easier than men to make the necessary adjustments to a world changing at an accelerating rate. Although men do not seem to resent women's diverse roles as wife, mother, homemaker, community volunteer and career woman, they have found it hard to accept the fact that women do all these things "with so much apparent adaptability, resourcefulness, versatility and flexibility."

Women have won nearly all the goals that the most aggressive among them have demanded, but their victories have created new problems, and cynics observe that primitive society may still be the happiest. The woman who works outside her home and divides her time between family and office has endless difficulties to overcome. High-powered careers admittedly are satisfying, but the average mother coping with the average family is often so frustrated that she gets little pleasure from her work, aside from the pay check. In a world where many children are committed to LSD, juvenile delinquency and Hippie escape; where street brawls, campus riots and broken homes abound, she lives with a sense of guilt and fear.

Sir Ashley Montagu maintains that the kind of intelligence with which women are endowed is the "ability to love, to laugh, to civilize." But as an anthropologist he warns them that they will cease to be equipped for the future if they continue "migrating toward that ultimate destiny of complete equality" and embrace masculine values. Like Dr. Calderone, he is inclined to think that men are "unconsciously afraid of the constitutional and intellectual strength" of women and that this is why men have downgraded women through the ages.

But the leveling process goes on, and there are always agitators in action to push the issue a little further. Changes in the abortion and divorce laws and the broadening of job opportunities continue to be targets with the mature woman, just as the issues of peace and racial equality engage the attention of the young. Women are as deeply concerned as men over political issues and are generally more ardent in their resistance to war and other forms of authority involving their families. None could deny that their influence is more pervasive than it ever was—on the campus as well as at the polls, in the board room and at the executive table, in Hippie pads and at guru colonies. Today they are in the forefront of the picture, and they zoomed into the political limelight in 1968 more visibly than ever before in American history. The pioneer women did it differently. Their public image was dim or nonexistent at the time, however great a share they had in building up the country and influencing the course of history. Now women in action are visible to the public and can be appraised by families watching in millions of homes.

The American man does not complain. In general he takes it all with calm good humor and accepts its benefits with pragmatic spirit. He no longer considers it a reflection on his manhood or earning ability to have his wife give aid with the family bills. Young professional men have found it of benefit in helping them up the ladder and in raising the family standard of living. In a sense it is a reversion to the early days of the nation when duties were shared on a fifty-fifty basis. Thus the contemporary man can walk the baby on Sunday, shop at the supermarket, cook a steak, wash the dishes and baby-sit when the need arises—a state of affairs that in the nineteenth century was good only for the cartoonist, lampooning the sad fate of the feminists' husbands.

In other parts of the world this social picture is viewed with some degree of scorn, and uxorial women will have none of it. They feel it falls short of the true feminine instinct of the wife and mother and tends to keep men in a subjugated state. But no American man would admit, except in jest, to being subjugated, and he seems to suffer less than his emancipated wife from the consequences of her life outside the home. She does not always find happiness in her freedom, and psychiatrists increasingly tell aimless and distraught patients to go home and scrub their kitchens, make an omelet or wash their curtains. The swing to using their heads instead of their hands carries its own penalty.

Although the working wife is a commonplace on the American scene today she has to face up to difficulties that do not diminish. She has the inescapable problem of her growing children and the severe shortage of help. Some of the professional sociologists insist that college degrees do not necessarily lead to high marks in motherhood any more than they do to top jobs. The career woman, perhaps working harder over her children than the frankly domestic type, is apt to find them outclassed on all levels—in behavior, in scholarship, in adjustment to life. The sons and daughters of the utterly ignorant and indifferent not infrequently do much better than the blue-ribbon child. A study made at Columbia by Eli Ginzberg, a professor of economics, showed that the cocktail party or bridge game for their mothers had a better rating with the young than preoccupation with a job. The former fell into the herd pattern of what other mothers were doing.

If one is to accept this debatable point of view it suggests that the better educated women are more out of step in their maternity. Pearl Buck, who rates top honors both academically and as a mother, believes that "amiable, ignorant, boring women make much better mothers than neurotic college graduates." She sees no chance that American women will be content "unless they are kept more ignorant or are given equal opportunity with men to use what they have been taught, and American men will not be really happy until their women do." Thousands of women, in Mrs. Buck's opinion, are upholding the medieval tradition in the United States more heartily than men, while the atmosphere around the highly educated is "gray with discontent."

Marshall McLuhan predicts that the coming age will be tribal rather than industrial. "The long-haired boys' appeal is not aesthetic, but sexual; not private, but corporate," he says. "An ability to free emotions, and not a fragmented 'all-maleness' provides today's most compelling erotic appeal." Arnold Toynbee has called the Hippies a "red warning light for the American way of life." Meanwhile Hippie enclaves range from New Delhi to San Francisco, and the public is acutely aware that their strange habits are not an ephemeral student fad like swallowing goldfish. There is no question of sex dominance, or career dominance, in the world of the Hippie. Love is the catchword, and all is share and share alike. They are the "Freudian proletariat," according to one sociologist. They are "expatriates living on our shores but beyond our society," says another.

In addressing the Radcliffe graduating class of 1967 Barbara Tuchman, herself a Radcliffe graduate of 1933, said: "Thirty years ago and earlier, it seems to me the individual did not consider himself as so important nor, in spite of the Depression, so aggrieved as many seem today. . . . The burden of the recent complaint seems to be that the college does not adjust itself to the individual's varying and changing needs. No, it does not; why should it? Life does not adjust to them either, as the complainants will eventually discover. I cannot remember anyone when I was in college being troubled about his individualism."

Mrs. Tuchman pointed out that in spite of the four great agents of change since 1933—nuclear power, television, electronics and the revolution in sexual morality—promiscuity, reversal of sex roles and topless costumes had happened somewhere, sometime before—in Sodom and Gomorrah or in the Samoa described by Margaret Mead. It is more than a cliché that *plus ça change, plus c'est la même chose.* Thus the revival of the "equal rights for women" cry has a strangely familiar if anachronistic ring in the depths of the struggle going on around the world for rights involving all humanity. The ripples of discontent and frustration have been stirred anew by Betty Friedan, author of *The Feminine Mystique* and head of a new organization called NOW (National Organization of Women). Mrs. Friedan has sparked a contemporary wave of feminism and spreads the idea that women are third-class citizens on every count and are getting nowhere. She debunks the image of the happy housewife and highlights the dismaying effect of academe on the feminine spirit. As Mrs. Friedan views it, 75 per cent of the twenty-eight million women in the job market are at rock bottom and never do anything to pull themselves up. "Women have traded their rights for their comforts and now are too comfortable to care," she says. "Wives and widows own the stocks and men vote them."

Nearly a hundred men, mostly lawyers, are members of Mrs. Friedan's organization. The core of the movement is absolute equality for women in all spheres, and an immediate issue is revision of existing abortion laws. Other organizations have questioned the justice of these laws, and many legislative measures affecting the status of women have been quietly put through in recent years. But Mrs. Friedan's latter-day exponents of the Susan Anthony tradition are finding new ways to proclaim their views, going right to the well-established fountainhead of publicity and wherever possible making polite nuisances of themselves. They showed originality in picketing the mighty *New York Times* to protest the dividing line it drew between Male and Female want ads. The *Times* took this novel picket line with equanimity, since picketing and dissent are more or less the order of the day and publicity is a well-understood gambit in this orbit. With a minimum of fuss the cause was won. But the Overeseas Press Club banished them for violating bylaws when they used the club premises to pass out leaflets urging the boycott of a company they accused of discriminating against women employees. A cluster of young career women promptly protested the ban. In 1968 to protest was to live.

The undeniable discontent of some of the most brilliant college graduates after marriage has not been overlooked in scholarly circles. The colleges in some instances invite women back in their mature years, and Mary Bunting includes in her wide domain the Radcliffe Institute for women who have chosen to suspend their professional careers to devote themselves to growing families. They return and work on independent research without severing the link with their domestic and community responsibilities. Mrs. Bunting, who has played the double role herself as mother and college president, and whose academic interests are strongly scientific, believes that much of the talent of American women is still being wasted.

The binding strings of tradition are being questioned even in the Catholic Church as ancient rules are relaxed. Nuns are changing their habits for the first time in centuries. They are moving out into the community, not only as teachers but as participants in the struggles of the day. Pope Paul VI appointed women members of the Sacred Congregations in 1968. But the Church lags behind society as a whole by excluding women from the priesthood. Dr. Mary Daly, the first woman theologian to teach at Boston College, in her book *The Church and the Second Sex* traces ecclesiastical misogynism to the inferior status of women in Jewish and Greek civilizations, and to the traditional image of God as a stern father figure. Even the most reputable Biblical scholars take it for granted that God is masculine, says Dr. Daly, and Eve in Genesis is pictured as a subordinate being to man, and a sinful temptress.

The strictures of the church were among the roadblocks that Margaret Sanger encountered in her long, hard fight for what she considered the inalienable right of women to decide how many children they should bear. Of all the American women who have backed causes, worked for freedom at all levels and initiated social movements, Mrs. Sanger has been one of the most significant for the world of the future. Among the pioneers and women of quiet determination who from time to time have shaken up the social structure and influenced the relationship of men and women on the American scene, she stands alone, a key figure who contributed the vital spark to what today has become a major political cause—control of the population explosion around the world. From small beginnings early in the twentieth century she was an internationally known figure at the time of her death in 1966.

The unfamiliar phrase "birth control" appeared in her paper *Woman Rebel* in 1914. It was a term that sank slowly into the public consciousness until it assumed the broader implications of Planned Parenthood in 1942. Now the movement is worldwide; the International Planned Parenthood Federation operates in one hundred countries.

In many ways Mrs. Sanger's cause was more disruptive than the old suffrage battle, for it caught both men and women in the most vital aspect of their relationship. It ran counter to church teaching and offended the puritanical American inheritance. It violated legal restrictions pushed through by Anthony Comstock in 1873, and for years it lacked social approval. It could not be trumpeted in the streets like the suffrage issue, for it did not lend itself to public clamor. When its echoes reached the newspapers their impact was apt to be shocking to a public not yet wholly free of Victorian inhibitions.

Most young American mothers now take birth control as much for granted as if it were part of the Bill of Rights, but Mrs. Sanger went to jail for her convictions before she was able to spread her message around the world. She had to win her way with the medical profession, with the legislatures of the land, with the churches and with the public. Doctors stayed aloof from entanglements in the early days of her struggle, and it was not until 1937 that the American Medical Association recognized birth control as legal medical practice.

Determined though she was to have the movement soundly based on medical principles, Mrs. Sanger was pictured as an irresponsible bohemian, backing a prurient cause. Nothing seemed to her to be further from the truth. "The greatest issue," she said, "is to raise the question of birth control out of the gutter of obscenity, where my opponents have put it, and get it into the light of intelligence and human understanding." Her deepest interest lay in research. She never lost hope that the perfect contraceptive would be found, and that eventually it would come within the reach of all the women who might need it. Happily she lived to see the widely advertised Pill in successful operation, and her advocates know that many of today's contraceptives are improved variations of simple devices she brought back to the United States from Holland in the 1920's.

There was nothing aggressive about Margaret Sanger. She was all woman, with floppy auburn hair and widely spaced gray eyes that gazed at the world with a certain wistfulness. In court she surprised magistrates and the press with her seemingly meek and diffident air. Actually, she had the same quiet and persistent force as Lucy Stone, and could blaze with anger, expressed in a flushed face and tense hands, yet without ever raising her voice. In her early days, before success gave her self-assurance, she seemed a shrinking figure, except in debate, when she could flip a quick Irish witticism that silenced even policemen. She dressed simply and even demurely, admitting in later years that she found it best to subdue her own personality while the battle raged. Hugh de Selincourt, an English admirer, said of her that she could be a stern Margaret "devoted with sheer tremendousness to a Cause," but she was also the Margaret of "jasmine tea and rose liqueur." But it took some time for the American public to appreciate the distinction.

She was married twice, first to William Sanger, whom she divorced in 1921 after years of separation and then to J. Noah H. Slee, an older man who adored her and lavished much of his Three-in-One Oil fortune on her work and her interests. Her two sons, Stuart and Grant, became successful doctors, but her only daughter, Peggy, died of pneumonia at a moment when Margaret was fighting one of her court cases. The man who most profoundly affected her thinking and steered her course was the noted English scientist of whom she wrote, "I have never felt about any person as I do about Havelock Ellis." Yet nothing swung her away from her single-minded determination to push the cause in which she believed so intensely. Like other women pioneers she was accused in time of making her cause a one-woman movement, and of focusing it around her own presence. As others moved into what had become a great humanitarian drive she had the bitter disillusionment of having to step aside from the organization she had founded.

The militant spirit identified with the movement from the beginning had been superseded by a program of more restrained social activity. Mrs. Sanger believed that federal action on birth control would be faster and wider in scope. Her critics preferred to work through the states. As the rich and the fashionable moved into the ranks, Mrs. Sanger's early radical associations were emphasized, and in turn the founder backed away from the doctrinaire program that had taken the place of her own quick-moving and sometimes sensational methods. Her struggles with the medical profession had drawn fire. After years of feuding she gave up the presidency of the American Birth Control League in 1928, but she remained the focus of the movement she had started. Before long she broadened the base and pushed research, carrying her message around the world.

Mrs. Sanger had a deep mystical sense and believed that she was born "to live, to act, to rebel." Her interest in birth control had its roots in her own early life. Her father, Michael Hennessey Higgins, was a lusty Irishman, an agnostic, a follower of Henry George and Robert Ingersoll. Their home was in Corning, New York, where he carved saints and angels for the local graveyard. Just as Lucy Stone reacted to seeing her mother work on the farm the night before she was confined, so Margaret suffered when her own tubercular mother died at forty-eight after bearing eleven children. Margaret was threatened with the same disease herself at the time of her marriage to William Sanger, but she moved to Saranac from a city apartment and fought it off.

During her first sixteen years Margaret learned from her father to fight for what she believed in, and the sights she later saw while nursing on New York's lower East Side showed her where her life interest should lie. After coping with many self-induced abortion cases and puerperal mishaps she gave up nursing and devoted herself to the study of contraceptive history. Her paper, *Woman*

Rebel, spearheaded her findings, and copies were banned by the Post Office when she detailed seven circumstances under which birth control should be practiced. In the summer of 1914 she was indicted on nine counts for sending contraceptive information through the mails. She stood almost alone as she faced this charge. Even the most progressive of her friends dared not voice their support. On the eve of her trial she fled to Europe without permission of the court. During her absence Anthony Comstock visited her house and bought a birth-control pamphlet from the unsuspecting William Sanger, who had to serve a month in jail for this infringement of the law—and did it willingly for Margaret's sake.

A new life began for her when she rented a small furnished room close to the British Museum. She proceeded to study the history of contraception as far back as the printed records would carry her. Soon she had a master hand steering her course along scientific channels, for Havelock Ellis had entered her life. Through her radical connections in the United States she had been taken up by the Fabian intellectuals of England. Speaking in Fabian Hall she used the phrase "birth control," which from then on became more generally used than Neo-Malthusianism.

Margaret seemed "all grace and spirit" to Ellis. He was fifty-five when she flashed across his path with all the intensity of her driving nature. They went to concerts together and lunched regularly in Soho. He left notes at her desk in the museum to guide her studies for the day. By degrees he taught her to view the subject as a matter of eugenics, vital to the family and to society as a whole. In spite of matrimonial entanglements they discussed marriage, but the birth-control movement had taken such possession of Margaret's spirit that deep personal interests could not thrive within her. "I think we should agree on the subject of love," Ellis wrote to her. "I think that passion is mostly a disastrous thing. . . . I mean by love something that is based on a true relationship but that has succeeded in avoiding the blind volcano of passion."

Mrs. Sanger enjoyed the suavities of country-house life in England when she visited Wantley in Sussex, a house that had belonged to Shelley's father and was owned by Hugh de Selincourt, a poet and novelist who concentrated on Shelley and Blake. Here she found writers, artists, musicians who tramped the moors or devoted their days to music and reading aloud. When introduced later to the more practical world in which H. G. Wells lived, she met such men as Arnold Bennett, Bernard Shaw, Bertrand Russell and a variety of scholars who clustered around Wells at Easton Glebe in Essex.

When she returned to the United States to answer to her indictment and to launch the birth-control movement in earnest she had fresh knowledge and scientific understanding behind her. Her own pamphlet *Family Limitation*, eventually translated into thirteen languages, was an eye opener to the public, although Robert Dale Owen and Charles Knowlton had written earlier on the subject. In 1876 Knowlton's book, which had gone unnoticed in his native America, became the focus of England's Neo-Malthusian movement. But by the 1920's, as far as women were concerned, Dr. Marie Stopes carried the torch in England and Margaret Sanger in the United States. They brought the subject down to the level of the home whereas the Malthusians had given it more classical treatment.

The war clouds had gathered in Europe as Margaret came home prepared to do battle. The indictment standing against her was quashed in 1916, and that year she and her sister, a nurse named Ethel Byrne, opened a birth-control clinic in the Brownsville section of Brooklyn—the first of its kind in the United States and the second in the world. (The Netherlands had the first.) The clinic was promptly raided, and Mrs. Byrne went on a hunger strike in jail, thereby arousing sympathy across the country. Mrs. Sanger, sentenced to thirty days in the workhouse, gave lectures on birth control to her fellow prisoners. Provocative headlines followed. The *Woman Rebel*, which had challenged the Comstock law, was followed by the *Birth Control Review*, to be published for the next twenty-three years. It was less explosive than its predecessor and was sold on street corners by towheaded, blue-eyed Kitty Marion. The stars of the theater knew her as a fixture in Times Square on the iciest of winter nights as well as the balmiest of summer evenings. The *Review* frequently quoted Havelock Ellis and H. G. Wells. Mrs. Sanger publicly and defiantly gave contraceptive information to women whom she felt needed it. "I could no more stop than I could change the color of my eyes," she wrote.

In 1917 she opened an office of her own on Fifth Avenue with the words "Birth Control" on the door. But the movement really caught fire after a meeting held in Town Hall in 1921 was broken up by the police. Mrs. Sanger was billed to speak on "Birth Control: Is It Moral?" A large and fashionable audience that filled the hall saw her being forcibly restrained from making her address. She was taken to the police station in a patrol wagon through a crowd of booing, protesting observers.

A storm blew up in the press over this, giving Mrs. Sanger the martyr halo for the time being. Helen Rogers Reid, of the New York *Herald Tribune,* and other notables of the journalistic world had viewed the strong-arm tactics used. The *World* noted editorially: "The issue Sunday evening was bigger than the right to advocate birth control. It is part of the eternal fight for free speech, free assembly and democratic government." Hundreds of editorials spread the message, and from being viewed as a fanatic and crackpot Mrs. Sanger was hailed as a defender of the Constitution. She charged the Catholic hierarchy with being responsible for silencing her and named the Monsignor whom she had seen leaning against the wings and giving the order to place her under arrest. Before she died she noted with satisfaction that the Vatican seemed to be modifying its position as a result of a three-year study of the subject, but two years after her death the issue was again acute when the Catholic Church reaffirmed its ban on birth control.

Public indignation over the Town Hall raid reached such a point that an investigation was ordered, but the matter soon was dropped —except by Mrs. Sanger, whose subsequent meeting in the Park Theater was a smashing success. Many of the city's notables turned out to give her their support. This was the year in which the American Birth Control League was organized to draw all the strings together. It was also the year in which she concentrated heavily on birth-control legislation, lobbying at Albany, spreading her propaganda, enlisting the interest of Samuel Rosenman, later a judge and adviser to President Franklin Roosevelt.

Soon she was touring the country as a speaker, weathering scorn and jeers in certain cities but finding hordes of eager women ready to fill her meeting halls and learn what she could teach them. The raid had swung the whole movement into a pattern of respectability, with strongly entrenched women ready to uphold Mrs. Sanger's standard. Her own presence, with her quiet demeanor and gentle manners, was reassuring to the doubting, and although trembling with stage fright at first, she weathered the most strenuous touring and began to think in terms of the larger world.

In the years that followed she traveled the world over, attending Neo-Malthusian conferences, helping to organize birth-control centers and stimulating the interest of national leaders in a cause that deeply affected the political structure of their countries. She began with Japan, a country that she revisited later to observe how the seed she had planted had flowered. "The greatest threat to the peace of the world is to be found in the teeming populations of Asia," she wrote prophetically in 1922. Thirty years later she joined Lady Dhanvanthi Rama Rau of India, Elise Ottesen-Jensen of Sweden and other birth-control pioneers in forming the International Planned Parenthood Federation. Within another decade—in 1962—the United Nations was discussing birth control for the first time under the encompassing title "Population Growth and Economic Development."

Mrs. Sanger went to Russia in 1934 but made no headway there. In the following year she visited India, where she talked to Nehru and Madame Pandit, who were sympathetic, and Gandhi, who did not seem to hear her. Many battles were fought on the home front as Mrs. Sanger backed research, spread scientific contraceptive information, helped to organize birth-control centers in various cities and worked ceaselessly to win the support of the medical profession. The Clinical Research Bureau she opened in 1923 provided a wealth of case histories and marital information. It became a laboratory for doctors, clergymen and social-service workers. When the sixth International Birth Control Conference was held in New York in 1925 more than a thousand doctors tried to gain admission, such was the interest in the clinical findings.

Thirty years before the publication of the Kinsey report this bureau was exploring patients' attitudes in the marriage relationship. Dr. Hannah M. Stone did courageous work in this field, aided by her husband, Dr. Abraham Stone. A crucial issue was settled in 1936 when Morris Ernst fought and won the One Package Case, involving contraceptives mailed to Dr. Hannah Stone by a Japanese doctor and ordered by Mrs. Sanger. When the judge ruled that the package should be delivered to Dr. Stone, both domestic and overseas mails were at last open for the transmission of contraceptive materials. This ended the Comstock legislation of 1873, and was a key victory for the birth-control movement. It was also a personal triumph for Mrs Sanger. In the following year the Town Hall Club, in whose auditorium she had once been forbidden to speak, awarded her its annual medal. More importantly, the medical profession moved cautiously into the fold.

Mrs. Sanger's own life had changed considerably with her second marriage, and she no longer had to cope with the financial worries that had always beset her. Slee pursued her for three years before she finally married him at a London registry in 1935. He offered her a prenuptial marriage settlement, which she refused, but he contributed handsomely to the birth-control movement and helped her in many practical ways, such as introducing office efficiency into her organization. She used the name Slee for social affairs only, since Margaret Sanger's name was unalterably linked with the birth-control movement. Like Fannie Hurst and her husband, the Slees kept separate quarters in the same apartment house in New York. His wedding gift to her was a stretch of land at Beacon, overlooking the Hudson, and there they built a gray fieldstone manor designed by Margaret to resemble Wantley. In her study, "Tree Tops," she continued to write articles and books. Outdoors were willow trees fringing the lake, a rock garden, a rose arbor and groves of lilac bushes.

The setting was strongly English for the busy American who ran her large household and took the train each day to New York to cope with her office work. Although she was constantly called away to strengthen weak links in the growing birth-control movement, the domestic picture was harmoniously preserved. At Beacon the Margaret Sanger of "jasmine tea and rose liqueur" could whip up an exotic salad, give a costume party for her children and grandchildren, dance on the grass like a professional or swim in the lake at midnight. She preferred the company of intellectuals, writers and artists to her husband's business friends. Although opera was one of her major interests, it left her husband cold. Both liked horseback riding. Slee was tall, ruddy and white-haired; visitors thought he had the look of an English squire. His own life was more closely identified with the Union League Club and the Episcopal Church than with the assorted gatherings at their Beacon home, but their hospitality was inclusive

After her husband's death Margaret moved to Tucson and lived in a fan-shaped house with an aluminum roof that shimmered in the desert sun. A steel fireplace was reflected in a curving pool, Chinese prints hung on the stark white walls, and Korean chests from her travels gave a solid touch to Margaret's sunny quarters. An enclosed porch opened on terrace and gardens. In 1966 Mrs. Sanger died there of arteriosclerosis after a life strenuously lived. She was often ill, and during the early days of her struggle she spent many months in Switzerland seeking health. After her daughter's death she turned for consolation to Indian philosophy, Rosicrucianism and astrology, like some other women protagonists of great movements, but in the end she came to rely solely on her own strength. Pearl Buck said of her, "She started the fire of a great freedom, and it will not burn down and no one can put it out . . . it is sure that her name will go down in history."

Her influence was still being strongly felt around the world as well as at home as the 1960's drew to a close. By then contraceptives were being sold legally to married couples in all states and to unmarried persons in every state except Massachusetts and Wisconsin. During 1967 more than 300,000 patients received direct birth-control help from the American centers, tripling the number helped in 1960. A significant decline was noted in the birth rate for low-income groups. By 1968 thirty-four states had adopted family-planning policies or legislation.

"When the history of our civilization is written," said H. G. Wells, "it will be a biological history and Margaret Sanger will be its heroine." One of the fundamentals of her teaching was the greater care that parents could give to well-spaced children. This was an argument with appeal for the American woman.

Probably no parents in the world today devote more time and thought to their offspring than those who live in the United States. They buy more books on child care, listen to more lectures, discuss the subject more searchingly than any other people. They pay tribute to their children and steer them into the accepted channels of culture, yet one of the anomalies of the era is the number of Hippies and drug addicts who have come from prosperous homes in the suburbs. Parents are told they are too permissive, too neglectful or too occupied with their own affairs. The critics abroad who insist that women dominate the scene in America are equally convinced that their children are the most spoiled on earth.

Few American men ever protest because their wives work, whether they work from necessity or by choice. It happens to be the way of life in the United States, accepted at every social level. But between the wholly submissive wife (and the species is not yet extinct) and the independent woman who prefers to work in the outside world may be found the universal feminine type, spreading her aura of family stability. More often than not she preserves some of the traditions of her ancestors. She runs her home with skill and charm. She devotes herself to community causes and keeps a weather eye on international affairs. She finds time to read, to talk to her children, to have hobbies, to show informed interest in her husband's work and to know what is going on in the world. The chances are that she is well turned out for all occasions. She is the unsung Daughter of Eve who is happy in her home. She does not feel the need of the limelight, nor does she worry about her rights. The picture sounds strangely old-fashioned, but it is in style again. There is no question of whose will prevails; decisions are forged by both husband and wife. It's idyllic when it works.

It was significant that the 1960's, with all their uproar and rebellion, reintroduced the image of the thoroughly domestic woman.

The focus had swung again to the home, the nursery, the kitchen, with women taking pride in a perfect dinner, in the houses they remodeled, the clothes they designed, the pictures they painted, the flowers they planted. Cook books are in high esteem, and Julia Child and Poppy Cannon are as much the goddesses of the kitchen as Fannie Farmer and Mrs. Beaton were early in the century. Needlepoint and crewel work have their place at the most fashionable parties, and the women's magazines play up the domestic arts more thoroughly than at any time since the 1880's—but with a difference. Modern art and décor, contemporary emphasis and dash, have supplanted the flowery bowers and starchy menus of the late nineteenth century. Split-level houses, condominiums and glass homes in the woods have taken the place of Tuscan villas and Gothic cottages, but the focus remains constant—husband, child and home.

Ambassador or factory worker, Cabinet officer or filing clerk, professor or waitress, artist or technician, voter or nonvoter, woman's chief concern is still her relationship with man. However far she may have traveled along the shining road of personal achievement she is chained to this reality. All men may be born equal, but men and women are born with a difference and, as Margaret Sanger put it, "A woman must be absolute mistress of her own body with the right to dispose of herself or to withhold herself." The right to vote has been only a small part of her long hard fight for a place in the sun, though it has made much else possible. However, in the final analysis her instincts fuse inevitably into her own particular art—procreation. Women are still the mothers of men, and in this fundamental respect their status has not changed from the beginning of time. In all else they are touching new horizons today, for better or for worse.

Notes

CHAPTER 1. ABIGAIL'S BID FOR INDEPENDENCE

Abigail Adams, *New Letters of Abigail Adams, 1788–1801*; "Abigail Adams, Commentator," Massachusetts Historical Society *Proceedings*, Boston, 1942; Charles Francis Adams (ed.), *Familiar Letters of John Adams and his wife, Abigail Adams during the Revolution*; Henry Adams, *The Education of Henry Adams*; Charles Francis Adams, *Diary of Charles Francis Adams*; James Truslow Adams, *The Adams Family*; John Quincy Adams, *Memoirs of John Quincy Adams*; Margaret L. Brown, "Anne Willing Bingham," *Bermuda Historical Quarterly*, August, 1949; "Mr. and Mrs. William Bingham of Philadelphia," *Pennsylvania Magazine of History and Biography*, 1937, Vol. 61; "Belinda" in *Post-Boy*, November 7, 1765; William Jay, *The Life of John Jay*, 2 vols; Samuel Eliot Morison, *The Oxford History of the American People*; Ann Hollingsworth Wharton, *Colonial Days and Dames* and *Social Life in the Early Republic*; Elizabeth F. Ellet, *The Women of the American Revolution, The Court Circles of the Republic* and *The Queens of American Society*; Katharine Susan Anthony, *Dolly Madison, Her Life and Times* and *First Lady of the Revolution*; James Thomas Flexner, *George Washington in the American Revolution, 1775–1783*; Douglas Southall Freeman, *George Washington*; Elswyth Thane, *Washington's Lady*; John Winthrop, *The History of New England from 1630–1649*; Arthur M. Schlesinger and Dixon Ryan Fox (eds.), *A History of American Life*, Vol. 10; Clinton Rossiter, *Seedtime of the Republic*; Gamaliel Bradford, *Wives*; Mary Sumner Benson, *Women in Eighteenth Century America*; Mary Caroline Crawford, *Romantic Days in the Early Republic* and *Social Life in Old New England*; Janet Whitney, *Abigail Adams*; "Impressions of a First Lady," *This Week*, January 10, 1965; Oliver Andrew, *Portraits of John and Abigail Adams*; Rebecca Franks' Letters, 1778 and 1781, *Pennsylvania Magazine of History and Biography*, XVI.

CHAPTER 2. THE EARLY PACEMAKERS

James Madison papers, Library of Congress; *Memoirs and Letters of Dolly Madison*, edited by her grandniece; Katharine Susan Anthony, *Dolly Madison, Her Life and Times*; and *First Lady of the Revolution*; Mary Sumner Benson, *Women in Eighteenth Century America*; Washington Irving, *Knickerbocker's History of New York*; Elizabeth L. Dean, *Dolly Madison, the Nation's Hostess*; Alice Morse Earle, *Home Life in Colonial Days*; Meade Minnegerode, *Some American Ladies*; Allan Nevins, *American Social History as Recorded by British Travellers*; Saul K. Padover, *The Complete Madison*; James Polk, *The Diary of a President 1845–1849*, edited by Allan Nevins; Mrs. Samuel Harrison Smith, *The First Forty Years of Washington Society*, edited by Gaillard Hunt; Mary Newton Stanard, *Colonial Virginia, Its People and Customs*; Thomas Jefferson Wertenbaker, *The Puritan Oligarchy: The Founding of American Civilization*; Anne Hollingsworth Wharton, *Colonial Days and Dames* and *Social Life in the Early Republic*; Mary French Caldwell, *General Jackson's Lady*; Elizabeth F. Ellet, *The Court Circles of the Republic, The Queens of American Society* and *The Women of the American Revolution*; Bess Furman, *White House Profile*; Laura C. Holloway, *The Ladies of the White House*; Van Wyck Brooks, *The World of Washington Irving*; Mary Caroline Crawford, *Romantic Days in the Early Republic*; Marshall B. Davidson, *Life in America*; Alice (Curtis) Desmond, *Glamorous Dolly Madison*; Sydney George Fisher, *Men, Women, and Manners in Colonial Times*; Jessie Benton Frémont, *Souvenir of My Time*; Ona Griffin Jeffries, *In and Out of the White House*; Amy (La Follette) Jensen, *The White House and its Thirty-Two Families*; Harriet Martineau, *Society in America*; Allan Nevins, *Grover Cleveland, The Emergence of Modern America 1865–1878*; George Bancroft, *History of the United States*; Arthur Styron, *The Last of the Cocked Hats*; Philip Hone, *The Diary of Philip Hone*, 2 vols.; Frank Moore, *The Diary of the American Revolution 1775–1781* and *The Rebellion Record, 1864–1868*; Ben Perley Poore, *Reminiscences of Sixty Years in the National Metropolis*, 2 vols.; Mary Clemmer Ames, *Ten Years in Washington*; Esther Singleton, *The Story of the White House*, 2 vols.; Margaret Leech, *Reveille in Washington* and *In the Days of McKinley*; Carl Sandburg and Paul M. Angle, *Mary Lincoln, Wife and Widow*; Ruth Painter Randall, *Mary Lincoln*; Ishbel Ross, *The General's Wife*; Mary A. Livermore, *My Story of the War*; Adam Badeau, *Grant in Peace*; Ulysses S. Grant, *Personal Memoirs of U. S. Grant*, 2 vols.; Rutherford Birchard Hayes, *Diary and Letters*; James A. Garfield, *The Works of James Abram Garfield*, edited by Burke A. Hinsdale; John Russell Young, *Men and Memories*; H. H. Kohlsaat, *From McKinley to*

Harding; Wilbur Cross and Ann Novotny, *White House Weddings;* Robert Seager, II, *And Tyler Too.*

CHAPTER 3. A NEW ERA BEGINS

Theodore Roosevelt papers in Library of Congress; William Howard Taft family papers in Library of Congress; *Theodore Roosevelt, An Autobiography;* Elting E. Morison (ed.), *The Letters of Theodore Roosevelt,* 8 vols.; Henry F. Pringle, *Theodore Roosevelt;* Lilian Rixey, *Bamie;* Anna Roosevelt Cowles, *Letters from Theodore Roosevelt to Anna Roosevelt Cowles, 1870–1918;* Alice Longworth, *Crowded Hours;* Archibald Butt, *Taft and Roosevelt;* Ellen Maury Slayden, *Washington Wife;* Henry L. Stoddard, *As I Knew Them;* Mark Sullivan, *Our Times: The United States, 1900–1925;* William Allen White, *Masks in a Pageant;* Irwin (Ike) Hoover, *Forty-two Years in the White House;* Hermann Hagedorn, *The Roosevelt Family of Sagamore Hill;* Herbert Hoover, *Memoirs of Herbert Hoover,* Vol. 2; Eugene Lyons, *Herbert Hoover;* Arthur M. Schlesinger and Dixon Ryan Fox (eds.), *A History of American Life,* Vol. 10; Charles Austin and Mary Beard, *The Rise of American Civilization,* 2 vols.; William J. and Mary Baird Bryan, *The Memoirs of William Jennings Bryan;* Henry F. Pringle, *The Life and Times of William Howard Taft;* Ishbel Ross, *An American Family: The Tafts 1678–1964;* Henry Steele Commager, *The American Mind;* Samuel Eliot Morison, *The Oxford History of the American People;* Ray Stannard Baker, *Woodrow Wilson, Life and Letters,* Vols. 3 and 4; Alden Hatch, *Edith Bolling Wilson: First Lady Extraordinary;* A. S. Link, *Wilson: The Road to the White House;* Edith Bolling Wilson, *My Memoir;* Eleanor Wilson McAdoo and M. J. Gaffey, *The Woodrow Wilsons;* Henry Cabot Lodge, *The Senate and the League of Nations;* Cary T. Grayson, *Woodrow Wilson, An Intimate Memoir;* Charles Willis Thompson, *Presidents I've Known and Two Near Presidents;* Andrew Sinclair, *The Available Man: Warren Gamaliel Harding;* Mary Randolph, *Presidents and First Ladies;* Claude M. Fuess, *Calvin Coolidge;* Ishbel Ross, *Grace Coolidge and Her Era;* Frances Parkinson Keyes, *Letters from a Senator's Wife;* Lloyd Morris, *Postscript to Yesterday;* Frederick Lewis Allen, *Only Yesterday;* Samuel Hopkins Adams, *The Incredible Era;* Gamaliel Bradford, *The Quick and the Dead;* Calvin Coolidge, *The Autobiography of Calvin Coolidge;* New York *Herald Tribune* files of the 1920's; Emily Taft Douglas, *Remember the Ladies.*

CHAPTER 4. POWER IN THE WHITE HOUSE

Eleanor Roosevelt, *Autobiography of Eleanor Roosevelt, It Seems to Me, This I Remember* and *You Learn by Living;* Eleanor Roosevelt and

Lorena A. Hickok, *Ladies of Courage*; Frances Perkins, *The Roosevelt I Knew*; Amy (La Follette) Jensen, *The White House and Its Thirty-Two Families*; Lloyd R. Morris, *Not So Long Ago*; Arthur M. Schlesinger, Jr., and Morton White, *Paths of American Thought*; Arthur M. Schlesinger and Dixon Ryan Fox (eds.), *A History of American Life*, Vol. 10; William Manchester, *The Death of a President*; Lloyd R. Morris, *Not So Long Ago*; Adlai Stevenson, "A Lady for All Seasons," *Saturday Review*, October 10, 1964; Mrs. James A. Halsted (Anna Roosevelt), "I Followed My Parents' Lead," New York *Post*, July 20, 1967; Margaret Truman with Margaret Cousins, *Souvenir*; Mary Van Renssalaer Thayer, "Triumph and Tragedy in the White House," *McCall's*, February, 1968, and *Jacqueline Bouvier Kennedy*; "Mother Defends RFK, Denies He's Ruthless," New York *Post*, April 25, 1968; June Weir, "Bobby's Irish Rose," *Women's Wear Daily*, May 9, 1968; Anne H. Lincoln, *The Kennedy White House Parties*; Marion K. Sanders, "New American Female; demi Feminism takes over," *Harper's Magazine*, July, 1965; Nancy Seely, "The Ten Living Daughters of United States Presidents," New York *Post*, July 21, 1967; "100 American Women of Accomplishment," *Harper's Bazaar*, September, 1967; Henry Brandon, "A Talk with the First Lady," *New York Times Magazine*, September 10, 1967; Stewart Alsop, *The Center: People and Power in Political Washington*; Phyllis Battelle, "Lady Bird's Anguish—Role in the Decision," New York *Daily Column*, April 4, 1968; Charles Rabb, "Months of Soul-Searching Before the Decision," New York *Daily News*, April 2, 1968; H. Sherrill, "Family Next Door in the Big White House," *New York Times Magazine*, July 31, 1966; Luci Johnson, "I've Been Forced to Grow Up," *Seventeen*, May, 1966; "Lynda Tells the Story of her Engagement," *McCall's*, November, 1967; "Wonderful Terrible Life of the President's Daughters," *Newsweek*, May 23, 1966; "Word from Miss Kitt," *Newsweek*, January 29, 1968; "Down to Eartha," *Time*, January 26, 1968; Inez Robb, "HHH Can Have His Wife's Egg Money, Anytime," New York *Daily Column*, April 26, 1968; Myra McPherson, "Governors' Wives Discover America in Style at the White House," *New York Times*, March 1, 1968; David K. Shipler, "Campaigners Lure Talented Women," *New York Times*, July 17, 1968; Laura Bergquist, "Ethel," *Look*, June 25, 1968; Kandy Shuman, "Ethel," *Women's Wear Daily*, June 7, 1968; "Survivor of Family Tragedies," *New York Times*, June 7, 1968; June Weir, "Bobby's Irish Rose," *Women's Wear Daily*, May 9, 1968; Judy Michaelson, "Ethel Kennedy," New York *Post*, June 8, 1968; "100 American Women of Accomplishment," *Harper's Bazaar*, September, 1967; Judy Michaelson, "Margaret Truman Daniel," New York *Post*, July 20, 1968; Eugenia Sheppard, "First Fashion Show at the White House," *Women's Wear Daily*, February 13, 1968; Harriet Van Horne, "Lady Bird," New

York *Post,* September 6, 1967; Miscellaneous items from *Life, Look, Time, Newsweek* and the *New York Times.*

CHAPTER 5. TROUBLEMAKERS AND PIONEERS

Henry Leland Chapman, "Mrs. Anne Hutchinson," a paper read before the New England Historical Genealogical Society, February 6, 1901; Otto Hufeland, *Anne Hutchinson's Refuge in the Wilderness,* a paper read before the Westchester County Historical Society, October 27, 1923; John Winthrop, *Antinomians and Familists Condemned by the Synod of Elders in New England* and *The History of New England from 1630–1649;* Edmund S. Morgan, "The Case Against Anne Hutchinson," *New England Quarterly,* 1937, Vol. 10; Charles M. Andrews, *Pilgrims and Puritans;* Edith Curtis, *Anne Hutchinson;* Charles W. Ferguson, *The Male Attitude;* Jared Sparks, *Lives of Ezra Stiles, John Fitch and Anne Hutchinson;* Winifred King Rugg, *Unafraid: A Life of Anne Hutchinson;* Marion Lena Starkey, *The Devil in Massachusetts;* Alice Morse Earle, *Customs and Fashions in Old New England* and *Margaret Winthrop;* Katharine Susan Anthony, *First Lady of the Revolution;* Mary Sumner Benson, *Women in Eighteenth Century America;* Sarah Josepha Hale, *Woman's Record, or Sketches of Distinguished Women from the Creation to the Present Day;* Thomas Jefferson Wertenbaker, *The Puritan Oligarchy: the Founding of American Civilization;* Charles Francis Adams (ed.), *Familiar Letters of John Adams and his wife Abigail Adams during the Revolution;* Harriet Martineau, *Society in America,* 3 vols.; Frances Milton Trollope, *Domestic Manners of the Americans;* Frances Wright D'Arusmont, *View of Society and Manners in America* and *Course of Popular Lectures;* Margaret Fuller Ossoli, *Memoirs of Margaret Fuller Ossoli;* Madeleine B. Stern, *The Life of Margaret Fuller;* Margaret Fuller, *Love Letters of Margaret Fuller;* Margaret Bell, *Margaret Fuller;* Horace Greeley, *Recollections of a Full Life* and *Autobiography;* Ishbel Ross, *Ladies of the Press; Kate Field's Washington;* Lilian Whiting, *Kate Field;* Jane Grey Swisshelm, *Half a Century;* Gail Hamilton, *Biography of James G. Blaine;* H. Augusta Dodge, *Gail Hamilton's Life in Letters,* 2 vols.; Emily Edson Briggs, *The Olivia Letters;* A. J. G. Perkins and Theresa Wolfson, *Frances Wright;* Julia Ward Howe, *Reminiscences, 1819–1899; Grace Greenwood's Leaves; Fanny Fern's Leaves;* Anne Royall's *Paul Pry;* Robert Dale Owen, "An Earnest Sowing of Wild Oats," *Atlantic Monthly,* July, 1874.

CHAPTER 6. BEAUTIES, SIRENS AND SPIES

Salmon Portland Chase papers, Library of Congress; Mary Merwin Phelps, *Kate Chase, Dominant Daughter;* Thomas Graham and Marva

Robins Belden, *So Fell the Angels*; Ruth Painter Randall, *Mary Lincoln*; Carl Sandburg, *Abraham Lincoln, the War Years*, 4 vols.; Ishbel Ross, *Proud Kate, The General's Wife* and *Rebel Rose*; Varina Davis correspondence in Confederate Memorial Hall, New Orleans; Valentine Museum, Richmond; Duke University; Confederate Museum, Richmond; Nannie Mayes Crump letters, Library of Congress; Lydia Johnston letters, Library of Congress; Mary Boykin Chesnut, *A Diary from Dixie*; Virginia Clay-Clopton, *A Belle of the Fifties*, edited by Ada Sterling; Varina Davis, *Jefferson Davis*, 2 vols.; Katharine M. Jones, *Heroines of Dixie*; Margaret Leech, *Reveille in Washington*; Frank Moore, *The Rebellion Record*; Sara Agnes Pryor (Mrs. Roger A.), *Reminiscences of Peace and War*; Henry Villard, *Memoirs*, 2 vols.; Allan Pinkerton, *The Spy of the Rebellion*; Varina Howell Davis, *Jefferson Davis. A Memoir by his Wife*; Hudson Strode, *Jefferson Davis*, 3 vols.; Elizabeth F. Ellet, *The Court Circles of the Republic*; Jesse R. Grant, *In the Days of My Father*; Constance Cary Harrison, *Recollections Grave and Gay*; Laura C. Holloway, *The Ladies of the White House*; J. B. Jones, *A Rebel Clerk's Diary*; E. D. Keyes, *Fifty Years Observation of Men and Events*; Robert Douthat Meade, *Judah P. Benjamin*; Jessie Benton Frémont, *Souvenir of My Time*; Julia Ward Howe, *Reminiscences 1819–1899*; Catherine Coffin Phillips, *Jessie Benton Frémont*; Catherine H. Birney, *Sarah and Angelina Grimké*; T. C. De Leon, *Belles, Beaux and Brains of the 60s*; *Frank Leslie Illustrated Newspaper* and *Harper's Weekly* files; "The Late Jessie Benton Frémont," *The Bookman*, February, 1903; Robert L. Duffus, "Frémont and Jessie," *The American Mercury*, November, 1925; "The Origin of the Frémont Exploration," *The Century Magazine*, 1890; Charles F. Lummis, "Jessie Benton Frémont, a Woman Who Has Lived History," *Overland Monthly*, Vol. XXXVII; "Half Forgotten Romances of History," *Washington Post*, September 24, 1934; "A Year of American Travel," *Harper's Magazine*, Vols. 55–56, 1878; Margaret Tims, *Jane Addams of Hull House*; James Weber Linn, *Jane Addams*; Jane Addams, *Twenty Years at Hull-house* and *The Spirit of Youth and the City Streets*.

CHAPTER 7. A CAUSE TAKES ROOT

Elizabeth Cady Stanton, *Elizabeth Cady Stanton Revealed in her Letters, Diary and Reminiscences*; Elizabeth Stanton, Susan B. Anthony and Matilda Joslyn Gage (eds.), *The History of Woman Suffrage*; Alma Lutz, *Susan B. Anthony* and *Created Equal*; Eleanor Flexner, *Century of Struggle*; Andrew Sinclair, *The Better Half*; Elinor Rice Hays, *Morning Star*; Julia Ward Howe, *Reminiscences, 1819–1899*; Inez Haynes

Irwin, *Angels and Amazons;* Mildred Adams, *The Right to be People;* Mary Beard, *America Through Women's Eyes, On Understanding Women* and *Women as a Force in History;* Alice Stone Blackwell, *Lucy Stone, Pioneer of Woman's Rights;* Fredrika Bremer, *Life, Letters and Posthumous Works of Fredrika Bremer;* Henry Addington Bruce, *Woman in the Making in America;* Beverly Benner Cassara (ed.), *American Women: The Changing Image;* Alexis de Tocqueville, *Democracy in America,* edited by P. Bradley; Mary Earhart, *Frances Willard;* Herbert Asbury, *Carry Nation;* Carleton Beals, *Cyclone Carry;* "Onward March of Carry Nation," *Current Literature,* March, 1901; Ishbel Ross, *Charmers and Cranks* and *Silhouette in Diamonds;* Ephraim George Squier correspondence, New York Historical Society; Madeleine B. Stern, *Purple Passage;* Files of *Woodhull & Claflin's Weekly;* Emanie Sachs, *The Terrible Siren;* Johanna Johnston, *Mrs. Satan;* Ida Husted Harper, *The Life and Work of Susan B. Anthony;* Dixon Wecter, *The Saga of American Society;* Lloyd Morris, *Incredible New York;* Robert Shaplen, *Free Love and Heavenly Sinners;* Mrs. Jane C. Croly (Jennie June), *The History of the Woman's Club Movement in America;* Elizabeth Bancroft Schlesinger, *The Nineteenth Century Woman's Dilemma and Jennie June;* Arthur M. Schlesinger and Dixon Ryan Fox (eds.), *A History of American Life,* Vol. 10; Arthur M. Schlesinger, Jr., and Morton White, *Paths of American Thought;* Maud Howe Elliott, *Uncle Sam Ward and his Circle;* Louise Hall Tharp, *The Peabody Sisters of Salem;* Emily Faithfull, *Three Visits to America;* Ruth Finley, *The Lady of Godey's;* Sarah Josepha Hale, *Woman's Record, or Sketches of Distinguished Women from the Creation to the Present Day;* Lady Duffus Hardy, *Through Cities and Prairie Lands;* Allan Nevins, *American Social History as Recorded by British Travelers* and *The Emergence of Modern America, 1865–1878;* Bellamy Partridge, *As We Were: Family Life in America, 1850–1900;* Harrison G. Rhodes, *History of the United States from the Compromise of 1850;* Yuri Suhl, *Ernestine Rose;* William E. Woodward, *The Way Our People Lived;* Ellen Key, *The Woman Movement;* John A. Kouwenhoven, *Adventures of America, 1857–1900;* Thomas Lately, *Sam Ward: King of the Lobby;* Mary E. Massey, *Bonnet Brigades;* Annie Nathan Meyer (ed.), *Woman's Work in America;* Mrs. Frank Leslie, "Are Our Girls Too Independent?" *Ladies Home Journal,* March, 1892; Mrs. Frank Leslie, "Which Is Woman's Happiest Hour?" *Ladies Home Journal,* August, 1890; Files of *Woodhull & Claflin's Weekly; Kate Field's Washington; New York Independent* scrapbooks, New York Public Library; *Frank Leslie's Illustrated Newspaper; Frank Leslie's Popular Monthly, Once a Week: Frank Leslie's Lady's Journal, Harper's Weekly* and *Harper's New Monthly Magazine.*

CHAPTER 8. THE HARD ROAD

Daisy Harriman, *From Pinafores to Politics*; Virginia C. Gildersleeve, *Many a Good Crusade*; Charles Austin and Mary Beard, *The Rise of American Civilization*, 2 vols.; Mary Beard (ed.), *America Through Women's Eyes, On Understanding Women* and *Women as a Force in History*; Alice Stone Blackwell, *Lucy Stone: Pioneer of Woman's Rights*; Henry Addington Bruce, *Woman in the Making in America*; Emily Taft Douglas, *Remember the Ladies*; Eleanor Flexner, *Century of Struggle*; Oscar Handlin (ed.), *This Was America*; Julia Ward Howe, *Reminiscences, 1819–1899*; M. A. De Wolfe Howe, *A Venture in Remembrance*; Inez Haynes Irwin, *The Story of the Woman's Party* and *Angels and Amazons*; Henry James, *The American Scene*; Oliver Jensen, *The Revolt of American Women*; Alice Longworth, *Crowded Hours*; Alma Lutz, *Created Equal* and *Susan B. Anthony*; Eleanor Wilson McAdoo and M. J. Gaffey, *The Woodrow Wilsons*; Meade Minnegerode, *Some American Ladies*; David Mitchell, *The Fighting Pankhursts*; Lloyd R. Morris, *Not So Long Ago* and *Postscript to Yesterday*; Mary Gray Peck, *Carrie Chapman Catt*; Agnes Rogers, *The American Procession* and *Women Are Here to Stay*; Ishbel Ross, *An American Family: The Tafts 1678– 1964* and *Charmers and Cranks*; Eleanor Roosevelt and Lorena A. Hickok, *Ladies of Courage*; Theodore Roosevelt, *An Autobiography*; Arthur M. Schlesinger and Dixon Ryan Fox (eds.), *A History of American Life*, Vol. 10; Madeleine B. Stern, *Purple Passage*; Mark Sullivan, *Our Times: The United States 1900–1925*; Ida M. Tarbell, *The Ways of Woman* and *The Business of Being a Woman*; Dixon Wecter, *The Saga of American Society*; Virginia Lee Warren, "The Colony Club: It's Still Exclusive," *New York Times*, July 21, 1968; Helen Woodward, *Through Many Windows*; Ida M. Tarbell, New York *World*, June 7 and 8, 1916; Doris Stevens, Omaha *Daily News*, June 29, 1919; "First Woman Gets Princeton Tenure," *New York Times*, May 6, 1968; "Wesleyan Will Begin Admitting Women in Fall," *New York Times*, May 15, 1968; "Yale Going Coed Next September," *New York Times*, November 14, 1968; Mrs. J. Borden Harriman obituary, *New York Times*, September 1, 1967; Files of *Life, Newsweek, Time, Vanity Fair, Vogue, Harper's Bazaar, Ladies Home Journal* and *McCall's*.

CHAPTER 9. THE FEMININE ESTABLISHMENT

Frances Perkins, *The Roosevelt I Knew*; Eleanor Roosevelt and Lorena A. Hickok, *Ladies of Courage*; Eleanor Roosevelt, *Autobiography of Eleanor Roosevelt*; Frances Perkins obituary, *New York Times*, May 15, 1965; Emily Taft Douglas, *Remember the Ladies*; Bess Furman, *White*

House Profile; Frank Graham, Jr., *Margaret Chase Smith;* David G. Loth, *A Long Way Forward: The Biography of Congresswoman Frances P. Bolton;* "Crusader's Widow," *Newsweek,* March 21, 1960; R. Cahn, "Madam Senator from Oregon," *Saturday Evening Post,* January 7, 1961; Mrs. Maurine Neuberger, *Newsweek,* May 31, 1965, *New York Times,* May 19, 1965; Mabel Walker Willebrandt, "First Impression," *Good Housekeeping,* May, 1928; "First Lady in Law," *Ladies Home Journal,* June, 1925; A. Strakosch, "Woman in Law," *Saturday Evening Post,* September 24, 1927; "The State Department's Poetic Powerhouse," *Look,* October 17, 1967; "Woman Politician Arrives," *Outlook,* June 27, 1928; Arthur M. Schlesinger, Jr., and Morton White, *Paths of American Thought;* Isabel Spatz Leighton (ed.), *The Aspirin Age;* Frances Parkinson Keyes, *Capital Kaleidoscope;* Walter Lord, *The Good Years;* Eric F. Goldman, *The Crucial Decade;* "100 Accomplished Women," *Harper's Bazaar,* September, 1967; "Three Ruths in Congress," *Woman's Journal,* December, 1928; Mrs. John T. Pratt, "Men Are Bad Housekeepers," *Harper's Magazine,* May, 1927; "Lady or the Tiger," *Ladies Home Journal,* May, 1928; Roy Reed, "Betty Furness Wants it to Read: Caveat Vendor," *New York Times;* "At Home with Betty Furness," *New York Post,* January 6, 1968; Ted Lewis, "Betty Talking Turkey, Critics Eating Crow," *New York Daily News,* November 24, 1967; Judy Michaelson, "Jeannette Rankin, Once More a Date in Washington," *New York Post,* December 23, 1967; "G.O.P. Woman Is Elected Hartford's Mayor," *New York Times,* November 8, 1967; Judy Michaelson, "Women in New York Politics," *New York Post,* February 24, 1964; Mrs. John Lindsay, *New York World-Telegram,* June 23, 1965, and *Women's Wear Daily,* November 3, 1967; Ouida Ferguson Nalle, *The Fergusons of Texas;* W. D. Hornaday, "Who Governs Texas?" *New York Herald Tribune,* February 1, 1925; W. Whitman, "Ma Ferguson. Can a Wife be Governor?" *Collier's,* September 5, 1925; "Petticoat Politics," *Collier's,* April 17, 1926; "Will Ma Ferguson Be Impeached?" *Outlook,* December 9, 1925; "Is Ma or Pa Governor of Texas?" *Literary Digest,* April 11, 1925; Mildred Adams, "Again the Fergusons Rouse the Texans," *New York Times,* October 23, 1932; "Miriam Amanda Ferguson," *Current Opinion,* October, 1924; *New York World,* May 29, 1925; *New York Times,* April 25, 1926, May 23, 1926, June 1, 1926, May 29, 1925; "Governor Lady: Autobiography of Nellie Tayloe Ross," *Good Housekeeping,* August, September and October, 1927; "First Woman Governor," *Woman Citizen,* November, 1926; "When a Woman Governor Campaigns," *Scribner's Monthly,* July, 1928; "Progress, Prohibition and the Democratic Party, *Scribner's Monthly,* May, 1928; Frank Graham, Jr., *Margaret Chase Smith;* "Mrs. Smith Misses Vote First Time in 13 Years," *New*

York Times, September 7, 1968; Data from Senator Smith; Henry F.
and Katharine Pringle, "He Followed Mom to Congress," Saturday
Evening Post, August 15, 1953; Data from Mrs. Frances P.
Bolton; Department of State Bulletins, November 16, December 7, 14 and 21, 1953;
Independent Woman, December, 1953; Margaret A. Kilgore, "Women
Have Come Long Way on Political Trail of Jeannette Rankin," Boston
Sunday Globe, November 29, 1964; "Lady Takes Over Newest Cabinet
Post," Life, June 15, 1953; "Lady in Command," Reader's Digest, August, 1953; Oveta Culp Hobby, "We All Have a Job to Do," Woman's
Home Companion, March, 1955; "Troubles of a Health Director," U.S.
News and World Report, June 10, 1955; Oveta Culp Hobby, "Houston:
The Race Is On," Saturday Review, May 22, 1965; New York Herald
Tribune files, 1953–55.

CHAPTER 10. CHARM SCHOOL

Henry Brandon, "I Talk with an 83-year-old Enfant Terrible," New
York Times Magazine, August 6, 1967; Alice Longworth, Crowded
Hours; June Bingham, "Her Witty Asides Put Washington Solemnity
Down," Washington Post, August 6, 1967; James Reston, Sketches in the
Sand; John Kobler, Luce, His Time, Life, and Fortune; Alden Hatch,
Ambassador Extraordinary Clare Boothe Luce; Clare Boothe Luce, Saints
for Now and Stuffed Shirts; Faye Henie, Au Clare de Luce; Portrait of a
Luminous Lady; Clare Boothe Luce, "Women Without Portfolio,"
McCall's, July, 1964, and March, 1965; Eleanor Roosevelt and Lorena
A. Hickok, Ladies of Courage; Letitia Baldridge, Roman Candle; Eugenia
Sheppard, "I Get Restless When I'm Not Doing Something" and "The
Best of Everything," Women's Wear Daily, December 8, 1967, and May
3, 1968; "Madame Ambassador Patricia Roberts Harris," New York
Times, October 6, 1967; Perle Mesta, "Heiresses of Susan B. Anthony,"
McCall's, February, 1965; Betty Beale, "Perle's Really the Hostess with
the Mostest," New York Daily Column, July 23, 1968; Kandy Shuman,
"The Perla," Women's Wear Daily, August 23, 1968; Ruth (Bryan)
Owen, "How Bryan's Daughter Runs for Congress," Literary Digest,
September 22, 1928; "Three Ruths in Congress," Woman's Journal,
December, 1928; "Ruth Bryan Owen," Woman's Journal, January, 1928;
Marietta Tree, "It's a Good Time to Be a Woman," Mademoiselle,
October, 1965; P. Devlin, "Penelope Tree," Vogue, October, 1967; "100
Accomplished American Women," Harper's Bazaar, September, 1967;
Marjorie Merriweather Post, "World Unique and Magnificent," Life,
November 5, 1965; Mary W. Lasker, "Elegant Frame for Masterpieces,"
House and Garden, July, 1966; Mary W. Lasker, "Unforgettable Character of Dusty Rhoads," Reader's Digest, April, 1965; Newsweek, Novem-

ber 9, 1964; *Time*, November 6, 1964, and June 4, 1965; Helen Dudar, "I'm Having a Fantastic Time," *New York Post*, April 27, 1968; Myra MacPherson, "The Women's Lobby Meets in Capital," *New York Times*, June 27, 1968; Marion K. Sanders, *Politics as a Spectator Sport*, *Harper's Magazine*, July, 1965.

CHAPTER 11. VIEW FROM THE SUMMIT

Margaret Mead, *Report of President Kennedy's Commission on the Status of Women*, 1963; Esther Peterson, "The Status of United States Women Today," *General Federation Clubwoman*, March, 1963; "100 Accomplished American Women," *Harper's Bazaar*, September, 1967; Dr. Mary Calderone, "Today's Women," *New York Times*, October 7, 1966; Eli Ginzberg and Alice Yoyalem, *Educated American Women* and *Life Styles of Educated Women*, from studies done in connection with the Columbia Conservation of Human Resources Projects, 1960–66; Kate Louchheim, *The Role of Women in American Life*, State Department report; "Women: Toward a Better World," *New York Times*, October 7, 1966; "Women at Work," *Time*, May 24, 1968; "The Talk of Vassar," *Newsweek*, June 13, 1966; Alice Gore King, *Career Opportunities for Women in Business*, 1963; Mary G. Roebling, *Newsweek*, July 11, 1966; Dr. Nancy G. Roman, "Women Active in United States Space Program," Department of Labor report, 1962; Margaret Mead, *Male and Female*; Oliver Jensen, *The Revolt of American Women*; Agnes Allen, *Women Are Here to Stay*; Mary Beard, *Women as a Force in History*; Annie Nathan Meyer (ed.), *Woman's Work in America*; Eleanor Flexner, *Century of Struggle*; Ashley Montagu, *The Natural Superiority of Women*; "Day Care for Children," *Newsweek*, August 28, 1967; *Graduate Education for Women: The Radcliffe Ph.D.*, report of Faculty Trustee Committee, 1956; "More Co-eds Retaining Jobs Despite Marriage and Children," *New York Times*, November 21, 1966; "America's Centimillionaires," *Fortune*, May, 1968; "Richest of the American Rich," *Time*, May 3, 1967; Hetty Green, "Why Women Are Not Moneymakers," *Harper's Bazaar*, March 10, 1900; Arthur H. Lewis, *The Day They Shook the Plum Tree*; "Queen Midas: Hetty Robinson Green," *New England Quarterly*, June, 1950; Virginia C. Gildersleeve, *Many a Good Crusade*; Hope MacLeod, "First Woman to 'Crash' the All-Male Big Board," *New York Post*, January 6, 1968; "A Mind for Money Pays off on Wall Street," *New York Post*, August 12, 1967; "Birth Rate Declines," Howard J. Rusk, *New York Times*, April 28, 1968; Mrs. John M. Cotton, *The Case of the Working Mother*; Eugenia Sheppard, "Mary Wells Lawrence," *Women's Wear Daily*, November 13, 1967 and May 3, 1968; Muriel McCooey, "She Gives Pizzazz to the Beautiful People,"

New York Post, March 30, 1968; "Women Judges," Time, January 29, 1965; Marilyn Bender, "The New Portia," New York Times, February 26, 1968; "Mrs. Fortas, Law is Her Life, Too," New York Times, July 25, 1968; Judy Michaelson, "The Law is Not Incompatible with Feminine Goals," New York Post, May 18, 1968; May Okon, "Judge Margaret Mary Mangan," New York Sunday News, August 13, 1967; Marilyn Mercer, "Is there Room at the Top?" Saturday Evening Post, July 27, 1968; J. D. Ratcliff, "Justice from the Heart," Christian Herald, November, 1968. Reports and pamphlets of the Departments of State, Labor, and Health, Education and Welfare.

CHAPTER 12. THE VOTE THAT COUNTS

Reports of Democratic and Republican National Women's Committees; Gallup Poll tracing pattern of voting in presidential elections 1952–64, and other Gallup Polls; Margaret Mead, President's Commission on the Status of Women; Marguerite J. Fisher and Betty Whitehead, "Women and National Party Organization," American Political Science Review, October, 1944; Samuel Grafton, "American Women in Politics," McCall's, September, 1962; Nona B. Brown, "Inquiry into the Feminine Mind," New York Times Magazine, April 12, 1964; Warner Olivier, "The League of Frightened Women," Saturday Evening Post, 1954; Katharine T. Kinkead, "A Reporter at Large," New Yorker, May 5, 1956; "League of Women Voters Opposes New Constitution," New York Times, September 30, 1967; "Assessment of Oak Lawn," The Wall Street Journal, October 17, 1963; Marguerite M. Wells, A Portrait of the League of Women Voters, published by Overseas Education Fund of the League, Washington, 1962; 40 Years of a Great Idea, Publication 266, League of Women Voters; The Big Water Fight by the League of Women Voters, Education Fund, Stephen Greene Press, Brattleboro, Vermont; Edwin B. Dooley, Mayor of Mamaroneck, "You Can Fight City Hall," Today's Living; New York Herald Tribune, November 25, 1956; Ray T. Davis, "The Power of a Woman," Catholic Digest, June, 1958; Compilation of Suffrage Events by League of Women Voters displayed in Pepsi-Cola Building, 1966; "This is Your New York City League," League of Women Voters of the City of New York, September, 1963; Town Hall meeting held in Community Church, New York, New York Post, February 2, 1968; Woman's Day, May, 1964; Newsweek, September 21, 1964, and July 5, 1965; Miami Herald, September 27, 1964; Edith Evans Asbury, "Housing Drive Set by Women Voters," New York Times, May 6, 1968. Pamphlets, scrapbooks and reports from the League of Women Voters of the City of New York, courtesy of Mrs. Orpha Zimmer. Pamphlets and clippings from the National League of Women Voters, courtesy of Miss Dorothy Rapp.

CHAPTER 13. THE TREE OF KNOWLEDGE

Marshall McLuhan and George B. Leonard, "The Future of Sex," *Look,* July 25, 1967; Arthur Schlesinger, Jr., "An Informal History of Love, U.S.A.," *Saturday Evening Post,* 1966; Margaret Mead, *Male and Female;* Margaret Mead and Ken Heyman, *Family;* Beverly Benner Cassara (ed.), *American Women: The Changing Image;* Merle Curti, *The Growth of American Thought;* Helene Deutsch, *The Psychology of Women;* Eric John Dingwall, *The American Woman;* Marynia Farnham and Ferdinand Lundberg, *Modern Woman: The Lost Sex;* Charles W. Ferguson, *The Male Attitude;* Betty Friedan, *The Feminine Mystique;* Oliver Jensen, *The Revolt of American Women;* Florence Rockwood Kluckhohn, *The American Family and the Feminine Role in Human Relations;* Ashley Montagu, *The Natural Superiority of Women;* "Man and Civilization: The Potential of Woman," a symposium edited by Seymour M. Farber and Roger H. L. Wilson, University of California at Berkeley, 1963; Harold Rosenberg, "Love, Self-Love," *Vogue,* May, 1967; Karl Stern, *The Flight from Woman;* Robert Stein (ed.), *Why Young Mothers Feel Trapped;* Dr. Eric Goldman, "The Oppressed Emancipated Woman," *Holiday,* May, 1962; Dorothy W. Cotton, *The Case for the Working Mother;* Paul Woodring, "View from the Campus," *Saturday Review,* January 20, 1968; "Women's Training Held Inflexible," *New York Times,* May 9, 1956; "Hippies," *Time,* July 7, 1967; Alice P. Cooper on Mary Bunting, *Saturday Review,* March 6, 1965; Barbara Wertheim Tuchman, "The Dare of History," Commencement Address at Radcliffe, June, 1967; Pearl S. Buck, "America's Mediaeval Women," *Harper's Magazine,* August, 1938; "The Second Feminist Wave" by Martha Weinman Lear, *New York Times Magazine,* March 10, 1968; Marya Mannes, "Let's Face It," *McCall's,* November, 1966; Dr. Roger Revelle, director of Harvard's Center for Population Studies, *New York Times,* December 15, 1967; Dr. Alexander Reid Martin, *The Unfinished Society;* "Women: Toward a Better World," conference held in 1966 with Dr. Mary Calderone, director of the Sex Information and Education Council of the United States; Gallup Poll on young voters, May, 1968; "Sex Focus on Sex Issue on Campus Decried," *New York Times,* May 14, 1968; Inez Robb, "Are Colleges Now Sanctuaries for Lawless?" *New York Daily Column,* May 13, 1968; Arthur J. Snider, "The Campus Sex Revolution: Is it More Talk than Action?" *New York Post,* May 22, 1967; "College Generation Gap," letters to editor, *Newsweek,* July 15, 1968; "Parents, You Better Tune In," *New York Times,* August 16, 1968;

Arthur A. Campbell, "The Role of Family Planning in the Reduction of Poverty," *Journal of Marriage and the Family,* Vol. XXX, No. 2, 1968; Alice Taylor Day, "Parenthood: Its New Responsibilities," *Smith Alumnae Quarterly,* November, 1964; "Oberlin College Poll Finds 40% of Girls Had Sex Relations," *New York Times,* June 16, 1968; Dr. Mary Daly, *The Church and the Second Sex;* "A Woman's Group Protests Ban by Overseas Press Club," *New York Times,* August 31, 1968; Planned Parenthood annual report, 1967; pamphlets, articles and reports, courtesy Planned Parenthood Federation of America; Havelock Ellis, *Impressions and Comments* and *My Life;* F. L. Delisle, *Friendship's Odyssey;* Lawrence Lader, *The Margaret Sanger Story and the Fight for Birth Control;* Margaret Sanger, *An Autobiography, My Fight for Birth Control* and *Woman and the New Race;* Margaret Sanger obituary, *New York Times,* September 7, 1966.

Bibliography

ADAMS, ABIGAIL. *New Letters of Abigail Adams, 1788–1801,* edited by Stewart Mitchell. Boston: Houghton Mifflin Company, 1947.

ADAMS, CHARLES FRANCIS. *Diary of Charles Francis Adams,* edited by Aida DiPace Donald and David Donald. 2 vols. Cambridge, Mass.: The Belknap Press, 1964.

ADAMS, CHARLES FRANCIS (ED.). *Familiar Letters of John Adams and his wife Abigail Adams during the Revolution.* Boston: Houghton Mifflin Company, 1875.

ADAMS, HENRY. *The Education of Henry Adams.* Boston: Houghton Mifflin Company, 1918.

ADAMS, JAMES TRUSLOW (ED.). *Album of American History.* 5 vols. New York: Charles Scribner's Sons, 1944–53.

———. *Provincial Society, 1690–1763.* New York: The Macmillan Company, 1927.

———. *The Adams Family.* Boston: Little, Brown & Company, 1930.

ADAMS, MILDRED. *The Right to be People.* Philadelphia: J. B. Lippincott Company, 1967.

ADAMS, SAMUEL HOPKINS. *The Incredible Era.* Boston: Houghton Mifflin Company, 1939.

ADDAMS, JANE. *The Long Road of Woman's Memory.* New York: The Macmillan Company, 1916.

———. *Twenty Years at Hull-House with autobiographical notes.* New York: The Macmillan Company, 1949.

———. *The Spirit of Youth and the City Streets.* New York: The Macmillan Company, 1909.

———. *Democracy and Social Ethics.* New York: The Macmillan Company, 1902.

ALLEN, FREDERICK LEWIS. *Only Yesterday.* New York: Harper & Brothers, 1931.

ALSOP, STEWART. *The Center: People and Power in Political Washington.* New York: Harper & Row, 1968.

313

AMORY, CLEVELAND. *Who Killed Society?* New York: Harper & Brothers, 1960.
————. *The Proper Bostonians.* New York: E. P. Dutton & Company, 1947.
ANBUREY, THOMAS. *Travels Through the Interior Parts of America.* Boston: Houghton Mifflin Company, 1923.
ANDREW, OLIVER. *Portraits of John and Abigail Adams.* Cambridge, Mass.: The Belknap Press, 1967.
ANDREWS, CHARLES M. *Colonial Folkways.* New Haven: Yale University Press, 1920.
————. *Pilgrims and Puritans.* New Haven: Yale University Press, 1919.
ANTHONY, KATHARINE SUSAN. *Dolly Madison, Her Life and Times.* Garden City, N.Y.: Doubleday, 1949.
————. *First Lady of the Revolution.* Garden City, N.Y.: Doubleday, 1958.
AUGUR, HELEN. *An American Jezebel.* New York: Brentano's, 1930.

BADEAU, ADAM. *Grant in Peace.* Hartford, Conn.: S. S. Scranton & Company, 1887.
BAKER, RAY STANNARD. *Woodrow Wilson, Life and Letters.* Vols. 3 and 4. Garden City, N.Y.: Doubleday, Doran & Company, 1931.
BALDRIDGE, LETITIA. *Roman Candle.* Boston: Houghton Mifflin Company, 1956.
BEARD, CHARLES AUSTIN, AND MARY. *The Rise of American Civilization.* 2 vols. New York: The Macmillan Company, 1933.
BEARD, MARY (ED.). *America Through Women's Eyes.* New York: The Macmillan Company, 1933.
————. *On Understanding Women.* New York: Longmans, Green & Company, 1931.
————. *Women as a Force in History.* New York: The Macmillan Company, 1946.
BEECHER, CATHARINE. *The American Woman's Home.* New York: J. B. Ford & Company, 1869.
BELDEN, THOMAS GRAHAM, AND MARVA BELDEN. *So Fell the Angels.* Boston: Little, Brown & Company, 1956.
BELL, MARGARET. *Margaret Fuller.* New York: Albert and Charles Boni, 1930.
BENSON, MARY SUMNER. *Women in Eighteenth Century America.* New York: Columbia University Press, 1935.
BIGELOW, JOHN. *Life of John Charles Frémont.* New York: Derby and Jackson, 1856.
BIRD, CAROLINE. *Invisible Scar.* New York: Mackay Publishing Corporation, 1965.

BIRNEY, CATHERINE H. *Sarah and Angelina Grimké.* Boston: Lee & Shepard, 1885.
BLACKWELL, ALICE STONE. *Lucy Stone: Pioneer of Woman's Rights.* Boston: Little, Brown & Company, 1930.
BLACKWELL, ELIZABETH. *Pioneer Work in Opening the Medical Profession to Women.* New York: E. P. Dutton & Company, 1895.
BOORSTIN, DANIEL J. *The Americans: The National Experience.* New York: Random House, 1965.
BOWEN, CATHERINE. *John Adams and the American Revolution.* Boston: Little, Brown & Company, 1950.
BOWERS, CLAUDE G. *The Tragic Era.* Boston: Houghton Mifflin Company, 1929.
BOWNE, ELIZA S. *A Girl's Life Eighty Years Ago.* New York: Charles Scribner's Sons, 1887.
BRADFORD, GAMALIEL. *Wives.* New York: Harper & Brothers, 1925.
BREMER, FREDRIKA. *Life, Letters and Posthumous Works of Fredrika Bremer,* edited by Charlotte Bremer, New York: Hurd & Houghton, 1868.
———. *The Homes of the New World.* New York: Harper & Brothers, 1853.
BROOKS, VAN WYCK. *The World of Washington Irving.* New York: E. P. Dutton & Company, 1944.
BROUN, HEYWOOD, AND MARGARET LEECH. *Anthony Comstock.* New York: Boni, 1927.
BROWN, STUART GERRY (ED.). *Autobiography of James Monroe.* Syracuse, N.Y.: Syracuse University Press, 1959.
BRUCE, HENRY ADDINGTON. *Woman in the Making in America.* Boston: Little, Brown & Company, 1912.
BRYAN, WILLIAM J., AND MARY BAIRD BRYAN. *The Memoirs of William Jennings Bryan.* Philadelphia: John C. Winston Company, 1925.
BUTLER, NICHOLAS MURRAY. *Across the Busy Years.* Charles Scribner's Sons, 1939.
BUTT, ARCHIBALD. *Taft and Roosevelt.* New York: Doran & Company, 1930.

CALDWELL, MARY FRENCH. *General Jackson's Lady.* Nashville, Tenn.: Kingsport Press, 1936.
CARSON, GERALD. *The Polite Americans.* New York: William Morrow & Company, 1966.
CASSARA, BEVERLY BENNER (ED.). *American Women: The Changing Image.* Boston: Beacon Press, 1962.
CHESNUT, MARY BOYKIN. *A Diary from Dixie.* Boston: Houghton Mifflin Company, 1949.

CHILD, LYDIA MARIA. *Letters of Lydia Maria Child.* Boston: Houghton Mifflin Company, 1883.

CLAY-CLOPTON, VIRGINIA. *A Belle of the Fifties,* edited by Ada Sterling. New York: Doubleday, Page & Company, 1904.

COHN, DAVID L. *The Good Old Days.* New York: Simon & Schuster, 1940.

COMMAGER, HENRY STEELE. *The American Mind.* New Haven: Yale University Press, 1950.

COTTON, DOROTHY W. *The Case for the Working Mother.* New York: Stein & Day, 1965.

COWLES, ANNA ROOSEVELT. *Letters from Theodore Roosevelt to Anna Roosevelt Cowles, 1870–1918.* New York: Charles Scribner's Sons, 1924.

CRAWFORD, MARY CAROLINE. *Romantic Days in the Early Republic.* Boston: Little, Brown & Company, 1912.

———. *Social Life in Old New England.* Boston: Little, Brown & Company, 1914.

CROSS, WILBUR, AND ANN NOVOTNY. *White House Weddings.* New York: Mackay Publishing Corporation, 1968.

CURTIS, EDITH. *Anne Hutchinson.* Cambridge, Mass.: Washburn & Thomas, 1930.

CURTIS, GEORGE TICKNOR. *Life of James Buchanan.* New York: Harper & Brothers, 1883.

DALY, MARY. *The Church and the Second Sex.* New York: Harper & Row, 1968.

D'ARUSMONT, FRANCES WRIGHT. *View of Society and Manners in America,* edited by Paul R. Baker. Cambridge, Mass.: Belknap Press, 1963.

DAVIDSON, MARSHALL B. *Life in America.* 2 vols. Boston: Houghton Mifflin Company, 1951.

DAVIS, VARINA. *Jefferson Davis.* 2 vols. New York: Belford Company, 1890.

DEAN, ELIZABETH L. *Dolly Madison, the Nation's Hostess.* Boston: Lothrop, Lee & Shepard, 1928.

DE LEON, T. C. *Belles, Beaux and Brains of the 1860s.* New York: G. W. Dillingham, 1907.

DELISLE, F. L. *Friendship's Odyssey.* London: Heinemann, 1946.

DESMOND, ALICE (CURTIS). *Glamorous Dolly Madison.* New York: Dodd, Mead & Company, 1946.

DE TOCQUEVILLE, ALEXIS. *Democracy in America,* edited by P. Bradley. New York: Alfred A. Knopf, 1945.

DEUTSCH, HELENE. *The Psychology of Women.* New York: Grune & Stratton, 1944–45.

DINGWALL, ERIC JOHN. *The American Woman.* New York: Rinehart, 1957.

DIXON, WILLIAM H. *New America.* Philadelphia: J. B. Lippincott & Company, 1867.

DOUGLAS, EMILY TAFT. *Remember the Ladies.* G. P. Putnam's Sons, 1966.

DOW, GEORGE F. *Domestic Life in New England in the Seventeenth Century.* Topsfield, Mass.: Perkins Press, 1925.

EARHART, MARY. *Frances Willard.* Chicago: University of Chicago Press, 1944.

EARLE, ALICE MORSE. *Customs and Fashions in Old New England.* New York: Charles Scribner's Sons, 1896.

———. *Home Life in Colonial Days.* New York: The Macmillan Company, 1898.

———. *Margaret Winthrop.* New York: Charles Scribner's Sons, 1895.

ELLET, ELIZABETH F. *The Court Circles of the Republic.* Hartford, Conn.: Hartford Publishing Company, 1869.

———. *The Queens of American Society.* New York: Charles Scribner's Sons, 1967.

———. *The Women of the American Revolution.* 2 vols. Philadelphia: George W. Jacobs & Company, 1900.

ELLIOTT, MAUD HOWE. *Uncle Sam Ward and his Circle.* New York: The Macmillan Company, 1938.

ELLIS, HAVELOCK. *My Life.* London: Heinemann, 1940.

FAITHFULL, EMILY. *Three Visits to America.* New York: Fowler & Wells Company, 1884.

FARNHAM, MARYNIA, AND FERDINAND LUNDBERG. *Modern Woman: The Lost Sex.* New York: Harper & Brothers, 1947.

FERGUSON, CHARLES W. *The Male Attitude.* Boston: Little, Brown & Company, 1966.

FINLEY, RUTH (EBRIGHT). *The Lady of Godey's.* Philadelphia: J. B. Lippincott Company, 1931.

FISHER, SYDNEY GEORGE. *Men, Women, and Manners in Colonial Times.* Philadelphia: J. B. Lippincott Company, 1898.

FLEXNER, ELEANOR. *Century of Struggle.* Cambridge, Mass.: The Belknap Press, 1959.

FLEXNER, JAMES THOMAS. *George Washington in the American Revolution, 1775–1783.* Boston: Little, Brown & Company, 1968.

FREEMAN, DOUGLAS SOUTHALL. *George Washington.* Vols. 5 and 7. Charles Scribner's Sons, 1948–57.

FRÉMONT, JESSIE BENTON. *Souvenir of My Time.* Boston: D. Lothrop & Company, 1887.

FRIEDAN, BETTY. *The Feminine Mystique.* New York: W. W. Norton & Company, 1963.

FUESS, CLAUDE M. *Calvin Coolidge.* Boston: Little, Brown & Company, 1940.

FULLER, MARGARET. *Love Letters of Margaret Fuller.* New York: D. Appleton & Company, 1903.

FURMAN, BESS. *White House Profile.* Indianapolis: The Bobbs-Merrill Company, 1951.

FURNESS, CLIFTON J. *The Genteel Female.* New York: Alfred A. Knopf, 1931.

GARFIELD, JAMES A. *The Works of James Abram Garfield,* edited by Burke A. Hinsdale. Boston: James R. Osgood & Company, 1882.

GILDERSLEEVE, VIRGINIA C. *Many a Good Crusade.* New York: The Macmillan Company, 1954.

GRAF, LE ROY P. *The Papers of Andrew Johnson,* edited by Ralph W. Haskins. Vol. 1. Knoxville, Tenn.: University of Tennessee Press, 1968.

GRAHAM, FRANK, JR. *Margaret Chase Smith.* New York: The John Day Company, 1964.

GRANT, JESSE R. *In the Days of My Father, General Grant.* New York: Harper & Brothers, 1925.

GRAYSON, CARY T. *Woodrow Wilson, an Intimate Memoir.* New York: Holt, Rinehart & Winston, 1960.

GREELEY, HORACE. *Recollections of a Busy Life.* New York: J. B. Ford & Company, 1868.

——. *The American Conflict.* Hartford, Conn.: O. D. Case & Company, 1864–67.

GREENHOW, ROSE O'NEAL. *My Imprisonment and the First Year of Abolition Rule at Washington.* London: Richard Bentley, 1963.

HALE, SARAH JOSEPHA (BUELL). *Woman's Record, or Sketches of Distinguished Women from the Creation to the Present Day.* New York: Harper & Brothers, 1853.

HALL, BASIL. *Travels in North America in the Years 1827 and 1828.* Philadelphia: Carey, Lea & Carey, 1829.

HAMILTON, HOLMAN. *Zachary Taylor.* Indianapolis: The Bobbs-Merrill Company, 1951.

HANDLIN, OSCAR (ED.). *This was America.* Cambridge, Mass.: Harvard University Press, 1949.

Bibliography 319

HARDY, LADY DUFFUS. *Through Cities and Prairie Lands.* New York: R. Worthington, 1881.

HARRIMAN, FLORENCE JAFFRAY HURST (MRS. J. BORDEN HARRIMAN). *From Pinafores to Politics.* New York: Henry Holt & Company, 1923.

HARRISON, CONSTANCE (CARY). *Recollections Grave and Gay.* New York: Charles Scribner's Sons, 1911.

HATCH, ALDEN. *Ambassador Extraordinary, Clare Boothe Luce.* New York: Holt, 1956.

———. *Edith Bolling Wilson: First Lady Extraordinary.* New York: Dodd, Mead & Company, 1961.

HAYES, ELINOR RICE. *Morning Star.* New York: Harcourt, Brace & World, 1961.

HAYES, RUTHERFORD BIRCHARD. *Diary and Letters.* Vol. 2. The Ohio State Archeological and Historical Society, 1922.

HENLE, FAYE. *Au Clare de Luce: Portrait of a Luminous Lady.* New York: S. Daye, 1943.

HIGGINSON, THOMAS WENTWORTH. *Margaret Fuller Ossoli.* Boston: Houghton Mifflin Company, 1884.

HOLBROOK, STEWART. *The Age of the Moguls.* Garden City, N.Y.: Doubleday, 1953.

HOLLIDAY, CARL. *Woman's Life in Colonial Days.* Boston: The Cornhill Publishing Company, 1922.

HOLLOWAY, LAURA C. *The Ladies of the White House.* Philadelphia: Bradley & Company, 1883.

HONE, PHILIP. *The Diary of Philip Hone.* 2 vols. New York: Dodd, Mead & Company, 1889.

HOOVER, HERBERT. *Memoirs of Herbert Hoover.* New York: The Macmillan Company, 1952.

HOOVER, IRWIN (IKE). *Forty-two Years in the White House.* Boston: Houghton Mifflin Company, 1934.

HORAN, JAMES D. *Desperate Women.* New York: G. P. Putnam's Sons, 1952.

HOUSE, E. M. *The Intimate Papers of Colonel House,* Vol. 4. Boston: Houghton Mifflin Company, 1928.

HOWE, JULIA WARD. *Reminiscences, 1819–1899.* Boston: Houghton Mifflin Company, 1899.

HOWE, M. A. DE WOLFE. *A Venture in Remembrance.* Boston: Little, Brown & Company, 1941.

HUNT, GAILLARD. *Life in America One Hundred Years Ago.* New York: Harper & Brothers, 1914.

IRVING, WASHINGTON. *Knickerbocker's History of New York.* New York: G. P. Putnam & Son, 1894.

IRWIN, INEZ HAYNES. *Angels and Amazons*. Garden City, N.Y.: Double-day, Doran & Company, 1933.
————. *The Story of the Woman's Party*. New York: Harcourt, Brace & Company, 1921.
IRWIN, WILL. *Herbert Hoover*. New York: The Century Company, 1928.

JAMES, HENRY. *The American Scene*. New York: Harper & Brothers, 1907.
JEFFRIES, ONA GRIFFIN. *In and Out of the White House*. New York: Wilfred Funk, 1960.
JENSEN, AMY (LA FOLLETTE). *The White House and its Thirty-two Families*. New York: McGraw-Hill Book Company, 1958.
JENSEN, OLIVER. *The Revolt of American Women*. New York: Harcourt, Brace & Company, 1952.
JOHNSTON, JOHANNA. *Mrs. Satan*. New York: G. P. Putnam's Sons, 1967.
JONES, J. B. *A Rebel Clerk's Diary*. 2 vols. Philadelphia: J. B. Lippincott, 1866.
JONES, KATHARINE M. *Heroines of Dixie*. Indianapolis: The Bobbs-Merrill Company, 1955.

KEY, ELLEN. *The Woman Movement*. New York: G. P. Putnam's Sons, 1912.
KEYES, E. D. *Fifty Years' Observation of Men and Events*. New York: Charles Scribner's Sons, 1884.
KING, ALICE GORE. *Career Opportunities for Women in Business*. E. P. Dutton & Company, 1963.
KLUCKHOHN, FLORENCE ROCKWOOD. *The American Family and the Feminine Role in Human Relations*, edited by Hugh Cabot and Joseph A. Kahl. Cambridge, Mass.: Harvard University Press, 1953.
KOBLER, JOHN. *Luce, His Time, Life, and Fortune*. Garden City, N.Y.: Doubleday, 1968.
KOHLSAAT, H. H. *From McKinley to Harding*. New York: Charles Scribner's Sons, 1923.
KOUWENHOVEN, JOHN A. *Adventures of America 1857–1900*. New York: Harper & Brothers, 1938.

LADER, LAWRENCE. *The Margaret Sanger Story*. Garden City, N.Y.: Doubleday, 1955.
LATELY, THOMAS. *Sam Ward: King of the Lobby*. Boston: Houghton Mifflin Company, 1965.
LAZARUS, EMMA. *Women in the Life and Time of Abraham Lincoln*.

Published by Emma Lazarus Federation of Jewish Clubs, December, 1963.

LEECH, MARGARET. *In the Days of McKinley.* New York: Harper & Brothers, 1959.

————. *Reveille in Washington, 1860–1865.* Harper & Brothers, 1941.

LEIGHTON, ISABEL (ED.). *The Aspirin Age.* New York: Simon & Schuster, 1949.

LEWIS, ARTHUR H. *The Day They Shook the Plum Tree.* New York: Harcourt, Brace & World, 1963.

LINCOLN, ANNE H. *The Kennedy White House Parties.* New York: The Viking Press, 1967.

LINK, A. S. *Wilson: The Road to the White House.* Princeton, N.J.: Princeton University Press, 1947.

LINN, JAMES WEBER. *Jane Addams.* New York: D. Appleton-Century Company, 1935.

LONGWORTH, ALICE. *Crowded Hours.* New York: Charles Scribner's Sons, 1933.

LOTH, DAVID G. *A Long Way Forward: The Biography of Congresswoman Frances P. Bolton.* New York: Longmans, Green, 1957.

LUCE, CLARE BOOTHE. *Saints for Now.* New York: Sheed & Ward, 1952.

————. *Stuffed Shirts.* New York: Liveright, 1931.

LUTZ, ALMA. *Created Equal. A Biography of Elizabeth Cady Stanton.* New York: The John Day Company, 1940.

————. *Susan B. Anthony.* Boston: Beacon Press, 1959.

LYNES, RUSSELL. *The Domesticated Americans.* New York: Harper & Brothers, 1957.

LYONS, EUGENE. *Herbert Hoover.* New York: Doubleday, 1947.

McADOO, ELEANOR WILSON, AND M. J. GAFFEY. *The Woodrow Wilsons.* New York: The Macmillan Company, 1937.

McELROY, ROBERT. *Grover Cleveland, the Man and the Statesman.* New York: Harper & Brothers, 1923.

MACKENZIE, WILLIAM L. *The Life and Times of Martin Van Buren.* Boston: Cooke & Company, 1846.

McKINLEY, SILAS BENT. *Old Rough and Ready.* New York: The Vanguard Press, 1946.

MANCHESTER, WILLIAM. *The Death of a President.* New York: Harper & Row, 1966.

MARTINEAU, HARRIET. *Society in America.* 3 vols. New York: Harper & Brothers, 1942.

MASSEY, MARY E. *Bonnet Brigades.* New York: Alfred A. Knopf, 1966.

MEAD, MARGARET. *Male and Female.* New York: William Morrow, 1949.

————. *President's Commission on the Status of Women.* New York: Charles Scribner's Sons, 1965.

MEAD, MARGARET, AND KEN HEYMAN. *Family.* New York: The Macmillan Company, 1965.

MEYER, ANNIE NATHAN (ED.). *Woman's Work in America.* New York: Henry Holt & Company, 1891.

MINNEGERODE, MEADE. *Some American Ladies.* New York: G. P. Putnam's Sons, 1926.

MITCHELL, DAVID. *The Fighting Pankhursts.* New York: The Macmillan Company, 1967.

MONTAGU, ASHLEY. *The Natural Superiority of Women.* New York: The Macmillan Company, 1953.

MOORE, FRANK. *The Diary of the American Revolution 1775–1781,* edited by John Anthony Scott. New York: Washington Square Press, 1967.

————. *The Rebellion Record.* New York: G. P. Putnam, 1861–63; D. Van Nostrand, 1864–68.

MORISON, ELTING E. (ED.). *The Letters of Theodore Roosevelt.* 8 vols. Cambridge, Mass., Harvard University Press, 1951–54.

MORISON, SAMUEL ELIOT. *The Oxford History of the American People.* New York: Oxford University Press, 1965.

MORRIS, LLOYD R. *Not So Long Ago.* New York: Random House, 1949.

————. *Postscript to Yesterday.* New York: Random House, 1947.

MYERS, GUSTAVUS. *History of the Great American Fortunes.* Chicago: G. H. Kerr & Company, 1911.

NALLE, OUIDA FERGUSON. *The Fergusons of Texas.* San Antonio: The Naylor Company, 1946.

NEVINS, ALLAN. *America Through British Eyes.* New York: Oxford University Press, 1948.

————. *American Social History as Recorded by British Travellers.* New York: Henry Holt & Company, 1923.

————. *Grover Cleveland.* New York: Dodd, Mead & Company, 1932.

————. *Frémont, Pathmarker of the West.* New York: Longmans, Green & Company, 1955.

————. *Frémont, the West's Greatest Adventurer.* New York: Harper & Brothers, 1928.

————. *The Emergence of Modern America 1865–1878.* New York: The Macmillan Company, 1927.

OSSOLI, MARGARET FULLER. *Memoirs of Margaret Fuller Ossoli.* Vol. 2. Boston: Phillips, Sampson & Company, 1851.

PADOVER, SAUL K. (ED.). *The Complete Madison.* New York: Harper & Brothers, 1953.

PARTRIDGE, BELLAMY. *As We Were: Family Life in America, 1850–1900.* New York: McGraw-Hill Book Company, 1946.

PECK, MARY GRAY. *Carrie Chapman Catt.* New York: H. W. Wilson Company, 1944.

PERKINS, A. J. G., AND THERESA WOLFSON. *Frances Wright, Free Enquirer.* New York: Harper & Brothers, 1939.

PERKINS, FRANCES. *The Roosevelt I Knew.* New York: The Viking Press, 1946.

PHELPS, MARY MERWIN. *Kate Chase, Dominant Daughter.* New York: Thomas Y. Crowell Company, 1935.

PHILLIPS, CATHERINE COFFIN. *Jessie Benton Frémont.* San Francisco: Printed by John Henry Nash, 1935.

POLK, JAMES. *The Diary of a President 1845–1849,* edited by Allan Nevins. New York: Longmans, Green & Company, 1929.

PRINGLE, HENRY F. *The Life and Times of William Howard Taft.* 2 vols. New York: Farrar & Rinehart, 1939.

PRYOR, SARA AGNES (MRS. ROGER A.). *Reminiscences of Peace and War.* New York: The Macmillan Company, 1904.

RANDALL, RUTH PAINTER. *Mary Lincoln.* Boston: Little, Brown & Company, 1953.

RESTON, JAMES. *Sketches in the Sand.* New York: Alfred A. Knopf, 1967.

RHODES, HARRISON G. *History of the United States from the Compromise of 1850.* New York: The Macmillan Company, 1892–1922.

RICHARDS, LAURA E. *Abigail Adams and Her Times.* New York: D. Appleton & Company, 1917.

RIXEY, LILIAN. *Bamie.* Indianapolis: Bobbs-Merrill Company, 1939.

ROGERS, AGNES. *The American Procession.* New York: Harper & Brothers, 1933.

———. *Women Are Here to Stay.* New York: Harper & Brothers, 1949.

ROOSEVELT, ELEANOR. *Autobiography of Eleanor Roosevelt.* New York: Harper & Row, 1961.

———. *It Seems to Me.* New York, W. W. Norton, 1954.

———. *It's Up to the Woman.* New York: Frederick A. Stokes Company, 1933.

———. *On My Own.* New York: Harper & Brothers, 1958.

———. *This I Remember.* New York: Harper & Brothers, 1949.

———. *This Is My Story.* New York: Harper & Brothers, 1937.

———. *Tomorrow Is Now.* New York: Harper & Row, 1963.

———. *You Learn by Living.* New York: Harper & Brothers, 1960.

ROOSEVELT, ELEANOR, AND LORENA A. HICKOK. *Ladies of Courage.* New York: G. P. Putnam's Sons, 1954.
ROOSEVELT, THEODORE. *An Autobiography.* New York: Charles Scribner's Sons, 1920.
ROSS, ISHBEL. *An American Family: The Tafts 1678–1964.* Cleveland: World Publishing Company, 1964.
————. *Angel of the Battlefield.* New York: Harper & Brothers, 1956.
————. *Child of Destiny.* New York: Harper & Brothers, 1949.
————. *First Lady of the South.* New York: Harper & Brothers, 1958.
————. *Grace Coolidge and Her Era.* New York: Dodd, Mead & Company, 1962.
————. *Ladies of the Press.* New York: Harper & Brothers, 1936.
————. *Proud Kate.* New York: Harper & Brothers, 1953.
————. *Rebel Rose.* New York: Harper & Brothers, 1954.
————. *The General's Wife.* New York: Dodd, Mead & Company, 1959.
ROSSITER, CLINTON. *Seedtime of the Republic.* New York: Harcourt, Brace & Company, 1953.
RUGG, WINNIFRED KING. *Unafraid: A Life of Anne Hutchinson.* Boston: Houghton Mifflin Company, 1930.

SACHS, EMANIE. *The Terrible Siren.* New York: Harper & Brothers, 1928.
SAMUELS, ERNEST. *Henry Adams: The Major Phase.* Cambridge, Mass.: The Belknap Press, 1964.
SANGER, MARGARET. *An Autobiography.* New York: W. W. Norton & Co., 1938.
SCHLESINGER, ARTHUR M., AND DIXON RYAN FOX (EDS.). *A History of American Life.* Vol. 10. New York: The Macmillan Company, 1938.
SCHLESINGER, ARTHUR M., JR., AND MORTON WHITE. *Paths of American Thought.* Boston: Houghton Mifflin Company, 1963.
SEAGER, ROBERT, II. *And Tyler Too.* New York: McGraw-Hill Book Company, 1963.
SHAPLEN, ROBERT. *Free Love and Heavenly Sinners.* New York: Alfred A. Knopf, 1954.
SIEVERS, HARRY J. *Benjamin Harrison.* Chicago: Henry Regnery Company, 1952.
SINCLAIR, ANDREW. *The Available Man: Warren Gamaliel Harding.* New York: The Macmillan Company, 1965.
————. *The Better Half.* New York: Harper & Row, 1965.
SINGLETON, ESTHER. *The Story of the White House.* 2 vols. New York: The McClure Company, 1907.
SLAYDEN, ELLEN MAURY. *Washington Life.* New York: Harper & Row, 1963.

SMITH, GENE. *When the Cheering Stopped.* New York: William Morrow & Company, 1964.
SMITH, PAGE. *John Adams.* Garden City, N.Y.: Doubleday, 1962.
SMITH, MRS. SAMUEL HARRISON. *The First Forty Years of Washington Society,* edited by Gaillard Hunt. New York: Charles Scribner's Sons, 1906.
SPARKS, JARED. *Lives of Ezra Stiles, John Fitch and Anne Hutchinson.* Boston: Charles C. Little and James Brown, 1847.
STANARD, MARY NEWTON. *Colonial Virginia, Its People and Customs.* Philadelphia: J. B. Lippincott, 1917.
STANTON, ELIZABETH CADY. *Elizabeth Cady Stanton Revealed in her Letters, Diary and Reminiscences,* edited by Theodore Stanton and Harriot Stanton Blatch. New York: Harper & Brothers, 1922.
STANTON, ELIZABETH CADY, SUSAN B. ANTHONY AND MATILDA JOSLYN GAGE (EDS.). *The History of Woman Suffrage.* New York: Fowler & Wells, 1881.
STARKEY, MARION LENA. *The Devil in Massachusetts.* New York: Alfred A. Knopf, 1949.
STARLING, COLONEL EDMUND W. *Starling of the White House,* as told to Thomas Sugrue. New York: Simon & Schuster, 1946.
STERN, KARL. *The Flight from Woman.* New York: Farrar, Straus & Giroux, 1965.
STERN, MADELEINE B. *The Life of Margaret Fuller.* New York: E. P. Dutton & Company, 1942.
STODDARD, HENRY L. *As I Knew Them.* New York: Harper & Brothers, 1927.
STRODE, HUDSON. *Jefferson Davis.* 3 vols. New York: Harcourt, Brace & Company, 1955–64.
STRYKER, LLOYD PAUL. *Andrew Johnson.* New York: The Macmillan Company, 1929.
STYRON, ARTHUR. *The Last of the Cocked Hats: James Monroe and the Virginia Dynasty.* Norman, Okla.: University of Oklahoma Press, 1945.
SUHL, YURI. *Ernestine Rose.* New York: Reynal & Company, 1959.
SULLIVAN, MARK. *Our Times: The United States 1900–1925 and 1926–1935. The War Begins, 1909–1914,* vol. V; *Over Here, 1914–1918,* vol. VI; *The Twenties,* vol. VII. New York: Charles Scribner's Sons, 1935.
SWISSHELM, JANE GREY. *Half a Century.* Chicago: Jansen, McClugg & Company, 1880.

TARBELL, IDA M. *The Ways of Woman.* New York: The Macmillan Company, 1915.

————. *The Business of Being a Woman.* New York: The Macmillan Company, 1912.

THANE, ELSWYTH. *Washington's Lady.* New York: Dodd, Mead & Company, 1960.

THARP, LOUISE HALL. *The Peabody Sisters of Salem.* Boston: Little, Brown, & Company, 1950.

THAYER, MARY VAN RENSSALAER. *Jacqueline Bouvier Kennedy.* Garden City, N.Y.: Doubleday, 1961.

TIMS, MARGARET. *Jane Addams of Hull House, 1860–1935.* New York: The Macmillan Company, 1961.

TROLLOPE, FRANCES MILTON. *Domestic Manners of the Americans.* New York: Alfred A. Knopf, 1949.

TRUMAN, MARGARET, WITH MARGARET COUSINS. *Souvenir.* New York: McGraw-Hill Book Company, 1956.

VILLARD, HENRY. *Memoirs of Henry Villard.* Boston: Houghton Mifflin Company, 1904.

WECTER, DIXON. *The Saga of American Society.* New York: Charles Scribner's Sons, 1937.

WELLS, MILDRED WHITE. *Unity in Diversity.* Washington, D.C.: Published by the General Federation of Women's Clubs, 1953.

WERTENBAKER, THOMAS JEFFERSON. *The Puritan Oligarchy: The Founding of American Civilization.* New York: Charles Scribner's Sons, 1947.

WHARTON, ANNE HOLLINGSWORTH. *Colonial Days and Dames.* Philadelphia: J. B. Lippincott Company, 1895.

————. *Social Life in the Early Republic.* Philadelphia: J. B. Lippincott Company, 1902.

WHITE, WILLIAM ALLEN. *Masks in a Pageant.* New York: The Macmillan Company, 1930.

WHITING, LILIAN. *Kate Field, A Record.* Boston: Little, Brown & Company, 1899.

WHITNEY, JANET. *Abigail Adams.* Boston: Little, Brown & Company, 1947.

WILSON, WILLIAM E. *The Angel and the Serpent.* Bloomington, Ind.: Indiana University Press, 1967.

WINSLOW, ANNE GREEN. *Diary of a Boston School Girl of 1771,* edited by Alice Morse Earle. Boston: Houghton Mifflin Company, 1894.

WINTHROP, JOHN. *The History of New England from 1630–1649.* Boston: Phelps & Farnham, 1826.

————. *Antinomians and Familists condemned by the Synod Elders in New England.* London: Printed for R. Smith, 1644.

WISE, WINIFRED ESTHER. *Jane Addams of Hull-House.* New York: Harcourt, Brace, 1935.

WOODWARD, HELEN. *Through Many Windows.* New York: Harper & Brothers, 1926.

WOODWARD, WILLIAM E. *The Way Our People Lived.* New York: E. P. Dutton & Company, 1944.

WRIGHT, FRANCIS. *Course of Popular Lectures.* New York: G. W. and A. J. Matsell, 1936.

———. *Views of Society and Manners in America,* edited by Paul R. Baker. Cambridge, Mass.: The Belknap Press, 1963.

Index

Abolition and abolitionists 122, 134, 138, 148–149, 157–158
Acheson, Dean, 89
Adams, Abby, 18
Adams, Abigail, 1–3, 6–21, 23–24, 29, 60, 68, 75, 111, 114–116, 128–129, 165, 227
  influence of, 2, 9–14, 19–20
Adams, Charles, 18
Adams, Henry, 6–7, 10, 58
Adams, John, 1–2, 8–20, 23, 60, 75, 114–116
Adams, John Quincy, 18–19, 28–30, 158
Adams, Louisa, 29–30
Adams, Samuel Hopkins, 70, 115
Adams, Thomas Boylston, 18
Addams, Jane, 150–154, 260
Adkins, Bertha S., 216
Advertising, women in, 245–246
Africa, 208
Aging, women and, 257
Alabama, 223
Alexander, Lady Kitty, 113
Allen, Florence E., 214, 254
Almy, Mary Gould, 117
Alsop, Stewart, 98
Alumnae Advisory Center, 251
Ambassadors, women, 213
American Anti-Slavery Society, 148
American Birth Control League, 290, 293
American Federation of Labor, 192
Anderson, Eugenie M., 232–233
Anderson, John Pierce, 232–233
Anderson, Marian, 83, 216
Anthony, Susan B., 46, 128, 140, 159–161, 163–174, 184, 187

Antinomian Controversy, 108, 110
Arnold, Matthew, 156
Arthur, Chester, 45
Arts, women and, 227, 236, 240–241
Aspinwall, Hannah, 28
Astor, Lady, 178, 188
Astor, Mrs. Vincent, 241

Bach, George R., 280
Backus, Mrs. Dana C., 275
Badeau, Adam, 39, 44–45
Baker, Newton D., 68, 209
Baker, Ray Stannard, 66
Banking, women in, 249
Baptists, 111
Barnard College, 179–182
Barton, Bruce, 74
Barton, Clara, 126, 137, 150, 168
Baruch, Bernard, 68
Baumgartner, Leona, 216
Beard, Mary, 186
Beauregard, General, 142–144
Beecher, Henry Ward, 125, 160
Beekman, Cornelia, 112
Belmont, Mrs. August, 241
Belmont, Mrs. O. H. P., 177, 185, 260
Benjamin, Judah P., 142
Benton, Thomas Hart, 145
Benton, Mrs. Thomas Hart, 32
Bickerdyke, Mary A., 137
Biddle, Colonel Clement, 112
Biddle, Rebecca, 112
Bingham, Anne Willing, 15
Birth control, 259, 276, 280, 287–297
Birth control clinics, 292–293
Black, Shirley Temple, 229
Blackwell, Alice Stone, 170, 184–185

Blackwell, Elizabeth, 123, 126, 138, 171, 227
Blackwell, Henry, 168–170
Blackwell, Samuel, 169
Blaine, Graham B., 280
Blaine, Mr. and Mrs. James G., 132
Blair, Frank, 146
Blatch, Harriot Stanton, 186
Bloomer, Amelia, 123, 160
Bloomers, 160–161
Bolton, Chester C., 207
Bolton, Frances P., 201, 203, 207–210

C.I.O., 190, 192, 203
Calderone, Mary, 282–283
Calhoun, John, 35
Calhoun, Mrs. John, 32
Cambodia, 96
Caraway, Hattie, 211
Career woman (see Business women)
Carlyle, Thomas, 122–123
Carpenter, Liz, 101
Cary, Alice and Phoebe, 126, 130
Catholic Church, 287, 293
Catt, Carrie Chapman, 184–185, 188, 274
Catt, George, 185
Catton, Bruce, 41
Chandler, Mrs. Norman ("Buffy"), 243
Chapman, Leo, 184
Charlotte, Queen, 14
Charm and charmers, 225–241
    in the White House, 3, 24, 91
Chase, Kate, 5, 39, 139–141, 146–147
Chase, Salmon P., 4–5, 39, 139
Chesnut, Mary Boykin, 142
Chicago, 255–256
    Columbian Fair in, 127–128, 152, 173, 175
    Slums in, 151–152
Child, David Lee, 134
Child, Lydia Maria, 125, 134, 148
Chisholm, Shirley, 211
Cincinnati Symphony Orchestra, 63
Civil rights, 98
Civil War, 36, 40, 42, 47, 132–133, 136–138, 140–145, 149–150, 163, 172, 184
Civilian Defense, 85

Claflin, Tennessee, 172
Clark, Mary Todhunter, 219
Clarke, Sara Jane (see Greenwood, Grace)
Clay, Henry, 32
Clemenceau, 66
Clemmer, Mary, 46
Cleveland, Frances Folsom, 3–4, 49–50
Cleveland, Grover, 49–50, 127
Cleveland, Rose Elizabeth, 49–50
Clifford, Clark, 94
Cline, Genevieve R., 254
Clubs for women, 172, 179
Coeducation, 183–184
Colby, Bainbridge, 188
College women, 278
    employed, 258–259
    marriage and, 259
Colony Club, New York, 179
Commission on the Status of Women, 250, 266, 270
Communism, 202–203, 212, 215
Community life, women in, 269–270, 297
Comstock, Anthony, 288, 291
Condorcet, Marquis de, 111
Confederacy, the, 36–37, 42, 141–142, 144
Connecticut, 212
Constitution, the, 12, 115, 163
    and suffrage amendment, 164, 188
Contraceptives, 276, 295
Conway, Moncure D., 174
Coolidge, Calvin, 72–78, 95, 213, 254
Coolidge, Calvin, Jr., 76
Coolidge, Grace, 3–5, 46, 72–78, 95
Cooper, Mrs. John Sherman, 229
Copley, John Singleton, 116, 156
Corbin, Abel Rathbone, 43–44
Cotton, John, 108, 110
Cowles, Anna Roosevelt, 53–54, 57, 59
Cowles, Commander William Sheffield, 55
Craig, May, 204
Cranch, Mary, 15–16
Cresswell, Elizabeth, 150
Crook, William H., 44
Culture, women and, 227
Curtis, Charles, 79
Custis, Daniel Parke, 7

Daly, Mary, 287
Daniel, Mrs. Clifton (*see* Truman, Margaret)
Daniels, Josephus, 68
D'Arusmont, Guillaume Sylvan Casimir Phiquepal, 121
Daugherty, Harry M., 71–72
Davenport, Russell and Marcia, 235
David, Richard, D., 35
Davis, James J., 76
Davis, Jefferson, 141–143
Davis, Paulina Wright, 158
Davis, Varina, 141–144
Davison, Henry P., 178
Debs, Eugene, 151
Declaration of Conscience, 202–203
De Gaulle, Charles, 94
Demorest, Madame, 129–130
Denmark, 232–233
Dent, Colonel Frederick, 41, 43
Depression, the, 79–80, 85, 137, 279
De Wolfe, Henry, 71
Dewson, Mary E., 83, 85, 193, 213–214
Dickinson, Anna E., 138, 234
Diplomats, wives of, 230–231
  women, 231–239
Distinguished Service Medal, 198
Divorce, 158, 171, 264
Dix, Dorothea, 138, 149
Dodge, Mary Abigail (*see* Hamilton, Gail)
Donelson, Emily, 30–32
Donelson, Colonel John, 30
Douglas, Helen Gahagan, 209, 212
Douglas, Melvin, 212
Douglas, Stephen A., 38, 145
Douglas, Mrs. Stephen A., 37, 145
Douglass, Anna Mae, 149
Douglass, Frederick, 149
Drinker, Hannah, 117
Drug addiction, 280, 282, 297,
Duke, Mrs. Angier Biddle, 230
Duniway, Abigail Scott, 162
Dyer, Mary, 111

Eastman, Crystal, 186
Eaton, Major John H., 32
Eaton, Peggy, 4, 32
Education of women, 117–118, 165, 182–184, 278–279

Edward VII, 37
Edwards, India, 214
Eisenhower, David, 90
Eisenhower, Dwight D., 87, 90–91, 195–197, 206, 208, 212–213, 215, 232, 235, 263
Eisenhower, Mamie, 4, 90–91
Ellis, Havelock, 289, 291–292
Emancipation Proclamation, 146, 167
Emerson, Ralph Waldo, 122
Emmet, Elida, 177
England, 9, 14, 29, 36–37, 55, 178, 188, 198, 291–292
Ernst, Morris, 295

Fall, Albert, 69
Farley, James A., 85
Farms and farming, 259, 270
Fashion, 245, 278
  politics and, 225–241
  (*See also* Society)
Female Anti-Slavery Society, 157
Femininity, 277, 289, 297
Feminism, 82–83, 118–135, 156, 176, 181, 252, 277
  (*See also* Woman suffrage)
Ferguson, James, 220–221, 223
Ferguson, Miriam Amanda, 219–224
Fergusson, Elizabeth Graeme, 117
Fern, Fanny, 130
Ferry, Thomas, W., 172
Field, Joseph M., 125
Field, Kate, 125–129, 135, 162
Fillmore, Mrs. Millard, 102
Fisk, Jim, 44
FitzGerald, Frances, 238
Fleischman, Doris, 168
Flower Children, 279, 282
Folsom, Oscar, 49
Foreign correspondents, 245
Foreign Service, women in, 231–239, 252
Forrestal, Michael, 96
Fortas, Carolyn Aggers, 252–253
Foster, Abby Kelly, 164
France, 10, 14–16, 28, 66, 178
Franklin, Benjamin, 117
Franklin, Sarah, 118
Franks, Rebecca, 113
Frazier, Mary, 29

Frémont, Jessie Benton, 27, 32, 145–148
Frémont, John C., 145–147
French, Eleanor Clark, 218–219
French, John, 219
Freud, Sigmund, 279
Friedan, Betty, 286
Fuller, Margaret 118, 121–125, 128, 130
Furness, Betty, 200–201, 266

Gage, Frances Dana, 134
Gage, Matilda Joslyn, 134
Gallatin, Albert, 18, 25
Gallatin, Mrs. Albert, 25
Galt, Norman, 64
Gann, Dolly, 79
Gannette, Deborah, 112
Gardiner, Alexander, 34–35
Gardiner, Julia (see Tyler, Julia)
Gardiner, Robert, 34
Gardiner, Senator David, 33
Gardiner's Island, 33
Gardner, John W., 258
Garfield, Eliza Ballou, 48
Garfield, James, 45, 48
Garfield, Lucretia, 48
Garrison, William Lloyd, 148
General Federation of Women's Clubs, 172
Generation gap, 281–282
Germany, 29
Gibson Girl, 175
Gildersleeve, Virginia, 179–183
Ginzberg, Eli, 284
Glamour, 228, 277
Goddard, Mary K., 150
Goldberg, Arthur, 233
Golden, Ruth, 244
Goldwater, Barry, 234
Gompers, Samuel, 178
Gould, Jay, 44
Governors, women, 219–224
Graham, Katherine, 243
Grant, Frederick Dent, 43, 45
Grant, Hannah, 114
Grant, Jane, 168
Grant, Jesse, 43
Grant, Julia, 45
Grant, Julia Dent, 3–5, 39–46, 95, 102, 163

Grant, Nellie, 43, 45
Grant, General Ulysses S., 4–5, 38, 40–45, 95, 114, 163
Grant, Virginia, 44
Grayson, Admiral Cary T., 66–69
Greeley, Horace, 46, 122–125, 130–131, 133, 158, 163
Green, Hetty, 248
Green, William, 192
Greene, Catherine, 113
Greene, Nathaniel, 113
Greenhow, Robert, 144
Greenhow, Rose O'Neal, 144–145
Greenwood, Grace, 132–133
Griffin, General Charles, 40
Griffin, Sallie, 40
Griffiths, Hannah, 117
Grimké, Angelina and Sarah, 122, 148–149
Group, The, 115
Guggenheim, Harry and Alicia, 243

Hale, Ruth, 168
Hale, Sarah Josepha, 129
Halleck, Seymour, 280
Halsted, Mrs. James A. (see Roosevelt, Anna)
Hamilton, Alexander, 18
Hamilton, Gail, 132
Hamilton, George, 103
Hanaford, Phoebe, 174
Hancock, Mrs. John, 112
Harding, Florence, 3–4, 50, 70–73
Harding, Warren G., 70–73
Harlech, Lord, 96
Harriman, Averell, 90, 253
Harriman, Mrs. Averell, 241
Harriman, Daisy, 175, 177–179, 260
Harris, Patricia Roberts, 231
Harrison, Benjamin, 127
Harrison, Mrs. Benjamin, 4
Haupt, Enid, 245
Hawthorne, Nathaniel, 123
Hay, Eliza, 28
Hay, John, 55, 58, 146–147
Hay, Mary Garrett, 184–185
Hayes, Lucy Webb ("Lemonade Lucy"), 3–5, 46–48, 60
Hayes, Rutherford, 45–46, 60
Hearst, Phoebe Apperson, 177, 244
Heiskill, Mr. and Mrs. Andrew, 244

Herron, John W., 59
Hibbins, Ann, 111
Higgins, Michael Hennessey, 290
Higginson, Thomas Wentworth, 169
Hippies, 279, 282, 285, 297
Hirshhorn, Joseph H., 100
Hitchcock, Enos, 118
Hitchcock, Gilbert M., 68–69
Hitt, Patricia Reilly, 201
Hobby, Oveta Culp, 195–200, 210, 243
Hobby, William P., 196, 198–199
Hoffman, Paul, 215
Hoge, Mrs. A. H., 137
Homemakers, 282–283, 297–298
Hone, Philip, 24
Honoré, Ida, 43, 45
Hoover, Herbert, 78–81, 213
Hoover, Irwin (Ike), 58, 70
Hoover, Lou Henry, 4, 78–80
Hostesses, 231–232
    political, 239–241
Hough, Henry Beetle and Elizabeth Howie, 262
House, Colonel E. M., 5, 65–67
Howe, Julia Ward, 122, 160, 168, 170–171, 173
Howe, Louis, 84
Hughes, Charles Evans, 61, 178, 187
Hughes, Sarah T., 253
Hull, Mrs. Lytle, 240
Hull House, 150–152, 190
Humphrey, Hubert, 244
Humphrey, Mrs. Hubert, 230
Hunt, Harriot K., 164
Hurst, Francis W. J., 177
Hutchinson, Anne, 108–111, 114
Hutchinson, William, 109

Ickes, Harold, 191
Independence Day, 14
India, 294
Industry, women in, 191
International Council of Women, 168
International Ladies Garment Workers Union, 259–260
International Planned Parenthood Federation, 288, 294
International Woman Suffrage Alliance, 184
Interstate Commerce Commission, 254

Invalids, 50–52, 64, 73
Irving, Washington, 24
Italy, 235

Jackson, Andrew, 4, 30–32
Jackson, Rachel Donelson Robards, 4, 30–32
Jaffray, Edward S., 178
James, Henry, 156
James, William, 153
Jay, Mrs. John, 15
Jazz Age, 74, 279
Jefferson, Thomas, 10–11, 15, 18–19, 21–23, 28, 59, 114–116, 118–119
Jews, 135
Johnson, Mrs. Andrew, 102
Johnson, Claudia Alta Taylor ("Lady Bird"), 3, 6, 11, 50, 57, 88, 97–103, 199, 227, 239
Johnson, Hugh, 191
Johnson, Joshua, 29
Johnson, Luci, 45, 98, 103
Johnson, Lynda, 98, 101, 103
Johnson, Lyndon B., 97–102, 196, 199–201, 213, 216, 229, 253
Johnston, Henry Elliot, 37
Johnston, General Joseph E., 141–143
Johnston, Lydia, 141
Jones, Margaret, 111
Journalists, women, 126–132, 135, 261–262
    (See also Newspapers)
Judges, women, 253–256
    Negro, 255–256
Junc, Jennie, 129–130, 183

Katz, Joseph, 280
Kellems, Vivian, 164
Kelly, Edna F., 211
Kennedy, Ethel, 104–105
Kennedy, Jacqueline, 3–4, 6, 21, 38, 54, 77, 91–97, 102, 204, 231
Kennedy, John F., 91–97, 103, 179, 204, 206, 211, 213, 233, 237, 249, 264, 266, 270
Kennedy, Robert, 96–97, 103–105, 269
Kennedy, Rose, 103–105, 230
Keyes, Colonel Erasmus D., 145
Khan, Ayub, 92
Khrushchev, Nikita, 94

King, Alice Gore, 251
King, Mrs. Martin Luther, Jr., 211
Kirchwey, Freda, 181
Kirk, Gabrielle, 255
Kitt, Eartha, 98
Kling, Amos O., 71
Knowlton, Charles, 292
Knox, Frank, 194
Knox, Major Henry, 112–113, 115
Knox, Lucy, 112–113
Kohlsaat, H. H., 51
Koontz, Elizabeth Duncan, 211
Kortwright, Captain Lawrence, 28

Labor, 190–191, 210
   (*See also* Trade unionism)
Lafayette, 24, 28–29, 113, 115, 119
Lafayette, Madame, 27–28
La Guardia, Mrs. Fiorello, 218
Laidlaw, Mrs. James Lees, 177, 275
Landor, Walter Savage, 125
Lane, Harriet, 36
Lansing, Robert, 67, 69
Lasker, Albert D., 239–240
Lasker, Mary, 239–240, 268
Lawrence, David, 68
Lawrence, Harding, 246
Lawyers, women, 252–256
   Negro, 255–256
Lazarus, Emma, 134–135
League of Nations, 66–67, 69, 72
League of Women Voters, 82, 199,
   271–275
Le Clair, Linda, 182
Lecturers, women, 120, 138, 145
Lee, Dorothy McCullough, 217
Lee, General Robert E., 143
Lend-Lease, 205, 208
Leopold, Alice K., 212
Leslie, Mrs. Frank, 128, 160, 176,
   185, 274
Lewis, John L., 190–191, 193–194
Lewis, William C., 204
Lexington, Battle of, 112, 117
Lincoln, Abraham, 3, 38–41, 131, 133,
   138–139, 146, 149
Lincoln, Mary Todd, 3–4, 38–41, 132,
   139, 143
Lincoln, Robert Todd, 38, 41
Lincoln, Willie, 39

Lindsay, Mayor and Mrs. John V.,
   218
Lippincott, Leander K., 133
Livermore, Mary, 137
Livingston, Mrs. Edward, 31
Locke, John, 117
Lockwood, Belva, 267
Lodge, Henry Cabot, 55–56, 58–59,
   65–66
Logan, Deborah, 117
London, 14, 28–29, 55, 66, 94, 186,
   238
Longworth, Alice Roosevelt, 4, 45, 53,
   56, 58–59, 72, 74, 76, 79, 92,
   133, 147, 229, 265
Longworth, Nicholas, 57
Lord, Mary Pillsbury, 216
Louchheim, Kate, 216–217, 262
Louisiana Purchase, 28–29
Luce, Clare Boothe, 231, 234–236, 266
Luce, Henry, 234–236
Lucy Stone League, 168
Luxembourg, 231–232
Lyon, Mary 167
Lyons, Lord, 37

McAfee, Mildred, 181–182
McCarthy, Eugene, 104, 219, 269
McCarthy, Mrs. Eugene, 226
McCarthy, Joseph, 202–203
Macaulay, Catharine, 116
McClellan, General George B., 5, 38,
   144
McIntosh, Mrs. Rustin (*see* Thomas,
   Millicent)
McKinley, Ida Saxton, 50–52, 95
McKinley, William, 5, 50–52, 60, 95,
   147
McLean, John, 34–35
McLuhan, Marshall, 276, 285
Madison, Dolley, 3–4, 6, 17, 21–27,
   75–76, 87, 92
Madison, James, 22, 24–26, 75, 116
Malone, Dudley Field, 70
Management, women in, 250
Manchester, William, 96
Mangan, Margaret Mary, 253–254
Mannes, Marya, 269
Manning, Mrs. Frederick J. (*see* Taft,
   Helen)
Marie of Rumania, Queen, 76

Marion, Kitty, 292
Married women, in the work force, 257–259
Marshall, General George C., 197, 203, 214
Martin, Alexander Reid, 281
Martineau, Harriet, 124
Mather, Cotton, 117
Mayors, women, 217
Mayors' wives, 217–218
Mazzini, 124
Mead, Margaret, 250, 266, 279, 286
Medal of Freedom award, 215
Mellon, Mrs. Paul, 240
Men, equality with, 283
  women's domination of, 277
  and working wives, 284, 297
Merman, Ethel, 232
Mesta, Perle, 231–232
Meyer, Agnes, 79, 182, 243
Meyer, Eugene, 243
Midgley, Mrs. Leslie, 201
Milholland, Inez, 177, 186–187
Milholland, Vida, 187
Millay, Edna St. Vincent, 177
Miller, Elizabeth Smith, 160
Millionaires, women, 247–248
Mitchell, Maria, 165
Momism, 279
Monroe, Elizabeth, 27–30
Monroe, James, 19, 27–30
Monroe Doctrine, 29
Montagu, Sir Ashley, 283
Moody, Lady Deborah, 111
Morgan, Anne, 177–179, 260
Morgan, Juliet, 177
Morgenthau, Mrs. Henry, 177, 260
Mormonism, 127, 162
Morris, Esther, 161–162
Morris, Margaret, 117
Morrow, Mrs. Dwight, 74, 77
Morse, Wayne, 234
Moskowitz, Belle, 215
Motherhood, 283–285
Motley, Constance B., 255
Motley, Joel, 255
Mott, James, 157
Mott, Lucretia, 121, 138, 148, 157, 160, 166
Murray, Judith Sargent, 117
Murray, Mrs. Robert, 112

Murray, William Vans, 16
Myers, Mrs. A. C., 141

N.R.A., 192
Nation, Carry, 166
National College Women's Equal Suffrage League, 179–180
National committeewomen, 267
National Equal Rights Party, 171–172
National Society Opposed to Woman Suffrage, 176
National Woman Suffrage Association, 168, 171, 174, 273–274
National Woman's Party, 76–77, 185–187
National Youth Administration, 85
Nazis, 179
Negroes, 83–84, 149, 210–211
  as career women, 255–257
  (See also Slaves and slavery)
Neo-Malthusians, 292, 294
Nepotism, 3, 34, 43, 47, 261
Neuberger, Maurine, 207, 268
New Deal, 85, 137
New Orleans World's Fair, 173
New York City, 14, 34, 54, 56, 175, 179, 185, 188, 257, 290, 293
New York State, 163, 185, 212–213, 254–256, 271
New York Stock Exchange, 248–249
Newspapers, owned and edited by women, 243–244, 262
  (See also Journalists)
Nichols, Clarina Howard, 134
Nixon, Julie, 90
Nixon, Richard M., 90, 201, 212, 264
Nixon, Mrs. Richard M., 102
Nobel Peace Prize, 150
Norton, Mary, 210
Norway, 178–179
NOW (National Organization of Women), 286
Nugent, Patrick, 103

Ochs, Adolph, 244
O'Day, Caroline, 85
Offenbach, Jacques, 155–156
Old-age pensions, 195
Onassis, Aristotle, 91, 96
O'Neale, Peggy (see Eaton, Peggy)
Ord, General Edward, 39–40

Ord, Mrs. Edward, 39
Oregon, 162, 217
Ossoli, Marchese Giovanni Angelo
    (*See* Fuller, Margaret)
Ottesen-Jensen, Elise, 294
Owen, Robert Dale, 119, 292
Owen, Ruth Bryan, 214, 232

Palmer, Mrs. Potter, 43, 127, 152, 173,
    175
Pankhurst, Emmeline, 159, 188
Parents, American, 282, 297
Paris, 28, 93–94
    Exposition of 1900, 152
    Peace conferences in, 66, 153, 178
Patterson, Alicia, 243
Patterson, Cissie, 244
Patterson, Mary King, 243
Paul, Alice, 77, 185–188
Paul VI, Pope, 287
Payne, John, 22
Payson, Mrs. Whitney, 240
Peabody, Mrs. Malcolm E., 237
Peabody, Sophia and Elizabeth, 125
Peace conferences, 66, 152–153, 178
Pearl Harbor, 194
Perkins, Frances, 83, 85–86, 190–195,
    213
Pershing, General, 77
Peterson, Esther, 200, 249
Peterson, Martha, 182
Philadelphia, 11, 15–17, 148
    Centennial of 1876, 172–173
Philanthropy, 189, 240–241
Pickens, Francis W., 35
Pierce, Franklin, 5
Pitcher, Molly, 112
Planned Parenthood, 288
Pocahontas, 108
Poets, women, 116–117, 134, 236
Polio vaccinations, 195–196
Political conventions, women at, 265–
    266
Politics, and fashion, 225–241
    and the law, 255–257
    women and, 1, 54, 59, 62, 68, 81,
        84, 90, 114, 138–140, 152, 175,
        181, 193, 195, 199, 201, 213–224,
        228–229, 235–237, 263–275, 283
    youth and, 282
Polk, James K., 21

Polk, Mrs. James K., 4
Poore, Ben Perley, 43
Post, Mrs. Merriweather, 240
Poston, Ersa, 256
Powel, Mrs. Samuel, 113
Pratt, Ruth, 212–213
Premarital relations, 278, 280–281
Presidential candidates, women as,
    267–269
Presidents, women who influenced, 36–
    37, 48, 59, 127
Presidents' wives, influential, 3–5, 9–
    14, 21, 24–25, 28, 32–36, 44–46,
    57, 59–62, 64–73, 78, 88–90, 98–
    99, 147
Press, the, 87
    (*See also* Newspapers)
Press agents, 33
Priest, Ivy Baker, 215–216
Prohibition, 72, 165
    (*See also* Temperance movement)
Propagandists, women, 111, 117, 123,
    145
Psychiatry, 281
Public life, women in, 217–218, 225
Public service, women in, 149–150,
    177–179, 189–224
Pullman strike of 1894, 151
Puritans, the, 108–109, 278

Quakers, 111–112, 153, 157, 166–167,
    180, 185

Radio, 245–246
Randolph, Mary, 75
Rankin, Jeannette, 210–211
Rappite communities, 119
Raskob, John J., 84
Rau, Lady Dhanvanthi Rama, 294
Real estate, women in, 249
Red Cross, 136, 168, 178
Reid, Helen Rogers (Mrs. Ogden),
    177, 182, 245, 293
Reid, Whitelaw, 55
Reid, Mrs. Whitelaw, 230
Reston, James, 230, 262
Reston, Sally, 262
Revolutionary War, 7, 9, 11, 14, 29,
    59, 111–112, 114–119, 135–136,
    138–139
Rhode Island, 110

Robards, Lewis, 30
Robb, Captain Charles S., 101, 103
Robinson, Corinne Roosevelt, 54, 59, 82
Roche, Josephine, 214
Rochefoucauld, Duc de la, 155
Rockefeller, Nelson A., 237, 241, 256, 264
Roebling, Mary G., 249
Rogers, Edith Nourse, 210
Rogers, Will, 74
Rohde, Börge, 232
Rome, 66, 124
Roosevelt, Alice Lee, 53, 56
Roosevelt, Anna, 87
Roosevelt, Edith Carow, 3–4, 25, 53–60, 62, 88
Roosevelt, Eleanor, 3–6, 11, 17, 38, 48, 52, 54, 57, 81–87, 91, 93, 96, 99, 102, 124, 191, 198, 213, 266
Roosevelt, Franklin D., 4, 57, 69, 81–86, 181, 190–195, 215, 254
Roosevelt, Sara Delano, 84
Roosevelt, Theodore, 3, 5, 36, 53–63, 65, 82, 174, 187, 211
Root, Elihu, 55, 61
Root, Mrs. Elihu, 176–177
Rosenberg, Anna M., 214–215
Rosenman, Samuel, 293
Ross, Nellie Tayloe, 214, 221–224
Royall, Anne, 30, 130, 135
Rudolph, Zebulon, 48
Rush, Benjamin, 117
Russell, William Howard, 37
Russia, 29
    working women in, 251–252
Rutherford, Margaret, 66

St. George, Katharine, 212
Salem, Massachusetts, 111
Salk, Jonas, 195–196
Sampson, Edith, 255–256
Sand, George, 124–125
Sanger, Margaret, 287–298
Sanger, William, 289–291
Sargent, A. A., 164
Sartoris, Algernon, 45
Sassower, Doris Lipson, 253
Schiff, Dorothy, 243
Schiff, Jacob H., 182, 243
Schneiderman, Rose, 260

Schuyler, Louisa Lee, 137
Schuyler, Mrs. Philip, 112–113
Seaton, William, 25
Selincourt, Hugh de, 289, 291
Semple, Letitia Tyler, 33
Sevareid, Eric, 98
Sex revolution, 276–282
Seymour, Horatio, 139–140
Shaw, Anna Howard, 184–185
Sheppard, Eugenia, 245
Shippen, Margaret, 113
Siebert, Muriel ("Mickie"), 248–249
Sihanouk, Prince, 96
Simkovitch, Mary, 260
Slaves and slavery, 116, 119, 134, 146, 148–149
Slee, J. Noah H. 289, 295–296
Slidell, Rosine, 142
Slocumb, Mary, 113
Slums, Chicago, 151–152
    London, 153
Smith, Al, 83–84, 188, 190
Smith, Clyde, 205
Smith, Julia and Abby, 164
Smith, Margaret Chase, 201–208, 267–268
Smith, Sophia, 183
Social Security, 191, 195
Social work, 150–154, 189
Society, and the suffrage movement, 175–179, 185
Sorosis Club, 129–130, 162, 172
Spain, 29, 51
Spanish-American War, 54, 136
Spence, Clara, 177
Spies, 144–145
Sprague, William, 139
Sprague, Mrs. (*see* Chase, Kate)
Stanford, Mrs. Leland, 177
Stanton, Edwin M., 40
Stanton, Elizabeth Cady, 128, 156–157, 159–160, 163–167, 171, 173–174, 184
Stanton, Henry, 156–157
State legislatures, 271
    women in, 212–214
Stearns, Frank, 76
Stevens, Doris, 70, 177, 186, 188, 236
Stevenson, Adlai, 81, 86–87, 90, 237–238, 252, 264
Stimson, Henry, 197

Stockton, Annie Boudinot, 177
Stone, Abraham and Hannah M., 295
Stone, Lucy, 128, 149, 160, 163, 165, 168–171, 173
Stopes, Marie, 292
Stowe, Harriet Beecher, 134
Strauss, Anna Lord, 273
Strikes, 151, 192, 292
Stuart, Gilbert, 26
Suffrage conventions, 158
Sullivan, Mark, 73
Sulzberger, Mrs. Arthur Hays, 182 244
Sweden, 178–179, 294
Swisshelm, Jane, 130–132
Symington, Stuart, 203

Taft, Charles, 60, 63
Taft, Helen, 63–64, 180
Taft, Helen Herron, 3, 5, 59–64, 95, 176
Taft, Henry, 60
Taft, Horace, 60
Taft, Robert A., 57, 60, 63, 203
Taft, William Howard, 3, 57–65, 72, 93, 95, 158, 176
Taft-Hartley Act, 203
Tarbell, Ida M., 260
Taxation, women and, 164
Taylor, Margaret, 5, 102
Taylor, Zachary, 5
Technology, 279
Television, 245–246
Temperance movement, 46–47, 165–167
Texas, 97, 219–221
    annexation of, 34–36
Thomas, F. W., 33–35
Thomas, M. Carey, 179–180
Thomas, Millicent (Mrs. Rustin McIntosh), 180, 261
Thompson, Charles Willis, 67
Thompson, Dorothy, 235
Tiffany, Katrina Ely, 176
Tilden, Samuel J., 140
Timberlake, John Bowie, 32
Tocqueville, Alexis de, 155
Todd, John, 22
Todd, Payne, 27
Tonga, 275
Toombs, Mrs. Robert, 141

Torrey, Delia, 158, 176
Torrey, Louise, 176
Toynbee, Arnold, 285
Trade unionism for women, 153, 171, 259–260
Trahey, Jane, 246–247
Transcendentalism, 122
Tree, Arthur Ronald Lambert Field, 238
Tree, Marietta, 229, 237–239
Tree, Penelope, 238
Trollope, Anthony, 125
Trollope, Mrs., 119
Truman, Bess Wallace, 4, 25, 87–90, 230
Truman, Harry, 57, 86–90, 182, 194, 212–215, 231–232
Truman, Margaret, 88–89, 244, 268
Truth, Sojourner, 149
Tubman, Harriet, 149
Tuchman, Barbara, 134, 285–286
Tumulty, Joseph, 68, 70
Tydings, Millard, 203
Tyler, John, 32–36, 131
Tyler, Julia Gardiner, 3, 32–36, 102
Tyler, Letitia Christian, 33
Tyler, Priscilla Cooper, 33

Uccella, Antonina P., 217
Underground Railroad, 149
Unemployment insurance, 191
Unions (*see* Trade unionism)
United Nations, 86–87, 208, 212, 216, 233, 237–238, 273
United Nations Charter, 181
United States Congress, 13, 271
    (*See also* U.S. House of Representatives; U.S. Senate)
United States Defense Department, 214–215
United States Department of Health, Education and Welfare, 195
United States Department of Labor, 190, 211, 249
    Women's Bureau, 258, 260
United States House of Representatives, women in, 201, 207–212, 234–235
United States Senate, women in, 201–207
United States State Department, 216

United States Treasury Department, 214
Utah, 162, 254

Van Buren, Martin, 4
Van Cortlandt, Pierre, 112
Vandenberg, Arthur, 181, 234
Vanderlip, Mrs. Frank, 177
Vane, Sir Harry, 110
Victoria, Queen, 33, 37, 45, 126, 175
Viereck, George Sylvester, 67
Vietnam war, 263, 268, 274, 279
Vote, women and the, 263–275
  (*See also* Woman suffrage)
Vreeland, Diana, 245

W.C.T.U., 165
  (*See also* Prohibition; Temperance movement)
Wadsworth, Mrs. James, 176
Wagner, Robert, 253
Wagner, Susan, 216, 239
Wald, Lillian, 260
Waldorf, Richard, 35
Walker, Mary, 161
Wallace, George C., 223–224
Wallace, Henry, 85–86
Wallace, Lurleen, 223–224
War of 1812, 26
Warren, James, 115
Warren, Mercy Otis, 7, 9, 111, 114–116, 128–129
Washington, Bennetta Bullock, 256–257
Washington, D.C., 16–17, 126, 146–147, 185–188
  burning of, 26
Washington, George, 7–8, 113–117
  Stuart portrait of, 26
Washington, Martha, 3, 6–8, 113, 115
Washington, Mary, 113
Wealth, women's share of, 227, 247–248
Webb, Sidney and Beatrice, 153
Webster, Daniel, 130, 132
Wells, H. G., 292, 297
Wells, Mary, 246
Wheatley, Phillis, 116
White, Henry, 66
White, James, J., 255
White, Katharine, 233

White, William Allen, 74, 78
White House, the, 2, 16–17, 27–30, 32, 35–37, 43, 47–49, 57–58, 63, 72, 75, 77, 80, 91–92, 94–95, 100, 102
Whitehouse, Mrs. Norman, 177
Wigfall, Charlotte, 141
Willard, Frances, 47, 165–167
Willebrandt, Mabel Walker, 214
Williams, Roger, 110–111
Willis, Nathaniel Parker, 131
Willkie, Wendell, 193, 235
Wilson, Edith Bolling Galt, 3–5, 64–70, 176
Wilson, Ellen Axson, 64
Wilson, James G., 42
Wilson, the Rev. John, 110
Wilson, Paul Caldwell, 190
Wilson, Woodrow, 3–4, 63–70, 176–177, 186–188
Winthrop, Hannah, 9, 115, 117
Winthrop, John, 9, 109–110
Wiseman, Sir William, 67
Wister, Sally, 117
Wives, of mayors, 217–218
  of presidents, 1–106, 227, 230
  of public figures, 225–227, 229–231
  working, 283–284, 297
Wollstonecraft, Mary, 116
Woman suffrage, 46, 59, 64, 70, 108, 111, 121, 123, 128, 143, 149, 155–174, 236
  as fashionable cause, 175–179, 185–186
  female opposition to, 176
  in the 20th century, 184–188
  women's colleges and, 179–183
Woman's Rights Convention of 1860, 163
Women, The (Luce), 234, 236
Women's Army Corps, 195, 197–198
Women's Army and Navy Reserve, 181
Women's colleges, 179–183
Women's International League, 154
Women's National Democratic Club, 179
Women's National Press Association, 134
Women's Trade Union League, 82, 260

Woodhull, Victoria, 125, 131, 135,
149, 160, 165, 171–172, 267
Woolley, Mary E., 179
World War I, 65–66, 136, 152, 178,
185, 187, 209, 211, 279
World War II, 137–138, 178–179,
181–182, 194–195, 197, 206, 215,
237, 257, 261, 264

Wright, Frances, 118–121, 128, 158,
160, 171, 234
Writers, American women, 236
Wyoming, 161, 221–222

Yale, Anne, 111
Young, Brigham, 127

Format by Katharine Sitterly
Set in Linotype Electra
Composed, printed and bound by American Book–Stratford Press, Inc.
HARPER & ROW, PUBLISHERS, INCORPORATED

69707172738765 4 3 2 1